FINDING LOST

SEASONS ONE & TWO

NIKKI STAFFORD

ECW Press

To Rob and Sydney

Published by ECW Press
2120 Queen Street East, Suite 200, Toronto, Ontario, Canada M4E 1E2
416.694.3348 / info@ecwpress.com

LIBRARY AND ARCHIVES CANADA CATALOGUING IN PUBLICATION

Stafford, Nikki, 1973–
Finding Lost : the unofficial guide / Nikki Stafford.

ISBN 978-1-55022-743-7
ALSO ISSUED AS: 978-1-55490-743-4 (PDF); 978-1-55490-276-7 (EPUB)

1. Lost (Television program).   I. Title.

PN1992.77.L67S73 2006   791.45'72   C2006-904109-1

Developing editor: Jennifer Hale
Cover and text design: Tania Craan
Typesetting: Gail Nina
Front cover photo: Nicola Sutton/Life File/Getty
Back cover photo: Sergio Pitamitz/Corbis

PRINTED AND BOUND IN THE UNITED STATES

ECW PRESS
ecwpress.com

Table of Contents

Acknowledgments

Thank you to everyone at ECW Press, especially Jack David for agreeing with me when I raved about *Lost* and said we should do a book on it; Gail Nina and Tania Craan; Crissy Boylan, my pal who not only typed in the changes to the book, but was so intent on not being spoiled she watched both seasons in less than 10 days (my hero!); and Nadine James, who started watching the show along with the episode guide as a test subject for how it would work.

To Gil Adamson, my editor extraordinaire, who worked diligently on the book in three parts, and never complained about getting everything piecemeal.

A huge thank you to Ryan Ozawa, who took most of the amazing Oahu location photos, helped me with the locations and captions, and answered every single question I had about Oahu (usually within minutes on e-mail). You rock. Special thanks also to John Fischer at About.com, who helped me out with the chapter when it was still just an idea, put me in touch with Ryan, suggested a map, and supplied me with some great location photos.

Thank you to RVTurnage and PenYours for allowing their whisper transcripts to be reprinted in the book.

A warm thanks to Ian Andrew, who saved me at the last minute when I didn't know what to do about the Oahu map. He carefully inserted all of the dots and numbers onto the map, and offered to add dolphins in the water, but we decided against it.

A big thank you to Fionna Boyle and Michelle Woolley for reading through the episode guides and offering comments, corrections, and additions (special thanks to Fionna for constantly forwarding me articles and tidbits she thought might help). Thanks also to Robyn Burnett, my colleague and friend, for suggesting the format of the book (chapters between the episodes), helping research the cast bios, and being there to offer advice.

Thanks to Mark at LostLinks.net for his support of the book, and for suggesting the radar screen used on the front cover. A big, big appreciation to all of the fans who maintain the plethora of mind-blowing *Lost* Web sites that allow other fans to delve deeper into the mysteries of the show, and discuss the show with the similarly obsessed.

Thanks to my family for their support (I think I'm finally going to get you to watch one of my shows, Dad). And to my friends, especially Suzanne Kingshott, who listened to me complain and gush about the book for eight months.

To my wonderful husband Robert, who was an immense help to me throughout this process, thank you. I couldn't have done this without your help. And thanks to my lovely and amazing daughter Sydney for not writing on too many of Mommy's notes when she was trying to work. And finally, as always, to Jennifer Hale: this book exists because of you.

Introduction: How Not to Get Lost

When *Buffy the Vampire Slayer* went off the air in May 2003, it was a sad, sad day for me and all the other fans of this smart, poignant, and funny show. A year later, *Angel* was canceled, and as I watched the finale in May 2004, I mourned the loss of Joss Whedon (the creator of both shows) on my weekly television schedule. How could any show possibly get me as interested as those two had? *Alias* was interesting, but when the writers decided to drop the more complex Rambaldi story line, I felt like the show lost something — especially when I'd been so diligently trying to put the puzzle pieces together for the previous three years.

And then, in September 2004, a plane crashed on a deserted island, and television has never been the same.

Lost is without a doubt the most fascinating, intricate show television viewers have seen in years. It appeals to both kinds of viewers: those who want to casually enjoy a show about a bunch of castaways trying to survive on a mysterious, supernatural island, making and breaking relationships as they go along; and those who watch the show on a deeper level, jotting down numbers, formulas, references, and bible verses as the show airs, and hopping onto the Internet to wikipedia everything and dissect each moment of the show with fellow online viewers. Both kinds of viewers can enjoy the show equally, and the writers are cunning enough to keep it interesting on both levels.

This book takes more of the latter approach, and tries to help join the dots of the puzzle. There are hundreds of Web sites, mailing lists, forums, chat rooms, and encyclopedic entries online to cover every aspect of *Lost,* and you could spend weeks getting lost with other viewers as you scope out every single possibility there is. This book is a compendium of theories, facts, and analyses to help out all types of viewers as they watch the show and read along. Where other books on *Lost* have either featured lots of glossy photos or academic analyses or collections of essays, I wanted to focus on the individual episodes themselves. As with my other books, *Finding Lost* will primarily be an episode guide, analyzing the development of characters and plotlines, asking questions along the way, and acting as a companion for viewers. I want you to read the episode guides as if you were discussing the shows with a friend.

Finding Lost is *not,* however, a substitute for watching the show. I will not provide plot summaries or transcripts or anything that would allow a reader to read my book instead of actually watching the show. You must watch the DVDs or the aired episodes. This book will provide a deeper understanding of the characters, the events, and the mysteries, but it will not be a replacement for *Lost* itself. No book could ever hope to do that.

The book is formatted episode by episode. Between each guide you will find some tidbit of information, either as a small sidebar of interest, or a larger chapter on the historical significance of something. Just as life on the island is interrupted by flashbacks of the characters, so too will the episode guide be broken up by these sections. You can skip them and come back to them later, or read through them to get a better understanding of the references or the actors playing the characters.

The sidebars are usually compilations of small themes or motifs in the episodes. The purpose of these is to connect some of the characters through their experiences, or just to have some fun with recurring motifs (like Sawyer's nicknames for people).

The book summaries provide a more in-depth study of the books referenced on the show. In some cases, the books are being read by a character (*A Wrinkle in Time, Watership Down, The Third Policeman, Our Mutual Friend, The Brothers Karamazov, Faster Friends*); in some, the book is simply referenced in conversation, but is important to the show (*Lord of the Flies, Heart of Darkness, The Turn of the Screw*), and in the case of *1984*, the book is alluded to on-screen, though never by the characters. In each of the book summaries, I will give a brief rundown of the plot, and point out the deeper meaning in each book (warning: the book chapters contain spoilers for important plot details in the books). I will then suggest some links to the show, but because many of the books appear early in the series and have much greater significance later on (like *A Wrinkle in Time*), I don't want to spoil anything for people, so I won't mention any specific links to plot details I haven't yet covered. Instead, read the book summaries carefully, because I've often pointed out details that would apply to various later episodes.

Some of the intermission chapters will touch on historical explanations of allusions on the show, such as the chapter on philosopher John Locke, or the synopsis of who B.F. Skinner was and why he's important to season 2. Others will take a facet of the episode and explore it more closely than you might have seen on the show.

The end of the book contains appendices outlining the links each character had to other characters before the plane crash; the best places to check out on the Internet for deep examination of the show, fun trivia, and damn good conversation with other *Lost* fans; and a special section on filming locations in Oahu, to allow fans to conduct their own tour of the places seen on the show, thanks to Oahu resident Ryan Ozawa.

The guides to the individual episodes will contain some spoilers for that particular episode, so I urge you to watch the episode before reading the guide to it. I've been careful not to spoil any episodes beyond what you're reading, so if you watch an episode, and then read the guide to it, you should be pretty safe from having any future surprises ruined. The episode guide will feature a one-line summary of the episode, and then an analysis. Following each analysis, you'll find special notes of interest, and they require some explanation:

Highlight: A moment in the show that was either really funny or left an impression on me that I couldn't forget after it ended.

Did You Notice?: A list of small moments in the episode that you might have missed, but are either important clues to later mysteries, or were just really cool.

Interesting Facts: These are little tidbits of information that are outside the show's canon, explaining allusions, references, or offering behind-the-scenes material.

Nitpick: Little things in the episode that bugged me. In past books I've done, I've occasionally had fans e-mail me saying, "Why would you say this?? The explanation for that happening is *right here*," and they can completely change my mind. But as I say in every book (and I'll say it again here), I've put these things in nitpicks because I couldn't come up with a rational explanation myself, but I'd love to hear them from anyone else. Nitpicks aren't necessarily wrong (those items appear in Oops). What makes the nitpicks section difficult regarding this series is that what appears to be an inconsistency now could be a deliberate plot point by the writers that will take on massive significance later. So I'm prepared for several of these to be debunked by the show.

Oops: These are mistakes that I don't think can be explained away.

4 8 15 16 23 42: In the late season 1 episode, "Numbers," Hurley reveals a set of numbers that have had an impact in his life, and it turns out those numbers have popped up everywhere, on the island and in the characters' lives before the crash. This section will try to catalogue them. I know there are a ton of them I'm missing, such as mathematical formulas whose solutions are one of these numbers, but I've tried to find as many as I could.

It's Just a Flesh Wound: In "Raised by Another," Hurley says to Jack, "It seems like someone's getting punched, or stabbed, or something every other day here." This is a list of all of the wounds incurred by the characters on the show.

Lost in Translation: Whenever a character speaks in another language that is not translated for us (mostly Jin), this section will provide a translation if I could find it. For the most complete Korean translations online, go to www.lostlinks. net, and check out the translations by fans from the ABC message boards and The Fuselage, or go directly to the The Fuselage and you'll find more translations that aren't available on this site. Thanks to all of the fans who have provided these to the non-Korean speakers like me.

Any Questions?: At the end of each episode, I've provided a list of questions that I think viewers should be asking themselves at that point. For anyone who's already seen the show to the end of season 2, many of the questions have been answered, but I've left them in here to show what questions should be arising at the end of each hour. Most of them are genuine questions I've been asking, and I hope they will be resolved in later seasons.

Ashes to Ashes: Whenever a character on the show dies, this section will provide a very brief obituary.

Music/Bands: This is a list of the popular music we hear on the show, whether it's on Hurley's CD player or in a flashback. In most cases I've provided in italics the name of the CD where you can find the song, but if I haven't, it's because it's a song that is featured on several compilations.

And there you have it, a guide to the guide. I hope you enjoy the book, and I welcome any corrections, nitpicks, praise (please? just a little?), and discussion at my e-mail address, nikki_stafford@yahoo.com. I cannot stress this strongly enough, however: The opinions in the following pages are completely my own, and if anyone out there has contrary opinions, I respect those. I don't expect everyone to have the same views as I do. What makes *Lost* so much fun to watch and discuss is how many possibilities this show presents to us. Ten fans can come away with 10 different interpretations of what they just saw, and that's what makes a show great, in my opinion.

Nikki Stafford
nikkistafford.blogspot.com
June 2006

"This is a waste of time": The Story of *Lost*

It was a show few people felt would ever actually happen. And once it was clear it *would* happen, critics cried out that it would fail. It was too risky, too weird, and simply too expensive to catch on with an increasingly fickle television audience that was more interested in *American Idol* than a complex story of a group of people stranded on an island. The concept, developed largely by Lloyd Braun, then the chairman of the ABC Television group, was to be called *Lost*, but even those controlling ABC felt it would be a disaster.

"A crazy project that's never going to work," was the take of Michael Eisner, the chairman and chief executive of the Walt Disney Co., the media giant that owns ABC. His second-in-command, Bob Iger, put it more succinctly: "This is a waste of time." The problems were evident: Too many characters and too many plotlines. The questions were equally apparent: Would people commit to a show that demanded such a heightened level of involvement, or had ABC dramatically overpaid for the pilot of a show that was doomed to failure?

The truth is that both Disney execs completely underestimated the possibilities and nuances of a show that thrives on the nuances of possibilities. They missed the show's endless series of options and its boundlessly interesting characters. They didn't feel audiences would be willing to dedicate valuable time and energy to a television program that was an enigma wrapped in a riddle. They could not have been more wrong.

There are just about as many theories about how *Lost* started as there are about the show's blurred plotline. The truth seems to be this: Lloyd Braun, a lawyer by training who had formerly managed Cher, was asked by Disney to join the company's subsidiary, Buena Vista Television. At the time, he was 39 and had been the force behind several key series, including HBO's mega hit *The Sopranos*.

Braun was so successful in his new role that he soon was handed the keys to the kingdom, in this case the position of group chairman of ABC, also owned by Disney. Not that ABC was a prize at the time — the network was struggling, and by 2003, it placed fourth among the major television networks. Braun was left fighting for his job and the only hope was to develop programs that brought viewers back to ABC. One concept he fostered during this period went on to become *Desperate Housewives*. The other idea he promoted was less refined. It involved survivors of a plane crash trapped on an island.

How Braun stumbled onto the *Lost* concept in 2003 is unclear. Some accounts suggest the idea of a show about survivors on an island had been pitched around Hollywood for a couple of seasons without attracting any takers. Braun was fascinated by the idea, though it had little substance beyond a vague notion and sketchy plotlines. A treatment was ordered, but was deemed unsatisfactory, followed by another attempt to nail down the concept. It was also summarily rejected.

Braun apparently was undeterred by the failure to find a workable concept, and as 2003 drew to a close, he continued to push forward with the idea. At the same time, his grip on power at ABC was coming into question. Eisner was not pleased with the network's continued struggles and Braun's inability to discover a hit program that would put ABC back in the limelight. But Braun was running out of time.

Networks traditionally give their new shows long lead times in order to deal with concerns about development, writing, and casting. The shows are written by October and presented to the network in December, when the decision is made which shows the network will finance. While other shows had already been scheduled for ABC, Braun's "Plane crashes on an island" concept was still just that — a concept. Searching for a concrete plan for his show, Braun turned to the network's upstart hotshot, J.J. Abrams.

Abrams was hardly a newcomer to Hollywood when Braun turned to him. In many ways he had been a golden boy since writing the script for Harrison Ford's 1991 star turn in *Regarding Henry*, when the 25-year-old was still known as Jeffrey Abrams. Other scripts followed, most of which were immediately forgettable, including Michael Bay's dismal *Armageddon*, which met critical disdain, but lucrative box office totals. Still no one saw Abrams' next turn coming. Nineteen ninety-eight found Abrams at the helm of a new show for the WB Network, entitled *Felicity*.

The story line didn't involve exploding asteroids or big Hollywood production values. Instead, it was about a high school senior who follows her crush to a college in New York. Abrams presented his main character, Felicity Porter, played with zest by Keri Russell, with a great range of dialogue and gave her believable everyday emotions.

The show was never destined to be the next *ER*; it was simply too intimate and too unique. But it did meet tremendous critical applause, much of it poured on Russell and Abrams. Abrams' success with *Felicity* caught the attention of Braun, who was looking for a writer who could help craft new programs that would resurrect ABC.

J.J. Abrams, at a fan convention, holds up a fan drawing of the Losties. (ALBERT L. ORTEGA)

"He's the whole package in every respect," Braun said. "He's obviously a brilliant writer who has creative, fleshed-out ideas. He's also a great producer, a great director, and just great to deal with day in and day out."

Not surprisingly, Braun managed to lure Abrams over to ABC to helm a new show about a female super spy called *Alias*. The show, starring then unknown Jennifer Garner, who had worked with Abrams on *Felicity*, debuted in September 2001 to critical accolades. The show became a must-watch for some, but its fantastic themes (ancient inventor creates plans for modern weapons), its elaborate plotlines (just how many people were related to Sydney Bristow on the show), and its convoluted nature kept it outside the mainstream. *Alias* became part of pop culture zeitgeist, but popularity on a massive scale remained elusive for Abrams.

By its third season, even Abrams admitted *Alias'* popularity might never match its critical appeal. "The show was about good guys working with the bad guys, many of whom thought they were good guys," he said. "But the baddest of the bad guys had to pretend he was good. That premise made it not only impenetrable to many viewers but also frustrating to write."

In an attempt to propel the show to a wider audience, Abrams reconsidered the concept and calmed some of *Alias*' more elaborate story lines. While it wasn't going to rival *CSI*, *Alias* became a modest hit for ABC in 2003 and 2004.

"I love the show too much and respect it too much to dumb it down or simplify it to the point of being lowest-common-denominator television," Abrams said. "If the network had said to me, 'you need to make the show simpler,' I would have said to them, 'Get someone else and do *VIP*.'"

With *Alias* firmly established, Abrams began work on a new show to be called *The Catch*. That was when he received the call from Braun in January 2004 about his "plane crashes on an island" concept, which the executive was still hoping to salvage and launch that September.

That Braun should turn to Abrams was not surprising. But the *Alias* creator was not entirely thrilled with the prospect of developing the show. "J.J. said, 'How can I possibly do another show this year? I'm running *Alias* and I've written this other show called *The Catch* and I don't have time to do this island show,'" recalls Damon Lindelof. "'I don't even know what it is. What's the show? A plane crashes on an island? Is that it? What's the series?'"

The truth was, a series didn't exist. Braun only had a concept, and even that was not particularly well developed. Lindelof has always been cagey on exactly how the show developed prior to his involvement.

"I don't want to get too into the details of what ABC was up to regarding this concept before J.J. and I got involved, out of respect for any other executives and/or writers who may have been involved in that process," he said in an interview just prior to the show's premiere. "Suffice to say, it was Lloyd Braun who came to J.J. with the series concept of 'plane crashes on island' in late January [2004]. J.J. was insane at the time, so he said the only way he could even think about getting involved would be to bring in another writer to spitball with — Enter me."

Not that Lindelof was well known. He had written for series such as *Nash Bridges* and *Crossing Jordan*. He had pitched a police concept to ABC in 2003 that was not taken, but ABC executives were impressed with his abilities as a writer and developer. He was asked to meet with them about the possibility of working with Abrams to add some detail and bring the "island concept" to life. "Let it be said, this was the fanboy dream. I'd been an *Alias* addict for almost three years at this point and had been pushing my agents and anyone who would listen just to get a meeting with J.J.," Lindelof said.

The pair immediately began brainstorming ideas for the show. Braun had envisioned some variation of *Cast Away*, Tom Hanks' star vehicle on the big screen, or even the television show *Survivor*.

But Abrams had other ideas. "What I like to do is to take a premise that's maybe a 'B' premise — castaways, spy stuff — and ask, 'How do we do this?'" Abrams said. "And inevitably, it's all about getting into the characters."

Soon after Braun pitched the idea, Lindelof and Abrams had a three-hour meeting and began discussing the concept. The island was a given. But what might go on there was still up in the air. The pair agreed the island had to become a central character to the drama.

Lost co-creator Damon Lindelof (SUE SCHNEIDER/MOONGLOW PHOTOS)

Time remained an issue. Abrams and Lindelof had only weeks to develop, write, cast, and shoot the pilot for the series. The treatment the pair developed — about a plane crash on an island and the stories of the individual survivors who also face daunting challenges from an unknown evil — sounded like a tough sell. It involved more than a dozen cast members and a big budget pilot. But the concept met with Braun's approval. "This, my friend, is *ER*," he was overheard telling his assistant.

In order to be ready for a premiere in September, Lindelof and Abrams had to meet deadlines unheard of for a new series. They were up to the task: in 11 weeks they wrote the pilot, established a cast, and shot the initial episode, a daunting two-hour pilot with an immense budget of $12.5 million.

Before anyone had even seen one frame of the show, which was now being called *Lost*, ABC was already putting some hype behind it.

"We're excited about the kind of drama that J.J. and Damon will be able to do in this world," Touchstone TV President Stephen McPherson told the *Hollywood Reporter*. "It's going to have Michael Crichton-esque elements of a thriller with strong characters. One of the biggest priorities in developing the piece is to have it done in a way that it can sustain over the long term as a regular series."

Unfortunately for Braun, without whom there would have been no *Lost*, he was not around to enjoy his success. With costs for the pilot mounting, and concerns that he had given a green light to a big budget series that lacked a coherent script, Braun's days at Disney were numbered. By March 2004, with the pilot being filmed, Braun returned from Hawaii where *Lost* was being shot. A few days later he was fired.

It's hard to say why *Lost* wasn't immediately scuttled after Braun's dismissal. Perhaps it was the costs; maybe only Eisner and Iger know. Either way, reports out of Web sites that followed the show (even before the pilot aired) made clear that several episodes were in the can as its premiere approached. Nonetheless, *Lost* became one of the rare occasions where fans — if that's what you call people who have yet to see a single episode of a show — launched an online campaign designed to save the series. The fans felt the series, which was set to premiere on September 22, 2004, would be destined for cancellation before it even started.

The initial appraisals of the show by television critics were mixed. Those jaded scribes who see TV programs before the public does were not certain what to make of *Lost*. At worst, it would be another flop for ABC, and a costly one at that.

"*Lost*, a drama series about people who get stranded on a strange island after a plane crash, was jokingly referred to as 'Lost It,' by media agency executives," said one media report after a screening. *New York Newsday* said ABC's new shows include, "*Lost*, a creepy-island plane-crash saga that looks like the flop *Dinotopia*."

Other critics sourly pointed out the show's shortcomings. "Miracles happen every day in the Church of J.J. For instance, although middle-aged women will not survive a plane crash on a remote island, miraculously all of the hot young ones will, as will all of the hot young men," wrote Lisa de Moraes, television reporter at the *Washington Post*. "Also surviving will be one young though fat male, one middle-aged man, and one precocious child."

Abrams said he understood some of their skepticism after only seeing the pilot, but asked they withhold judgment until they had some sense of how the wild and intricate plot would start to unravel. *Lost* was more than a show about a monster on an island, he assured them, and the characters and their stories would provide the satisfaction and fascination the viewers were looking for — if they gave the show a chance. "If you have a monster and you call it a monster,

Co-creator Jeffrey Lieber, Maggie Grace, Josh Holloway, Damon Lindelof, co-creator
Carlton Cuse, and writer/producer Javier Grillo-Marxuach hang out at a fan convention.
(ALBERT L. ORTEGA)

then it's sort of disposable and silly and feels kind of irrelevant or gimmicky,"
Abrams said while trying to explain his vision prior to the premiere. "If you have
something that represents terror and represents fear and represents the darkness
of this place, to me, that's incredibly valuable."

It was clear that *Lost* would challenge those viewers who tuned in on a weekly
basis. After all, there were more than a dozen key cast members, and keeping the
plotlines straight was a genuine concern. After all, complex television programs
often have difficulty expanding beyond an initial audience. No one wants to start
a book partway through, so there was a concern at the network that if the show
didn't immediately attract a huge audience, it couldn't do so as time went on. It
was expected that latecomers would be, well, lost by the complex web of characters, character histories, and plots that were weaved into the show.

Despite these concerns, neither Abrams nor Lindelof were making any apolo-
gies. "I love the show. But this is a drama. You know, at the end of the day, what
are our stories going to be? Jeff Probst isn't going to be walking out of the jungle
and telling them what to do," Lindelof said, admitting in another interview that,

The first season cast of *Lost* on the set in Hawaii in April 2005.
(JEAN CUMMINGS/SHOOTING STAR)

"People prefer franchise dramas like *CSI* or *Law & Order*, shows where the audience knows what they'll get, shows that they don't have to watch every week. What they don't want are serialized stories, character-based shows, or horror elements."

One thing was clear: *Lost* wasn't going to pander to the lowest common denominator. The audience that tuned in weekly to see *Everybody Loves Raymond* would likely not be attracted to *Lost*, a factor Abrams and Lindelof not only accepted but found liberating.

With the critics circling and ABC lowering its expectations, Abrams and his crew of writers remained upbeat and positive. They knew they had created a show that was unlike anything television had seen, with its mix of soap opera, humor, and *X-Files*-style science fiction. "To me, if this show were on, I would watch it," Abrams said.

It turned out Abrams wasn't the only one interested in tuning in to *Lost*. When the show premiered on September 22, 2004, viewers turned their TV sets to *Lost* in unprecedented numbers. Second only to a new spin-off of the *CSI* series, *Lost* drew 18.6 million viewers for its premiere, tapping deeply into the much-desired youth demographic. One week later, the show's initial success was reconfirmed when 17 million tuned in for the second episode. The show that had been written off as a failure by some of Disney's key executives was now a certifiable hit. It also garnered critical attention. In its first season, *Lost* went on to win nominations for 12 prime-time Emmy awards and became ABC's fastest-selling show internationally.

For Braun, the show's original backer who would land an executive position with Internet search engine Yahoo!, *Lost*'s success was bittersweet: "It feels like you were at the craps table, you were walking out the door, your bags are packed, you're about to step on the plane and someone says, 'Excuse me, you just won.' What? No way!"

SEASON ONE – September 2004–May 2005

Recurring characters in season 1: L. Scott Caldwell (Rose), Fredric Lane (Marshal), John Terry (Christian Shephard), William Mapother (Ethan Rom), Mira Furlan (Danielle Rousseau)

1.1   Pilot, Part 1

Original air date: September 22, 2004
Teleplay by: J.J. Abrams, Damon Lindelof
Story by: Jeffrey Lieber, J.J. Abrams, Damon Lindelof
Directed by: J.J. Abrams
Guest cast: Greg Grunberg (Pilot), Kimberley Joseph (Flight Attendant #1), Jon Dixon (Flight Attendant #2), Michelle Arthur (Flight Attendant #3), Dale Radomski (Tourniquet Man), Geoff Heise (Man), Barbara Vidinha (Woman)

Flashback: Jack

A plane crashes on a deserted island, and 48 people survive.

The scene opens on a man's eye, in which you can see the reflection of bamboo. He's lying in a jungle, wearing a business suit, and looks around in shock and terror. A golden Lab comes trotting toward him, and then bolts past him. As the

The fuselage of Oceanic Flight 815, which is stored on the island. (RYAN OZAWA)

realization of what has happened washes over the man, he jumps up and begins running toward a beach. The camera stays on him, not showing us what he sees, until he runs past a piece of jet engine whirring in the sand. As the camera turns to show us what this man can see, we witness the horrors of a plane crash on a deserted island, complete with fire, smoke, deafening noise, screams, and shocked survivors wandering aimlessly on the shoreline. It's a glorious moment of television.

From the show's opening seconds, the writers play up the show's title: all of the characters seem hopelessly lost. Jack, the doctor who was in the jungle, is the first character we see; he's followed by Charlie, wandering near the jet engine, looking completely befuddled; Jin, yelling Sun's name; Michael, calling out for Walt; Shannon, in a panic, screaming for Boone. In a matter of minutes, Jack manages to pull a man out from under the wreckage (with Locke), calm a pregnant Claire (with Hurley), and resuscitate a woman who appeared to be dead (with Boone). Only when he's taken care of everyone else in immediate danger does he wander away like an injured animal to finally deal with his own wound (with Kate). Jack is a surgeon, and he's been trained to care for other people first; and that pattern will continue throughout the series, where he lets the group dictate his actions rather than making his own decisions. This opening sequence, which makes even the tensest episode of M*A*S*H look like a walk in the park, gives us glimpses of most of the major characters. Sawyer and Sayid are not part of the big opening moment, but the show soon cuts to them, and our first impressions of them are actually pretty accurate — Sayid is a take-charge guy who knows how to get things done, and Sawyer turns himself into a nonchalant bystander, seeming like he'll help no one but himself.

"Pilot, Part 1," like the series in general, is about fear. There are few things more frightening than being utterly lost in a foreign place among strangers, unsure if you'll be able to survive. But J.J. Abrams & Co. aren't satisfied with just a tiny thing like a plane crash on a deserted island; they throw in wild animals, mysterious voices . . . and a tree-crushin', banshee-howlin', people-evisceratin' *monster* to boot. And that's just in the first episode. The pilot of the plane tells everyone that they're so off course that any search-and-rescue team is looking for them in the wrong place, eliminating all hope of someone coming to their aid quickly, and it's that moment when the fear sets in for all of them. As Jack tells Kate when he first meets her, the trick is to conquer that fear and not let it overtake you. This comment will become integral to the overall plot of the show, especially in season 2.

Jack is immediately set up as the alpha male. Matthew Fox plays this character as a somber, damaged person who doesn't want to be the leader, but once the burden is bestowed upon him he becomes The Boss. The series' first shot is of him, his is the first flashback we see (when we see what happens on the plane for the first time), and he gets more lines than anyone else on the show. Later, Locke and Sayid will also step in as leaders of the group, but for now, it's all Jack. We see him as a man with incredible self-control (his story of his first surgery where he only "allowed" himself to be scared for five seconds establishes his Type A personality), but he'll soon discover that controlling everyone around him might not be as easy.

The rest of the characters remain vague. Kate looks like she could be a girly-girl, but within seconds of being introduced to the audience, we realize she just wants to be one of the guys, and will try desperately to prove that she can succeed as one. Charlie is a friendly but self-deprecating British former rock star; Locke is a mysterious man who might be a little bit insane; Boone is a guy who's willing to help out everyone, but he's a little dense; Shannon is a snotty princess whose most useful contribution to the group is lending her sunblock; Jin keeps his wife Sun on a short leash, and doesn't want anything to do with the others; Hurley is a puppy dog whose presence makes others feel safe. Of course, first impressions are deceiving, and by the very next episode, almost all of these assumptions we've made about the characters will turn out to be completely wrong. Vincent, the golden Lab, is the second "character" we see after Jack, and as long as he is with Walt, Walt is safe; but whenever Vincent leaves him, Walt is in danger. Dogs have always been a symbol of protection and loyalty, and it is believed they have a sixth sense, and can detect danger before it occurs (dogs have been known to become anxious about their owners moments before their owners suffer a heart attack). Dogs are guides, and Native American beliefs state that when a dog appears, you should follow it and he'll lead you to safety. Vincent appears to Jack but Jack doesn't follow. Vincent will continue to pop up at integral moments, but we'll later discover he isn't the only character who can detect something before it happens (see page 321).

As with every episode of the series, viewers will walk away with more questions than answers. "Pilot, Part 1" is more of an establishing episode than one that will generate questions, but they're still there. The biggest question being, of course, what the heck is that monster? Throughout this season and the next, we'll be privy to various theories from castaways and other people, but for now, it's a menacing, terrifying beast. Yet, for all its fear-inducing rage, it's nothing compared to what else awaits these people.

Highlight: Hurley: "You think we should do something about the [sees Walt] uh . . . B-O-D-Y-S?"

Did You Notice?:
- In the very first scene, Jack pulls back his jacket and realizes he's wounded, but we don't see the gash.
- The "O" in the Oceanic logo looks like a giant eye.
- When Kate emerges from the jungle, she is rubbing her wrist.
- When Kate helps out Jack and he tells her the story of his first surgery, she says the first thing she would have done is run, and he says, "You're not running now." This tiny, subtle dialogue doesn't mean much to us now, but it'll become integral to Kate's character. Also, watch the way Kate looks at the plane that Jack constructs out of a leaf. It'll become important in "Whatever the Case May Be."
- Take a close look at the black smoke swirling around the plane; at first it appears to just be black smoke from the fire within the fuselage, but on closer inspection it's very wispy and seems to shoot up into the air with some purpose (see "Exodus, Part 2").
- When Charlie trips in the jungle you can hear the clinking and whirr like a chain gearing up. In "Exodus, Part 2," we'll finally see what the chain sound does, but in this case Jack prevents it from happening.

- Several people have cuts on the right sides of their faces or eyes.

Interesting Facts: Greg Grunberg, who plays the pilot, has known J.J. Abrams since they were in kindergarten, and has had roles in almost all of Abrams' projects, including prominent ones in *Alias* and *Felicity*. He only makes a brief appearance in *Lost* because Abrams was developing another series for him at the time — *The Catch* — but that show's pilot was never picked up. Also, Locke looks at Kate and smiles with an orange peel over his teeth, and then he looks down and eats it. This moment echoes a scene in *The Godfather*, where Don Corleone (Marlon Brando) is playing with his grandson in the tomato garden, puts an orange peel over his teeth and growls like a monster, which makes his grandson cry. He laughs, and takes it out of his mouth, and his grandson runs through the garden laughing while Corleone collapses and dies of a heart attack.

Nitpicks: After the explosion caused by the falling wing, why didn't everything in the interior of the fuselage catch on fire? It remains relatively intact, as we see when the survivors enter it later. Also, we see a lot of seriously hurt people on the beach, yet the only person Jack continues to take care of is the marshal. You'd think the guy with the leg caught under the piece of the plane would have required some sort of long-term care beyond Jack simply removing the tourniquet, as he says he did in the next episode.

4 8 15 16 23 42: Claire is **8** months pregnant; Jack tells Kate about the time he was doing a spinal surgery on a **16**-year-old girl; Jack figures the plane was at 40,000 feet when it began dropping; when they find the pilot in the plane Jack tells him they've been on the island for **16** hours; there are **48** survivors (**4** & **8**); the pilot has **4** stripes on his shoulder (**8** if you count both shoulders).

It's Just a Flesh Wound: Several survivors are sporting wounds from the crash in this episode. Jack: two gashes on his lower right cheek, two on his upper left cheek, scrapes on his knuckles, and a huge slice across his ribs under his left arm; Locke: one large slice on the right side of his face, over and under his eye; Claire: a large scrape on her chin and scrapes on both knees; Hurley: a cut over his left eye; Boone: a scrape on his lower left cheek (although that could have been incurred before the crash); Kate: cuts on her knuckles and marks on her wrists; Sawyer: scrapes on his knuckles; Jin: a large cut along his right cheekbone; Sun: cut above her left eyebrow; Marshal: has a piece of shrapnel embedded in his stomach and a severe head wound; Rose: a bruise on the left side of her forehead.

Lost in Translation: When Jin and Sun are huddling under the piece of the plane in the rain and another man tries to join them, Jin holds up his hand and says, "No, no, no, there's no room for you. Go somewhere else."

Any Questions?:

- There's a guy running by the jet engine when Locke yells to him to get away from the jet engine. The guy stops, looks toward Locke, and gets sucked in. One can't help but wonder, if Locke had kept his mouth shut, would that guy have just continued running and have been okay?

- What was Jack doing out in the jungle when most of the other people landed on the beach? We see in the flashback that when the turbulence got bad on the plane, Jack fastened his seatbelt, so how did it become unfastened, somehow flinging him from the plane? Rose was sitting right next to him, and she ended up on the beach. And if he was flung from the plane at an enormous speed, why didn't the impact crush him? As we see when he first becomes conscious and pulls out his tiny liquor bottle, the impact didn't even break it. Did he land on the beach and get dragged into the jungle by something/someone else? Did he land on the beach and wander deliriously into the jungle and pass out there? Or, is there a more sinister explanation?

- How did so many people walk away from this crash with barely a scratch? Sayid will later say that the plane did a cartwheel through the jungle, yet it didn't appear to cut a swath in the trees, and there are few broken bones or serious injuries among the people who actually survive the crash.

- If you listen carefully to the discussion some of the castaways have on the beach the morning after the monster's first appearance, Charlie thinks it's monkeys, and Rose curiously mentions that she thinks she recognizes the sound the monster makes from somewhere. Where, the Brooklyn Zoo? Construction?

Ashes to Ashes: Hundreds perish in the crash and subsequent explosion on the beach. The plane was carrying 300 to 350 people to begin with (according to one of the official Web sites for the show). We see several of them in the fuselage, hanging from the seats, dead.

Music/Bands: The majestic score for *Lost* is composed by Michael Giacchino.

1.2   Pilot, Part 2

Original air date: September 29, 2004
Teleplay by: J.J. Abrams, Damon Lindelof
Story by: Jeffrey Lieber, J.J. Abrams, Damon Lindelof
Directed by: J.J. Abrams
Guest cast: Greg Grunberg (Pilot), Kimberley Joseph (Flight Attendant #1), Jon Dixon (Flight Attendant #2), Michelle Arthur (Flight Attendant #3)

Flashbacks: Charlie, Kate

Using the transceiver, a group of castaways tries to send out a signal for help, but what they discover will change everything; meanwhile, Jack tries to save the life of a U.S. Marshal who has been seriously injured in the crash.

Where the first half of *Lost*'s two-hour pilot focused on the crash, this one zooms in on the characters themselves. Through flashbacks that show two new perspectives of the crash, we discover what Kate and Charlie were both up to when the plane began its downward spiral. Charlie's secret isn't very surprising, but Kate's is a revelation. Her escalating lies throughout the season will constantly get other people in trouble, just as they did before she became stranded on this island.

Locke finally speaks in this episode, and he will become the show's central figure when it comes to unlocking the mysteries of the island (pun intended). The first person he talks to is Walt, and fittingly, he tells him about backgammon. Locke likes to play games, literally and figuratively, and his super-creepy, "You wanna know a secret?" proposition to Walt definitely causes discomfort in the viewer, especially because Walt is a young boy. But watch how Locke treats Walt: he never acts like Walt is too young to understand something, and talks to him like he would anyone else on the island. It's fitting that he's playing backgammon, not only because of the light and dark reference, which is a recurring theme of the show, but because it's an ancient game of trying to escape a small area, which parallels the plight of the survivors. Each player has 15 checkers, which they use to pass through 24 points to eventually remove all of their checkers from the board. The first person to take away all their pieces wins. Just as the "tabula" (board) in backgammon must be cleared of all checker pieces, many survivors are looking to the island as a fresh start (and are looking to escape it).

What is most interesting about this episode is that, as hope begins to fade that an immediate rescue is on the way, people begin to revert to stereotypes that existed back in their home countries. All of these characters, as Locke will later say, have a clean slate on the island, a chance to start over, but they will be unable to leave behind who they were. Sawyer makes racist comments about Sayid, and Sayid calls Sawyer a redneck. As the group of castaways goes on a trek to find a radio signal, they alternately help each other and fight with each other. Kate and Charlie are harboring secrets, and as we saw in the previous episode, Jack was drinking pretty heavily for some reason. We've spent two hours scratching the surface of who these people *are*, and now it's finally time to flash back to who they *were*.

Highlight: The plane breaking in half in Kate's flashback. The special effects are breathtaking, and make you feel like you're right there, on the plane.

Did You Notice?:

- Right before the plane went down, Charlie, Kate, and Jack all imbibed something.
- The marshal uses nicknames for everyone, just like Sawyer does.
- Claire's necklace is the Chinese symbol "ai," which means love. As a soon-to-be mother, she may be the only person on the island who represents unconditional love.
- When Walt is reading his comic book, he sees a picture of a polar bear. Soon after, a group of people encounters one in the jungle. This link will become important in "Special."

Interesting Fact: The comic book that Walt is reading is a Spanish version of Green Lantern and Flash in *Faster Friends, Part 1* (see sidebar, page 93; there are spoilers for the rest of season 1 in the synopsis).

Oops: Charlie gets up and runs to the toilets through economy, business class, and first class. When the flight attendants pass through economy, you don't see Jack, Rose, or Locke sitting in the section (they've been chasing him too long at that point to be in the back section of the plane still). Later, in Jack's flashback, the "fasten seatbelts" sign comes on, and a few seconds later we see the passengers fly up in the air. In Charlie's flashback, the sign comes on, he gets to the bathroom, gets his fix, considers flushing the evidence, and *then* he flies up into the air. Also, the scene in the jungle where Sawyer kills the polar bear was obviously filmed long before the other scenes in the first two episodes. In the jungle, Sawyer has almost no facial hair, Sayid has a few days of stubble, and Charlie has a light

The cast makes an appearance (sans Sayid's beard) to promote ABC's newest show.

moustache and heavier beard. Elsewhere in these episodes, Sayid has a thick moustache, Charlie's moustache is the same thickness as his beard, and Sawyer has far more stubble than he does in the jungle. Finally, the first time we hear the iteration number, the man clearly says, "Iteration 7294531," but the second time, he says "Iteration 17294532," which is the correct number. Clearly the voice actor forgot the "one" the first time around.

4 8 15 16 23 42: Hurley tells Sayid he had a buddy in the **104**th Airborne in the Gulf War. Sayid says the Frenchwoman's message has been playing for **16** years. In backgammon, each player has **15** checkers, and the board has 24 spaces (24 is a reversed **42**). To keep track of the stakes of the game, players use a doubling cube, which has on it the numbers 2, **4**, **8**, **16**, 32 (a reverse **23**), and 64. The transceiver's model number is ABT-520. If you assign numbers to each letter of the alphabet, then A=1, B=2, and T=20; 1 + 2 + 20 = **23**.

It's Just a Flesh Wound: Kate has a bruise on the upper right side of her forehead, which may have happened at the cockpit, since it wasn't showing after the crash in the previous episode. Sawyer gets a cut above his right eye from his fight with Sayid.

Lost in Translation: A rough translation of the Frenchwoman's multiple transmissions is, "If there is anyone who can hear this, they are dead. I am going to try to go near the black rock; would you help us? They are all dead. Would you help us? It is outside. Would you help us, would you help us? If there is anyone who can hear this, I have told him to go up to the black rock. Would you help us — they are all dead, they are dead, it has killed them, it has killed them all. I have told him to go up to the black rock."

When Michael approaches Sun and asks her if she's seen Walt, she says, "I'm sorry, I don't speak English. I don't understand any English. I don't speak English." Then Jin shouts to her, "Your top button is undone. Button it." When Kate is bathing in the ocean, Sun says to her, "Excuse me, but I think they're ready for you. They're looking for you, over there." When Jin offers Hurley the sea urchins, he says, "These are sea urchins. We have plenty to go around for everyone. Please try one. Eat! These will help keep your strength up. Please eat!" When Jin offers one to Claire, he says, "Please try one of these. These will be good for your condition. Please try one, eat." After she eats one, he says, "Have another." And when she grabs his hand out of excitement that she's just felt the baby kick, he objects, "Please don't. No, don't do that. Oh, oh . . . let go of my hand, please. Don't do that."

Any Questions?:

- In Charlie's flashback, when the plane begins to plummet, he throws open the bathroom door and trips onto the floor. He barely dodges the drink cart before struggling up to strap himself into the second row of seats . . . in first class. I don't think the writers had him run all the way to first class for no reason; he straps himself into the one section of the plane where everyone died. How did he survive and end up on the beach with everyone else?

- Despite what Sayid and Shannon say, her message is not actually the same each time; if you listen closely, you'll hear her saying something either slightly different or completely different each time, making it four different messages. If, in fact, there are four messages (and it's not simply a production oversight) and they play one after the other, rather than the same one, then it means the amount of time she's been there should be divided by four, which would indicate she's been there for four years, not 16. Is this the case, or is it a production error?

- What letter is Sawyer reading?

Matthew Fox (Jack Shephard)

Arguably the most well known of the cast members to sign on to *Lost*, Matthew Fox was never intended for the role of Dr. Jack Shephard. He auditioned for the character of Sawyer, but J.J. Abrams had other ideas.

"With his look, confidence and kindness, he felt like the guy who could take you through this mysterious adventure," Abrams explained, pegging Fox in the role of Shephard, the know-it-all doctor and central figure in the cast. The only problem was that Fox had no idea who the character was.

"It was one of the few times in my career I've ever gone to meet somebody without reading a script," Fox said. "It was top secret, and nobody was allowed to read it. So I went in just knowing about Abrams, literally nothing else. I never go in that blind. Upon meeting me, I think he really saw me as Jack Shephard. I said, 'That's great, but I don't know who Jack Shephard is.'

"He sat me down and he gave me a script on the spot. I was trying to read it, but he kept running into the room every 20 minutes and asking me if I liked it. I said 'I'm absolutely loving it, but you've got to let me finish it.'"

With that, Fox landed his defining role as an actor to date in a career that already had its fair share of successes.

The middle child of Loretta and Francis Fox, Matthew was raised on his family horse ranch in Crowheart, Wyoming. It didn't take long for Fox to outgrow the rural nature of Wyoming. With his father's encouragement, he moved to Massachusetts following high school, eventually landing at Columbia University, where he majored in economics with his eyes on a job on Wall Street. The move presented Fox with a myriad of opportunities. "It opened my mind and my concept of the world," he said. "Wyoming is very provincial and has a way of keeping people there."

After graduating, Fox interviewed for jobs within the investment field. It became clear early on that he wasn't set for the life of a stockbroker. One early interview went well, until Fox realized he just didn't fit the mold. "I looked down, and I had those fuckin' penny loafers on, with pants that were, like, this much too short on me," Fox said. "And they all had exactly the same pair of Oxford shoes on. And in that moment, I was like, 'There's no way I can do this.'"

Not sure what his next move would be, Fox met a girl named Margherita Ronchi in New York in 1987. She became his girlfriend (and later his wife) and supported Fox after he determined he wanted to become an actor and entered The School for Film and Television. "She's always been incredibly supportive and sometimes even a little bit

A younger Matthew Fox, while promoting *Party of Five*. (YORAM KAHANA/SHOOTING STAR)

jealous that I found that thing that I was so dedicated to, and had a thing I wanted to grow at, learn about, and succeed in."

Success didn't come easily. After graduating, Fox landed some roles on forgettable series like *Wings*, before being cast in a supporting role in the movie *My Boyfriend's Back*. But his breakthrough came in 1994 with the television series *Party of Five*, in which he played Charlie, the brother who had to look after his siblings after their parents were killed. The show, which had a significant cult following, brought stardom for the often brooding Fox, whose celebrity led him to be featured in everything from the "Got Milk?" advertising campaign to *People* magazine's list of the 50 Most Beautiful People. Throughout it all, Fox was uncomfortable with his new stature as a Hollywood heartthrob. "I fought fame for a long time," he said. "People think you are just like that character and make judgments about you. I was very distrustful of people. But I've grown up a bit."

The party ended in 2000, leaving Fox uncertain about his next move. He shaved his head and attempted to distance himself from the success and audience he had garnered with *Party of Five*. "I wanted people to forget about me in that show," he said, "and come back doing something different."

He joined an L.A. repertory company, but eventually returned to television with the doomed show *Haunted*. By 2004, he had landed the role of Jack on *Lost* where he quickly became one of the best-liked cast members on the show, hosting barbeques for the crew and his fellow actors.

"He's a jock and a hard-core tattooed dude, and he's sensitive, and he's a dad, and the guy you want to get shit-housed with," says Damon Lindelof. "It's all the same guy. You can have man-love with Foxy, and it's all good."

1.3 Tabula Rasa

Original air date: October 6, 2004
Written by: Damon Lindelof
Directed by: Jack Bender
Guest cast: Nick Tate (Ray)

Flashback: Kate

As the marshal lies in agony in Jack's care, Sayid tries to organize the people; meanwhile, we flash back to Kate's past and discover why she was on the plane with the marshal.

So . . . it turns out Kate, the gal-who's-just-one-of-the-guys, has a mysterious past (by the end of the season, we'll be able to say that about every major character). In only three episodes, we've seen her convince everyone that she is completely harmless, while the marshal's words and her past suggest otherwise. Is Kate a chronic liar? Or is she a genuinely good person who made a mistake? She seems to sincerely worry about the marshal's health and how much he's suffering, and she also seemed honest when she said she hoped Ray would get his reward money. This season will give us two more Kate flashbacks that will allow us to delve more deeply into the character.

Sayid steps up into a major role in this episode. With Jack absent from their trek to find a radio signal, Sayid appoints himself leader of the small group, and makes the decision that what they discover on the hill will not be repeated to the other castaways. When they all return to the beach, Sayid stands on a platform and gathers everyone around, trying to rally them together to work as a team. It's the first time anyone has stepped up to take charge in any noticeable way; up to this point, everyone has assumed a rescue team is coming. But now that rescue seems unlikely, they need to find out if they can survive on this island. Later, Sayid comes up to Jack and reports to him, as if he's still in the Iraqi Republican Guard, reporting to his superior officer. By informing Jack what the people are saying and what their concerns are, he comes to him as the voice of the people, like an elected leader — one who must report to someone higher up. Sayid seems like the natural one to lead them, so why is Jack the one everyone will turn to? Because Sayid has dark skin? Because he's Iraqi?

While Sayid is establishing himself as a military/political presence, Jack continues to be the doctor whose sole purpose on the island is to maintain the health of the castaways. But what is Sawyer's role? He's an interesting character (see

Evangeline Lilly, on the *Lost* set in Hawaii. (YORAM KAHANA/SHOOTING STAR)

"Confidence Man"), but what makes him fascinating is not how others see him, but how he sees himself. In this episode he tells Jack that if Jack represents civilization, he'll represent the wild man. Yet he's not as wild as he'd like to think he is. While Jack berates him for looting the plane and stealing from dead people, isn't he simply doing what Sayid told everyone to do? They need to gather anything that can be of use on the island. At this point, the only person Sawyer really cares about is himself, and he has no intention of giving his loot to anyone else, but in future episodes, the very things he took from the plane will become essential items.

And in the end, it's Sawyer who steps up to do what Jack doesn't seem able to do. As we'll find out in future episodes, Jack cannot let go of things easily, and his Hippocratic oath is to save people and "do no harm." But on the island, things change. Here, doctors help you die.

It's already become obvious that Jack is a judgmental person who needs to trust people completely before he'll open up to them. When Kate comes back from the trek and informs him of the Frenchwoman's transmission, he doesn't show the anxiety that she expected from him. Instead, he stands and waits for her to completely come clean with him, and when she doesn't, he turns on her. The final scene with Jack and Kate is an interesting one, as he echoes a comment that Ray makes earlier in the episode. Jack reassures Kate that all is forgiven, and on the island, they can all start over and not be held accountable for who they were or what they did before they got there. But Jack is lying: he does care, and he will make Kate pay for who she was, again and again.

Highlight: The look on Michael's face when the rain stops.

Did You Notice?:

- Watch very closely at the end of the episode, when Walt is walking across the wing of the plane on the ground and Michael is just about to bring his dog back. On the side of the plane in the background, you can see the hexagon symbol that will become very familiar in season 2.

Interesting Fact: Interestingly, the Ancient Romans played a form of backgammon they called Tabula (Latin for board), which refers back to the previous episode. The basis of John Locke's philosophical theory was that each person was a *tabula rasa* (see page 30).

Nitpick: Sun brings over a suitcase to Jin and says she thinks it's his, and he says it isn't. Wouldn't Sun know what her husband's luggage looked like? Or is he so alien to her that even that is kept from her?

Oops: The pilot episode was clearly filmed long before the rest, which is normal in Hollywood. Walt's hair in this episode is a lot thicker than it was in the previous episode. It looks like it's been growing for two months since the pilot. Michael's looks a lot thicker as well. Sawyer had short hair in the pilot; now it consists of long layers, and his bangs go past his eyes. Sayid's hair has grown from just below his ears to almost shoulder-length. Also, when Claire and Charlie are on the beach, and Claire wonders if they wandered all the way up the mountain for nothing, the camera cuts back to Charlie and you can see that Claire is clearly talking, like it was the previous line shot from a different angle, but we can't hear her.

4 8 15 16 23 42: In Kate's flashback, Ray tells her the closest town is **15** kilometers away and his wife died **8** months earlier. The reward for Kate's capture is $**23**,000. Kate's mug shot number is 961136, which not only contains a reversed **16**, but is perfectly divisible by **4**, **8**, and **16**.

It's Just a Flesh Wound: At the end of the episode, Sayid throws some fruit to Sawyer and we see a long gash on his right arm, which is probably from the plane crash and we just couldn't see it before now.

Any Questions?:

- What is the significance of Ray's prosthetic arm? The writers have clearly put this in for some reason. Does it tie in with the fact that most people have wounds on their right sides? Especially the ones with something to hide? Will it feature in another person's flashback (e.g., we find out he's Claire's father or something? Crazier things have happened . . .)?

- How does Kate walk away from the accident with barely a scratch if she wasn't wearing a seatbelt?

- The gun only had one bullet, but what about the clip? Boone took the magazine from Sayid and Sayid leapt up and demanded it back, like there were bullets in it.
- Why does Charlie change FATE to LATE?

Ashes to Ashes: Marshal Edward Mars was escorting fugitive Kate Austen back to the U.S. when he was seriously injured in the crash with a piece of shrapnel lodging itself into his abdomen. It took two men to put him out of his misery. (But he was a bit of a bastard, so, no tears here.)

Music/Bands: As Kate and Ray are driving, they're listening to Patsy Cline's "Leavin' on Your Mind." At the end of the episode, Hurley is listening to Joe Purdy's "Wash Away" (*Julie Blue*).

Evangeline Lilly (Kate Austen)

Unlike *Lost*, which was pitched as a big-budget blockbuster film that everyone in Hollywood was talking about well before the series appeared on the small screen, no one had ever heard of Evangeline Lilly when she auditioned for a role in the series.

That was understandable. Even Lilly didn't expect to get the part. After all, her experience up until *Lost* was largely in roles on series like the short-lived *Tru Calling*, where Lilly was simply "uncredited," or on *Smallville*, where she was "Wade's girlfriend."

But the girl from rural Western Canada turned heads upon appearing to audition for J.J. Abrams.

"J.J. [Abrams] saw the tape I sent in from Vancouver to audition for the show, and basically it was his guts and courage to say, 'I've never seen this girl work, and I don't know what she's all about, but I'm going to take a chance and go with my gut instinct and take her on as Kate Austen,'" Lilly explained soon after *Lost* premiered. "For me, it's been a real honor. . . . I'm so grateful."

Since taking the role of Kate, Lilly has gone from being an unknown to being a notable Hollywood celebrity, leaving the tabloids to speculate on her relationship with Dominic Monaghan. It is a far cry from her childhood and teenage years spent in Canada.

Born in 1979, Lilly's father was a home economics teacher, while her mother ran a daycare center. The three girls in the family were raised by their father as "surrogate sons," she says. There was lots of physical activity, including swimming, running, and more. "We've got lots of land to play in [in Canada], and we do," she explained.

It didn't take long for people to notice Lilly's stunning beauty, though she didn't find it pleasant at the time. When she was 16, many started noticing her for her looks, something she found distracting and difficult to deal with.

"I spent many nights crying myself to sleep wishing I was ugly because of the way men leered and disrespected me, because they assumed things about my mental capacity or my physical willingness based on the way I looked." It got worse when she landed in university and spent time waiting tables. "I felt like a whore. You feel like they're paying to stare at your ass when you're walking away from the table."

Dominic Monaghan began dating Evangeline Lilly soon after they began working together, and they're now engaged. (CHRISTINA RADISH)

While her looks were getting her unwanted attention, Lilly's acting skills weren't suggesting to anyone that she was Hollywood bound. She took two years of drama in school and appeared in one play.

During her time studying for a degree in international relations at the University of British Columbia in Vancouver, Lilly's first big break came. While spending time in the holiday town of Kelowna, she was "discovered" by Ford Models agent Jeff Palffy. She turned down the offer to model, insulted that she was only being judged on her appearance.

In the meantime, she worked a number of menial jobs, including a stint as a flight attendant. "We used to go into airplane simulators when I was training, and they would simulate what a drop out of the sky would feel like," she said in an interview after *Lost* appeared. "I'd have my hands thrown in the air and be whooping while people behind me were vomiting. It's fun — take it for the ride."

Perhaps it was jobs like this that convinced Lilly that modeling wasn't that bad after all. She signed with Ford and began doing commercials, something she didn't enjoy.

"I always loved acting and being in front of people like that, but the industry is so corrupt and immoral. And I just didn't know where I would fit in."

But a career in acting or modeling was not what Lilly had in mind. With a devout Christian upbringing, she was preparing to work as a missionary following the conclusion of her schooling.

"I always planned to do humanitarian aid work or mission work when I got my degree," she says. "When I was 18, I went to the Philippines for three weeks working at Bible camps as a tutor and a physical education instructor for juvenile delinquents."

But Lilly never commenced her missionary work. Instead, her work at Ford led to a series of bit roles in a variety of television programs and commercials. With the work not amounting to much, and with friends saying she was sabotaging any chance she had at success, Lilly started taking acting lessons and submitted an audition tape to Abrams for the new *Lost* series. Abrams was looking for an unknown actress to cast in the role of Kate. He had been through dozens of tapes in the hopes of snagging the right woman for the role of the beautiful and dangerous fugitive, before stumbling across Lilly's entry. As an unknown, cast in such a central role for the series, Abrams warned her she would be under tremendous scrutiny.

"You have no idea what's about to happen. If you don't really want this, run," Abrams is reported to have told her. But Lilly wanted the part, and displayed an ability as an actress that belied her lack of experience.

"She's amazing," costar Matthew Fox says. "Stepping into the lead of a show with no experience? Her poise and confidence are remarkable."

Given the show's success, Lilly has become tabloid fodder, especially given her romantic relationship with costar Monaghan, whom she didn't even recognize when she first met him.

"I remember my first audition in L.A. and I was sitting in a room with him. I'm a die-hard *Lord of the Rings* fan, but I had no idea who he was. No idea. I saw him and thought, 'Huh, that guy is kind of familiar. That's really odd.' An hour later, I was still waiting to go in, because that's the way those auditions are, and somebody made a comment about *Lord of the Rings*. And he started talking like he knew all about it. So, I was thinking, 'Who are you?' And all of a sudden it clued in, oh my goodness, you were Merry in *Lord of the Rings*!"

Lilly's inexperience did prove difficult to overcome. Abrams said she occasionally lacked confidence in her first season, and would often rehearse scenes time and again. "It reminded me how wildly green she was," he says. "And she had mannerisms she had to unlearn, like crinkling up her forehead in a crazy way."

Lilly continues to recognize her shortcomings and work to get beyond them. The first year of *Lost* was difficult, she admits, but it was also clear that she had become a central and important part of the show's success.

"The first year was very hard. I was surrounded by breathtaking actors, and I felt very insecure about performing next to them. I thought I was going to fall flat on my face," she explained. "The first year I just kept thinking, 'Well, there has to be a point, a reason I'm here.' Otherwise, it wouldn't have happened the way it happened: in such a magical and spontaneous way."

1.4   Walkabout

Original air date: October 13, 2004
Written by: David Fury
Directed by: Jack Bender
Guest cast: John Simon Jones (Travel Agent), Billy Ray Gallion (Randy), Stephen J. Rafferty (Warren)

Flashback: Locke

While Sayid, Kate, and Boone attempt to triangulate the radio signal, the others decide to burn the fuselage and the bodies; flashbacks reveal Locke's secret, and the reason why he seems far more content on the island than the other survivors do.

"Don't tell me what I can't do." Everyone on the island carries emotional baggage from their lives before they stepped onto the plane. As such, they all have fears of what the others will think of them, fears sparked by how they were treated by others in their "past lives." Kate is scared of people discovering what she did and thinking she's a bad person, so she creates a persona and is constantly on the move, making it harder for people to figure her out. She's overeager to help, going on treks, assisting Jack, and later being involved in some extraordinary events. But for Locke, it's a fear of being told he can't do something.

Through flashbacks, Locke seems to be pretty consistent with what we've seen of him on the island — he's got an almost military presence; he's probably delusional; and with a mention of a therapist, we wonder if there may be psychiatric problems. On the island, he's remained quiet, keeping to himself, spouting the occasional foreboding message to anyone who will listen (i.e., Walt), and establishing himself as a loner and an outsider. In "Walkabout," he attempts to conquer old perceptions of himself by becoming a helpful and essential member of the group. (If this were *Survivor*, Locke would be the weird guy everyone wants to vote off, but doesn't because he helps keep them alive.) But he finds something far more meaningful in the jungle than just respect from the others. His behavior after what appears to be a religious experience will be entirely different.

The end of this episode is extraordinary, the first of many strokes of writing brilliance (and who better to deliver that stroke than David Fury, former writer and executive producer of *Buffy the Vampire Slayer* and *Angel*). As we flash back to discover the reason why Locke was in Sydney, the episode takes an unforeseen twist, and suddenly all those perceptions we had of Locke — that he's a physical, military guy; that he has a psychiatric therapist — fall away, and we discover *Lost* will be a show full of surprises.

The final moments of the episode are beautiful, with the music swelling as we see the major difference between past Locke, and present Locke, and we realize why he's been acting the way he has. Like everyone else, Locke was being defeated by life before he got on the plane, but he doesn't see the crash as another in a long line of unlucky occurrences. Where the island has been everyone else's hell, it's Locke's salvation. The island has trapped these survivors within its shores, within its jungles, but it has freed Locke. He has become a new man, baptized on an island that has given him a second chance. While Jack remains a man of science, Locke has become a man of faith.

Highlight: The final flashback in the travel agent's office. It's beautifully acted by Terry O'Quinn, and contains the twist of the episode.

Did You Notice?:

- Jack says he's not big on rubbing it in, which isn't true.
- When Claire is conducting the memorial service, the camera cuts to Charlie and Locke talking but you can hear Claire mention one of the dead, named Howard, had been assigned seat 23C. That was the seat Jack had moved to and was sitting in when the plane crashed.

Nitpick: When Locke is out tracking the boar and explaining to everyone how you follow the tracks, why doesn't Kate speak up? We'll learn in a future episode that she's an expert tracker, but she stays silent in this episode. Also, Sayid rightfully objects to Jack's idea of burning all of the bodies in the plane, saying Jack is clearly not taking into consideration what their wishes would be (see "The

The "Walkabout" travel agency was a vacant retail space in downtown Honolulu that was dressed specifically for the episode.
(RYAN OZAWA)

Greater Good"). Jack says he wants the fire to cast a signal, but what about burying the bodies and still burning the fuselage? It's moments like this where the others have every right to question Jack's decision-making, especially when he uses as an excuse that he doesn't want wild animals digging up the bodies, yet we later find out he buried the marshal. Finally, Kate tells Jack that she's a vegetarian, but in her flashback in "Tabula Rasa," we see her eating bacon and eggs when she first meets Ray. Was she lying to Jack in this episode, or is this an oversight on the part of the writers?

Oops: Obviously to avoid ruining the big twist, when the camera pans back in Locke's flashback where he's speaking to Helen, there's no wheelchair beside the bed, or anywhere in the room for that matter. How did he get into the bed? Also, Locke tells the story of Norman Croucher, a man who, despite having two artificial legs, managed to climb Mt. Everest. However, Croucher has never climbed Mt. Everest. He's climbed the Andes, the Himalayas, and several other large mountains, but never Everest. Why would Locke get a detail like that wrong? It seems the writers haven't done their research.

4 8 15 16 23 42: Jack says he was in seat **23**A. Locke tells Helen they've been speaking to each other for **8** months. He's been in the wheelchair for **4** years. Jack mentions that the plane crashed **4** days ago. Kate incurs **4** scratches on her face from avoiding a boar attack. In one of Locke's flashbacks, he calls Helen, a dial-a-date who costs $89.95 per hour.

It's Just a Flesh Wound: Charlie is grazed by a boar when the survivors find them in the plane. Michael is gored by a boar on his right leg, and Kate gets four scratches on her cheek when she jumps out of its way.

Lost in Translation: When Michael asks Sun to watch Walt, she says, "I will take care of your son." She then turns to Walt and says, "Don't worry, your father will be fine."

Any Questions?:

- How did Locke end up in the wheelchair?
- When he's on the phone to Helen, we see him lean over and turn off a TENS machine that's on a bedside table. Did he have *some* feeling in his legs?
- Is Rose delusional or is her husband really still alive? And if he is, could her comment about everyone assuming the people in the tail section are dead — "They're probably thinking the same thing about us" — be true?
- Who does Jack see in the jungle?
- What does Locke see in the jungle, and why does it affect him the way it does?

John Locke (1632–1704)

Considered one of the most influential of the Enlightenment thinkers, Locke believed that people had a right to use reason and common sense to search for truth, rather than just accept authoritarian rules. He coined the phrase "life, liberty, and estate," three things he believed every human being was entitled to. He posited that a government should be beholden to its people, and was only a proper government if it upheld its people's rights to life, liberty, and estate. If it didn't do so, it was within the people's rights to rebel against such authoritarianism. His theories influenced both the French and American Revolutions.

Locke's seminal publication was *An Essay Concerning Human Understanding*, to this day required reading for political science scholars. In it he stated that at birth, we have no innate knowledge and are instead a blank slate (or *tabula rasa*) upon which experience writes. All ideas are borne of experience, which can be divided into two kinds: sensation and reflection. Sensation is what tells us about the world around us — what we see, hear, touch, taste, and smell. Reflection is how our internal minds process information and make us conscious of the mental process. Locke explores how the physical world is made up of atoms that combine to form the world around us, and how ideas similarly combine to create knowledge. He then takes all of his statements and tries to explain the nature of knowledge. To Locke, knowledge is simply the agreement or disagreement of ideas, and that knowledge exists in degrees, by which we can say for certain what things are. The existence of ourselves is the *first degree* of knowledge — he subscribes to the Cartesian philosophy "I think, therefore I am" (i.e., the fact that we are standing here, and know it, is proof of our existence). From there, the *second degree* proves to us that God exists: If I exist, then someone must have created me, therefore God exists. The third degree of knowledge is our sensitive comprehension of external objects, the world around us, and our reasoning that if we can sense them in some way, they must exist. Locke maintains that man has been given knowledge to comprehend his world, but failing that, he must always use judgment. He writes, "Reason must be our last judge and guide in everything."

Locke's other important work is *Two Treatises of Government*, specifically the second treatise, where he defines a state of nature, and supports an individualistic law of society. In the seventeenth century, the work of Thomas Hobbes had gained popularity, but was controversial (see page 147). Locke's theory was an answer to this. He believed man is naturally good, and things like evil and greed are learned through experience; they are not innate within us. Locke writes that since God created man, man is God's property, to do with what he will. God has determined survival as our end, and therefore, we must use the means — life, liberty, health, and property — to achieve that end. Since, as mentioned, these are our natural rights, we must expect that no one can take those rights away from us, nor can we take anyone else's rights from them. All men are born free and equal, and must uphold their rights without violating those of anyone else. In a state of nature, all men are free to live independently, naturally, freely, loving our fellow creatures. However, when one person attempts to violate the rights of another, they enter a state of war, and the person who is being violated has the right to enter into that war to protect his rights. Locke defines slavery as a possible result of war — the victor in a war can kill the one he has defeated, or he can enslave him.

Locke talks a lot about property, and believes that in the first state of nature

— hunting and gathering — that which is caught or picked belongs to the person who caught or picked it. An apple is not a piece of property until someone picks it, and then it belongs to that person. Making one person go and pick apples for other people turns that person into a slave. One can do this as long as: he is not taking anything from anyone else, he leaves as much or more afterward (i.e., he can't pick the last apple), and he doesn't take so much that it might rot or spoil before he can use it.

The next stage of the state of nature is agriculture and farming. He who plants the seeds and tills the land is putting his labor into it, therefore he owns what he's sown. The third stage is the introduction of money, which changes everything. If someone buys apples with money, some of the apples may spoil or rot, but he owns them because he paid for them. His labor didn't go into the creation of them, and the introduction of money creates economic inequality. However, money can be useful in the sense that if one man tills the soil to create an apple tree, but cannot eat all of the apples before they rot, then he can sell the remaining apples to someone else who could use them. In this way, money can become useful in a state of nature.

So . . . what does all of this have to do with *Lost*'s John Locke, the guy with "four hundred knives" who used to be in a wheelchair? Like his namesake, Locke believes in fairness, and in individualism. In upcoming episodes, Sayid and Jack will be dividing the group and coming up with different tactics to organize and corral the survivors. Locke will remain separate from all of that, acting as the hunter-gatherer (the first stage of the state of nature) and bringing things back to the group. Like his historical namesake, he believes in God, but he's actually seen some form of what he believes God to be, so not only does his faith stem from the second degree of knowledge — that there must be a God if he himself exists — but from the third, using one's senses to understand the external world. Locke uses reason, and calmly sits and philosophizes with Jack, Sawyer, Boone, Claire, and several others, using anecdotes and parables to prove his points. His repetitive mantra — "Don't tell me what I can't do" — suggests he feels violated in those moments, that by telling him he can't do something, you are trampling his basic human rights of life, liberty, and the pursuit of happiness. He believes that the island is giving everyone a blank slate, and that people are essentially good but can change thanks to society (watch how his attitude to Charlie will change from season 1 to season 2). He will maintain his hunter-gatherer state, even when Sun will move on to the agricultural one, building a garden in the jungle. He has no time for Sawyer, the man who hoards property, because it goes against everything the philosopher John Locke believed in.

And when push comes to shove, as we will see in season 2, John Locke knows how to shove back.

1.5   White Rabbit

Original air date: October 20, 2004
Written by: Christian Taylor
Directed by: Kevin Hooks
Guest cast: Veronica Hamel (Jack's Mother), John O'Hara (Young Jack), Sev Palmer (Meathead), Andy Trask (Hotel Manager), Geoff Heise (Doctor), Meilinda Soerjoko (Ticket Agent)

Flashback: Jack

The survivors are running out of water, leading Jack on a search for a drinking supply as he follows a mysterious man through the jungle.

In Lewis Carroll's classic tale for children (and adults), *Alice's Adventures in Wonderland*, a white rabbit leads Alice down a deep hole to a world of nonsense and surrealism. What she discovers doesn't mean much to a little girl, but adults who read the book are treated to a terse commentary on Victorian social customs and educational system. As Alice navigates the fantastical land and meets a crying Mock Turtle, a regal Dodo bird, a grinning Cheshire Cat, an abusive Duchess, and a stoned Caterpillar, she attempts to make sense of the nonsense around her by using what she has learned in school, only to discover her lessons are almost as nonsensical as Wonderland itself. In the end, it turns out to be nothing but a dream. "Curiouser and curiouser."

The same could be said for *Lost*, which adds new layers of mystery and weirdness with each episode. Just as the White Rabbit led Alice deeper and deeper into Wonderland, the image of Jack's father leads him deeper into the jungle, forcing him to look into himself to discover who he is. Through a childhood flashback we see that Jack doesn't easily back down or let go, even when it's in his best interest to do so (we'll see more of this behavior in "Do No Harm"). We also see the parents Jack has had to deal with: a father who puts immense pressure on

In *Lost*, the Sydney International Airport is played by the Hawaiian Convention Center. (RYAN OZAWA)

Matthew Fox, on the set of *Lost*. In "White Rabbit," Jack follows a haunting image from his past into the heart of the jungle. (YORAM KAHANA/SHOOTING STAR)

him, and a mother who appears to blame Jack for her husband's problems. It's amazing he turned out to be as together as he is (or seems to be). His father had warned him when Jack was a child that Jack shouldn't try to play the hero, because he can't deal with the fallout if he fails, but when his father couldn't take care of himself, Jack is forced to take care of him, and we discover why Jack was on that plane from Sydney.

Despite telling Kate that the island is a place of new beginnings, Jack is clearly haunted by his father, and beholden to a mind-set that won't allow him to back down. When he confesses to Locke that he's worried he's going crazy and maybe should consider ending this nonsense, we know before Locke tells him to that Jack will persevere and see this thing to its bitter end. It's what Jack does. The scene between Jack and Locke is one of the first key moments in the series, where we see Locke turning into a religious man who worships the island itself, and Jack looking at him with skepticism.

The pressures of the island are starting to get to Jack, and understandably so. He's the only character who is not getting a break from his old life while on the island — he's a full-time doctor, on call 24/7, and he feels the pressure of his vocation as strongly, if not more so, than he did before the crash. Watch how many times people turn to Jack as if he were their spiritual guide, the one who has to help them not just physically, but emotionally. In the previous episode, Boone tells him Rose has been sitting alone on the beach, and Jack wonders aloud what Boone expects him to do. In this episode, Boone's accusations come as a blow to both Jack and the viewer, when Boone asks, "Who appointed you as our savior?" The answer is — everyone. From the moment they crashed on the island, the castaways have turned to Jack for medical attention, advice, solace, and help of every kind, and often he's tried to escape their neediness. There will be several times when Jack will become a self-righteous jerk on the island, but because of his vocation, he is the obvious choice as leader.

Ultimately, Jack follows his White Rabbit to one amazing discovery, and another shocking one, and he has an epiphany. His father is dead, and Jack is no longer under his thumb or hidden in his shadow. Soon Jack will step up and take his place as the official "shepherd" of the flock, but what he will propose will divide the group in a way that could threaten their survival.

Highlight: Sawyer trying to charge Shannon $5,000 for sand-flea repellant.

Did You Notice?:

- Charlie's tattoo says, "Living is easy with eyes closed," a line from The Beatles' "Strawberry Fields Forever." Dominic Monaghan actually had the tattoo before starring on *Lost*, but the writers couldn't have come up with a more appropriate motto for his character — and for the show itself.
- Jack's speech about getting organized and cataloguing things on the island is almost exactly the same as Sayid's in the previous episode, yet everyone listens like Jack is saying this stuff for the first time.
- Geoff Heise, who plays the doctor in the morgue, appears in "Pilot, Part 1," as a survivor on the beach (you see him in the first four minutes running along the beach, yelling back at someone, "Stay away from the gas! Stay there!"). Did the casting agents just use the same guy and hope no one would notice, or is there some significance to him showing up twice? Was the morgue doctor actually on the plane with Jack?

Interesting Fact: When Jack gets to the caves, there are little china dolls scattered everywhere, a very surreal moment. This could be a reference to Czech director Jan Svankmajer's stop-motion animation classic, *Alice*, a nightmarish and brilliant adaptation of *Alice's Adventures in Wonderland*. Whenever Alice eats or drinks anything that makes her small, she changes from a live girl into a little china doll.

Nitpick: Why are Boone and Jack the only two people who attempt to save Joanna? We know several of them can swim. Also, when Jack visits the morgue, it's odd that the doctor would say Jack's father died of a myocardial infarction, and then explain that it means a sizeable and fatal heart attack. Perhaps the doctor didn't realize that Jack is a doctor as well, but if he didn't, he would simply have said he died of a heart attack. Finally, when Jack begins smashing the casket to bits, it comes apart like punchboard. With two doctors in the family, why couldn't the Shephards have afforded a nicer casket?

4 8 15 16 23 42: When Kate jumps Sawyer, he says he made this birthday wish 4 years ago. Charlie jokes with Claire that Locke had 400 knives in his knife case.

Lost in Translation: When Sayid questions Jin and Sun about the water, Jin yells at him, "Beat it, S.O.B. If you touch my wife one more time, I will kill you."

Any Questions?:

- Was Boone telling the truth in "Pilot, Part 1" when he said he was a lifeguard?
- Why did Jack's father leave his wallet in the hotel room? Did something happen to him that was perhaps more calculated than just a heart attack?
- Claire mentions that she's looked through 20 suitcases and has yet to find a hairbrush; why are there no hairbrushes? It seems like a strange line of dialogue for the writers to have just thrown in there.
- Is Kate really a Gemini or is it just another lie? It would be interesting if she is, since a Gemini is the sign of twins, i.e., two faces.
- How did Locke happen to be at the very spot on the cliff where Jack went over?
- What exactly did Locke see in the previous episode, and what did he mean when he said he's looked into the eye of the island, and what he saw was beautiful?
- Why was someone shipping a crate of china dolls? Were they from the Oceanic plane crash or another one?
- Where is Jack's father's body? Theories abound about what happens at the end of this episode. Maybe after fighting with the airline agent, Jack lost the fight and they wouldn't allow the corpse to board with him after all,

which is more realistic than an agent allowing a dead body on board out of pity for the alleged son. But if that's the case, why did Jack get on the plane? Why did he seem so shocked when the corpse wasn't in the casket? Another theory is that the body fell out during the crash. Or maybe someone on the island has already taken the body. Or, more sinister, maybe he isn't dead after all? Jack saw the body in the morgue, but considering how preposterous other occurrences in the show have seemed, maybe Jack didn't see what he thought he saw. It's a big question mark, and fans will have to take a close look at upcoming clues to figure it out.

Ashes to Ashes: Joanna, a swimmer who was supposed to have been on an earlier flight, dies when a strong undertow pulls her away from shore.

Lord of the Flies by William Golding (1954)

One of the most famous books about a plane crash on a deserted island is *Lord of the Flies*, which is certainly a literary predecessor to *Lost*.

The novel is set during a war. A plane of English boys who were being evacuated crashes into a deserted island, and what begins as an ordered existence eventually devolves into chaos and madness. The main characters of the book are Ralph, who is designated the leader and who tries to maintain order and civility; Jack, who is the hunter of the group and who has little time for Ralph's lectures; Simon, the good, kind child who helps keep the younger boys calm; Piggy, the overweight, smart kid with glasses who becomes Ralph's right-hand man; Roger, Jack's henchman and bully, who doesn't seem to have any goodness in him; and a group of six-year-olds, who are referred to as the "littluns" by the others.

At the beginning of the book, Ralph is chosen to be the leader of the group, which infuriates Jack. Ralph finds a conch shell on the beach, and states that it will represent order on the island: whoever is holding the conch shell has the sole right to speak, and everyone else must be quiet. Jack becomes the hunter, and is in charge of finding food for the group. They light a fire using Piggy's glasses, and hope that a plane will see their signal. The first night, one of the littluns claims to have seen a "beastie" in the jungle, and while Ralph and the others don't believe him, the monster will take on a greater significance as the novel progresses.

As the divide between Ralph's group and Jack's group becomes larger, Ralph begins to lose his grip on maintaining order on the island. When a ship goes by and Ralph realizes Jack's let the signal fire go out, it sparks a fury in him that builds throughout the rest of the novel. Jack, meanwhile, has killed a wild pig, which gives him the power and respect that Ralph seems to be losing. As the boys dance a ritualistic bloodthirsty dance around the fire to celebrate their kill, Ralph holds the conch and pleads with them to listen, but the group of hunters no longer listens to him. Jack hits Piggy and breaks one of the lenses of his glasses, which is an allegorical blow against intellectualism.

One night, an aerial battle rages over the island, even though the boys sleep through it, and a pilot parachutes out of his plane, but is killed in the air and lands in a tree on the island. Two boys find him the next evening, but all they see is the large parachute blowing in the wind, with the body of the pilot rising and falling as if he were still alive. They race back to the group to report that they've found the beastie. Jack and Ralph lead an expedition into the jungle to locate the monster, and Jack insists they go up the cliff at night. When they see the parachute blowing in the breeze — again mistaking it for something it's not — they rush back to tell the others. The next morning, Jack holds the conch shell and tells everyone what they have found. Piggy is skeptical, Ralph is defeated, and the littluns are terrified. Jack forms a splinter group of hunters and invites anyone to come to his tribe. Several boys go because he offers them food and protection, and Ralph can't offer them anything but civilized behavior. Jack slaughters a pig, and puts its head on a stake in the jungle as an offering to the monster, and they prepare for a feast.

Simon, who has been the quiet reflective one until now, wanders into the jungle and finds the pig. He sits before it, and hallucinates that it's talking to him. It calls itself the Lord of the Flies, and says it exists within all of them, and it's going to have some fun with Simon. He faints from terror.

Ralph and Piggy go to Jack's camp during the feast to try to talk to him, but the boys are engaged in a ritualistic feast, and begin dancing around the fire, celebrating their kill. As the dance becomes more frenzied, even Ralph and Piggy join in, giving in to their more savage sides. Meanwhile, Simon wakes up and finds the parachutist. He grabs the parachute to take it back to the others and prove that there was never a monster on the island. As he emerges from the jungle, Jack declares him the beast, and they all set upon him, brutally killing him.

The next morning, Ralph feels guilty, and Piggy begins to explain away what happened, as if they weren't responsible. Jack sets upon them and takes Piggy's glasses, thereby stealing the last bit of power Ralph had — the ability to make fire. Ralph and Piggy return to Jack's camp to confront him, but in the ensuing argument, Roger hurls a boulder that hits the now-blind Piggy, crushes the conch, and sends Piggy over the cliff to his death. Ralph, realizing that civilization is now dead on the island and that everyone else has descended into savagery, runs into the jungle, with the boys on his heels. He finds the sow's head on a stake, and, accepting that he, too, has an evil side, grabs the stake with the intent to use it. The boys light the jungle on fire to smoke Ralph out, and as he races out onto the beach he discovers a naval officer standing there. He saw the fire from the water, and is appalled to find that such good English boys could turn into such savages in a short period of time. What his hypocritical statement fails to address is that he himself is engaged in a war the boys were initially trying to escape, and that they've given in to the same impulses that cause men to war amongst themselves. Ralph collapses on the beach in tears, realizing his innocence has been subsumed by the evil that existed within all of them.

Lord of the Flies is a Hobbesian nightmare that subscribes to the notion that all men are evil in nature, and without any order, they will give in to the darker side of themselves. There's a scene early in the novel where Roger is pelting one of the littluns with rocks, until he hears the imaginary voices of his parents and teachers telling him not to. It's only when the boys are so removed from society they think civilized behavior was a figment of their imaginations that they can completely embrace the savagery that existed in all of them. By the end of *Lord of the Flies*, we realize the littluns were correct all along: There *was* a beast on the island, but it was internal, not concrete, and the more they became caught up in killing the imaginary external monster, the more the beast within each one of them was able to flourish.

While *Lost* is a show about adults, not children, on a deserted island, the basic concepts are the same. Jack has just found a cave in the jungle, and his discovery will force survivors to choose sides and split up. Unlike the children of Golding's novel, however, the adults on *Lost* have lived in society for so long that they have the customs of society ingrained within them. They're not about to grab sticks and begin chasing each other through the jungle with the intent to kill (at least, not yet). But over the first two seasons of the show, we will watch these customs break down, and the people on the island will begin reverting to instinct rather than what society expects them to do. The first is John Locke, who, as the hunter in the group, is most like Golding's character Jack (Jack is a nickname for John). Throughout season 1 we'll watch him break away from the rest of the group; but he has few aspirations for leadership, unlike the Jack of the novel. Jack Shephard, on the other hand, resembles Ralph in his more sensible, civilized leadership, yet like the children in the novel, the characters on the island keep turning to other people when they disagree with Jack's leadership. Just as the littluns must go along with the decisions that the bigger boys make, so too do the voiceless castaways have to do whatever the main characters say in this episode — Sayid, Locke, Jack, and Sawyer seem to make the rules because they're the most powerful men, and the rest of the characters go along with it.

In the novel, the main enemy is a "beastie" on the island who turns out to be the *id* of the children. On *Lost*, the monster is a real thing that lurks in the jungle. But as the next two seasons will unfold, we'll find out more about the monster, and it will ultimately be far more akin to the one in *Lord of the Flies*. Jack tells Kate in "Pilot, Part 1" to let the fear in only momentarily, but the longer they are on the island, the more these characters will succumb to their deepest fears, and it will make them look at the darkness within themselves.

1.6   House of the Rising Sun

Original air date: October 27, 2004
Written by: Javier Grillo-Marxuach
Directed by: Michael Zinberg
Guest cast: Sora Jung (Decorator)

Flashback: Sun

As Jack and Sayid argue over whether to stay on the beach or move to the caves, Sun remembers what life used to be like with Jin.

"Two players, two sides. One is light, one is dark." Locke's ominous words in "Pilot, Part 2," as previously discussed, will become integral to the show, and the feud that breaks out between Sayid and Jack in this episode is the first major war between black and white. Throughout this episode, both men will make their moves, as if the survivors are backgammon pieces they can shift around as they please. Sayid believes strongly that rescue is coming, and he doesn't want to miss it when it does. Jack, on the other hand, believes everyone should focus on how they are going to live on this island, because he has much less faith that help is on its way. By suggesting people should move a mile inland to the caves where they will have access to fresh water, he divides the camp between those who are desperate to get off, and those who may be finding solace and freedom on the island — the pessimists, as Sawyer puts it. Sayid asks Jack at one point, "Is there a reason you didn't consult us when you decided to start your own civilization?" As discussed in the previous episode, Jack has had leadership foisted upon him, and has finally accepted it. But in doing so, watch how many people will question his decision-making. He's been informally chosen, but not democratically elected, and his main frustration will be that people expect him to make the difficult decisions, but ask permission first.

Sayid and Jack's relationship troubles are new, but Sun and Jin's have been ongoing. Over the past five episodes, Sun and Jin have been established as That Korean Couple, where he is controlling and nasty, she is submissive and fearful, and no one can understand a word they say. In this episode, we finally see another side of Jin, and Sun's backstory shows us that things weren't always the way they are now. In previous flashbacks, we've discovered things about each character that they don't want others to find out, but in Sun's, we find out the only person she worries about discovering her secret is Jin. Theirs is a portrait of a whirlwind romance, a controlling father, and a difficult marriage. What creates the tension between them isn't actually from problems within, but without — namely Sun's father, Mr. Paik. Sun doesn't know what Jin does for her father, but she suspects it's dangerous, immoral, and illegal, and Jin's reluctance to tell her anything only makes her suspicions worse. Up to now viewers have seen her as a sheepish woman with a domineering husband, though we get glimpses of tiny rebellions on her part. In her flashback, however, we discover that her secret involved both courage and defiance.

Back at the caves, Kate, Charlie, Locke, and Jack make a shocking discovery, and realize there was someone stranded on the island even before the last group of people. Locke refers to their finding as "our very own Adam and Eve," which could also be a comment on the main story of the episode. Adam was thrown out of the Garden of Eden because Eve gave into temptation, according to the biblical account, just as Jin was drawn into the world of Mr. Paik's corruption because of his love for Sun (thereby ruining his own plans for future paradise). Is the island itself a Garden of Eden, or is it the dark world Adam and Eve faced when they ate the fruit of knowledge?

While Sayid is trying to suss out who's on side with him, he is also carrying out an investigation into a seemingly unwarranted attack on Michael by Jin. Like Jack, he makes harsh decisions of his own and designates himself the island's hand of justice. Sun realizes that if she doesn't reveal her secret to someone, her husband could be in trouble, so she turns to Michael. He's an interesting choice — Michael is having serious problems communicating with his son, yet he's now able to speak to one of the two most incommunicative characters. And while he believes Koreans in the U.S. hate black people, Jin and Sun aren't American. Sun turns to Michael because she's worried about her husband and wants the others to know he's not a bad person. Deep down, we know she still loves Jin.

Which is the epiphany she has in the airport. As she prepares to execute her brave plan, she takes one last glance back at her husband, the way Orpheus looked back at Eurydice as he was leading her to freedom. But where Eurydice vanished back into hell, Sun returns to Jin . . . and goes to hell with him. An excellent episode, with a beautiful, mournful musical score.

Highlight: Locke's unexpected review of Drive Shaft's two albums.

Did You Notice?:

- Jin is handcuffed to the side of the plane for attacking Michael, yet in this season alone we will see one castaway commit murder, and another one attempt it, and both will get off scot-free. Both of those characters will be white. Apparently, the racism that exists in the outside world has been carried to the island.
- The "decorator" tells Sun that after one week missing, she'll be assumed dead and will finally be free. The survivors have been missing for eight days, a suggestion that maybe she and Jin are free.

Oops: When Jin first rushes into the bathroom, he's covered in blood, but many of the bloodstains disappear and reappear throughout the scene. Also, we see Kate take her shirt off in the cave near the bodies, but Charlie brings it in with him and says she left it outside.

4 8 15 16 23 42: Walt's birthday is August 24 (**08**/24, with 24 being a reverse **42**); Charlie says it's been **8** days since he's played his guitar; Sun must make her escape at the airport at 11:**15**; as Sun rejoins Jin at the airport, you hear an announcement for Flight 125 (1 + 2 + 5 = **8**).

It's Just a Flesh Wound: Charlie, Locke, Kate, and Jack (but mostly Charlie) suffer bee stings; Jin's wrist is badly chafed from the handcuff.

Any Questions?:

- Who are the two people in the caves? Why do they have two polished stones in a pouch, one black and one white?
- Why was Jin covered in blood?
- Who is Mr. Paik and what exactly does he do?
- How did Jin and Sun meet in the first place, having come from two very different worlds?
- Why does Kate choose to stay on the beach? What does she mean when she tells Jack she can't dig in? It's interesting that by staying on the beach, Kate is indicating that she wants to be rescued. Why? On the island she's free, but in the outside world she'll be put in prison, so why is she so intent on rescue?

Music/Bands: The episode's title is a reference to a traditional song made famous by UK band The Animals in 1964. At the end of the episode, Hurley is listening to Willie Nelson's "Are You Sure?" (versions of this song appear on various Nelson compilations, but if you want the version that appeared in the episode, it's on *Crazy: The Demo Sessions*). What a perfect song to end the episode.

Yunjin Kim (Sun Kwon)

Sometimes referred to as "the Korean Julia Roberts," actress Yunjin Kim is the biggest star of *Lost* — at least among her established fanbase and in Korea. "I know that in Koreatown in L.A., things practically shut down when the show is on because people want to tune in to see these two Koreans go at each other," says Kim. "I heard that people dressed up as Sun and Jin for Halloween last year, too."

In fact, in Korea the show is dubbed from its English, while the conversations of Jin and Sun remain in Korean, an unusual occurrence considering the other characters are not supposed to be able to understand Jin, though they are all speaking the same language.

Born November 7, 1973, in Seoul, South Korea, Yunjin (pronounced Yoon-jin), Kim immigrated to the United States at the age of 10 with her family. In an attempt to find

Yunjin Kim originally tried out for the part of Kate, but so impressed everyone they created a role just for her. (STHANLEE MIRADOR/ SHOOTING STAR)

friends in her adopted homeland, Kim joined a musical production of *My Fair Lady*. "I was cast as only an extra, but that day, I stood on the stage and sang loudly in my own voice," she says. "When singing and acting on stage, I didn't feel the least bit awkward. I felt so at home under the lights . . . Something about being on stage just felt right."

She would attend the New York High School of Performing Arts before training at Boston University and the British American Drama Academy, where she graduated alongside *Lost* season 2 costar Cynthia Watros (Libby). Along the way Kim became a trained dancer, studying ballet and jazz.

Following graduation, she garnered some small roles on MTV and ABC, as well as on Broadway. However, it took a 1996 Korean series, called *A Gorgeous Vacation*, to make her a star — at least in Korea. By the time she did *Wedding Dress*, a 1997 miniseries, Kim was living full-time in Korea. "Even then, I had no idea I would live in Korea," she says. "I thought I would finish the film and go back to the United States."

She continued to work in Korea and Hong Kong before auditioning for the role of Kate on *Lost*. Like many of the roles in the series, J.J. Abrams liked Kim, and fashioned a role specifically for her. "You know, the role didn't exist before I met with J.J.," she explains. "He thought it would be interesting to have a Korean couple on the plane, but only after we met. So that's really flattering."

However, Kim wasn't thrilled with her character's relationship with Jin, her husband on the show. She felt the way the relationship was initially presented was out of date and not a contemporary example of a Korean marriage. "It's not my ideal of a relationship. It started out being very stereotypical in the beginning, and I was concerned about that. You know, Korean men are not like that anymore. That was back in the 1950s," she says.

However, the characters both developed over the course of the first season. "You're fighting with stereotypes of many things," she says. "But the reason why we went that way, it was for Sun to start out a certain way, and for her to make some kind of transition. J.J. knows. He knows Asian women. So he took her as far as he could at the end of the episode, so he could bring her back."

In the end, according to Kim, *Lost* is about more than simply a plane crash on an island. It is about the development of the characters and their evolution as people. "*Lost* is about so many different things. From the beginning, when they ask what the show is about, I always say, 'Like the title, you have lost people on a deserted island. Whether they're trying to find their way home, or themselves, or [they're] letting go of the past, putting some closure.' I think the title gives away a lot."

1.7   The Moth

Original air date: November 3, 2004
Written by: Jennifer Johnson, Paul Dini
Directed by: Jack Bender
Guest cast: Neil Hopkins (Liam), Christian Bowman (Steve), Dustin Watchman (Scott), Glenn Cannon (Priest)

Flashback: Charlie

While Charlie withdraws from heroin and reflects on how he became an addict in the first place, Jack becomes trapped in a cave-in, and Charlie may be the only person who can save him.

Since the castaways crashed on the island, Charlie has buzzed about, trying to talk to people, wondering when someone is going to recognize him for the rock star he thinks he is, but he never makes any real connections or friends. His heroin addiction makes him jumpy and unpredictable, and the knowledge that his limited supply will soon run out is adding inevitable stress. In "The Moth," we discover Charlie "used to be" (and probably still is) a religious man, so it's only fitting that Locke, the island's disciple, should be the one to step up and help Charlie break his habit.

Charlie's forced withdrawal has reaped an immediate reward — he's gotten his beloved guitar back. And when he plays it, we flash back to the story of Drive Shaft. The band, fronted by two brothers, is set up a lot like another British band,

Oasis, right down to the lead singers sharing the same name. As in that band, the front man is a bit of a talentless wank who gets into fights and drinks a lot, while the real talent has a penchant for The Beatles and stays in the background, writing lyrics that don't make sense, singing backup, and playing an instrument. Unlike Noel Gallagher, however, Charlie never actually gets to share the limelight with Liam, and after one hit single, the band is completely forgotten. It's an Oasis beginning with a Kula Shaker ending. (Who, you might ask? Exactly.) It's a fun story line, and one that happens all too often in the British music business. With fickle papers touting bands of the month/week/hour, and musical trends lasting less than a year, countless British bands have arrived, conquered the charts once, and disappeared before even getting a chance to exhibit any lasting power.

The not-so-fun aspect of the story, however, is what happens to these fledgling rock stars. Some, like Liam, are able to move on, find jobs, and treat their one-time stardom as a bit o' fun they had while they were young. Others, like Charlie, spend the rest of their lives trying to get back even a small taste of the rush that stardom gave them, the way drug addicts are always looking to reexperience the glory of their first fix. Sadly, the music biz belongs to the young, and Charlie has been eaten up and spat out by a public that has long ago moved onto the Next Big Thing. More devastating to him, though, is his brother's lack of sympathy or understanding of what Charlie is going through. In this and subsequent Charlie episodes, we'll discover his fear is that he will be seen as useless, unable to take care of others. In "The Moth," then, he becomes determined to look useful to the other survivors by helping save Jack's life.

When Charlie confesses his addiction to Jack, it's like a burden is lifted from him, for it was his original blasphemous statement — "I'm a bloody rock god!" — that put Jack in this position in the first place. By elevating himself to the level of a deity, Charlie was brought crashing down to reality by circumstance. In the final flashback, Charlie looks at his brother and says, "You *never* looked out for me," as if he'd spent his life taking care of others, but no one had cared what happened to him. It's the defining moment of his past. When Jack tells Charlie he's not alone, and Jack will help him through this, it's just what he needs to hear — someone else will finally help look out for him.

Locke, the spiritual man, is the one who is responsible for Charlie finding salvation, however, for he is the one who forces Charlie into a frenzied, desperate state, begging Locke to give him back his crutch. Locke uses the metaphor of a moth emerging from a cocoon to describe Charlie's situation, and it works beau-

The church where Charlie goes for confession and talks with his brother in "The Moth" is
Parke Chapel in Honolulu. (RYAN OZAWA)

tifully (although it's a little overused by the end of the episode, bordering on
cheesy). Not only does Charlie have the potential to move beyond his mediocre
rock past and into a promising artistic future, but Locke chooses an insect that
inhabits the island to show Charlie what he has in common with his environment.

Unfortunately, what Locke doesn't mention is that a moth is also attracted to
flames, and Charlie has just as much potential to destroy, as to redeem, himself.

Highlight: Charlie's confession to the priest.

Did You Notice?:

- The people who go to the caves are Jack, Charlie, Locke, Jin, Sun, and
  Hurley. Those who stay on the beach are Sayid, Kate, Sawyer, Michael,
  Walt, Shannon, Boone, and Claire. A few of the beach people will switch
  in upcoming episodes.
- The priest tells Charlie that life is a series of choices, which is exactly what
  Locke tells him.
- This is the first time we see Scott and Steve, a pairing that will become a
  running joke on the show. He's the second Steve to be mentioned — in
  "Walkabout," when Claire is helping conduct the funeral service, she men-
  tions there was another Steve on board the plane who was engaged to
  Kristen.

- Sayid mentions to Kate that it's strange they all walked away from the crash with barely a scratch, which is one of the first times someone states outright that there was something paranormal or unnatural about the crash.
- Sayid tells Kate that he'll take the high ground, which is an interesting comment on his character — he often takes the moral high ground, too.
- Charlie says to Jack, "I'm here to rescue you," which is a line from *Star Wars*, when Luke Skywalker first shows up to save Princess Leia.

Interesting Facts: Damon Lindelof claims to have seen a television show where a drunk audience member got up and shouted, "You all everybody, acting like you're stupid people wearing expensive clothes." Those become the only lyrics to Drive Shaft's hit tune.

In the previous episode, Locke took Charlie's stash away from him, and has told him he will only return it if Charlie asks for it three times. The number three is significant in many world religions, most importantly, in Charlie's case, in Christianity, where it represents the Holy Trinity. The doctrine describes how God exists as the communion of three entities: the Father, the Son, and the Holy Spirit. The scenario between Locke and Charlie is reminiscent of St. Peter denying Christ three times before the crucifixion. At the Last Supper, Christ told Peter he would deny him three times, and Peter said he would die by Christ's side rather than deny him. But at Christ's trial, Peter sat with the servants, and when three people asked him if he was one of the disciples of Jesus of Galilee, he said three times that he didn't know the man. When Peter realizes what he's done, he weeps. In a twisted version of these events, Locke tells Charlie he will deny him three times, making Charlie the Christ to Locke's Peter, and it is through Locke's denial that Charlie finds a resurrection of sorts.

Nitpick: Sayid finds some bottle rockets that have been smuggled onto the airplane. Since most territories in Australia have actually banned public sale of fireworks, it would be a very difficult country to smuggle fireworks *out* of, and probably more common to be smuggling them in. Also, Michael says he's been in construction for eight years, but in a flashback we'll discover he was working in construction before Walt was born, which was 10 years ago.

4 8 15 16 23 42: Kate says they crashed **8** days ago. Michael has **8** years of construction experience. He needs **4** people working at a time to dig out the rocks. Charlie tells Liam he has an **8**-week tour opening for a band called Meat Coat all set up.

It's Just a Flesh Wound: Jack dislocates his shoulder; Sayid is struck in the back of the head; Charlie goes through the physical pain of withdrawal.

Any Questions?:

- Why is Kate's mug shot a fax? Was it taken in Australia where the marshal caught her (in which case a fax wouldn't make much sense), or was it taken before in the U.S. and sent to the marshal in Australia (in which case she's been caught and charged before)?
- Why does everyone automatically assume the Frenchwoman wasn't rescued? Couldn't she have gotten off the island by chance and not returned to the spot of the transmission to turn it off?
- In "Tabula Rasa," Charlie told Locke that he was in a band, and Locke doesn't say anything back to him, yet in this episode he reveals that he knows a lot about Drive Shaft. Why didn't he say, "Yes, I know," to Charlie in "Tabula Rasa"? Was he waiting for his moment?

Music/Bands: "You All Everybody" by Drive Shaft (available at ABC.com's *Lost* site).

Dominic Monaghan (Charlie Pace)

Having appeared in three of the biggest movies in history, no one would have guessed that Dominic Monaghan struggled to find work in the year leading up to *Lost*. Monaghan had spent more than two years filming the *Lord of the Rings* trilogy, but found himself saddled with poor management and was unable to take advantage of his high visibility in the industry.

The man who is best known for playing a hobbit was searching for other movie work when the script for *Lost* came to his attention. The only problem was that, like many of the other actors who would land roles on the show, there didn't immediately seem to be a part for him. Legend has it that Monaghan auditioned for the part of Sawyer, but he corrects that impression. "There wasn't really a part for me so I went in with these pages that were just for someone generic and it happened to be Sawyer, but I was never going to read for Sawyer. The guys said, 'no, you can't be Sawyer.'" The character that really appealed to him — that of the washed-up rock star, Charlie — was deemed too old for the young actor.

"When we started looking to cast the role of Charlie, our idea was that he'd be a has-been rock star in his early forties," says Damon Lindelof. "Dom came in and read for us,

In the summer preceding the premiere of *Lost*, there was a lot of buzz about Dominic Monaghan – a movie actor from the multiple-Oscar-winning *Lord of the Rings* – being a star of the show. (SUE SCHNEIDER/ MOONGLOW PHOTOS)

and five minutes later we were figuring out how to make the character much younger. He was just that good."

With that luck, Monaghan avoided being typecast as a member of "the shire" for the rest of his life.

Born in Berlin in 1976, Monaghan and his family moved to Manchester, England, when he was 11. The time in Germany made Monaghan fluent in German, and also provided him with the ability to mimic accents.

Manchester, the industrial city that has been home to a vibrant music community, was not an easy place to grow up, Monaghan says. "Manchester's a rough place," he says. "It's guys walking around in thick anoraks in the pouring rain, smoking that last cigarette, and jonesing for a fight."

He attended Aquinas College, a Catholic sixth form school in Stockport where he studied English literature, drama, and geography and found a calling in acting. He performed in several plays, including Charles Dickens' *A Christmas Carol,* and soon started acting with the Manchester Youth Theatre. His work with the group caught the attention of a talent agent, who sent him to an audition for the television show *Hetty Wainthropp Investigates*. At the age of 18, he landed a role on the show. But with his quick rise came some difficulty, including an arrest for stealing a movie. "Not even a good movie," he explains. "I didn't have the brains to steal *Apocalypse Now*. I had been drinking all day."

A fan of the *Lord of the Rings* since he was a child, Monaghan auditioned for the role of Frodo Baggins when the film started casting. Involved in a play at the time that required him to shave his head, he was mugged on the way to the audition. "I was a skinhead, I had a cold, and I had been beaten up in the Tube," he says. Despite that, he received a callback, landed the part of Merry, and moved to New Zealand.

"I had a week to go back and sell my house, say good-bye to my friends," he explains. For two straight years, Monaghan shot the three movies that made up the series, and then had to endure an additional nine weeks of reshoots. Despite the time it took to shoot the films, Monaghan has no regrets: "I can plot, very clearly, how my life changed based on that movie. It started with saying yes to Pete Jackson."

However, once the series was finished, Monaghan found himself in Los Angeles without work. "My first year in Los Angeles was pretty hellish," he says. "I came over here after the high point of *Lord of the Rings*, and I saw all my friends jumping around to jobs, and I had nothing." His manager wasn't lining up any new work, and Monaghan was living in a bad part of town with his money quickly running out. "I didn't have a car, and living in L.A. without a car, well, is difficult. I couldn't get a car because I didn't have an American bank account and could not get credit. . . . So at that point, I was just hanging out at my place all day, playing *Grand Theft Auto III*. I was waiting for the phone I didn't have to ring."

As luck would have it, *Lost* filled the void. Monaghan, a big music fan, has embraced the role of Charlie, adding nuances to the character to bring the drug-addled former rock star to life. "The frustration of Charlie's situation means he has a lot going on in his head," Monaghan says. "Charlie is lost, and I can understand that almost too well. The [woes] you carry around with you as an actor always helps you flesh out a character. "

Initially the most visible member of the *Lost* cast (leading up to the pilot, every article mentioned him), Monaghan remains in the headlines, partially due to his relationship with fellow cast member Evangeline Lilly.

Now two years into playing Charlie, Monaghan still finds the character compelling. "Yeah, he is a screwup, and also in my mind, he's a wild card, the joker in the pack," the actor explains. "We don't necessarily know where he's headed. He's not, for me, as black and white as characters like Jack or Hurley, who seem like intrinsically good characters, or people like Ethan or Locke, who seem a little more sinister. It appears to me that Charlie is really cutting straight down the middle — in one episode, he'll be a good guy and a hero, and in the next he'll fail. For me as an actor, sitting on the fence is a great place to be. I've said that from the start."

1.8   Confidence Man

Original air date: November 10, 2004
Written by: Damon Lindelof

Directed by: Tucker Gates

Guest cast: Michael DeLuise (David), Kristin Richardson (Jessica), Billy Mayo (Kilo), Jim Woitas (Boy)

Flashback: Sawyer

When Shannon begins suffering asthma attacks that leave her unable to breathe, Jack and Sayid take drastic measures to force Sawyer to give them asthma inhalers from his stash.

Despite the fact that *everyone* is keeping secrets on this island, Sawyer is someone who has devoted his life to being a mystery. He keeps up a joking exterior, but if anyone responds to him, he immediately shuts down and gives them an icy glare. Kate is the only person for whom he'll drop the act, but even that exposure is guarded.

The secret Sawyer harbors is different from those of the others — where they are looking for a second chance and they hide their dark selves, Sawyer enhances and exaggerates his to make people hate him. We find out that Sawyer has adopted the name of the man who destroyed his family when he was a young boy. In flashbacks, we realize he hasn't just taken on Mr. Sawyer's surname, but also his persona. After a lifetime spent trying to find this man, he instead has chosen a more attainable path — he's become the man he's hunting. He forces others to loathe and punish him in a way he feels befits the real Sawyer, somehow believing that in doing so, he's hurting the real Sawyer. But after being this guy for so long, Sawyer's begun to hate himself, which is a dangerous and sad result.

Up to this episode, Sawyer has come off as a bully, a jerk, a redneck, and a racist; and yet Josh Holloway imbues him with a charm that makes him likeable. Kate is clearly attracted to him and repelled by him simultaneously, and her ambivalence brings him both pleasure and pain. He revels in making her squeamish, as he does in this episode by suggesting he'll trade the inhalers for a kiss, but when she gives in and moves her face toward his, you can see his look of longing. All of Sawyer's relationships have been meaningless, and Kate is different from the other women he's used and conned in the past. But when she looks like she's sympathizing with him, he growls at her not to pity him. He cannot let her feel sorry for him, because if she does, it means the real Sawyer is also deserving of pity. And he can't allow himself to fall in love with her, or it means the real Sawyer is permitted to fall in love, too.

The scene where Sayid and Jack, frustrated by Sawyer's clowning around, take him to the jungle to torture him, is brutal and vicious. It's also full of desperation and emotional turmoil. The actors handle the scene amazingly well, especially Holloway and Andrews. Jack has pledged to save lives and make people more comfortable, not to physically attack anyone. Sayid may have tortured people before, but there's something gentle and mournful about him that suggests it was a part of his life he'd put to rest. And to top off the scene, Sawyer wants them to bring the pain, because every bamboo shoot under his fingernails will be one under the real Sawyer's, or so he believes.

"Just pretend everything is okay and keep smiling." "I can barely hold up my arm." "And it's going to get a lot worse if you don't give me those inhalers." (STHANLEE MIRADOR/ SHOOTING STAR)

Has Sawyer really gone so far into the head of the man who originally hurt him that he can't separate himself from the other con man any longer? It seems so, until we see the final flashback. Just as he's about to do the very thing he hates another man for doing, he sees an image of who he once was, before his life had been turned upside-down, and it jolts him back into reality. Sawyer is not a nice guy, and he'll see to it that others hate him as much as he hates himself, but somewhere in there still lurks an innocent boy who just might be saved.

Highlight: Hurley's reaction when Jack manages to calm Shannon down and avert her asthma attack: "Wow, man. That was awesome. I mean, that was like a . . . Jedi moment."

Did You Notice?:

- Sawyer has clearly been named after Mark Twain's character, Tom Sawyer, who was a rascally con man himself. Both of them con people by making them think they came up with the idea in the first place. Where Sawyer steals money, Tom gets local kids to paint a fence for him. Tom has a much deeper mean streak, like Sawyer. In one story, when he runs away and finds out his family and friends think he's dead, he cruelly shows up at his own funeral to watch the mourners, only to suddenly leap out and surprise them.

- The kiss between Sawyer and Kate doesn't exactly look obligatory on her part.
- In the previous episode, Sawyer tells Kate all it would take for him to be respected like Jack would be some Band-Aids and peroxide, which is exactly what Jack uses to clean up Sayid's head and Boone's face in this episode.
- Sayid pins Sawyer to the ground in a Christ pose.
- When Sayid leaves, he does so because he hates himself for what he just did, which is exactly Sawyer's problem.

Interesting Facts: Although there have been no conclusive studies yet, pregnant and breastfeeding women are often asked by their doctors to abstain from peanut products, because there is a concern that an early exposure to peanut butter for the child — even in the womb — could lead to a peanut allergy later in life. So it's perfect that Charlie brings Claire *imaginary* peanut butter. Also, among the things Charlie says he misses is Banoffi Pie. Banoffi Pie originated in a restaurant in East Sussex in England called The Hungry Monk, in 1972. It has a pastry base, covered in a thick toffee, then sliced bananas, and topped with whipped cream. You can find the recipe at the restaurant's Web site, at www.hungrymonk.co.uk.

Nitpicks: Sawyer says the copy of *Watership Down* washed up on shore and had gone into the ocean with a bunch of other luggage, but if that were the case, it would have been bloated and seriously warped, whereas it looks like a book he's taken off a bookshelf. Either he's lying, or the pristine book is a production error.

Oops: This is the first episode where the timeline is mistaken, and that mistake continues throughout the series. By the end of the season, the castaways will have been on the island for over 40 days, but if you follow the timeline carefully from episode to episode, you realize they're adding in days that don't exist. In "The Moth," Kate tells Jack that they've been on the island for 8 days. Then she and Sayid go out into the jungle to try to triangulate the radio signal. He gets hit in the head around sunset, lies unconscious, and somehow stumbles back to the cave, early the next morning. This episode opens with him returning to the cave, so it would be day 9. But when Charlie and Hurley are out walking in the jungle that same day, Charlie says they've been on the island for two weeks. He's wrong, but the timeline of the show will continue from his mistake.

4 8 15 16 23 42: Boone says he had **4** refills of Shannon's asthma medicine. Kate says the incident with Sawyer's parents happened when he was **8** or 9 years old. Sawyer tells the woman in the flashback that he needs $160,000 to complete his investment transaction.

It's Just a Flesh Wound: Sawyer beats up Boone, who incurs facial bruises and cuts. Sawyer gets a cut lip from Jack, a head wound from being hit with a plank, has bamboo shoots stuck under his fingernails, and his artery is cut when Sayid stabs him in the bicep. (Sawyer's probably had better days.)

Any Questions?:

Sawyer remains a fan favorite – especially among the ladies. (CHRISTINA RADISH)

- Was Sawyer planning on conning Kilo, the guy in the pool hall who'd lent him the money in the flashback?
- Where *has* all the money gone from his previous cons? He says he likes to spend it, but if he's making almost $100,000 per con, that's a lot of spending. Has he been investing it in something?
- How did Sawyer manage to find out the name of the guy who'd ruined his family?
- Who raised him?
- Why did he need $6,000 at age 19?

Music/Bands: At the end of the episode, we hear "I Shall Not Walk Alone," by The Blind Boys of Alabama (*Higher Ground*).

 Watership Down by Richard Adams (1972)

Watership Down is the story of a group of rabbits who leave their warren to make a home elsewhere after their original warren is threatened by a housing development. The book's protagonist is Hazel, whose smaller brother Fiver has a sixth sense and knows that something is going to happen. Hazel gathers a band of refugees, including Bigwig, who is one of the largest rabbits and who has a military sense; Blackberry, who possesses the intelligence to help them adapt to new situations; and Dandelion, who is the storyteller and keeps them occupied when they're scared.

The original rabbit warren consists of a leader and an army called the Owsla that surrounds him (of which Bigwig is a part). The leader refuses to listen to Hazel and Fiver when they warn him of impending doom, showing that he might have been able to provide them with a safe place to grow up, but he's ineffective in desperate situations. As they leave, the other rabbits designate Hazel the leader, and he's an effective one because he not only listens to everyone's concerns, but he recognizes his own limitations, turning to Bigwig for military advice and Blackberry for plans to get out of dangerous situations.

Along the way, Dandelion keeps the group entertained with stories of El-ahrairah, a legendary folk hero among the rabbits. El-ahrairah is known for his trickery, and uses it to get himself out of dangerous situations. In the book, trickery is looked upon not as a form of deceit, but as using one's intelligence over brute force. In the world of *Watership Down*, the con man can be the hero.

Forms of government and finding one's way "home" are the two main themes of this book, and both are established from the outset. After some initial adventures, the rabbits find a seemingly ideal warren, but something about it seems wrong. The rabbits soon discover that the warren is actually run by men who leave snares out for the rabbits (Bigwig is caught in one) and fatten them up with carrots. The rabbits they encounter there act strangely because they live in constant fear of death, and laugh maniacally and tell fantastical poems to escape their dreary existence.

The group moves on and eventually finds their way to Watership Down, a warren that seems to be perfect, with one exception — they don't have any does, or female rabbits, to mate with. There's no way they could start a new warren if there's no chance of future generations, so they set out to find does. After an initial attempt to free some caged rabbits is only partly successful, they discover a warren called Efrafa, and they send a group over to scope it out. When they realize Efrafa is run by a ruthless leader named General Woundwort, who has a bloodthirsty passion for war, they devise a plan to infiltrate the warren, steal some does, and escape. Bigwig (who escaped from the snare) poses as a potential candidate for Woundwort's Owsla, and he manages to find several rabbits that are unhappy living in Woundwort's tyrannical regime, and they manage to escape, with Woundwort's army on their tails. While they eventually make it back to the warren, Woundwort's Owsla find their way there, too, and a battle is waged on their home turf, with their brains winning out over Woundwort's brawn. Several generations of rabbits thrive in Watership Down, respecting Hazel as their benevolent leader, and recognizing that home can be the place you make, and not the place you came from.

It is fitting that Sawyer is the one who reads *Watership Down*. Not only is El-ahrairah hailed as a hero (which would make Sawyer proud, since he obtains things through trickery just as the rabbit does), but the book is about what makes a good leader. Sawyer constantly questions Jack's leadership skills, and doesn't like taking direction from anyone (except, occasionally, Kate). Jack is a reluctant leader, but people turn to him because they think he'll make the most sensible suggestions, and he's the most essential member of the "tribe." However, despite acknowledging that he doesn't want to be a leader, Jack tends to make some dictatorial moves, and when he does, things always go haywire. Like Hazel, Jack will eventually learn that he must find the strengths of each member of the group and rely on those, and if someone knows more than he does about something (like Locke and hunting) then he should give that person free reign to lead the others. But for now, Jack will assume he is the one to control everything.

The book is also about learning to leave behind everything you know and make a new place your home. We're already seeing the castaways beginning to make this place their home, and they are finding ways to adapt to this new and scary existence. Yet as Jack keeps reminding them (and in this way he is similar to Hazel), if they all stick together, like the rabbits do in *Watership Down*, they can be stronger. In *Watership Down*, the rabbits purposely set off to find a new life, whereas on *Lost*, the castaways were thrown unwillingly into it. However, the longer they spend on the island, the more they realize they all *were* looking for something new, they just didn't know it.

1.9   Solitary

Original air date: November 17, 2004
Written by: David Fury

Directed by: Greg Yaitanes

Guest cast: Andrea Gabriel (Nadia), Scott Paulin (Sullivan), Navid Negahban (Omar), Xavier Alaniz (Prisoner)

Flashback: Sayid

Sayid exiles himself out of shame for what he did to Sawyer, and in the jungle, discovers the dispatcher of the 16-year-old transmission.

Each of us wants to be left alone sometimes, and as our lives get fuller and more complicated, it becomes more difficult to find those few solitary moments. But no one wants to be completely alone, and that difference is what this episode is about. In many ways, everyone on the island is a solitary creature, keeping secrets from the others and only revealing themselves in small doses. In "Solitary," Sayid enters a self-imposed exile out of shame, and he's not on his own for long before he discovers there is someone else living on the island — and *she* has been in solitary confinement for over 16 years.

Through flashbacks, we see Sayid was stretching the truth when he said he was a communications officer in the Republican Guard. By "communications," he meant his job was getting information by torturing people. He seemed to be able to shut down his emotions in order to get the job done . . . until someone from his past reappeared. The relationship between Sayid and Nadia is never fully fleshed out, leaving us with many questions, but the mystery makes the flashbacks more effective. All we know is that they knew each other as children, and now she's a suspected insurgent and it's up to Sayid to get the truth out of her.

In the present, the tables are turned when Sayid is captured and strapped to a table by Rousseau, the Frenchwoman whose distress call Sayid discovered in "Pilot, Part 2." Rousseau is a bag of unanswered questions herself, but having lived on her own for so long, she's extremely paranoid, she might be insane, and she's forgotten how to interact with people (she attacks Sayid, caresses him, yells at him, all in the same minute). Yet in many ways, she's a lot like Sayid — she's using her knowledge from before she came to the island to try to get off the island in the same way Sayid is using his expertise with electronics to try to radio for help. More importantly, both have lost people who were close to them, and are obsessed with trying to find them again.

Meanwhile, back at the crash site, Hurley decides it's time for everyone to stop being so darn serious as he puts together a two-hole golf course and invites everyone to the first "Island Open." Golf is an apt game for them to be playing, for it provides the perfect metaphor for everyone's struggles on the island. Golf is one of the few sports that is truly solitary, where golfers compete against their own best score, rather than each other. More importantly, it's a game that pits player against course, not player against player, and a bad lie in a bunker or a tree blocking the way to the green is a far greater hazard for a player than how the other guy is doing. Similarly, so far, the group of survivors has been pitted against the perils of the island, not any human enemy . . . until now.

Naveen Andrews was best known to North American audiences for his role in *The English Patient* before starring in *Lost*. (YORAM KAHANA/SHOOTING STAR)

When Rousseau tells Sayid about "the Others," it alters the dynamic of the entire show. It's also an intriguing name for them, because it raises the "self/other" distinction often used in feminist and postcolonial literary theory. Not only is "other" a term often used for a minority (making it appropriate that Sayid is the one with the first exposure to them), but it's also a term that all of the survivors toss around to describe each other. Jin has told Sun she doesn't need "the others." Shannon translates the transmission as saying "the others are dead." When the small band of travelers hears the transmission, they discuss whether or not they should tell "the others." When the marshal is screaming in pain, Sayid tells Jack that "the others" are getting upset. When Hurley and Charlie find out the water is running low, Charlie cautions him not to tell "the others." "The others" is a term the survivors (and everyone, in everyday life) uses to make an "us and them" distinction. Rousseau's paranoia makes us wonder, then, do these Others exist, or has Rousseau just put a kernel in Sayid's mind that will make him — and everyone else — begin to question who they can trust?

Highlight: Sawyer's reaction when he hears that Jack is playing golf on the island. "Doctor playing golf. Woo boy, howdy, now I've heard everything. What's next, cop eating a donut?"

Did You Notice?:

- Sayid sees a shirt with the word "Rousseau" on it, and it's obviously there so viewers will recognize the spelling as being the same as the French philosopher, and not "Russo" (see page 62).
- Scott and Steve are in the crowd watching the golf game; you can see them to the right of the screen as Kate approaches Jack and asks about the ladies' tees.
- Nadia's note on the back of the photo says she'll see him in the next life, if not in this one. Is the island the next life, and if so, will he somehow find Nadia here?
- Boone is wearing a shirt with the Chinese characters for 84, which is significant because of the **8** and the **4**; it's a reversed 48, which is the number of survivors initially on the island; and it conjures up Orwell's novel *1984*, which this show is beginning to echo more and more (see page 313).

Interesting Fact: Mira Furlan, who plays Rousseau, is a Croatian actress who moved to the United States in the early 1990s to escape the political turmoil in Yugoslavia at the time. She has appeared in dozens of films in her homeland and in the U.S., and is best known to cult television viewers as Ambassador Delenn from *Babylon 5*.

4 8 15 16 23 42: Sayid tells Nadia there's a supply truck 40 meters outside the door.

It's Just a Flesh Wound: Sayid gets a piece of bamboo stuck in his right leg, and incurs a wound over his right eye.

Any Questions?:

- Michael shows Jack some amazing plans for a shower where he can divert the washing water away from the drinking water. How come he never actually builds it?
- Is Rousseau crazy, or is she one of the few people completely telling the truth?
- If the Others exist, who are they? How did they get on the island? How long have they been there?
- Is Alex still alive?
- Where did Rousseau learn so many languages? (She asks Sayid, "Where is Alex?" in several different languages at first, trying to determine which one he actually speaks.) What was her team researching? Why were they in Tahiti? What was the malfunction on the ship that caused them to crash into the island?

"Solitary" Whisper Transcript

When Sayid enters the jungle at the end of "Solitary," he hears indecipherable whispers. Well, indecipherable to us, but not to two viewers — RVTurnage and PenYours — who record the tracks, isolate the whispers, and manage to transcribe them. By isolating the surround sound tracks and breaking them into left, right, and center audio files, these two fans independently transcribe what they hear, and then compare notes to make sure they heard the same thing before publishing their findings online. What they have uncovered is a fascinating key to the Others — they know more about the survivors than we might think.

Lucky the man can't run
He's a crash survivor
Why only isolate him
I said we do . . . he's coming
(Click)
You have no idea how he got here?
(Radio static)
(Beeping sound — could be alarm, Morse code, computer, etc.)

Right here
He's right behind me
It's okay
Who cares
Help him when?
Crash survivor
Why only isolate him?
Standing orders . . . go
You have no idea

He's coming
Security issue
You have no idea how he got here?
Skip it

- What does Rousseau inject into Sayid, and where did she get it? Where is she getting the electricity to zap Sayid?
- Is Rousseau one of the Others?
- Why didn't Rousseau hear the plane crash or even feel it in the earth, especially since the craft was so huge and ended up in so many pieces around the island?
- When Sayid tells Rousseau what is written on the back of the photo, she

looks surprised and elated, like she recognizes the saying. Has someone said that to her, too?

- Did Sayid torture Nadia?
- Did Jack sink his putt?

Jean-Jacques Rousseau (1712–1778)

Jean-Jacques Rousseau was arguably the most influential of the Enlightenment thinkers. He believed that in a state of nature, man was neither good nor bad, but was a "noble savage" who used reason for self-preservation. He stated that man was corrupted by society, which he deemed to be an artificial construct. His most famous statement, "Man is born free, and everywhere is in chains," illustrates his beliefs that man is born without any of society's influences, but is forced into them immediately. In this way, his philosophy was similar to Locke's theory that man was a blank slate to be written upon by society.

In his *Discourse on the Origin and Basis of Inequality*, Rousseau argued that the only way to understand man is to picture him in a state of nature, stripped of society's trappings. He believed man would originate as a solitary being, working for his own self-preservation. He would occasionally join up with others to build a shelter or hunt for food, but there were no friendships or lasting attachments, and he would return to his solitary existence. As populations grow, socialization comes in, and lasting connections are made. The beginnings of families and friendships leads to permanent homes and private property, and also an awareness of other people's opinions. Until now, man only worried about survival, but now he sees the way others see him, and it offers him a kind of love and pride in himself and others. As societies become more complex, and agriculture and metallurgy are introduced, societies are divided into groups of people — those who do the physical labor and those who do the mental work and are the leaders — and therein lies the origin of inequality. Social classes are formed, and a social contract is established by the wealthy. The poor agree to it because the powerful reassure them it will protect them, and as a result, the rich get richer and the poor get poorer.

In *The Social Contract*, Rousseau outlined what he believed the ideal social contract should be. Where he had outlined earlier that in a social setting man becomes worried about what others think, he believes under an unfair social contract as outlined above, those feelings turn to competition, which leads to inequality among men. Instead, he believed that people should not be under the thumb of a wealthy monarchy, but instead should be able to choose their leader, and that leader should represent the general will of the people. He saw the new social contract being carried out by a sovereign, who protected the people and carried out their general will; by a group of magistrates, who answered to the people and who ensured the sovereign was protecting them; and by the citizens themselves, who let their will be known. Though this might look like democracy, he believed that there should not be a representative legislature that would make the laws on the people's behalf, but that the people should make the laws directly and see to it that their leader follows their mandate. Under Rousseau's social contract, people sacrifice their individual will for the general will, but while they give up a small part of their freedom, they become free as individuals by allowing their general will to be heard.

Rousseau's ideas formed the basis of the French Revolution and have been influential in several governments and democracies, though his philosophy has come under criticism for its apparent self-contradiction. How is the individual truly free under a contract where he must sacrifice his individuality? How can personal interests flourish if the government is only meant to support the overall well-being of the population? Proponents of Rousseau's philosophies would argue that there is no contradiction, and that by forcing the leader to listen to the people's general will, an individual's rights are protected. As soon as a leader is no longer protecting the general will, the citizens have the right to unseat him and bring in a new one. *The Social Contract* wasn't the only aspect of Rousseau that was controversial — his very life seemed to be a series of contradictions. He wrote his first discourse on the arts, stating that the arts were unnecessary in society and corrupted the individual, yet he also wrote a well-known opera and was a talented musician. He wrote a fictional work entitled *Emile* on how children should be educated (it remains influential even today), yet he took each of the five children he had with his lifelong partner to an orphanage the moment they were weaned, protesting that he wouldn't have been a good father to them. That said, Rousseau still has his admirers today, and his views have influenced more of today's democracies than other Enlightenment thinkers.

On the island, the society that has been developing has mimicked some of Rousseau's descriptions of man in a state of nature without a social contract. In the beginning (and even now) some characters befriend others to hunt or build a shelter, but abandon them when they are no longer any use. Certain characters are beginning to rise up as more powerful members of the group, and they are the ones making the rules. Jack is "elected" leader, so to speak, but the moment his views don't coincide with the general will, people turn to someone else. More important, however, is the connection between philosopher Rousseau and his namesake, Danielle Rousseau. She remains in a state of nature, shunning the society that she believes will corrupt (or kill) her. She is neither good nor evil, and every time we see her she's a bundle of contradictions. Like Rousseau, she didn't raise her child, although unlike Rousseau, it wasn't her decision. She will become one of the most complex characters on the show, just as Rousseau's complex and not always comprehensible philosophies are still being debated today.

1.10   Raised by Another

Original air date: December 1, 2004
Written by: Lynne E. Litt
Directed by: Marita Grabiak
Guest cast: Nick Jameson (Psychic), Keir O'Donnell (Thomas), Jenny Chang (Rachel), Lisa Fraser (Arlene), Barry Whitfield (Slavitt)

Flashback: Claire
When Claire begins having vivid dreams that someone is trying to hurt her baby, Jack tries to calm her down while Charlie vows to take care of her.

As the creepy gets creepier, the paranoia that Sayid was introduced to last episode has now spread through the camp when Claire becomes convinced there is a potential attacker among their group. Jack tries to reason with her, which only makes her more anxious and suspicious, while Charlie takes the more tactful route, believing Claire's story and reassuring her that he'll keep watch over her.

Disturbing dreams are very common in pregnant women, especially in the last trimester. Women at the end of their pregnancies have vivid nightmares involving their baby, which many psychologists and childcare experts say is nature's way of preparing the mother for the rigors and constant worries of motherhood. Women dream of forgetting their baby in public places or losing it altogether; of not taking care of the baby properly, like forgetting to feed it; or being attacked and hurt by others, which is a sign of vulnerability. These sorts of dreams grow out of the anxieties new moms feel when they realize someone will be entirely dependent on them — a very daunting experience. So it's natural that Jack immediately sees Claire's dream as par for the course.

The details of Claire's dream are fascinating, though, and offer an intimate look at her psyche. The sound of a crying baby in a dream can be interpreted as a realization that a part of yourself is vulnerable. There are several moments with black-and-white imagery — Locke's eyes, the backs of the Tarot cards he's dealing, the white crib against the black night — which indicates the purity and innocence of the unborn child

Aw, see? He's not that bad! William Mapother plays the mysterious Ethan Rom.
(ALBERT L. ORTEGA)

against the evil of the island that surrounds it. Dreaming of playing cards usually points to a belief that whoever is playing has mastered bluffing and the use of strategy: does Claire believe that of Locke? Though we don't see the Tarot cards Locke is laying out, there's a distinct sound of a sword unsheathing, which could mean he's looking at the Sword suit. Swords in Tarot cards indicate intellect, thought, and reason — three qualities one could definitely say belong to Locke — but more importantly, the element they are associated with is Air. Since Claire arrived on this mysterious island via an airplane, it would make sense that she would be dealt Sword cards. (The cards can also be laid on the table to represent disharmony and unhappiness.) The sight of blood in a dream usually signifies the dreamer must use caution, and that something bad is going to happen. Finally, a dead baby can be interpreted to mean the dreamer senses the end of something that was a part of them.

So what does all of this mean? In Claire's flashbacks, we see that she has been vulnerable through most of her pregnancy, as her pathetic boyfriend wanted to play house and then walked away before it became too real for him. We see that Claire was tough, and able to bounce back quickly and resolve to do what's best for her baby (a characteristic of her personality that's entirely in character from what we've seen). But when a psychic suddenly sees something in his reading that causes him to panic and later phone her repeatedly out of desperation, her resolve begins to break down, and confusion sets in about what is the right thing to do. Her dream appears to be her subconscious warning her that someone is after her, and that she must protect her baby. It's showing her what could happen if she doesn't. It could also be Claire's deep-seated fears that she won't be a good enough mother, because she tried to give the baby up for adoption. She realizes her entire life is going to change, and it's going to happen on a island in the middle of nowhere.

Emilie de Ravin plays Claire with a goodness and sweetness that is almost unwavering. Although she's not one of the more prominent characters on the show, Claire is immensely important because of the baby she is carrying. Although she initially dismisses the psychic as nuts, she can't help but wonder if maybe he's acting in earnest. If the psychic is telling the truth, could Claire's unborn child have an important role to play on the island?

Unfortunately, just as Claire initially doubted the psychic, Jack doubts the validity of her fears. And when he finally realizes she wasn't hallucinating, it's too late.

Highlight: Hurley telling Ethan he loves Canada, then not being able to think of a single reason why.

Did You Notice?:
- The title of this episode sounds like "Raised by an Other."
- When Claire sees the plane mobile, you can hear the turbulence from the plane going down.
- Ethan Rom's name is an anagram for Other Man.
- Ethan said he was from Ontario, but he never actually said Canada. He could have meant Ontario in California or Ohio.
- Claire tells the couple in her flashback that she wants them to sing "Catch a Falling Star" to her baby. The song title could pertain to Charlie, since he's a fallen star.

Interesting Facts: What Claire experiences in the jungle is called Braxton-

Hicks contractions, and they are false contractions that usually begin happening one or two weeks before a baby's actual delivery. They are almost as painful as real contractions (in some cases they do actually serve to begin dilating the cervix), but for the most part, their occurrence is not a sign of impending labor. Also, while Charlie's dream sounds funny to us, it also points to something pretty serious about his own subconscious. Dreaming of being a bus driver tends to mean you believe you're moving forward too quickly in your life. He shot to stardom at a young age, and feels like his best years are behind him already. Teeth falling out is a very common occurrence in dreams, and most psychologists agree that it symbolizes that you're worried of making a fool of yourself, or being unattractive to others, or being powerless — all things that could apply to Charlie. Charlie said his mother was in the back of the bus, and dreaming of one's mother could indicate a nurturing aspect of your own character (which would certainly be the case with Charlie) or it could indicate a problem freeing yourself from your mother (also a problem with Charlie, as we'll see). Finally, he says he could smell bacon throughout, and bacon appearing in a dream usually indicates a worry about earning a living and supplying loved ones with the essentials needed in their lives. Perhaps Charlie worries that he can't take care of Claire because he can't supply her with what the baby would need. So Charlie's dream, too, is actually packed with important symbolism for his character. Or, he could have been really stoned at the time and all of this is moot.

Nitpick: Jack tells Claire that if she continues to panic, it could bring on early labor and he doesn't have the equipment to deal with that. Claire's due date is one or two weeks away, meaning she'll be 40 weeks at that point. A baby is considered full term at 37 weeks, and any baby born after that time will usually have no complications at all. Jack's comment is a little ridiculous, as he seems to be insinuating that if she gave birth now, the baby would be grossly premature. Of course, Jack is a spinal surgeon, and not an OB-GYN, but this is pretty basic knowledge to anyone with a baby, much less a medical degree.

4 8 15 16 23 42: During her nightmare, Claire dug her fingernails a 1/4 inch into her palms. Claire takes the pregnancy test when her period has been late for 6 weeks, which means she conceived **8** weeks earlier (conception typically happens two weeks before a woman's period begins). The psychic gives Claire $12,000 (**8** + **4** = 12), which is $8,000 less than what the second half of her payment was going to be from the other adoptive couple. Claire tells the psychic to stop calling her, and mentions he's been bothering her for **4** months.

Any Questions?:

- Thomas mentions that Claire has daddy abandonment issues: What is he referring to? When did her father leave? Was she raised by her mother alone or by someone else? Thomas also says that Claire's mother has practically disowned her. Why?
- Did Claire really go to an OB-GYN regularly? She seems to be a little avoidy when Jack asks her about it.
- Why was Locke in Claire's dream? Because he was the one with Ethan? Because he's seen as the logical and intellectual one? Does she subconsciously suspect he would hurt her? Or is he some kind of father figure to her?
- What exactly did the psychic see?
- Why is Shannon so hostile and angry when Hurley is interviewing her? Did something happen beforehand that we don't know about? She's throwing her clothes around and snapping at everyone.
- The lawyer says that Claire will get an additional $20,000 after she gives birth. How much were they offering her up front?

Emilie de Ravin (Claire Littleton)

As Claire, the only actual Australian among the crash survivors, Emilie de Ravin gets to do something that has become increasingly rare for the young actress: use her actual Australian accent.

Losing her native speech pattern, incidentally, was something de Ravin had concentrated on when she first arrived in Hollywood. "I was doing the American accent in an American show — so in America's mindset, I was American. So the issue of being Australian never came up."

In many ways, auditioning for Claire would have seemed like the most obvious role for de Ravin, but that wasn't the path she followed. When she heard J.J. Abrams was casting for *Lost*, de Ravin read — in an American accent — for the role of Shannon, the poor little rich girl. Though she didn't get the part, she impressed the producers enough that they offered her the role of Claire, which at the time was only expected to be a recurring character. In fact, Abrams had never actually met de Ravin before casting her as Claire.

"I was in Canada shooting two movies, but this project came along and I loved J.J.

Abrams' work," she said. "So I put myself on tape for him and we ended up talking about it on the phone until I eventually got the job. I stopped in Los Angeles to change suitcases and flew straight to Hawaii to start shooting. It was a lot of trust on both our parts because I'd never read the script before I got there and he'd never met me."

Like much of the cast, de Ravin found the haste with which the plot and scripts developed in early 2004 to be challenging. She also found the conditions of Hawaii — hot and muggy — made her role even more demanding. "In many ways, the filming is actually like the drama. You endure the muggiest weather in the rainforest, and there are bugs everywhere that will completely devour you unless you wear copious amounts of insect repellent — it's very remote," she explains. "You're really exposed to the elements.

Before *Lost*, Emilie de Ravin was already known to cult television fans as Tess on *Roswell*. (PSEUDOIMAGE/SHOOTING STAR)

"The only other living creatures you see are the wild boar that hang round the catering tables. Mind you, unlike in the series, they are very sweet and we feed them bread."

Lost isn't de Ravin's first brush with celebrity. She grew up pursuing a passion for ballet, before making a decision to try her luck at acting. "[Ballet] takes a lot of work," de Ravin says. "It's your whole life, really. So when I began to realize that I didn't know if dancing was everything I hoped it would be, when I started asking, 'Will all this really be my whole career?' and I wasn't quite sure what the answer was, I guess I started thinking about other things I'd like to do for the first time. I knew I liked performing and thinking about different roles, so I thought I might just look into the acting side. I reasoned that if it didn't work out I was young enough to go back to dance."

She took intensive workshop classes in her native Australia at the National Institute of Dramatic Art and attended Prime Time Actors Studio in Los Angeles in 1998. The pursuit of work led de Ravin to Los Angeles full-time a year later, much to the concern of her mother. "I went there by myself, then Mum came out when I knew I was going to stay," she remembers. "She helped me find a place and helped me move in. I was always very independent, so while it was scary, it was also exciting. It was a challenge, which I like."

Her break didn't take long in coming. Only days after the move, de Ravin met with casting agents and landed the role of the alien Tess Harding on the television series *Roswell*. Her character, who broke up one of the show's main love stories, was hated by many viewers, but de Ravin found the role of Tess to be extremely nuanced. "When I read the script, even before I shot anything, I thought she was interesting," de Ravin explains. "She had no human side to her at first, none whatsoever. It's hard because you can't just say, 'Okay, I'm going to draw from this life experience' because, obviously, I haven't had any alien experiences and I haven't had that many life experiences as a human."

After her character was written off during the third season of the show, de Ravin was free to pursue new opportunities. However, an immigration issue limited her ability to find work. Once she was able to audition, she only found roles on failed television pilots before Abrams and *Lost* presented her next opportunity.

Interestingly, de Ravin is one of the only cast members to maintain a home in Los Angeles, flying back and forth to the set on a regular basis, and finding time to appear in the 2006 cult hit movie, *Brick*. Throughout all the air travel, she attempts to keep her mind clear of how *Lost*'s survivors ended up on the island in the first place.

"I just try not to think about that. Plus, I keep telling myself it would be too clichéd if something like that happened to any of us."

1.11 All the Best Cowboys Have Daddy Issues

Original air date: December 8, 2004
Written by: Javier Grillo-Marxuach
Directed by: Stephen Williams
Guest cast: Michael Adamshick (Anesthesiologist), Jackie Maraya (Andrea), Matt Moore (Husband), Mark Stitham (Head Doctor)

Flashback: Jack
With Charlie and Claire missing, several castaways go out in search of them, and along the way they begin to learn more about each other.

For the first 10 episodes of the series, we've gotten to know the characters and some are emerging as major ones — Kate, Jack, Locke, Charlie, Sawyer, and Sayid. These are the characters who will get more than one flashback episode this season, and who are becoming leaders and initiative-takers. Now that we've seen all of their initial flashbacks, "All the Best Cowboys" is the first episode to feature a second full flashback for the same character, so rather than focus on who that character is, the writers shift the emphasis to looking at the developing relationships on the island. The title of this episode, while long and cumbersome, could apply not only to Jack, but to all of the characters. Everyone seems to have serious parent problems (see page 73). But as we witnessed in "White Rabbit," Jack's daddy issues run deep. He has turned his life and vocation into a mirror image of his father's, and as such, he's in danger of turning into Dad all the time. His guilt about doing so catches up to him in this episode, and he shows hostility to anyone who reminds him of his father, Christian.

The most obvious target of his antagonism is Locke. Up til now, Locke has saved Jack's life and emerged as a hunter/warrior, one whom most of the others trust to keep them fed and safe. When Jack was chasing an image of his father through the jungle, it was Locke who talked him through his mixed feelings and encouraged him to go on. But suddenly, Jack begins to treat Locke like an interloper who won't allow him to step up and be the only strong male. Despite Locke's background and expertise, and his pleas for Jack to return to the caves to be the doctor so Locke can be the hunter, Jack refuses to back off or listen to anyone. Jack seems to have moved beyond "helpful leader" and become more of a dictator.

Why does Jack act the way he does? Does he not trust Locke because Locke was the one who hung around Ethan? Is he so full of guilt for not believing Claire that he's refusing to let others help fix what he thinks he did? Or does Locke somehow remind him of his father? When Locke first catches up to Jack in the jungle, he tells him it was a good thing Jack was going in circles because it made him easier to find. This subtle criticism of Jack's hunting skills is the sort of jab Jack's father would have relished. Although Locke was correct to point out that Jack's not a hunter, being embarrassed in front of the others wasn't what Jack needed. As we see in flashbacks, Jack was an ace surgeon, but his father was chief. He was always slightly better than Jack in everyone else's estimation, and even when Jack knew this was no longer the case, he couldn't bring himself to do anything about it until he realized he was being treated like a patsy.

This memory of his father tricking him is probably what triggers his cruel treat-

Jack is haunted by guilt and anger toward his father, and lashes out at other characters as a result. (PSEUDOIMAGE/SHOOTING STAR)

ment of Kate in this episode, which is an extension of the way he questioned her in "Tabula Rasa," but is far more hurtful and demeaning this time around. His conduct toward her will only worsen in the next episode. When Jack and Kate catch up to Ethan, Jack focuses his resentment on him, muttering, "I won't let him do this again." His comment is a little bewildering at first, but Jack is remembering his dad's false assurances, and he realizes Ethan's threats may be false, too. The bottom line is, Ethan is putting a pregnant woman's life in danger, just as his father had, but it is Jack who will live with the guilt if anything happens to her.

Sawyer and Sayid meet again for the first time since Sayid tortured him, which was about a week ago, according to Kate. Their relationship began with hostility and stereotyping and it's only gotten worse. Yet somehow, in the time they've been apart, there seems to have evolved a mutual understanding, something even bordering on respect. Sayid doesn't appear to hold a grudge against Sawyer, and Sawyer has done something to show he is trying to help maintain Sayid's efforts to get them off the island by keeping the bonfires burning. The very fact that Sawyer has opted to stay on the beach rather than go to the caves proves that, a knife in the arm notwithstanding, Sawyer still prefers Sayid to Jack.

When Kate and Jack finally find Charlie, the scene is terrifying. Later, Jack will be accused of not being able to let go of anything, and this scene is a perfect example of him refusing to give up, even when it seems futile not to. The question is, can you imagine what would have happened if he had? As the sky opens and the rain begins to fall, this scene is like a baptism for Jack, because while he's hostile to others throughout the episode for reminding him of his father, the person who reminds him most of Christian is himself. By doing what he does in this scene, he's able to do something Christian was unable to do at the end of his career.

Parent Issues

Bad parenting seems to be an ongoing theme of the show (warning: this contains spoilers for upcoming episodes in seasons 1 and 2):

Jack: His father tells him when he is young that he doesn't have what it takes, and both he and Jack's mother blame him for a mistake his father makes.

Sawyer: His mother had an affair when Sawyer was a child, and when his father found out, he killed his wife, and then himself.

Claire: Her father abandoned her when she was a child, and her mother is no longer in her life.

Walt: His mother left Michael when Walt was a baby, and he was raised by another man who didn't want to be his father. Michael is now trying to make up for it.

Locke: His parents gave him up for adoption when he was a child, and he was raised by several foster families. His father came back into his life only to take something from him. His mother suffers from mental problems and betrayed her son for money.

Kate: Kate's father, Sam, thinks the world of her (yay!) . . . but he isn't her father at all (sigh). Her mother, Diane, had had an affair with another man, Wayne, and got pregnant. Sam left when Kate was five, Diane married Wayne, and Kate grew up thinking Wayne was her abusive stepfather, wondering why her father didn't take her with him.

Jin: His father is a loving man, but Jin is ashamed of what he does for a living, and thinks he's lower class.

Sun: Her pushy mother constantly tries to match Sun up with men of a higher class, and her father is a very dangerous man who abuses his daughter's love for her husband.

Charlie: His father was a harsh man who thought Charlie was wasting his life being a musician, and while his mother encouraged his talent, she put huge pressures on him.

Shannon: Her mother died when she was young, and her father remarried a tyrannical woman who hated Shannon because of her closeness to her father.

Boone: Boone's mother was largely absent during his childhood. Instead he had a nanny named Theresa, but his mistreatment of her led to her death.

Hurley: His mother loves him, and he loves her, but she's disappointed in him and wishes he'd do more with his life.

Sayid: His father was a hero of some kind, but it's not clear why. When Sayid is reminded of it in "One of Them," he noticeably flinches, like his father's heroism is something he's never been able to live up to.

This is a great episode that is *key* for character development, and shows us that ongoing flashbacks will eventually answer questions raised in earlier ones.

Highlight: Boone explains to Locke that a "Red Shirt" on *Star Trek* was the guy who always got killed when the captain sent them on away missions. Locke's response is priceless: "Sounds like a piss-poor captain."

Did You Notice?:

- In early episodes, Boone seemed to gravitate to Jack and work alongside him, but now he's moved on to Locke, as if he senses that Locke is the more important man on the island.
- When it begins to rain, Locke looks up and holds his arms out, which is exactly what he did when it began to rain in "Pilot, Part 1."
- Jack jumps up and fights Ethan after Ethan basically tells him to stay down, just like he did as a kid in the flashback in "White Rabbit."
- Jack's father's name is Christian, which no doubt has some significance on the island, a place where religion and faith are very important.

Nitpick: Boone knows the details of a bit of Trekkie trivia like what a Red Shirt is, yet he refers to Mr. Spock as "the guy with the pointy ears." Also, why does Jack have a permanent five o'clock shadow, even when he's in surgery? You'd think he'd clean up a bit for such an important job. Finally, Sayid says to Sawyer, "Have you got something to say to me, Sawyer, or are you going to continue asking me questions you know I don't have the answers to?" Yet up to that point, Sawyer had been asking legitimate questions that Sayid had been answering. Why would Sayid say that?

4 8 15 16 23 42: Kate says that she and her father spent **8** hours tracking deer one day. When playing backgammon, Walt rolls a **4** and a 3. Hurley says he placed 17th in a backgammon tournament once (1 + 7 = **8**).

It's Just a Flesh Wound: Jack has cuts on his head from Ethan hitting him, and a bruise on his cheek. Charlie's face is bruised and his neck is bruised and red. His ribs and chest are probably sore from the CPR (he's lucky nothing is broken).

Any Questions?:

- Jack wonders aloud how one man could have dragged off two people, and it's a good question that goes unanswered. Did Ethan have help? Did he knock them unconscious? Did he have some of the same drugs Rousseau put into Sayid?
- The last time we saw Shannon, she said there was no way she was moving to the "rape caves," yet now that's where she and Boone are. How did he convince her to go? Why is she so hostile suddenly? Before the previous episode, we saw her suffering from asthma and a worried Boone sitting by her side. Now she's just being bitchy. What happened?

- What did Hurley mean when he said, "Back home, I'm known as something of a warrior myself"?
- Locke tells Kate she's just full of surprises — what other surprises has she given Locke? He doesn't even know that she was the marshal's prisoner.
- Ethan seems to have inhuman strength when he fights Jack. Why is he so strong?
- Why can't Charlie remember anything?
- Charlie says "they" just wanted Claire. Who are "they"? When did the Others join Ethan after he'd taken Charlie and Claire? If Charlie remembers there was more than one person, does he have any recollection of any of the Others?
- The Others clearly want Claire because of her baby. Rousseau had mentioned they had taken her baby Alex. Why do they keep stealing children?
- What did Locke mean when he says to Boone at the end of the episode, "Don't you feel it? You know, *it.*"
- What is the thing that Boone and Locke find at the end of the episode? Were they meant to find it like this?

1.12   Whatever the Case May Be

Original air date: January 5, 2005
Written by: Damon Lindelof and Jennifer Johnson
Directed by: Jack Bender
Guest cast: Victor Browne (Shooter), Tim Halligan (Hutton), Dezmond Gilla (Baseball Hat), Achilles Gacis (Six Foot Five), Michael Vendrell (Trucker)

Flashback: Kate

When Kate finds a metal briefcase that she claims belongs to her, she becomes determined to open it.

There have been many points in human history where man severely messed things up. But given the chance to start over, would humankind just make the same mistakes? Is human nature just incorrigible? Throughout the history of Western civilization in particular, men have been the ones in charge, and women are largely marginalized. Men were hunters, then conquerors, kings, and presi-

The Chinatown Branch of First Hawaiian Bank was used as the setting for the bank Kate robs in New Mexico. (RYAN OZAWA)

dents. The original tradition of marriage involved a woman being passed from her father to her husband, taking the last name of her new husband to show she was his property and no longer her father's. Several religions paint women as the root of all evil and command their subservience to men.

In "Whatever the Case May Be," this marginalization of women begins to play itself out on the island. We've already seen Sun being bossed around by Jin, who treats her like a piece of his property. Claire has been manipulated by two different men — Thomas and the psychic — before making it to the island. Shannon doesn't contribute anything to anyone, but that doesn't entitle Boone to talk to her as rudely as he does. The one woman who stands apart from the others is Kate, the tomboy who is constantly trying to prove she's as strong and essential as any man on the island. But in this episode, it's like the men resent her for trying to be like them, because she's suddenly bullied, ordered around, questioned, and treated like a child. Jack and Sawyer make it clear they don't trust Kate, while keeping reams of secrets of their own.

The opening scene shows Kate and Sawyer frolicking in an oasis-like waterfall and swimming hole. It's one of the few times we ever see Kate completely laid-back and enjoying herself. The fun ends abruptly when Sawyer suspects her of lying to him, and he takes the case from her, determined to get it open. Clearly Kate wants what's inside, and perhaps if Sawyer can get whatever it is before she does, he'll have some power over her. But ultimately, what will that get him? The scenes of Sawyer and Kate playing an ongoing, flirty tug-o'-war over the case are fun to watch — especially for Kate/Sawyer shippers — but Kate stops being amused and turns to Jack for help. For Kate, it's out of the frying pan, into the hot burning oil of the deep fryer. Where Sawyer turned Kate's desire for the case into his own little sick game to watch her squirm, Jack decides to make Kate truly suffer.

The case itself clearly symbolizes Kate. She's a locked case to everyone, and the marshal holds the key to her past. Both Jack and Sawyer would do anything to crack her tough exterior, but while Sawyer would prefer to do it in a physical way, Jack would rather reach out to her emotionally, which is why he acts the way he does in this episode. But his rudeness goes a little too far.

Ever since "Tabula Rasa," Jack has felt hurt and betrayed by Kate. But even if she had owned up to him and admitted she'd been on the plane with the marshal, would he trust her any more now? The only difference between Kate and the other passengers on that plane is that she was *caught* for her transgressions. Since the third day on the island, though, Kate has always been truthful (or so it seems . . . you can never be too sure)

The lovely Evangeline Lilly. (CHRISTINA RADISH)

and helps everyone out. But Jack won't let her forget her lie. In the previous episode, he grilled her on why she was such a good tracker, and when she told him the reason, she turned the tables on him. He, of course, never answered her question. In this episode he's rude to her, questions her, refuses to take her at her word for *anything*, and acts like he's her judge and jury. It's one thing to be a leader; it's quite another to make everyone subservient. At the end of the episode, Jack screams at Kate to tell the truth "just this once." At the end of "Tabula Rasa," Kate offered to tell Jack what she did, but he said no, the island would be her second chance. (Well, apparently not.) She told him about Rousseau's transmission, and she told him how she got her tracking skills. When he asks her why the plane means something to her, she says it's because it belonged to the man she loved, which is the truth. Jack, on the other hand, has barely told Kate a thing, but when Kate needs something that's inside the case, he doesn't respect that need, and controls and berates her throughout the episode. From now on, he'll wear the key to the case around his neck as a constant reminder to Kate that he is in charge.

The Sayid and Shannon situation is the complete opposite. Shannon is a whiny young woman who seems to willingly play the stereotype of the helpless, useless, vapid girl. When given an extremely important task, she gets frustrated, starts to cry, and storms off in a huff. While Jack punishes Kate, Sayid indulges Shannon and shows a lot of patience.

Finally, Rose returns in this episode and jolts Charlie out of his shock and depression. In her matter-of-fact way, she helps bring him back to the one thing that had helped him and kept him afloat when he was younger — his faith. In this pairing, Rose is the one who has the upper hand. She takes Charlie under her wing as a parent would a child. There are no sexual dynamics, no gender hierarchies, just one survivor helping another, proving that all kinds of relationships exist on this island.

Despite everything Jack and Sawyer put Kate through, we know she gives as good as she gets. For every man on the island who treats her badly, there are probably two or three in the real world who have been hurt or betrayed by her. Could her treatment on the island be some kind of karmic payback for how she has treated the men in her past life?

Highlight: Sawyer and Kate goofing around in the water.

Did You Notice?:

- When Charlie says he's trying to protect Claire, it's a sweet but unlikely gesture; when Jack says it, it's gallant. When Locke says it, we totally believe him. Yet when Sawyer tells Kate he's following her to protect her, it sounds ridiculous.
- Rousseau's notes are a metaphor for the show's plot: a bunch of numbers and references that don't make sense.

Interesting Fact: The song that Shannon sings at the end is Charles Trenet's "La Mer," a song from 1946 that was used in *Finding Nemo*. Appropriately, the movie is about a fish who is lost, and trying to find his way to Sydney, Australia (see page 181).

Nitpick: There are a lot of nitpicks in this episode. Kate's bikini wax seems to have held up astonishingly well after three weeks on the island, considering that before the crash she was in custody, and before *that* she was living in the outback in Australia. (I was going to say Kate's G-string was gratuitous, but since I enjoyed Sawyer's low-rise jeans underwater, that would make me a hypocrite, so

I won't.) Shannon tells Sayid about a child she lived with who watched *Finding Nemo* (the computer movie with the fish, as she puts it) 900 times, to the point where she can remember every word of the final song in French. So why doesn't she remember the title? Were the writers legally unable to name the movie? Also, the obvious product placement of the "Halliburton" was a bit much — notice that very few characters referred to it as a "briefcase," but instead use its brand name, including Michael and Hurley joking about how *impossible* it is to open a Halliburton, that sturdy aluminum briefcase that is every passenger's best friend. Ugh. Finally, Rose tells Charlie he's being selfish by not contributing to the island, but in "Walkabout" Jack has to go out and deal with her while everyone else is cleaning up the wreckage of the fuselage. She doesn't help or contribute in any way in that episode, and she wasn't actually in shock like Charlie is.

Oops: Either Jack's bluffing when he talks to Sawyer, or he shows that once again he makes a much better spinal surgeon than a GP. He tells Sawyer that if he doesn't give him the case, he'll take him off cefalexin, the antibiotic he's put him on for his arm. However, like most antibiotics, cefalexin is prescribed in a 7–10 day cycle. Sawyer's arm was stabbed 12 days ago, according to the show's timeline, so he would no longer require the antibiotic.

4 8 15 16 23 42: The "Halliburton" contains 4 guns, with ammo. In Kate's flashback she opens the safety deposit box **815** (the same number as the flight). Shannon says Locke and Boone have been going to the jungle for 4 days.

It's Just a Flesh Wound: Sawyer has a bruise on his knee from Kate throwing a rock at him, hurts his arm trying to open the case, and probably has bruises on his forehead from Kate headbutting him. We see a wound on the back of Sayid's shoulder, presumably from his torture at the hands of Rousseau.

Any Questions?:

- Why has everyone seemingly abandoned the search for Claire? Boone and Locke have shifted their interest to what's under the earth, Kate's off looking for fruit, and everyone else is more worried about the luggage than the life of a young woman.
- The tides suddenly shift, carrying all of the luggage and belongings out into the ocean. Sayid says it can't be normal, despite Sawyer warning him this would happen four days earlier. What caused it?
- Why did Kate go to Jack for help? Why not Locke or Sayid? Is she *looking* for verbal abuse?

When *Lost* first started, the weirdness on the island and the obscure allusions and references immediately made fans think that this show couldn't be read on a surface level. Instead, conspiracy theorists put their thinking caps on and began to formulate scenarios of what was *really* happening on the island. These are some of the theories that ran rampant in season 1, and by season 2, some of them are still viable, while others have been disproved (see page 248):

Everyone died in the plane crash and are now in a purgatory, stuck here until they redeem themselves. This was one of the earliest and most popular theories among fans, because there was so much to back it up. In "Pilot, Part 2," Jack actually makes the statement, "Three days ago, we all died. We should all be able to start over." Every person on the plane was broken in some way, and they all have something they must work out in their lives. Life before they boarded the plane was spinning out of control, and the hand of God or some higher power interceded, took down the plane, and immediately sent some people to heaven, some to hell, but withheld judgment for 48 survivors, instead putting them on a strange island to work out their problems. In future episodes, you'll see that just when a character seems to have finally reconciled a problem in their lives, they die, which fueled the popularity of this theory.

Aliens are somehow involved, and they are controlling the events. Since this theory is so difficult to prove either way, it could be entirely correct. Maybe someone on the plane was an alien disguised as human who triggered something that allowed his fellow Martians to hijack the plane and take it somewhere else. This theory recalls the *Twilight Zone* episode, "Stopover in a Quiet Town," where a couple finds themselves wandering around a strange house that looks mysteriously phony, and every once in a while they hear a little girl laughing. The big twist at the end of the episode is that they've been abducted by giant aliens, and given to their daughter, who has put them into her dollhouse as little living dolls.

There's some sort of weird scientific experiment. Someone who's a big fan of philosophy and science has chosen these people specifically by tracking them through the years, forcing them to cross paths in some way, and getting them onto the plane. The people are now all on the island and are being monitored by scientists, who throw them into strange and terrifying situations to see how they'll adapt. They've introduced polar bears and can make the trees suddenly disappear into the earth. It's an interesting theory, and one that finds legs in season 2.

There has been a nuclear holocaust that caused the plane to break apart in the air and crash, and now these people are the only human beings alive on Earth. *Lost* never shows us the outside world in any way, and therefore a holocaust could be a possibility. It wouldn't explain why these characters were all linked before they got on the plane, or the strange anomalies on the island, or the monster, or the dreams. But maybe they were all part of the nuclear fallout.

Everything we see on the island is probably a hallucination. The show begins on Jack's eye, and there is a popular sentiment that everything we see is from his point of view. Everyone on the island represents a part of his personality. Working against this theory is the intricate nature of each of the backstories, and the fact that Jack doesn't really seem to know anyone very well. Why would we see flashbacks to Kate's life that reveal what she did, and then have Jack question what she did? If it were part of his imagination, he would already know. If, at the end of four or five seasons, Jack suddenly wakes up to find Patrick Duffy getting out of a shower, I'm going to throw out my television for good.

1.13   Hearts and Minds

Original air date: January 12, 2005
Written by: Carlton Cuse, Javier Grillo-Marxuach
Directed by: Rod Holcomb
Guest cast: Charles Mesure (Bryan), Adam Leadbetter (Malcolm), Kelly Rice (Nicole)

Flashback: Boone

As the survivors begin to wonder what Boone and Locke are doing on their hunting trips, Locke decides to let the island teach Boone a lesson about himself.

The title of this episode is thought provoking in the context of the show's plot. Even the most reasonable person can allow their heart to rule their mind. How many times in our lives do we know we shouldn't be doing something, but out of sympathy, pity, love, or lust, we do it anyway? In Boone's case, he has always seemed like a guy who bosses his sister around, but in this episode we realize their relationship is not what they make it out to be.

Since Locke's spiritual awakening, he seems to be falling deeper under the spell of the island, and he's becoming a little eerie. Now that he and Boone have discovered a hatch in the jungle, opening it has become an all-out obsession for him. He comes to believe the island is testing him in some way, and he has enormous faith that if he can open the hatch, he will prove himself a worthy disciple.

But just as Jack seems to believe that being the island doctor gives him carte blanche to rule over everyone, Locke seems to presume that because he's the man of faith, he has a right to force people into dangerous, terrifying, and compromising situations in an effort to steer them toward an epiphany like the one he had. We realize Locke has been telling lies to cover up the existence of the hatch, mostly by explaining away their expeditions as hunting excursions to find boar. After a week with no pork, the castaways are starting to wonder why Locke and Boone aren't delivering. Hurley, Kate, and Sayid all ask about Locke, and Jack begins his own inquiry to see if he can figure out if Locke is trustworthy. Locke spins one story to Sayid, a different one to Jack, and he tricks Boone into a life-threatening situation. When will his lies catch up with him?

While Locke and Boone are off in the jungle not hunting boar, Jin and Sun are contributing to the group by fishing and planting a garden, respectively. As Kate helps Sun, she discovers her secret and we see just how frightened she is that Jin cannot find out. She's not afraid that he'll hurt her — she's afraid of hurting him. Hurley again acts as comic relief in this episode, and the scene where he and Jin are involved in an emergency situation and neither one can understand the other is hysterical. Since Sun's flashbacks, the writers have allowed Jin to be a little more likeable, but he won't become a truly sympathetic character until ". . . In Translation."

As the mirth happens on the beach, however, Boone is enduring a personal hell, care of Locke. It's appropriate that Locke applies the paste to his head, because he needs Boone to let his head start ruling his heart. Locke may have tricked Boone into his current situation, but it's not the first time Boone has been tricked. As we see in a flashback, Boone has his reasons to resent Shannon for what she's done, but he can't help loving her. (In a future episode, we'll see that Shannon has her reasons, too.) His love for her is affecting him now that she's with Sayid and he's put into a situation where he must come to terms with it. His epiphany, however, is very different from the spiritual awakening Locke has had on the island, but it does achieve what Locke wanted.

Locke's comment at the end — "I gave you an experience that was vital to your survival on this island" — is vague, but also foreshadows upcoming episodes. Is Locke telling the truth, or has he got it all backwards? Locke has opened Boone's eyes to his own truth within, and now he must use Boone's revelation to open the hatch.

Maggie Grace and Ian Somerhalder are dating in real life, which seems to creep out a lot of fans. Don't worry: they're not really related. (CHRISTINA RADISH)

Highlight: Hurley begging Jin to pee on his foot.

Did You Notice?:

- In the flashback, Boone's girlfriend looks exactly like Shannon.
- The Michelangelo story that Locke tells involves an abusive father, which follows the trend of most of the parenting stories we've seen on the show.
- Jin appears to be using as his fishing net the netting used in the cargo hold to keep the luggage in place. (Usually the straps on the cargo netting would be much wider and thicker, but let's just overlook that.)
- The men spend most of their time in the jungle, learning how to live in the wild, while the women are trying to tame and cultivate it by making a garden.

- The monster's appearance is usually preceded by the sound of birds' wings fluttering.
- Boone's bruises clearly weren't from the crash, but from the beating he got from Bryan shortly before boarding.

Interesting Facts: Locke mentioned that he learned to make a homemade compass when he was a Webelos. A Webelos is the fifth level of Cub Scout, after Tiger Cubs, Bobcat, Wolf, and Bear, and after about two years, he moves on to the Boy Scout level. Also, Locke's Michelangelo story is close to the truth, if a little embellished. Michelangelo's mother died when he was young, and Michelangelo wrote, "When I told my father I wanted to be an artist, he flew into a rage, 'artists are laborers, no better than shoemakers.'" However, the commission for creating the statue of *David* was a long process, and despite Locke's story, Michelangelo wasn't just handed a hunk of uncarved marble. The block was carved in 1464 by sculptor Agostino di Duccio, who gave up after two years. The block then lay unused for 10 years before a second sculptor, Antonio Rossellini, tried and quit after a few months. Others, like Leonardo da Vinci, were brought in, but it was a 26-year-old Michelangelo who stepped forward in 1501, and was finished in 1504. According to his diaries, he writes, "The City Council asked me to carve a colossal David from a nineteen-foot block of marble — and damaged to boot! I locked myself away in a workshop behind the cathedral, hammered and chiseled at the towering block for three long years." Michelangelo created the statue believing he was liberating the human body that was encased in stone, and to do that, he had to have pictured it ahead of time, as Locke says.

Nitpick: A couple of the characters behave in ways that are inconsistent with what we've seen of them in the previous episode. Jack treated Kate like a common criminal in the last episode, and in this one he's jokey and sweet with her (and by the next episode he'll return to his previous behavior). When Jack talks to Charlie as they're building the fire, Charlie seems more like his old self again, too, despite everything that's just happened.

4 8 15 16 23 42: In Locke's story he said Michelangelo looked at the block of marble for **4** months, and the block of marble was **18** feet high. The camp is **4** miles west of where the hatch is located. When Shannon's father married Boone's mother, she was **8** years old. When Boone arrives in Sydney, he tells Shannon he just spent **15** hours on a plane. When Boone confronts Bryan about breaking up with Shannon, he walks by a tank with the numbers 1, **4**, and 0 on it. The 4 is in red.

It's Just a Flesh Wound: Hurley steps on a sea urchin.

Lost in Translation: When Hurley asks Jin if he can fish with him, Jin says jokingly to him, "I don't play with amateurs, please go away." After Hurley steps on the sea urchin, Jin figures out that that's what he's done, and then helps him onto the beach, looks at it, and says, "I have to pull it out." When Hurley insists that Jin pee on his foot, Jin figures out what he means, and says, "What are you doing? No, [that's] stupid."

Any Questions?:

- Shannon is reading *Watership Down* at the beginning of the episode. How did she get it from Sawyer? Did it cost her $5,000?
- Locke tells Boone they want to keep Sayid on their side. The only split in the camp so far was between Sayid and Jack with the location of the survivors, and Locke and Boone both chose the caves, with Jack. Clearly Locke detects an ideological split happening, which to him is far more detrimental.
- How did Locke know he would need the paste later? What is in the paste? Where did he learn to make such a thing? He seems surprised at what the paste "showed" Boone; what was he expecting it to do?
- Locke is usually an extremely careful person, so why does he tell one story to Sayid (that Boone gave him the day off) and another one to Jack (that he hadn't seen Boone all day)? And wouldn't Sayid see the ridiculousness in the statement that *Boone* gave *Locke* the day off?
- Locke tells Sayid he doesn't need a compass, "not anymore." What does he mean?
- Sayid mentions that north is obvious to them, but Locke's compass points in a different direction. Is the compass defective, or is there something strange about the island? Why don't Sayid and Jack think of the myriad possibilities, rather than just writing off the compass as defective?
- When was Shannon married?
- Why was Shannon in Sydney in the first place? Did she move there for a reason and find Bryan there, or did she meet Bryan in the U.S. and then move to Sydney?
- Did Bryan really take off with the money or has she put it away somewhere and left Bryan instead?
- Did Boone just leave the body in the water when he went back to camp?

Ashes to Ashes: Shannon Rutherford, 20, who was . . . oh, never mind.

Ian Somerhalder (Boone Carlyle)

It all happened so quickly. Teenage model. Teenage actor. Star on ABC's new series *Lost*.

Born in 1978 and raised in the ranch town of Covington, Louisiana, Ian Somerhalder was plucked from obscurity and made a star before he was even 18. The son of a massage therapist and a building contractor, with a mixed racial background that included Native American, Somerhalder was modeling by the time he was 15. It was an unusual atmosphere for a teen. Due to a modeling contract that forced him to fly to New York twice a week, Somerhalder was unable to attend school regularly. By the age of 16 he felt he was through with modeling, but the lure of the job brought him back into the business a year later. The face of Guess jeans for two years, Somerhalder had no problem paying his bills.

"I'd done a job in London and gotten paid in pounds and had exchanged it for dollars and had all this cash on me," he explains. "They almost didn't let me back in the country; it was too much to claim. It was in my boots and my socks and my underwear, in my cargo-pants pockets, in my luggage. About thirty-five thousand dollars."

Needless to say, not everyone understood or was accepting of Somerhalder's choices during the period. High school friends often spurned him because of his success as a model. "I lost many friends because of it," he says. "The ones that did stick however, are very close to me now. It seems as though people don't know what to make of the fashion industry or the people in it. My guess is that the difficulty lies within understanding a business based on sex, and where the lines of sexuality are personified in magazines and text as a 'gray area,' while younger guys, especially in high school, can't get their head around being in that environment."

His newfound wealth led to a life of endless parties, including an arrest in New Orleans when he was 17 for public (and underage) intoxication. Interested in entering acting, Somerhalder put an end to his party days. "I used to party," he says. "But it got to be all I did. I had to give it up — it can be overwhelming, you know."

By the time he was 19, Somerhalder had largely given up modeling and had refocused himself on a career in acting. Modeling, it turned out, just wasn't a permanent calling. "It was amazing to be able to travel around and make money and meet a lot of wonderful people, but it just wasn't where I was going to end up."

He took two years to study his craft. When he emerged in 2000 on the short-lived series *Young Americans*, Somerhalder found his good looks made him a hit — with male viewers. After two episodes, he'd received thousands of e-mails, mostly from gay male fans. The actor would use this appeal in other roles where he played gay characters. "I'm not gay, but some of my best roles have been. When it comes to sexuality, I'm fearless.

And if you're comfortable with that, you can get away with anything."

He would follow up his role on *Young Americans* with appearances on *Smallville* and a starring turn in the movie *The Rules of Attraction*, before being the first actor cast for *Lost* in the part of Boone, the rich kid who yearns for his stepsister (with whom he eventually hooked up romantically off the show).

In order to make the role a success, Somerhalder had to forget much of what he already knew. Having grown up on a ranch, the actor was comfortable in the rough-and-tumble world that Boone had to inhabit after the plane crash. However, the world of the island was supposed to be entirely foreign to Boone.

Ian Somerhalder was a model before being one of the first actors cast on *Lost*.

(STHANLEE MIRADOR/SHOOTING STAR)

"I grew up in Louisiana. We had horses and land. You learn how to survive. You understand the way things work in the woods; if you need to build a fire, tie a rope, make a rope out of something else. He didn't know any of these things. He was very fragile in that environment, where I wouldn't have been."

1.14   Special

Original air date: January 19, 2005
Written by: David Fury
Directed by: Greg Yaitanes
Guest cast: Tamara Taylor (Susan), David Starzyk (Brian), Monica Garcia (Nurse), Natasha Goss (Dagne)

Flashback: Michael and Walt

Michael becomes worried when he can't find Walt, and recalls why he has been absent throughout Walt's short life.

Michael Dawson: Bad father or unfortunate husband? "Special" is an episode with no easy answers, because it is all about subjective relationships: romantic partnerships, father and son, mother and son. Each relationship seems to adversely affect the others, making people miserable around one another. In the beginning of the episode, Hurley remarks to Jack that Michael clearly hates being a father. What Hurley doesn't realize is, Michael has never been given the chance to be one.

Michael's flashbacks are some of the most emotionally painful ones yet, because he is never in control. His partner Susan appears to be a good mother, but that image disintegrates when she's willing to cut the child's ties with his father. Susan may come off as kind and sympathetic, but she's also calculated. She gives her surname to the baby and refuses to marry Michael, as if she were just using him to get pregnant and doesn't need him anymore. When she hooks up with Brian Porter, Michael realizes she wasn't just leaving him for a better job.

Michael obviously loves his son, but he knows a court will side with Susan. He can't keep track of where the boy is, so that, by the time Susan tells him she wants Brian to adopt Walt, Michael seems to have accepted that he's not an asset to Walt, and Susan's plan will provide Walt with a better life. It's a heartbreaking scene, and Susan's question to Michael — "Why are you holding on to Walt, for him or for you?" — is unfair. No parent should be forced to make the decision Michael does. Susan maintains a careerist attitude throughout, but while having more money also means she can provide more for her son, a child's stability is about more than money, possessions, and private schools.

The flashbacks in this episode aren't all Michael's — in one, we finally see why Walt is "special." As he tries to get his parents' attention so they'll look at a picture of an Australian bird, he becomes frustrated — and finally does something that forces them to see the bird. This power over his environment explains several weird occurrences on the island: In "Pilot, Part 2," Walt was reading a *Flash* comic with a polar bear in it. When he saw the picture, he possibly willed it into being. He does it again in this episode. In "Tabula Rasa," Michael tells Walt he'll look for Vincent as soon as the rain has stopped. Walt looks out, and makes it stop immediately. In "All the Best Cowboys Have Daddy Issues," Walt is playing backgammon with Hurley and every time he says what dice he needs to roll, he rolls exactly those ones. And in this episode, when Locke tells him to picture the path the knife will take, he throws it perfectly into the tree. Walt has the ability to exert an immense control over his environment; in this way he is the opposite of his father. However, Walt doesn't appear to realize he has this gift.

Locke, on the other hand, has gleaned a sense of Walt's capabilities. Perhaps he sensed it when they were playing backgammon, or maybe he saw the comic book and realized what had happened in the jungle, but somehow, he realizes Walt is gifted, and that his gifts could be a huge advantage to them on the island. By showing him how to throw a knife properly, he's allowing Walt to recognize his powers and learn to exercise control over them — not get into situations like he does in this episode, where he may have accidentally summoned a polar bear who chases after him. Locke treats Walt like an adult with a special skill, and Michael treats him like a child who's been through a rough period and needs protection. Is either of them wrong? Is either of them right?

Highlight: Charlie trying not to read the diary, and opening and closing the book. Dominic Monaghan's comic timing in this scene is impeccable.

Did You Notice?:

- Again, Vincent senses that danger is coming, and he runs away. Walt is safe when Vincent is around, but as soon as the dog leaves, Walt is in grave danger. Notice how concerned the dog looks just before Walt throws the knife at the tree.
- Walt's first initial (W) is an upside-down version's of Michael's (M), as if to show they're exact opposites.
- If you look at the ceiling above Michael's head when the nanny hands him the box of letters, there's an octagon design made out of wood (this will be important in season 2).
- If you freeze-frame Claire's diary entry, you can see her entry the day before she got on the plane, where she says tomorrow is going to suck, and with her big belly, she's going to try to get into business class (we'll find out in "Exodus, Part 2" that she's unsuccessful). She mentions there's a DVD that she needs to return to Blockbuster. On the other side you can see her packing list (which includes make-up, "bathroom stuff," brush, water, books, camera, gum, hat, jerky, CDs and player, and candy) and she's drawn drops of water along the side (which might be tears). In block letters she's written "I HATE HIM" across the bottom. As Charlie turns the pages, you read another entry that says, "Today I realized I really like Charlie. There's something about him that's just so adorable and sweet. Even in a scary place like this, Charlie makes me feel safe."

- This is the second Brian on the show. The first was Shannon's boyfriend Bryan in "Hearts and Minds."

Interesting Fact: The frame in the comic that Walt reads aloud is (in the English version of the comic) where the younger Green Lantern encounters a polar bear in the Arctic and says, "Oh. One of those bearskin rugs . . . with the bear still in it," and he creates an image of a much larger monster to scare away the bear. However, as garbled as Walt's Spanish is, it doesn't sound like he's reading that. From what I can pick up, he says something about making up a polar bear, which is not a line in the comic. This is probably a big clue to viewers that the polar bears may be appearing because Walt is willing them into existence.

Nitpick: This episode seemed to go against the established conventions for flashbacks so far. The episode opens on Michael's eye, so we assume the flashbacks therein will be from his perspective. However, the flashback to the bird hitting the window is one only Walt would be privy to, not Michael. *But . . .* the flashback isn't really from Walt's perspective. What happens in this scene is more important to Michael and Brian than it is to Walt: If Walt were remembering something, it would be something that was significant to him, not to others. The writers clearly needed to alert us to Walt's specialness, but in doing so, they messed up slightly. Also, in "Solitary," when Rousseau hears a loud noise outside, she grabs her rifle and says to Sayid, "If we're lucky, it's one of the bears." This would indicate she regularly sees bears on the island, and if so, Walt didn't actually conjure up the polar bears. But this episode seems to be saying he did.

Oops: At the beginning of the episode, the sun in the sky indicates it's mid-morning, and Charlie is looking for Claire's bags. When Kate and Charlie find them and are looking through them on the beach much later, it's sunrise.

4 8 15 16 23 42: Boone is wearing a T-shirt with **4** aces on it. Michael sent Walt cards every year for **8** years.

It's Just a Flesh Wound: Sawyer gets a punch in the face from Charlie, and returns it in kind, cutting Charlie's mouth.

Any Questions?:
- In "All the Best Cowboys Have Daddy Issues," Walt suggests they take Vincent out into the jungle to help find Claire, but Michael says no. With Walt and Vincent's special abilities, would they have been able to find her?
- Jack speaks authoritatively on the difficulties of raising children; has he ever had any, or is he thinking of his father?

- Does Walt have any clue that he is capable of making things happen with his mind? He doesn't seem to, but Locke makes a mysterious comment that Walt "knows his own mind."
- When Susan first tells Michael that she's taking Walt, she mentions that they've "been through so much in such a short time." What does she mean?
- The first time Walt seemed to will the polar bear into existence, it appeared to other people, but this time it chased him. Why?
- When Michael was hit by a car in New York, was that bad luck, or was it somehow meant to happen?
- When Walt follows Locke into the caves despite his father telling him not to, does he do so because he looks up to Locke as a hero, or does he have a genuine sense that Locke might be able to help him?
- Right before the bird incident in Walt's flashback, Walt is staring closely at Vincent. What is he doing?
- Why doesn't Walt call Brian "Dad"?
- What sort of illness did Susan get that killed her in less than two weeks? Did Walt have anything to do with it?
- Brian tells Michael that he didn't want to adopt Walt, and admits he only did it so he could get Susan in the deal. Did Susan know this?
- What personal effects belonging to Susan did the nanny give to Michael?
- The nanny gives Michael the wooden box of letters and says it's something *she* thinks Walt should have (not Susan). How did she know about them? Did Susan really want Walt to have them, or is the nanny making a decision on her own?
- When Charlie's looking through Claire's diary, you can see "I HATE HIM" written across the bottom of one of the pages. Who is she referring to?
- Why was Claire having dreams about the black rock? Does she have psychic abilities?

Malcolm David Kelley (Walt Lloyd)

He's pivotal to the plot of *Lost*, but few had even taken notice of Malcolm David Kelley before he took the role of the unusual boy wonder Walt in 2004.

Malcolm David Kelley's Walt is one of the most mysterious characters on the island. (STHANLEE MIRADOR/SHOOTING STAR)

Born in California in 1992, Kelley was in foster care for nearly the entirety of his first year before being adopted by the Kelley family. His sister, Sydney, was adopted two months later. Despite his difficult start in life, Kelley found a calling in the entertainment industry by the age of five, and had appeared in television series, including *Malcolm in the Middle*, by the age of seven.

His motion picture credits include roles in *Antwone Fisher* in 2002 and *You Got Served* in 2004, as well as commercial work. He received a casting call for *Lost*, and was immediately deemed appropriate for Walt, the boy with mysterious abilities. "I only had an audition and a call-back," Kelley explains. "They called me back a week later and told me I got it and I was going to Hawaii. I was excited. It's so far away and everything."

Kelley has fallen into the role, becoming close with Harold Perrineau, who plays his father on the show. "I hang out with him, his wife, and his daughter all the time," says Kelley. He also enjoys spending time with Madison, the dog that plays Vincent on the show. "It's a female dog which is pretty cool," he says by way of explanation. "It's my first time working with a dog. I had a dog. It was a Dalmatian, but she died. Her name was Lucky."

The biggest challenge for Kelley has been adapting to the situation of living away from home. His parents come to visit regularly, and his grandmother has also helped out by staying with him. But for a child whose life and career are still in front of him, Kelley is drinking in the experiences he gains while shooting the show.

"I've never been on a boat like that before, so that was my first time, and I was kind of freaked out the first time we did it," he says of the conclusion to season 1. "But, I was cool. We were pretty far out there, too. I didn't get in the water, but just in case I fell in, in between takes, they gave me a life vest."

✍ Green Lantern and Flash: Faster Friends, Part 1 (1997)

The comic book that Walt is reading (and we now know belonged to Hurley) is a Spanish version of Green Lantern and Flash in *Faster Friends, Part 1*. In the Flash comic book that Walt is always reading, the story tells of an alien who came to Earth 50 years earlier and the Flash (Jay Garrick) and Green Lantern (Alan Scott) were brought in to holster the threat. The government agent who had hired them to lasso the alien, whom they've dubbed Alien X, then dispatches them without even a thank-you. The Flash and Green Lantern take the alien's spaceship and bury it in the Arctic so the government can't claim it. For 50 years the government has been conducting experiments on the alien, filling his body with diseases. Now that he has only a few weeks to live, Alien X finally breaks free, captures Garrick and Scott, and demands that they take him to his ship and help him uncover it. Meanwhile, the new, younger Flash (Barry Allen) and Green Lantern (Hal Jordan) are recruited to help save Jay and Alan, who are older and weaker and cannot fight against the mind tricks the alien plays on them. They manage to locate Jay and Alan on the ship in the Arctic (along the way Barry fights a polar bear), but the alien uses Jay and Alan to fight Barry and Hal, and meanwhile he jumps to the controls of the ship and sends out an "invitation." Everyone escapes from the ship after gaining control of their senses, and Barry offers an olive branch to Alien X, admitting that what was done to him was wrong, but taking revenge on innocent people won't make it any better. But what's done is done, and Alien X blows up his spaceship, killing himself. Now it's up to the Flashes and Green Lanterns to find out what this invitation was that Alien X sent out before dying . . . and readers must wait for Part 2 to discover what it was.

The polar bear that tries to stop the Green Lantern becomes pivotal to the first season of *Lost*, and there's a strong suggestion that Walt was the one who called the bear forth just by picturing it in his "mind's eye," as Locke puts it. If you take a look at the comic (the hard copy is difficult to find, but you can read the entire thing online, page by page, at www.lostlinks.net/comic/comic1.htm), there are a few other similarities. Jay and Alan had buried the alien's spaceship underground, and when Locke and Boone have dug out a lot of the hatch, it's rounded like the ship, and has been purposely buried there a few decades earlier. There's a frame near the beginning where Alien X is strapped to a table, much like Sayid is in "Solitary." The doctors who have been conducting experiments on Alien X have been injecting him with something, which Rousseau did, but we'll also see several other people doing this in season 2. Perhaps as the show continues, we'll find many more similarities — is there a government connection to what's happening on the island? An alien one? Was the crash premeditated, and if so, was it out of revenge for something? Are the people on the island versions of Alien X? Since Alien X seems hostile to the people on Earth, who have captured, tortured, and experimented on him, when in fact he came in peace, could the suggestion be that Ethan — who was accused, attacked, and killed by the people on the island — similarly came in peace and didn't actually mean any harm?

1.15   Homecoming

Original air date: February 9, 2005
Written by: Damon Lindelof
Directed by: Kevin Hooks
Guest cast: Jim Piddock (Francis Price Heatherton), Sally Strecker (Lucy), Darren Richardson (Tommy), Eric Griffith (Buyer)

Flashback: Charlie

When Claire comes back to the caves, Ethan demands they return her or he'll begin killing them all.

Like Jack, Charlie tends to take responsibility for things that are beyond his control. When Claire disappeared over a week ago, he became despondent, mulling over in his head how he could have saved her. In "The Moth," Charlie's flashbacks showed how he was betrayed by his brother and dragged into a world that destroyed him. His fear was that he would be useless to others and fall into the background. In "Homecoming," his motivation is more specific — he wants to be able to take care of people. His salvation in "The Moth" wasn't that he was able to admit his heroin addiction to Jack, but that he was able to find a way to rescue Jack from the cave-in and take care of him. Until now, he's been feeling guilty that he wasn't able to take care of Claire, but now that she's back, he'll get a second chance.

Claire's mind has erased every memory since the plane crash. When she

Charlie Pace poses backstage at a Drive Shaft concert with two of his fans.

(ALBERT L. ORTEGA)

landed on the island, she was calm, laid-back, and friendly; but now she's scared, paranoid, and wary of others. The only one who remembers is Ethan, and he has returned in proper slimy form. So far, Ethan is our only glimpse of an Other, and if he's any indication of the rest of the tribe, they're a scary lot. He has super-human strength, fights like a trained fighter, is wily, and seems omniscient.

This episode shows us how the group strategizes under pressure. Sayid, Locke, and Jack step up as the triumvirate of decision-makers. Sawyer is a "soldier" who comes along and does his duty when told, but he's not involved in the planning. Kate tries to be involved, but is shut out until Sawyer recruits her. And Charlie is seen by the decision-makers as emotional and too involved to be a part of the ambush. Every time he objects to a decision, he's overruled by those who "know better."

The flashback to Charlie's con of Lucy Heatherton didn't really illuminate much of his character (we already knew he was a junkie and that he wants to feel useful), other than the discussion he has with her father, who says he also used to be in a rock band before he decided to quit and become responsible. We see a dim light bulb go on in Charlie's head telling him he should do the same thing. What it *was* good for was explaining the continuing problems Charlie's had with his brother and Drive Shaft, and that even though he was the very backbone of the band, he's been denied the financial benefits of success. All his life he's tried to care for those around him, but for reasons beyond his control, he was never able to keep them out of harm's way. Perhaps the reason he keeps screwing up is because he doesn't know what it feels like to be taken care of, so how can he return the favor? At the end of this episode, Charlie finally does what he thinks will protect Claire, but what he does will probably put her — and everyone else — in even greater danger.

Highlight: Charlie's photocopier demonstration.

Did You Notice?:

- During the commotion when Claire is being brought into the caves, Jin asks Sun what's going on, as if he suspects she knows and understands.
- Ethan shows up with four scratches on his face, like several other people have had, including Jack and Kate, but where most people have incurred wounds on the right sides of their faces, Ethan's is on the left.
- Jin says he was attacked because of "the others" but he's referring to the other survivors.
- Ethan uses a slingshot, a primitive weapon that immediately suggests a David and Goliath situation, but that would make the Losties the "bad guys."
- Charlie will often look into a mirror right before he makes a difficult choice, and he almost always chooses the wrong thing. This is not just an ongoing Charlie motif, but another Alice reference, since in *Through the Looking Glass*, everything in the looking-glass world is backwards. Whenever Charlie looks into a mirror his world flips upside down in the same way. In "The Moth," he looked into a mirror before taking heroin for the first time, and in this episode, he glances into a mirror before stealing the cigarette holder.
- Sayid tells everyone they want to keep Ethan alive, so despite his crisis of conscience in "Solitary," he probably plans to torture him for information.
- Charlie shoots Ethan in the heart, as if to show how personal all of this was to him.
- The only thing that Claire remembers from before wasn't real.

Interesting Facts: Lucy Heatherton says her father is buying a paper company up in Slough. J.J. Abrams is a huge fan of the BBC series, *The Office* (going so far as to get its star, Ricky Gervais, to appear in an episode of *Alias*). The show is a mockumentary about a paper company in Slough. Also, William Mapother (Ethan) is Tom Cruise's cousin. No wonder Ethan is a bit of a spaz.

Nitpick: In the previous episode, Charlie says Claire's been gone over a week. In this episode, one day later, Boone says she's been gone almost two. Also, everyone reassures Claire that they'll be near her, protecting her at five points, yet it takes an eternity for anyone to get close to her once Ethan begins to chase her. Finally, Ethan is wily, so how did he fall for such an obvious trap as the one they set for him?

Oops: If you are looking down the beach with the water on the right and the sand on the left, they've used the sun coming up in that direction, and they've also used it as sunset.

4 8 15 16 23 42: Tommy chooses number **234** on the jukebox for the Drive Shaft song. Ethan has **4** scratches on his face. Locke sets the bags of garbage at **4** corners of the perimeter. The photocopier that Charlie tries to sell is the Heatherton **815** (same number as the flight).

It's Just a Flesh Wound: Claire has a serious scratch on her forehead; Jin incurs a wound on his upper left pectoral muscle from the slingshot.

Any Questions?:

- Charlie says he's amazed by how Tommy amasses information. How *does* he get his info? Where did Charlie meet Tommy in the first place?
- Okay, this is going to be a little confusing, and is a very hotly debated topic on *Lost* message boards, but here goes: The guy who is dead is Steve, not Scott. Christian Bowman plays Steve on the show (in "The Moth," Bowman is the one who steps forward and identifies himself as Steve), and Dustin Watchman plays Scott. In this episode, Hurley says Scott is dead, and he gives the eulogy at the funeral for Scott, yet when Sayid turns over the body on the beach, it's Christian Bowman playing the part. Bowman is no longer on the show (despite his name showing up to throw off fans), but Watchman is still working on the set (often appearing uncredited). On *The Fuselage* threaded message board, Watchman has posted and reassured fans that, yes, he *is* Scott, it says so on his contract, and he is still on the show. The writers didn't actually make a mistake, because they went to the trouble of using a body double at the funeral to make it look like Scott was

attending his own burial (Watchman is also the source of this information after fans bombarded him with questions about whether or not he's standing in the background). An article that followed the episode's airing said that in future episodes, we would find out the nature of Scott and Steve's relationship and why they were traveling together. *So* . . . this begs several questions: Why does Scott pretend he is Steve, and let everyone think that he's actually dead? When Hurley is giving the eulogy, he's reading from a wallet, so he must have Scott's ID . . . meaning the real Scott (the guy who's still alive) has switched IDs and is pretending to be Steve on purpose. Did he commit a crime before getting on the plane? What *is* the nature of his relationship with Steve (the guy who's dead)? Are they brothers? Are they lovers? If so, why isn't he a little more shaken up over it? Why doesn't anyone think it's weird that Hurley is giving the eulogy and not Scott (who they think is Steve)? Will we see more of Scott (who will from this point on be called Steve) or is this a story line that will just remain a background joke, never to be explored? Are you confused yet? No wonder online fandom refers to them as "Sceve."

- Where is Jack when they discover Sceve's body on the beach? Jack's nowhere to be seen, and he doesn't appear to be at the funeral, either.
- At the end of the previous episode, Claire was conscious when she emerged from the jungle, yet when Locke carries her into the caves, she's unconscious. What happened to her? Did Locke have anything to do with her being taken? Notice he's the one who asks Jack if there's any chance Claire will get her memory back.

Ashes to Ashes: Scott Jackson (well, not really . . .), killed by Ethan (or so we think . . . the sinister nature of the Scott/Steve thing makes me wonder). He was a sales guy at an Internet company and had won a two-week all-expenses-paid vacation to Sydney for his sales performance. He looks exactly like another guy named Steve (who is actually Scott). We also remember Ethan Rom, who died of gunshot wounds to his chest. His name probably isn't Ethan, either. I give up.

Heart of Darkness **by Joseph Conrad (1902)**

Heart of Darkness is about a journey into the deepest, darkest recesses of both the earth and the mind. When Joseph Conrad wrote this novel, arguably the first important work of fiction of the twentieth century, Europeans were beginning to lose their hold on world domination. Colonies in the far reaches of the world were rebelling against European rule and the corrupted power that the European ambassadors were lording over them. Imperialism was about bringing light to the dark world — they brought their "civilized" behaviors, traditions, and methods to tame the "savages" they found.

Marlow is a sailor who tells the story of a journey he'd taken years earlier into the Congo on behalf of the Company, a Belgian outfit that collects articles from the Congo to trade on the world market. When he arrives at the station to meet the Company accountant, he finds it in a horrible state, and the accountant tells him about a Mr. Kurtz whom he will undoubtedly encounter on his journey into the Congo. Before he travels up the Congo, he meets the "civilized" white people, who consist of the Company manager, who is a menacing man; a group of lazy agents who are hoping for advancement but never actually do anything (Marlow calls them the Pilgrims because they carry long staffs and have a religious aura about them); a brickmaker who never seems to make any bricks because he's perpetually waiting for materials to arrive. Marlow is surprised when he meets a group of cannibals who will join his expedition into the interior, and finds them by far the most level-headed group of people he's encountered yet.

Throughout his adventures, he begins to hear more and more about Kurtz, and people are saying he's gone mad, or he's a genius, or he's a threat to other employees of the Company. The accountant seems to be one of the few people who admires Kurtz, and he tells Marlow that he's sent back more ivory than all of the other traders put together. Marlow becomes obsessed with Kurtz, and during his stay at the station (where his boat is repaired) and his trip down the Congo, he witnesses the "savages" being brutalized and repressed, and he begins to reflect more on human nature and how power corrupts. If Kurtz really is mad, as Marlow intuits, is it insane to think that imperialism is wrong? Is it crazy to disagree with the brutal methods of the Company?

When he finally gets to the Inner Station, he and his colleagues (who just survived an ambush by natives in the jungle) are met by a Russian trader who seems slightly unhinged, who keeps ranting about Kurtz and how he has expanded his mind (think Dennis Hopper's character in *Apocalypse Now*, which is a modern retelling of *Heart of Darkness*). The natives worship Kurtz, who finally comes out on a stretcher. Marlow takes him onto his ship. A native woman emerges from the jungle, weighed down with ivory jewelry, and the Russian trader tells them she's Kurtz's mistress. In the middle of the night, Kurtz disappears, and Marlow finds him crawling on all fours through the jungle back toward the natives. He manages to get Kurtz back to the steamer.

As the ship travels back down the Congo toward the Outer Station, Kurtz shares his various views and philosophies with Marlow, that are at times fascinating, at other times disappointing, because it seems Kurtz wasn't some sort of godlike genius: he was just a man looking for fame and fortune. He wanted to stay with the natives because they thought he was a god. Marlow draws a parallel between imperialism and madness in this context: just as Kurtz went mad because he had no one to answer to but himself, the idea of imperialism is mad because there are no checks and balances, and with absolute power comes inevitable corruption.

Kurtz entrusts his papers and writings to Marlow, and among them is a pamphlet about how to civilize the natives, upon which he's written in block letters, "Exterminate all the brutes!" Kurtz doesn't actually treat the natives any better than the Company does, but the difference is, he's honest about what he does. The Company refers to their practices as trade and civilization, and Kurtz refers to it as taking ivory by force and repression. Kurtz's illness gets increasingly worse during the trip. At one point Marlow checks in on him, and sees him lying there with his eyes wide open. He cries, "The horror! The horror!" and dies. Marlow comes down with a similar sickness and almost succumbs the way Kurtz did, but in his lowest moment, his major regret is that he won't have something profound to say the way Kurtz did.

A year later, he goes to see Kurtz's fiancée to give her Kurtz's remaining papers. He meets other relatives of Kurtz's and they all talk about him as a musician or an artist, and it disappoints Marlow that other people have had experiences with a side of Kurtz he knows nothing about. He realizes man is essentially impenetrable. The heart of darkness is not just in the jungle, but in everyone, and mankind will continue to stumble through history because one can never know another person. When Kurtz's fiancée asks Marlow to tell her what his last words were, Marlow can't bring himself to let her know what Kurtz had discovered deep in the Congo, and instead lies that Kurtz had uttered her name. He decides it's better to leave her in ignorance than reveal to her the savagery of the world, and of man himself.

Heart of Darkness is more a metaphor than a book with a plot, and its link to *Lost* lies in that metaphor. Just as Marlow is forced to look at the darkness within himself and those around him, the characters on *Lost* are haunted by the bad things they've done in the past, and in various ways the island forces them to face those things head-on. The characters fear what may happen if they venture too far into the jungle, for they believe something evil and nasty lurks out there. It could be the monster, it could be the mysterious Others, but either way, their fear is real. However, the Others and the monster sometimes seem manageable compared to the personal darkness they all seem to harbor within.

1.16 Outlaws

Original air date: February 16, 2005
Written by: Drew Goddard
Directed by: Jack Bender
Guest cast: Robert Patrick (Hibbs), Stewart Finlay-McLennan (Laurence), Jeff Perry (Frank Duckett), Susse Budde (Mom), Gordon Hardie (Boy), Brittany Perrineau (Woman), Alex Mason (Bartender)

Flashback: Sawyer
Sawyer goes after a boar he believes is personally attacking him.

"Outlaws" is about karma, which is Sanskrit for "to do," or deed. Karma is the central tenet to the dharma-based religions (see page 174) and the simple explanation — I hope I don't sound like Earl Hickey here — is if you do good things, good things will happen to you; if you do evil things, bad things will befall you. Karma is the sum total of the actions in one's life; one good thing doesn't cancel out a series of bad ones. In Buddhism, it is believed that everything a person has done until the present moment creates who one is right now, and everything one does from this point on creates one's future state of being.

In Sawyer's case, we discover that he's killed a man, and now lives with the immense guilt of what he's done. When a boar destroys his tent and doesn't touch

Josh Holloway and Maggie Grace at a fan convention. (ALBERT L. ORTEGA)

anyone else's, he decides it's time to go after the boar. In Hinduism and Buddhism, karma ties in with reincarnation. The Western notion of reincarnation assumes that if you were a good person, you'll be reincarnated as a king or a cat (i.e., some kind of being that is treated like royalty), but if you were bad you'll be reincarnated as a cockroach. Sawyer seems to believe the boar is the reincarnation of the man he killed, yet rather than try to make amends of some kind (offer it food, give it a tarp), he decides to kill it. Again. While it's obvious Kate enjoys watching Sawyer suffer, she also seems to want to be near him, and helps him track the boar into the jungle. The scene of them playing "I never" by the fireside with tiny liquor bottles is a great one, and one of the few times we ever hear a fireside conversation (after having seen so many of them in the final music montages of the episodes). In the beginning her comments are simply meant to draw him out, while Sawyer is playing the game for real, but soon he follows her lead until the "game" becomes increasingly hurtful.

Charlie is also haunted by what he did. After waiting so long for Claire to come back, now he can't look her — or anyone else — in the eye. Some of the castaways were murderers in their past lives; Charlie's the only one who has *become* one on the island. (One could argue that Jack has killed someone as well, but his euthanization of the marshal was a completely different matter). In "Whatever the Case May Be," Charlie turned back to his faith with the help of Rose. But in the week that followed, that faith has broken away, like the pieces of himself that he lost, and now he probably feels as alone as he did when he was on heroin. Sayid, who is living with his own demons, his memories of what happened in Iraq and elsewhere, sympathizes with Charlie.

One of the most direct links between characters on the island happens in Sawyer's flashback, when we see him in a bar drinking with Jack's dad, Christian Shephard. Christian is trapped in his own karmic hell — his drinking caused the death of an innocent woman and her unborn child, and now it's slowly causing his own death. Without realizing it, Christian encourages Sawyer to follow through on an evil act, one Sawyer had been talking himself out of, thereby cementing Sawyer's karma as well. Yet Christian seems to realize what he's done to himself and to others, and he's regretful. But he doesn't have the guts to do anything about it.

By the end of the episode, Sawyer decides that sometimes a boar is just a boar. But when he hears the whispering in the jungle, he begins to realize what Sayid has already figured out — the island/jungle/Others know his deepest fears.

Josh Holloway goofs around for the camera.
(ALBERT L. ORTEGA)

Highlight: Kate confronting Sawyer in the jungle and telling him that while he was supposed to be tracking a boar, she's followed him as he tracked humans, a rockslide, birds . . . and himself.

Did You Notice?:

- Christian tells Sawyer that Sydney is as close as one can get to hell without being burned, and since every person on that plane was in Sydney before the plane left the airport, his comment could have foreshadowed what was going to happen to them; it's not Sydney that's closest to hell, it's the island. If the island represents a place of redemption, it's important to note that Christian died before boarding.

- Christian mentions he's misplaced his wallet, so Sawyer pays for his drinks. Presumably, since in "White Rabbit" we see Jack go to Christian's hotel room and find his wallet there, this is the moment where Christian literally drinks himself to death . . . courtesy of Sawyer.
- Locke tells the story of his sister Jeannie, and he seems to believe it, but when Kate asks him if the dog was his sister, he says, "Well, that would be silly." He often comes close to revealing his faith like this, but always pulls back as if he's worried others might think he's strange for doing so.
- Sawyer shoots Duckett in the chest, just like he shot the marshal. He obviously thought the marshal would die as quickly as Duckett did.
- This is the second Frank on the show; the first one was Lucy Heatherton's father Francis in "Homecoming."

Interesting Facts: Hibbs is played by Robert Patrick, well known to sci-fi fans as Special Agent John Doggett on *The X-Files*, T-1000 in *Terminator 2: Judgment Day*, and smaller roles on *Stargate: Atlantis* and several other movies and television series. Also, the woman who comes into the hotel room with Sawyer before he notices Hibbs is in the room is played by Brittany Perrineau, who is the real-life wife of Harold Perrineau, the actor who plays Michael.

Oops: As Hurley and Charlie are digging, you can tell parts of the scene were filmed at the end of the day, and the shots filmed from in front of them were later at night with bright lights to simulate the daytime. During the "I never" game, Kate says she never had a one-night stand, and Sawyer nearly finishes the bottle. On her next dare, his bottle is almost full again.

4 8 15 16 23 42: Hurley mentions that Charlie shot Ethan in the chest **4** times.

It's Just a Flesh Wound: A boar runs into Sawyer's leg in the jungle; Kate kicks him in the shin later.

Any Questions?:
- Was Sawyer planning on conning the woman he's with? Was it possible he was trying to get some lottery money from her? (See "Numbers.")
- How did Sawyer meet Hibbs? What happened between them? What was the Tampa job?
- Christian asks if Sawyer's business will ease his suffering, and if so, he should get on with it. Is Christian sitting at a bar drinking himself to death on purpose, thinking his death could ease the suffering of others?
- Sawyer tells Christian his real name; perhaps sine he got so close to the man

who he thought was the real Sawyer, he was preparing to drop his fictional name?

- When was Kate married? To whom?
- Why doesn't Kate later have carte blanche with Sawyer? She helped him track the boar to its wallow, and even though she abandoned him, she led him right to the boar, which was the agreement.

Josh Holloway (Sawyer)

For Josh Holloway, struggling actor and former model, his break into the acting business came through the role of Sawyer, the unlikable confidence man. The problem was that the character was so difficult to appreciate, even for Holloway, that he was certain Sawyer would meet some awful demise, which would surely be applauded by viewers.

"When I read the first script I was like 'Oh my God, I might as well not even unpack my bags. [Sawyer] is going to be hated.'" The star decided to make the most of his story line and accentuate any positive aspects of his character. He adds, "They gave me just a tiny bit of humanity and I blew it up as much as I could. I was like, 'Please be the guy you love to hate, not the guy you hate, because if you're the guy they hate . . .'

So I was trying my best to do that, and fans responded."

It was a long time coming for Holloway, born in California, but raised in Georgia. He found a degree of success on runways and in photo shoots as a model, but always hoped for something greater. That's not surprising, considering the actor comes from a family of overachievers. Holloway is the second of four brothers, and his siblings all work successfully within the computer software sector.

While the path to a career was clear for his brothers, it was less obvious for Josh. After attending high school in Georgia and working a series of tedious jobs, including picking up dead chickens on a farm and working in a department store, he attended the University of Georgia. But, like Sawyer, school held little interest for Holloway, who dropped out after a single year and moved to New York to pursue a career as a fashion model.

Fame didn't come quickly. Instead, Holloway drifted to Europe where jobs were tough to come by and even making enough money for food was difficult. "I was starving actually for the first couple of years. I was stealing food and jumping trains in Italy. I traveled all over Europe, but I ended up living in Bologna and speaking only Italian. It was very strange."

Eventually he landed gigs modeling for Calvin Klein and Perry Ellis. But he was more intrigued by acting, landing early roles as "the purse snatcher" in Aerosmith's video for "Crazy." But his first role in a series was a bit part in the pilot for the *Buffy the Vampire Slayer* spin-off, *Angel*. A series of forgettable small roles on forgettable shows like *Walker, Texas Ranger* and in unsuccessful movies followed. Nothing indicated that Holloway would be anything more than another pretty face lost in the beauty of Hollywood's unemployed. It was all too much for Holloway at the time. He wanted to marry his long-time girlfriend, Yessica Kumula, but was concerned he wouldn't he able to help support them with his sporadic acting work. He considered quitting and pursuing something more "legitimate."

"I was ready to marry my girl, or at least ask her, but I didn't think I had anything to bring to the table. I couldn't do it until then — it's just the way I was raised, I guess." He admits it was his breaking point.

"Eight years in this town, they've broken me in half so many times," he said. "I find myself in a heap on the floor going, 'You know what? Give up this dream, dude. It's done. They're killing you.' I've gotten so close for so many years on so many things. I've done seven independent movies, so I was doing about a movie a year. I'd just get a taste and just a little encouragement from the universe to continue. It was just enough to keep me in."

Thankfully, Holloway's break finally fell in his lap. As Abrams frantically tried to cast his embryonic show, a call went out to Holloway asking him to audition for the role of Sawyer in the new series called *Lost*.

"It was late and I was working on a small part at another set for a TV show pilot when my then girlfriend, now wife, called because she received the sides for the *Lost* pilot in our fax machine at home," he recalled. "The audition was for the very next morning, therefore she faxed over the material so I could study for it. I went in the next day, and the rest is history."

As part of the role of Sawyer, the shifty, amoral drifter, Holloway was asked to beef up his Southern accent, something he'd worked hard to lose. He also made slight shifts in the character of Sawyer. Initially written as a "Prada-wearing New York conman," Holloway had a different take on how Sawyer should be presented.

"I thought Prada would look rubbish after a day on the beach and it wouldn't age well. I made him a little softer and a little scruffier. Girls love a messed-up tough guy."

The model for Sawyer is actually a cross between Han Solo and Wolverine from *X-Men*, Holloway would later admit: "A little more edge and anger to him, but with the lovable scoundrel that Han Solo was."

In truth, Holloway has enjoyed playing the rogue, something he expects to do for some time. "Sawyer is basically my alter ego. He can say what he wanted when he wanted. I can't."

1.17 . . . In Translation

Original air date: February 23, 2005
Written by: Javier Grillo-Marxuach, Leonard Dick
Directed by: Tucker Gates
Guest cast: Byron Chung (Mr. Paik), John Shin (Mr. Kwon), Joey Yu (Byung Han), Chil Kong (White Suit), John Choi (Butler), Kiya Lee (Byung's wife), Angelica Perreira (Byung's Daughter), Tess Young (Best Friend)

Flashback: Jin

When someone sets Michael's raft on fire, all eyes turn to Jin as the culprit.

If "Outlaws" is an episode about karma, ". . . In Translation" is about starting over. "Tabula Rasa" touched on the idea of the blank slate, where everyone had a second chance on the island. Some characters, most notably Locke, saw their second chance immediately, and Locke has become The Believer, the one who sees the island as a place of redemption. Others, however, have taken longer to discover the advantages of the island; or, in the case of Jin, perhaps he, too, has seen it all along, but only now are we able to get a glimpse into his thoughts.

What makes this episode unique is that it's the only time we see exactly the same flashback we've already seen, but shown from a different perspective. For months, viewers have seen Jin as the cold husband of sweet Sun, ordering her around, unable to communicate with anyone but his wife, and largely keeping to himself. We have a few comic moments with him (Claire putting his hand on her belly; Hurley begging him to pee on his foot) but basically his role is to glower at Sun and grunt something in Korean, often without any translation given to the viewer. The writers have said they leave much of what Jin says unsubtitled on purpose — they want to recreate for the non-Korean-speaking viewer the confusion the other castaways feel when they try to talk to him. (This is why moments that are just between Jin and Sun are subtitled, because she understands him.) However, what that has done is made Jin foreign to us, and makes us unable to side with him or sympathize with him. The writers have forced this one character

Michael and Jin start off on the wrong foot as enemies, but become friends.

(CHRISTINA RADISH)

into the unenviable position of being "the foreign guy," which is unfair to the character; apparently, when it comes to Jin, the writers have decided to control when we're going to like that guy.

The time is now. In "House of the Rising Sun," Sun's memories were of her relationship with Jin, and how it seemed to disintegrate to the point of hopelessness. Her memories are full of questions that remain unanswered for her, but we finally get some answers now. Jin's memories of the past few years focus on his own incompetence — through his memories, we finally understand that he thought he was not worthy of Sun. He loved her deeply, he was controlled by her tyrannical father, and he was ashamed of his own. Jin was a tender and gentle man who changed himself to get the girl, but the change in him is the very thing that is driving the girl away. He remembers how he disappointed those around him, mostly Sun. And we discover — surprisingly — that Sun wasn't the only one intending to make a break at the airport. The difference is, his escape *included* Sun.

The islanders, unfortunately, only see the harsh side of Jin. Forced into a situation in which he can't understand anyone and is beginning to grow suspicious of his wife, he has become icy and belligerent. When the raft goes up in flames, Jin (again) becomes imprisoned by the others. As things start to seriously become very *Lord of the Flies*, as Sawyer puts it, Sun steps up in a way that surprises everyone, most of all her husband. The looks on both their faces — especially now that we know the real Jin — are heartrending.

The one person who seems to believe Jin is innocent is Locke. He reminds everyone that they can't be fighting amongst themselves when there's another clear enemy on the island. As mentioned, Locke sees the island as being redemptive, and at the end of this episode he talks with Walt, who feels the same way. For those castaways who found the real world a confusing and hostile place, the island could actually be seen as a sanctuary, a place they might not want to leave. Perhaps, until now, Jin saw the island as the only place he and Sun could escape the hand of Mr. Paik.

When Jin discovers Sun's secret, her worst fears come true. Without Sun, the only person with whom he could communicate, Jin is forced to make an effort with the others and his first English word — "boat" — shows where his new focus is. Rather than feel isolated, however, Sun tastes freedom for the first time in her life. As she stands on the beach and lets the wind remove her wrap, she is unencumbered by her husband, her father, or society. It's time for her, too, to start over.

Highlight: Hurley approaching Jin when he's playing golf with rocks, and suggesting he try sea urchins, because "they have more ping."

Did You Notice?:

- When Jin goes to Byung Han's house the first time to tell him Mr. Paik is displeased, Hurley is on the television show that Han's daughter is watching.
- The dog Byung Han gives to Jin is Bpo Bpo, the dog Jin gives to Sun in "House of the Rising Sun."
- Jin is a lot like Sawyer in that something that happened to him as a child makes him overly sensitive to children. Just as Sawyer backed out of his con in "Confidence Man" when the little boy came into the room, and Sawyer was reminded of himself as a boy, Jin is filled with regret when he sees Byung Han's daughter crying. He'd just beaten Han, and he realizes that she saw her father being humiliated, just as he was ashamed of his father when he was a child.
- When Jin is brought to the beach and there is much confusion around Michael, we *finally* hear the commotion from Jin's point of view — they make it sound like everyone is speaking another language by playing each audio track backwards. This proves that Jin doesn't understand English, despite fan theories that he can.
- Walt burned Michael's raft, just as he'd seen Michael burn his comic book.

Interesting Fact: The title of this episode alludes to Sofia Coppola's *Lost in*

Translation, the 2003 movie starring Bill Murray and Scarlett Johansson about two people who meet up in Japan and can't understand a word of the language around them, but come to a quiet understanding of each other.

Oops: When Jin gives Sun Bpo Bpo as a gift in "House of the Rising Sun," he's a tiny puppy. But when Byung Han first gives the dog to him in this episode, he's a lot bigger.

4 8 15 16 23 42: The raft will hold only **4** people. After Jin goes to Byung Han's house the second time, the associate in the back seat tells him to drive **8** kilometers away.

It's Just a Flesh Wound: Sun slaps Michael's face. Jin burns his hands, is kicked in the head by Sawyer, and has his face beaten to a pulp by Michael, cutting his mouth and bloodying his nose.

Lost in Translation: When Jin sees Sun on the beach in the bikini, he runs up to her and says, "What are you doing here? Why are you wearing that?" She tells him she just wants to go for a swim, and he says, "You have another bathing suit, why this one?" She tells him to stop it, and he grabs her arm and says, "Let's go, hurry." She asks where, and he tells her that everyone is looking at her, and she needs to go change. She tries to hush him, telling him he's being too loud, and she falls down in the sand. He tells her to get up, and she says, "Why are you doing this?" He asks her, "Don't you understand what I'm saying?" and Michael comes running down the beach. He turns to Michael and tells him this isn't his problem, and adds, "Who are you to talk to me like that?" Later, when Sawyer captures Jin and brings him to the beach for reckoning, Jin looks at Sun and says, "You don't believe me, either?" and he looks at Michael and says simply, "I didn't do it." Michael thinks he's said something nasty, and responds, "You say something to me?" Jin pleads with him, "I didn't do it, I didn't start the fire . . . do you understand?" and Michael punches him. Jin looks back up and says, "When I reached the boat, it was already on fire." Michael punches him again. Jin looks back up and yells at Michael, "I tried to stop the fire, that's what happened to my hands." It's at this point Sun realizes her husband is innocent, and she jumps in and reveals her secret to everyone. When you know what Jin is saying in this scene, it makes Michael's treatment of him all the more sad.

Any Questions?:

- How has Sun been sheltered from her father's life in organized crime?
- Locke tells Shannon it's time she move on from Boone, the same way he told Boone to move on from her. Why does he care so much that they separate?
- Why does Sun choose to speak her most heartfelt and meaningful words to

Jin in English, which she knows he doesn't understand? Is it because she still doesn't want him to know that she was going to leave him? Was it so the audience could truly feel her pain by hearing it in English?

- When Jin attacked Michael in "House of the Rising Sun," was it really in character? We see now that beating Byung Han was a very painful thing for Jin to do, emotionally, so why would he have beat up Michael so violently?

Music/Bands: During the final scene on the beach, Hurley is listening to Damien Rice's "Delicate," from his 2003 debut CD, *O*.

Daniel Dae Kim (Jin Kwon)

While he may play a character on *Lost* who rarely speaks English, Daniel Dae Kim's expertise and experience in handling the complicated character of Jin speaks loudly and clearly of the actor's abilities.

The son of a doctor father and a mother who studied English in Korea, Kim grew up living the quintessential immigrant experience. In the town of Easton, Pennsylvania, Korean-speaking immigrants were unusual. It didn't take long for Kim to feel the sting of racism. "I suffered the usual racial slurs in school," he says. "But I also played a lot of sports, so I had the pleasure of hearing them on the playing field as well. I'm sure it's a pretty common story among Asian-Americans, though."

As is the case with many new immigrants, Kim's parents had high aspirations for their son. But it didn't take long for Kim to realize what they wanted him to do wasn't the appropriate path for him. "Well, my mom and dad had a traditional upbringing in Korea, and my dad's a doctor, so I think they hoped I'd become a professional as well," he says. "After college I actually was going to go to law school or work on Wall Street like all good Korean-American children. I got offers from a couple of firms, but I decided I couldn't go through with it. Yeah, there was some friction [with my parents] for a few years, and that was tough."

Instead, Kim decided to pursue acting, something he'd become serious about while pursuing his undergraduate degree at Haverford College/Bryn Mawr College.

After finishing his degree, he went to New York University in the hopes of finishing a graduate program in theater. Though his parents were not pleased with his decision to forego the professional career, they backed Kim once they realized he was dedicated to the idea of acting.

For the first half of the season, it was difficult for Daniel Dae Kim to play the loathsome Jin Kwon, but after "…In Translation," the audience perception of his character changed drastically. (ALBERT L. ORTEGA)

"When I decided to go back to NYU to get my master's degree [in acting], they realized I was serious about my career choice. I'm happy to report they've been fans ever since." Prior to entertaining a career in acting, Kim met his wife, Mia, who made the needed sacrifices to allow the aspiring thespian to follow his dream. "I met her even before I had acted in my first thing or even wanted to be an actor," Kim says. "So she stuck with me through everything, and you don't find that very often in a woman or a man. People have their own paths they have to go on, and she made a lot of sacrifices for me. And that's one of the reasons I love her."

The skills he learned at NYU turned out to be extremely useful as Kim left school and started to look for work."I think my time at NYU was invaluable," he says. "I really credit the program there with making me a professional actor. I still use the tools and the skills that I learned there every single day when I'm on set."

With loans to pay, and realizing it would be tough to make a living in the New York acting scene, Kim and Mia moved to Los Angeles in 1997, the year after the birth of the couple's first son. Success came slowly, but surely. Mindful that roles for Asian-Americans were difficult to come by, Kim took small parts on television and in movies. Small appearances on *Seinfeld* and *NYPD Blue* came, as did bit parts in *Spider-Man 2*, *The Hulk*, and *Crash*. But his break came in the world of Jack Bauer and *24*, as well as on *Angel*. Playing the role of the evil lawyer Gavin Park on *Angel* gave Kim the notice he'd been lacking until that point. Given the zest that he threw into the role, it was not surprising when J.J. Abrams and *Lost* came calling in 2004. As with many of the characters in *Lost*, in the early going, the role of Jin was already evolving in Abrams' mind as he scouted potential actors. For Kim, the idea of playing a Korean was a relief, after having played other Asian nationalities on TV and in movies. The only drawback — Kim's Korean was extremely rusty, a hurdle he had to quickly overcome, since the character he played would communicate only in Korean.

To help create a realistic portrayal, Kim's costar on *Lost* — Yunjin Kim, who plays his wife and is fluent in Korean — coached him on his delivery. Even then, Kim found his accent was incorrect for the character of Jin. "My entire family is from Pusan, which is the deep south of Korea. So all of us there speak with an accent equivalent to someone from Georgia."

The role has not been without its critics. Many Asian viewers felt the character of Jin was simply reinforcing racial stereotypes of Asian men. It was difficult for Kim not to take the comments personally; but in time, viewers warmed to the character. "Initially, I was stung by it," he said. "I rejected a lot of roles that were one-dimensional and put Asian-Americans in a bad light, so to receive the amount of criticism I did when the show came out, was hurtful."

But as the character was more clearly defined for viewers, the perception of Jin has shifted. "The mail has been really positive," Kim said as the show entered its second season. "I think it was the fact you got to see a lot of different colors. He wasn't just this overbearing, domineering husband."

Given the opportunity to use his skills on a character as complex as Jin, a man torn by inner conflict, has been a revelation for Kim, who has carefully considered his character's motivations and thoughts.

"I think Jin knows that he's not well-liked on the island. It's part of why he stays away from people, especially because being the outsider is completely contrary to his nature. Look at his early life, how charming and friendly he is. Look at the kind, gentle nature of his father. To me, that's Jin. I also think buried somewhere under there, Jin harbors a certain level of self-hatred. I wouldn't be surprised if he wanted to make manifest some of the pain he'd been feeling on the inside since the crash."

1.18   Numbers

Original air date: March 2, 2005
Written by: David Fury, Brent Fletcher
Directed by: Daniel Attias
Guest cast: Lillian Hurst (Carmen Reyes), Jayne Taini (Martha Toomey), Ron Marasco (Ken Halperin), Ron Bottita (Leonard), Dann Seki (Dr. Curtis),

Michael Adamschick (Lottery Official), Archie Ahuna (Tito), Derrick Bulatao (Diego), Joy Minaai (Reporter), Brittany Perrineau (Lotto Girl), Maya Pruett (Nurse)

Flashback: Hurley

When Hurley finds a familiar series of numbers among Rousseau's papers, he remembers how they ruined his life — by helping him win the lottery.

Until now, Hurley's been the sweet, loveable, funny fan favorite with half of the show's best lines (Sawyer gets the other half). He seems completely harmless, and not really connected to any of the strange paranormal circumstances on the island. We just assume that in his previous life he was a laid-back, music-lovin' dude who probably slacked off, and enjoyed life. But in "Numbers," all that changes. The guy's a freakin' millionaire!

Jorge Garcia has the pleasure of playing the most beloved character on the show.
(CHRISTINA RADISH)

This is an episode that explores the notion of luck, and whether it's something we can control, or if it just happens to us. People who are down on their luck tend to believe in bad luck happening to them, that outside forces somehow put them into their lowly position. People who are happy generally believe they made their own luck, and can point out all of the things they did to make their lives as happy and comfortable as they are. When Hurley wins a whopping lottery by playing the numbers 4 8 15 16 23 42, he believes his life will turn around, but as his luck improves, everyone else's disappears. Family members are hurt, killed, and break up, and Hurley thinks the money is cursed. It's when his accountant tells him he's doubled his net worth through shrewd investments (which involved deaths, other people starving, etc.) that Hurley concludes not only that everyone else's bad luck is bringing him good things, but that the numbers are cursed.

Newspapers and magazines could be filled with the true-life stories of lotto

The large house that Hurley bought for his mother is located on Hunakai St. between Onaha and Koloa streets in Kahala. (RYAN OZAWA)

winners having bad luck. The sudden windfall of cash causes people with no money-sense to spend so lavishly and foolishly that they not only burn through their lottery winnings, but the rest of their savings as well, eventually declaring bankruptcy. Lottery winners are often shunned by jealous friends and family, and many believe they should be sharing their winnings. They become targets of thieves, scam artists, and people with bad investment ideas. The lottery world is full of winners who wish they'd never played.

As Hurley heads off into the jungle to demand an explanation from Rousseau, Locke asks Claire for some help on something he's building. The scenes between these two may seem innocuous at first, but there may be more going on. Locke hasn't had much of anything to do with Claire until he brought her to the caves after her abduction, and now that the Others have made it clear they think Claire's baby is important, maybe Locke is starting to believe the same thing. He wonders if she's regained her memory (a question he already asked Jack), and he talks to her about her pregnancy and the fact she was going to give the baby up for adoption. Locke is one of the most mysterious and unpredictable characters on the island, and he becomes even more so in season 2. He's a warrior, yet he had a menial job working for a box company. One minute he's extremely gentle, the next volatile. Some castaways believe he's the only person they can trust, others trust him the least. He could be the father figure that Claire needs, or he could be dangerous — when it comes to the island, Locke always puts "its" needs before anyone else's. It's interesting that before Claire knows what he's building, she guesses it's a trap, but instead, Locke has essentially built a box to house Claire's child. No matter how strange Locke acts, though, there's something about the way Terry O'Quinn plays the character that makes fans love him.

Which brings us back to Hurley. In a flashback, we see him return to Lenny, the insane guy who first heard those numbers 16 years earlier and is repeating them incessantly, and when Lenny hears what Hurley has done, he says, "You've opened the box." His comment seems like the maniacal ravings of a guy in a mental institution, until we see the very same series of numbers on the *ultimate* unopened box — the hatch.

Highlight: Hurley returning to the group and telling Sayid that Rousseau "says hey."

Did You Notice?:

- The woman who announces the lottery numbers on the television is the woman that Sawyer is with at the beginning of "Outlaws," when he enters a hotel room with her only to discover Hibbs is in the room.
- Hurley says that his grandfather worked 3 jobs for 52 years, which, if you multiply the numbers, comes out to exactly Hurley's lottery winnings (156).
- Hurley says the first thing he wants to do is give his grandfather the rest he deserves, and his grandfather instantly gets it.
- When Hurley's in the Hummer with his ma, he's wearing a medallion around his neck that is the Chinese symbol for prosperity.
- Hurley is the owner of a box company in Tustin, which means he's officially Locke's boss.
- Locke says he's good at putting bits and pieces together, which suggests he's starting to piece together what's going on with the Others and Claire's baby.
- In every scene where Jorge Garcia appears with Matthew Fox, Fox looks like he's on the verge of laughter, which is great to see, since Jack doesn't smile much.

4 8 15 16 23 42
Or, How I Learned to Stop Worrying and Love the Numbers

After "Numbers" aired, fans raced to their tapes and TiVOs of the previous episodes to see if they could find earlier occurrences of the numbers they'd missed the first time (they weren't disappointed). Since then, theories have abounded on what the significance of the numbers might be. Could the answer to all the mysteries of the show lie in these digits? After all, in the *Hitchhiker's Guide to the Galaxy* series, Douglas Adams tells the story of a superior race of scientists who fashion a supercomputer to answer one question: What is the answer to life, the universe, and everything? After seven and a half million years, it finally spits out the answer: "42." Could this be significant to *Lost*? (Probably not, but hey, who doesn't love referencing Douglas Adams?) The following are the most plausible theories yet:

It's a telephone number (481-516-2342).

It's the coordinates of where the people are located. If you go to Google Earth, and type in latitude 4.815, longitude 162.342, Google Earth will reposition itself to an area in the South Pacific, just southwest of a tiny island called Kosrae. Could this be where the island is hidden? There are several possibilities here: if you type in 48.15 latitude, 162.342 longitude, you end up just off the coast of Siberia (see "Live Together, Die Alone"). If you remove 16, and type in 4.815 latitude, 2.342 longitude, you end up just off the coast of Nigeria, which would explain how a very small Nigerian plane could make its way to the island (see "Deus Ex Machina" and "23rd Psalm").

It's what the world population was at some point in 1984, the same date as George Orwell's dystopian novel (see page 313). According to the online site World Population clock (www.ibiblio.org/lunarbin/worldpop) the world population hit 4,815,162,342 some time in May of that year.

The numbers correlate to the Psalms in the Bible: Psalm 4 is an "Evening Prayer for Help"; Psalm 8 is "God's Glory and Man's Dignity"; Psalm 15 explains "What God Requires"; Psalm 16 is "A Prayer of Confidence"; Psalm 23 is the most beloved of Psalms, "The Lord Our Shepherd"; Psalm 42 (the only one of these not in Book 1) is "The Prayer of a Man in Exile."

The numbers refer to Shakespearean sonnets. Sonnet 4 is urging a man not to waste his beauty, but to pass it on to future generations by having children. Sonnet 8 compares the harmonies in music to family harmony, and again states the man is sad because he doesn't have a family. In 15 the poet again talks about the man's beauty and states that where time may fade the man's beauty, his poetry can immortalize him. Sonnet 16 is a continuation of the previous sonnet, where the poet realizes that maybe his poetry will never do justice to his beauty, and again urges him (as in 4 and 8) to start a family so his looks may last for generations. Sonnet 23 is the poet's explanation of why he loves his subject so much, and he urges the man to look into a mirror to see his beauty with his own eyes. The 42nd sonnet is the last in a trio of sonnets where the poet writes about how the man has stolen his mistress, and he feels betrayed by both. In this final sonnet of the group, he makes excuses for his lover, but by the end of it, it's clear he's all alone. To add to the Shakespeare theory, Shakespeare died April (the 4th month) 23, 1616.

Or . . . the numbers were just chosen randomly by the writers to make us come up with various theories while they sit back and guffaw behind their computer screens to see how many of these numbers they can plant.

Nitpick: Hurley says that nothing ever happens to him and he's full of good luck, but why doesn't he consider the death of his grandfather to be something bad that's happened to him? And if his good luck causes other people's bad luck, why did he jump off the pressure switch, confident that nothing bad would happen? Didn't he stop to think that maybe his good luck (surviving the trap) might be someone else's bad luck (one of the other guys getting hurt)?

4 8 15 16 23 42: They don't appear in this episode. Kidding. Apart from the obvious uses of the numbers, the accountant says there was a fire in a sneaker factory that Hurley owned in Canada, and "**8** . . . some . . . people were killed." When Hurley visits Lenny in the hospital, Lenny is playing Connect Four. The game contains **42** circles where you have to connect **4** of the same colored checkers in a row. When Hurley first walks in, Lenny has dropped **16** checkers into the game, and there are **8** of each color. Sam Toomey has been dead for **4** years. The original transmission of the numbers that Lenny and Sam heard was **16** years ago.

Any Questions?:

- What do the numbers mean?
- The lottery official is played by Michael Adamshick, who played the anesthesiologist in "All the Best Cowboys Have Daddy Issues." Is it the same character, or just the same actor playing two different roles?
- This episode, despite being Hurley's flashback, does not open with a closeup on his eye. Is there something different about him and his flashback?
- Hurley says that he's put his family through a lot lately; what is he referring to?
- Where is Hurley's father? Has he died or are his parents divorced? (The fact his mother is such a strict Catholic would suggest the former.)
- Was Hurley in the mental institution with Leonard, or did he work there? If he was in the institution, does he still suffer from mental illness? Is it possible that this flashback isn't actually real?
- If Sam Toomey and Lenny heard the transmission at a listening post in the Pacific 16 years ago, as did Rousseau's science team, why hasn't anyone heard Rousseau's transmission if it was sent out from the same place?
- What did Martha Toomey mean when she said Sam used the numbers to guess the number of beans in the jar? If she means he guessed 4,815,162,342 beans, that jar would have been *way* bigger than a pony.
- Why hasn't Sayid sought out where Rousseau's transmission originates so he can go and change it?

- When Sayid was captured by Rousseau, he was near the cable. Did Rousseau carry him on her back across the bridge? Where did she find that kind of strength? Did she have help somehow?
- Who was transmitting those numbers 16 years ago, and why?
- How much money did Hurley actually win in the lottery? He tells Charlie that he's worth $156 million, but in one scene his accountant says he's nearly doubled his net worth, so was the lottery $80 million?

Music/Bands: The rap song that is playing in Hurley's Hummer was probably written for the show, because it's unavailable anywhere else.

1.19   Deus Ex Machina

Original air date: March 30, 2005
Written by: Carlton Cuse, Damon Lindelof
Directed by: Robert Mandel
Guest cast: Swoosie Kurtz (Emily Locke), Kevin Tighe (Anthony Cooper), Lawrence A. Mandley (Frainey), George O'Hanlon (Eddie), Julie Ow (Nurse), Tyler Burns Laudowicz (Kid)

Flashback: Locke

Locke believes the island has sent him a sign of how to get into the hatch, and he and Boone follow his gut instinct — to a disastrous end.

The term *deus ex machina* is a Latin phrase that comes from a Greek term used in theater, where a god would suddenly appear and decide the outcome of the play. (The "*machina*" was a mechanism of pulleys and ropes, and the god would often appear to creak down out of the sky.) A more modern definition of the term is when, in fiction or drama, a person or thing is suddenly introduced that seems to have come out of nowhere and is completely contrived, but serves to resolve the story line. (Think of the police showing up at the end of *Monty Python and the Holy Grail*, preventing the knights from actually storming the castle.) In this episode, the title seems to point to the sudden convenient discovery of an airplane that came out of nowhere, but at the same time, how is that any less believable than anything else that has happened on the island?

Since Locke's experience in "Walkabout," he seems to have come to believe he's

Kevin Tighe, who plays Locke's father Anthony Cooper, first found fame in *Emergency!*, an early 1970s television series. He's since appeared in films such as *Eight Men Out*, *What's Eating Gilbert Grape*, and *Better Off Dead*. (YORAM KAHANA/SHOOTING STAR)

a Chosen One, and he's been tested many times by things that have happened on the island, but he never wavers. He worships the island as if it is his god, and given the choice, would probably stay here forever. In the real world, he couldn't walk, but the island has given him a miracle, and he has pledged his allegiance to it in return. But suddenly, his miracle is fading, and now will be his true test of faith.

Locke's experience on the island isn't the first time he's acted like this, however, and in this episode we flash back to a painful event in Locke's life that helped shape who he is now. We discover that Locke was tossed around several foster homes as a child, although we never see any of his foster families. His birth parents gave him up, and no one wanted to adopt him. He's already told Sayid in "Heart and Minds," "I wasn't the most popular kid," and now we realize he meant that in terms of family as well as friends. When his birth mother and father reenter his life, they turn it upside down. Locke is so desperate for someone to love him and accept him that he turns to his new father wholeheartedly. When his mother tells him that he was immaculately conceived, his father laughs and says, "Well, I guess that makes me God," and if you watch the rest of the episode with that comment in mind, you realize Locke didn't love his birth father, he *worshiped* him. He and Anthony laugh off Emily's comment about immaculate conception as the talk of a crazy person (she had been institutionalized several times), but Locke still turns their reunion into an issue of faith.

When Locke's trebuchet falters, he shouts, "This was supposed to work!" as if he thought the island was attacking him personally by not letting it work. In the flashback, he tells Anthony, "This was meant to be," believing that destiny and fate have brought them together. In the previous episode, Claire asked Locke if he believed in luck, but he avoided her question. There's a fine line between the concepts of fate and luck: Luck refers to a force that brings success or adversity, whereas fate or destiny refers to anything that was pre-determined and out of our control.

Terry O'Quinn, who plays Locke, the island's disciple. (CHRISTINA RADISH)

Locke's ideas of fate and destiny (and Hurley's conception of luck) are important keys to this series: Were these people destined to be in a plane crash on this island, with events playing out as they are? Did the hand of God (or something else) cause things to happen, or are these just unlucky people?

Throughout his life, Locke has had one hard knock after another, rejected by his parents, by various foster families, by friends, and by women when he was older. He lost the use of his legs, and then was refused the walkabout tour. Things have never gone right for Locke, and he's turned to higher powers to try to understand why. While Hurley points to his numbers as his own curse, Locke looks at the wider scope of things, believing that destiny and fate have dealt him a bad hand, but, as Sawyer explored the idea of free will with his karmic boar, Locke seems to believe that if he makes enough sacrifices and passes every test, his destiny will change. When he met Anthony Cooper, he thought this man would give him back his chance to get to know his father, and he didn't realize that he would just take something away from him. The island was the first thing that gave him something, rather than taking something away — his ability to walk was returned to him. But just as he begins to think his new god has betrayed him as well by taking away his new ability to walk, he receives another sign. Locke's ability to walk is directly tied to his faith, and when it wavers, so do his legs. The next time we see him, we know that his faith has been completely restored.

Highlight: The look on Sawyer's face when Jack diagnoses him with hyperopia.

Did You Notice?:

- At the beginning of the episode, we flash back to when Locke was an employee of a toy store, and he's explaining the concept of Mousetrap to a child. His explanation is not only an important metaphor for what is going on on the island, but also foreshadows what will happen to him in this episode.
- There's a "lost dog" poster on Locke's windshield in one flashback, which not only has the title of the show and the word GOD spelled backwards, but the dog also looks a little bit like Vincent.
- Emily describes Locke as "special," which is the same way Brian Porter described Walt in "Special."
- There's a sound of pottery breaking in Locke's dream, perhaps foreshadowing Boone throwing the statue out of the plane.
- Jack tells Sawyer that he's farsighted, which is an apt metaphor for the character: Sawyer's always been so focused on the far-off future, when he'll finally get his revenge, that he never focuses on the joy of the moment. Even when he's on his cons, he's looking to the endgame, rather than actually trying to start a relationship with any of his marks.
- Swoosie Kurtz is a strange casting choice for Locke's mother: in real life, the actress is only eight years older than O'Quinn (there are the numbers again!).

Interesting Fact: The real John Locke (see page 30) studied medicine, and in 1666 he met up with the 1st Earl of Shaftesbury, who was suffering from a serious liver infection. He persuaded Locke to become his personal physician, and Locke moved into Shaftesbury's home. When the infection became worse, Locke performed a risky but successful surgery to remove the cyst from Shaftesbury's liver, and Shaftesbury proclaimed that John Locke had saved his life. The Earl's name was Anthony Ashley Cooper.

4 8 15 16 23 42: There were several occurrences of the numbers in this episode. At the beginning, Emily asks Locke where the footballs are, and he says aisle **8** for regulation, **15** for Nerf. When the private investigator shows Locke Emily's psychiatric profile, it has many of the numbers all over it. Her driver's license expires 03/20 (20 + 3 = **23**); her address is 2448 (a reverse **42** plus a **4** and an **8**); her birthday is 10/**15**; her weight is **115**; her admission number to the institution has three **4**s in it, with the first two numbers being **8** and **4**; her previous admission number was 46 **48 15** (note the first number is the current number of survivors on the island, and is **42** + **4**); the date she was admitted was 10/5 (10 +

5 = **15**); the area code of her aunt is **323**. Later, when Locke goes to his father's house, his license plate number is 2ABM**487** (if you assign numbers to the letters of the alphabet, A=1, B=2, M=13, which added equals **16**). Boone says that the accident with his nanny happened when he was 6. Since he's 22 now, the accident happened **16** years ago. Locke says they've been on the island **4** weeks.

It's Just a Flesh Wound: Locke's leg gets a piece of shrapnel in it; Boone incurs several life-threatening wounds in his fall.

Any Questions?:

- As Locke is running through the parking lot chasing his mother, a tan Bonneville backs up suddenly and hits him. If you go back to "Special," you'll see it's exactly the same car that hits Michael — the window frames look the same, and it's the same color, probably a late '80s model, or 1990 at the very latest. Is it the same car, driven by the same person? Is someone trying to alter their fates, since it happened at vital moments for each man? Who is driving that car?

- When the investigator hands Locke Emily's admittance paper to the mental hospital, across the top it says "Santa Rosa Mental Health Institute," which is exactly the same hospital Hurley stayed at. Presumably, they were not there at the same time, but Leonard would have been. Was Emily exposed to the numbers as well? Is this how Hurley and Locke are linked together in the crash?

- Cooper has photos and artifacts around his house from exotic locations, like he's a world traveler. Has he been to the island?

- Anthony Cooper says to Locke that he tried the family thing a couple of times and it didn't work: does this mean that Locke has half brothers and sisters?

- Locke is using the compass that he gave to Sayid in "Hearts and Minds." Sayid complained to Jack in that episode that the compass was faulty: did he mention that to Locke before giving it back to him?

- Locke's crazy dream happens after the shrapnel entered his leg; was there something on the shrapnel akin to his paste that caused him to have that vision?

- Who is the Nigerian priest, and why was he in a plane full of heroin?

- How did a small Beechcraft get all the way from Nigeria to an island in the South Pacific without refueling? Are the castaways really where the pilot said they were?

- How did Boone know that the statues contained heroin before he'd even broken one of them open?

- When Boone makes his desperate call on the radio, and says, "We're the survivors of Oceanic Flight 815," listen closely and you'll hear the other person say, "*We're* the survivors of Oceanic Flight 815!" Are there other survivors on the island who answered Boone's radio call?
- Will Charlie find the Virgin Mary statues full of heroin?
- Boone mutters to Jack, "They built a hatch." Who does he mean by "they"?
- Why did Locke end up in the wheelchair? Did it have something to do with the kidney transplant?

Terry O'Quinn (John Locke)

In early 2004, veteran character actor Terry O'Quinn was worried about his lagging career. A stint on J.J. Abrams' chick spy series *Alias* had come to an end and O'Quinn and his wife, Lori, had to make difficult decisions about how they would go forward. "I was at home in Maryland, no work, nothing going on," O'Quinn says. "I told Lori, 'We gotta toughen up. We can fold, or we can lean on each other and play the cards that were dealt us.'"

That's when Abrams, who was a fan of O'Quinn's, asked the actor to consider a part in his new script. "I told Lori, 'Things are at a crossroads. And if *Lost* isn't the crossroads, it's the bridge to the other side.' I believe in fate."

However, not all was copasetic. Upon seeing the script for the pilot, he realized the character he would play — named Locke — would hardly utter a word through the first two hours, and he was worried he'd be unable to make any notable impact on early viewers. Despite the misgivings, he took the part at Abram's urging, and went on to become one of the most intriguing and beguiling characters on television.

"I didn't know anything about the show, and J.J. asked me if I'd be interested in doing a series, and I said, 'Yes.' J.J. said, 'This role is something different and it will give you a chance to spread your wings a little more,' and that excited me very much."

With that, O'Quinn and his wife auctioned off their belongings and sold their 10,000 square foot house in Maryland as preparation for the move to Hawaii. It was a huge step in his career. "We've been married for 25 years and lived in Maryland most of that time, but our sons are both grown and moved to the west coast," O'Quinn said just after *Lost* began filming. "We have a big old house and want to cut loose some anchors and drift a while."

Even as he raised the anchor, O'Quinn could not have known that Abrams' show would bring him more acclaim than he had had throughout the first 25 years of his career.

Born in 1952 as Terry Quinn (he changed his name to avoid confusion with another actor), he grew up in a small town in northern Michigan. He fell into acting while at Central Michigan University in the early 1970s. Bored with his experience at school, O'Quinn took to acting as a recreation exercise, but soon found he had a natural ability.

By the time he was finished school, O'Quinn had been introduced to an agent in New York. Though not the typical leading man (his hairline receded in his early twenties, and he has appeared with his head shaved throughout much of his career), it didn't take long for the actor to find roles on television and in movies. Though many of the shows have

Terry O'Quinn, seen here on the set of *Lost*, did not have to audition for the role of John Locke. (YORAM KAHANA/SHOOTING STAR)

been long forgotten, he also had parts on hits like *Remington Steele* and *Miami Vice*.

In 1979, preparing for a role in Michael Cimino's Western epic and legendary cinematic disaster *Heaven's Gate*, he met and married his wife Lori, whose parents had helped him learn to ride horses for his part in the film. He credits Lori with keeping him on the straight and narrow over the course of his career. "If I hadn't met my wife when I was 27, I'd be an old, sick alcoholic living in a small, dirty apartment with a huge pornography collection. Instead, I live in a beautiful house in Hawaii and have two beautiful sons. Besides, after you get through the first 25 years of marriage, it's pretty much smooth sailing."

For more than two decades, O'Quinn appeared in a wide variety of film and television productions. The only problem was, he didn't make much money. "I've worked a lot. But, in all honesty, I didn't work for much," he explains.

By 1999 he had landed a regular role in *X-Files* spin-off *Millennium*. But the series failed to last, leaving O'Quinn once again looking for work. Four years later, after continuing to work in small roles on television, O'Quinn received a call to appear on J.J. Abrams' *Alias*.

"There was an implication that it might be beneath me to audition, which is something I never understood," he recalls. "If it's what you do best, why would you want to hold it back and make them guess how good you are, when you can go in and *show* them how good you are?"

While everyone on the cast of *Alias*, as well as the show's producers and creator, liked O'Quinn, his role didn't last. O'Quinn took roles in *The West Wing* and *Law & Order*, but Abrams still held the actor in great regard and became determined to cast him as Locke when *Lost* went into development in 2004. Unlike for *Alias*, there was no audition for O'Quinn; he was simply offered the role of Locke, the philosophical character with a complex and perplexing past.

Even as *Lost* rose in the ratings, making O'Quinn one of the most visible actors on the show, he stayed out of the limelight, and away from his costars. The actor says he likes to keep up the aura of mystery that surrounds his character.

"I'm kind of the senior citizen of the show. As to my partying days, I think I punched that ticket all the way out. I walk for miles on the beach and I love it. I people-watch and read a lot. I play guitar and swim and ride my bike."

In fact, O'Quinn says he has a lot in common with Locke, including a faith-based outlook on life. "That's the point at which the show as an experience began to parallel my own, in that I had to go on faith. You'll see coming up, there are times when Locke's faith is tested, and mine is, too. I don't ask what's coming up, I just wait for it, and I'm excited every time I get a script."

"My sense of Locke is that he's fatalistic," adds O'Quinn. "He feels that he has a destiny, that there's a mission that we're sent here to fulfill. And his mission is being revealed. That may make him powerful; it may make him dangerous; it may make him wonderful."

1.20   Do No Harm

Original air date: April 6, 2005
Written by: Janet Tamaro
Directed by: Stephen Williams
Guest cast: Zack Ward (Marc), Julie Bowen (Sarah), Clarence Logan (Minister), John Tilton (Tux Shop Owner)

Flashback: Jack

Jack vows to save Boone's life before he realizes how serious his injuries are, and as he works on his patient, he remembers the circumstances surrounding his wedding.

Since the Lostaways first landed on the island, Jack has been under immense pressure, as explored in "All the Best Cowboys Have Daddy Issues." He's saved many lives, treated wounds, and is even the person folks turn to for emotional support and aid. There are times when he doesn't seem to have a lot of patience, and he expects a lot from people in return and becomes resentful when they don't deliver. Jack hasn't changed at all since the plane crash. Where others are looking to the island as a new beginning, or pretending they're someone they're not, Jack is an open book, acting and speaking exactly the same way he did before. A few years earlier, he was engaged to a woman named Sarah, whose life he had saved after a car accident. She falls in love with the doctor who performed the miracle, not the man. At their engagement party, she holds up a glass and toasts, "To Jack, my hero."

And therein lies Jack's problem: he's expected to be a superhero, not a man. Heroism is momentary but Jack has tried to maintain his hero status, and so far it's doable because he doesn't acknowledge his limits. Everyone puts Jack on a pedestal, so the only way to go is down. Sawyer is the only one who rolls his eyes and sees Jack as the flawed person he really is, but, ironically, Sawyer's first nickname for Jack was "Hero." The problem is, a hero has to be one all the time, and never gets a break (unless he puts on some glasses and a suit and calls himself Clark Kent). Jack is on call full-time on the island. The reason his engagement to Sarah is coming back to him at this point is that, once again, he has someone who depends on him for a miracle, and he's promised to deliver.

Boone started off as Jack's loyal sidekick, the nurse to his doctor. But when Locke stepped up as the warrior, Boone decided he was the more attractive one to be following, and he switched loyalties. Now his very life depends on whether or not Jack is the superman he originally thought he was.

Meanwhile, as the male crisis unfolds in the cave, there's a female one happening in the jungle. Claire has gone into labor, and with Jack deciding to pump his own blood into Boone, Kate is left with no choice but to deliver the baby herself. The scenes with her and Claire are wonderfully done — it's so rare on this show to see two women having a serious discussion or being involved in any of the goings-on of the island, because the island is a very patriarchal place.

When faced with the birth of her child, all of Claire's worries and insecurities throughout the pregnancy hit her at once, and she begins working against Kate, trying to halt the birth of the baby, worried that the baby might know that she didn't want it. As Kate steps up, and is able to talk Claire through the daunting sit-

Good-bye, Boone. (YORAM KAHANA/SHOOTING STAR)

uation she's in, she shows what a good, thoughtful person she can be, which makes one wonder if she's telling the truth about her conviction, and has been wrongfully accused.

Sun and Jin become assistants in both crises. Sun assists with the male situation, where they're trying to prevent a death, and Jin helps out with the female one, helping bring new life into the world. Both of them become quiet heroes in this episode, as Jin combats his lack of communication skills to notify Jack of what's going on in the jungle, while Sun comes to the rescue numerous times when Jack is too wrapped up in his own terror to think straight. There's a brief moment, however, when Sun is translating for Jin, and we see a flash of disgust and resentment pass over his face, as if he feels like he's lowered himself in some way to allow someone else to speak for him.

Jack has always put everyone else's needs before his own, as if he's desperate to please everyone. He marries Sarah to make her happy and proud of him. He has become a doctor because that's what his father expected of him. Now, as he's working on Boone, he promises Boone, Sun, and Charlie that there's no way he will let Boone die, even while, deep down, he knows there's no way he can follow through on that promise. All of Jack's life, he has made promises before stopping to think whether or not he can deliver. He has spent his life being the person everyone else wants him to be, to the point where he's forgotten who he really is, just like a superhero does.

The ending of this episode is sad and poignant. Boone is the first major character we lose on the show, and while Shannon didn't think she needed him, she does. Whenever he's gone, she's a different person, dependent, clingy, and paranoid. Now he's gone forever, and it's only when she sits down and stares at his body that she realizes how she truly feels. When Boone was given a chance to imagine how he would feel upon Shannon's death in "Hearts and Minds," he admitted that he felt relief. As Shannon sits at his side, she looks utterly lost.

Highlight: Jin and Charlie rejoicing at the baby's birth.

Did You Notice?:

- Jack's best man is Marc Silverman, the kid who was getting beaten up at the beginning of "White Rabbit."
- Sawyer seems to be more of a team player these days: he had to be tortured for Shannon's asthma inhalers in "Confidence Man" (and it turned out he didn't even have them), but in this episode, Kate asks him for all of his alcohol and he turns it over, no questions asked. Wow.
- It's ironic that Jack turns to his father to voice his concern that he won't be the husband and father he needs to be in this relationship, when Jack has worried all his life that he can't be the son his father needs him to be.
- Boone reminds Jack of his promise to save him, and says, "I'm letting you off the hook," which is what Rose says to Jack in "Walkabout" when she reminds him that he promised to keep her company until her husband returned.

Interesting Facts: Zack Ward, who plays Marc, Jack's best man, is best known to audiences as the evil Scut Farkus in the 1983 film (and Christmas television staple) *A Christmas Story*. Also, compartment syndrome, which is Jack's diagnosis of Boone's leg condition, is caused by the swelling of a muscle under pressure, which becomes too big for the connective tissue surrounding it, so the tension of the muscle pushing against the surrounding tissue causes immense pain. The swelling is often brought on by a fracture and can cut off the arterial blood supply. The condition could be seen as a metaphor for various aspects of this episode. All of the characters are in close quarters, and the tension between them is being caused by the pressure of each one of them wanting to do their own thing. They were originally all on the beach, but now they're separated a long distance, which is causing rifts and problems. Fractures are occurring within the group, in this episode most notably between Jack and Locke, and that could cut off the supply of essentials that each man brings to the group.

Nitpick: For a woman who just gave birth with no anesthetic after several hours of labor, Claire seems to be walking a little too painlessly when she strides out onto the beach the following morning, carrying her baby. Most women would be hobbling and would probably require some assistance, especially with the uneven ground. And why is it that whenever Jack asks someone to do something in this episode, they just stand there all slackjawed for a moment before actually doing something? He tells Kate to get T-shirts at the end of the previous episode, and

Lives Saved, Lives Lost

Jack shows an immense amount of guilt over Boone's death, but he has saved several lives on the island:

- Rose, using CPR immediately following the plane crash
- A man with his leg caught under the plane, whom Jack rescues by pulling him out and tying a tourniquet on the leg
- Claire and Hurley by getting them out from under the falling wing
- Boone from drowning during his failed rescue attempt
- Shannon from her asthma attack
- Sawyer by treating his arm after Sayid's interrogation
- Charlie with CPR after Ethan tries to kill him

Who knows how many other lives he's saved by applying some simple peroxide and avoiding infection? But Jack will only remember the losses:

- The marshal, who died of an infection from shrapnel
- Joanna, who drowned
- Boone, who died of severe trauma to his leg

Jack's guilt doesn't last long, however, and he immediately turns his rage toward John Locke, whom he thinks is a killer. Locke says in "Hearts and Minds," "I wasn't the most popular kid." He's not the most popular adult, either, because despite what Jack thinks, he's saved lives, too:

- Jack from falling over the cliff
- Charlie from heroin addiction
- Walt and Michael from a polar bear attack

But his complicity in Boone's death will be the thing he needs to answer for, and it will spark a war between him and Jack.

she just stands there until he shouts at her. He needs Sun to grab some scissors, and she does exactly the same thing until he shouts at her as well. He asks Hurley for help, and Hurley's mouth hangs open until Jack snaps him out of it. And when he asks Kate to get the alcohol, she stands there *again* until he yells that he needs it now. Do all of these people have serious hearing problems? Yes, Boone's condition is shocking, but they've all seen bad things — they've been in a serious plane crash, for goodness sake.

Oops: When giving birth, a woman has to push as hard as she can to get the baby's head out, but once the head comes out, she must resist pushing to prevent the baby from shooting out of the canal suddenly. Jack's instructions to Kate are the opposite, reminding us again that he's not an OB-GYN (see "Raised by Another").

4 8 15 16 23 42: As Jack is adjusting Marc's tie, Marc says he'll be fine after **8** beers. When Charlie polls the camp for their blood type, only **4** people actually know what theirs is. In the flashback where Jack and Sarah are sitting at a piano at the hotel the night before their wedding, she's wearing a shirt with two **4**s on it (which add up to **8**).

It's Just a Flesh Wound: Boone's injuries from the previous episode include a fractured leg, and in this episode the leg causes his blood to pool and become deadly, and then his lung collapses. Jack has a cut in his arm from inserting the needle to give blood to Boone. Claire probably incurs a few wounds of her own.

Any Questions?:

- Where is Locke throughout the episode?
- Kate tells Claire that her baby is "all of us." Is this a hint about the importance of Claire's baby? Is it the reason they're all on the island like this? Is the baby representative somehow of all of the Lostaways?
- What was Boone going to tell Jack to tell Shannon? Why does he keep saying he's sorry?
- Jin seemed extremely happy to see the baby, and also seemed briefly interested when Claire put his hand on her belly in "Pilot, Part 2." Did he and Sun want children? Did they ever lose any?
- Locke told Boone in "Hearts and Minds" that he needed to give him an experience that would be vital to his survival on the island, and now Boone's dead. So what exactly did Locke mean by that statement?

Ashes to Ashes: Boone Carlyle, 22, dies of injuries incurred when the small plane he was investigating falls off a cliff and drops about 30 feet, yet he had survived the initial plane crash that put him on the island. He had been in Sydney to rescue his sister Shannon, and he was the CFO of a wedding company that his mother runs in the U.S.

1.21   The Greater Good

Original air date: May 4, 2005
Written by: Leonard Dick
Directed by: David Grossman
Guest cast: Donnie Keshawarz (Essam), Jenny Gago (Agent Cole), Dariush Kashani (Haddad), David Patterson (Agent Hewitt), Ali Shaheed Amini (Yusef), Warren Kundis (Imam)

Flashback: Sayid

Jack believes that Locke is responsible for Boone's death, and Locke takes Sayid to the plane in the jungle.

There's an irony to the title of this episode. While both Locke and Sayid believe that they're working for the greater good, it's been revealed in both cases that they are only thinking of themselves and actually thwarting the greater good in order to attain what they want. In Sayid's flashback we see how he betrayed a friend and tricked him into becoming a terrorist in order to be reunited with the woman he loved. The CIA — an organization that is trying to bring down terrorists by creating more of them, apparently (and a body that sacrifices the rights of the individual for the greater good) — pressures Sayid into betraying his own values by dangling over him the one thing he wants more than anything: Nadia. As Sayid turns to Essam and begins to feed him a bunch of dogma about the importance of becoming a martyr for the "greater good," we know it's eating him up that he's doing this, but that doesn't stop him from doing it.

Shannon grapples with the reality of Boone's death, and starts to fall apart. Luckily, Sayid is there for her, because otherwise, who knows what would have happened to her character in this situation. The problem is, the relationship between Sayid and Shannon isn't very believable. Sayid is an intelligent man who has been through hell, and in his 35 or so years, he's seen many things and has a maturity and understanding far beyond most people on the island. He has spent the last 13 years pining after Nadia, and about a month before this episode takes place, he forces a friend to become a criminal just so he can have the chance to see her. So why does he fall for the first bimbo who smiles at him after the crash?

In season 2, we'll find out there's more to Shannon than meets the eye, but when Sayid falls for her, she's done nothing but whine, tan the fronts of her legs, whine, stomp around, refuse to contribute to efforts to get off the island, cry, turn over and tan the backs of her legs, whine, follow Boone around like a puppy, cry, complain that Boone's cramping her style, whine, and insist that Boone stay by her side. What does Sayid see in this person? Shannon's action in this episode is one of the first things we see her do, and it's done out of fear and grief. She needs to blame someone for Boone's death, and by doing what she does, she believes she's looking out for Boone the way he always looked out for her.

Naveen Andrews gives a friendly kiss to Maggie Grace, who looks like a Hollywood starlet. (CHRISTINA RADISH)

Jack has announced to everyone that Locke is a liar, and we see that when Locke and Jack go to war, the Losties will side with Jack and abandon Locke. Unlike Sayid, who knew he was acting in his own self-interest, Locke seriously believes he's working for everyone's best interest, and that by keeping the survivors on the island and trying to break into the hatch, he can introduce them to a new life, one that he believes will be better than the ones they had before. Shockingly, he admits to being the one who hit Sayid over the head in "The Moth" when Sayid was trying to triangulate the signal. But like Sayid, Locke is acting selfishly, and not thinking of the others. He's turned into a bit of a terrorist himself, hurting and betraying those around him just to get what he wants. He believes that if he's separated from the island, he'll probably lose his ability to walk again, and his new chance at life will be gone. He has many questions about why he's been brought here, and what it all means, and he's hoping that the discovery of what's in the hatch might answer those questions. Unfortunately, Boone was sacrificed for Locke's needs, just like Essam was killed for Sayid's.

Highlight: Charlie chasing Sawyer around the beach when he realizes Sawyer's voice makes Turnip-Head stop crying.

Did You Notice?:

- When Locke is talking about something important, he often closes his right eye, the one that also has the scar around it.
- Claire's baby, Aaron, is a few hours old and is already twice the size of the baby we saw her give birth to. Most babies *lose* weight post-birth.
- The last time we saw Charlie and Sawyer together, they were punching each other in the head over Claire's diary, and now they seem like mates.
- Locke comes over to talk to Shannon with his shirt still covered in Boone's blood, showing he's not exactly Mr. Sensitive.
- Something has clearly changed in Kate and Jack's relationship — he didn't even consider her the culprit when he realized the key around his neck was missing.
- Shannon shoots Locke in the head out of revenge, and in the next episode she's wandering around scot-free, but in "House of the Rising Sun," Jin punched Michael and he was handcuffed to a plane. So . . . if the jailer is your boyfriend you're off the hook?

Interesting Fact: When Sayid first enters Essam's apartment, one of his friends is playing the video game, *Half-Life*, which is a first-person shooter where the player is a scientist who has accidentally opened a portal to an alien dimension. Trapped in an underground testing facility, the character must fight his way out using a series of weapons.

Nitpick: Kate means well when she slips Jack the sleeping pills, but it could have been risky if he'd had any sort of negative reaction to them. Finally, why does Locke tell Sayid that he assumes the radio wouldn't work anymore because of the plane falling off a cliff, despite the fact it somehow survived the original, horrible plane crash?

4 8 15 16 23 42: Sayid was held for 18 hours in a holding cell in Heathrow by the CIA. They say 300 pounds of C-4 has gone missing. The license plate of the van in Sayid's flashback is ALK 125 (assign numbers to ALK and the sum is 24, which is a reversed **42**, and 1 + 2 + 5 = **8**). Sawyer reads to Turnip-Head about a car with a **32**-valve, V-**8** engine, with **4**00 horses and a **4.4**L capacity.

Any Questions?:

- What happened to Sayid in the years between 1997 and 2004? Why did he leave Iraq?
- Why was he at the Heathrow Airport when the CIA picked him up?
- Locke tells Shannon that he knows what it's like to lose family. Is he refer-

ring to his parents, or someone else we haven't yet seen in flashback?

- Why does the CIA refer to Essam as a terrorist, when they were the ones who turned him into one?
- If Sayid's reason for being on the plane to L.A. was to find Nadia, why does he say in "Solitary" that Nadia is dead?
- Is Locke lying about his reasons for hitting Sayid in the head in "The Moth"? In "Pilot, Part 2," the people who hear the Frenchwoman's transmission are Kate, Charlie, Sayid, Boone, Shannon, and Sawyer. When they come back to the beach, Kate tells Jack, but no one else knows, and they have agreed to tell no one. Locke is never told about the Frenchwoman's transmission. Yet in this episode, he tells Sayid that he hit him because they were chasing a transmission that said "It killed them all," and he worried it would cause widespread panic. How did he know that's what it said? Was Locke told about it somewhere between "Pilot, Part 2" and "The Moth" and we never saw him get the information? Does he have insider information that we don't know about? Was it a mistake by the writers?
- Why didn't Locke destroy all the heroin, knowing Charlie's past and the temptation it would present?
- If Claire's baby is an important key to why they are all on the island (one of the major conspiracy theories among viewers) then is there significance to the fact the baby is only calmed by Sawyer's voice?

Music/Bands: Hurley sings James Brown's "I Got You (I Feel Good)."

Naveen Andrews (Sayid Jarrah)

He's endured social stigma, fathering a child at 16, a drug problem, and a difficult upbringing. Considering all the challenges Naveen Andrews has faced in his lifetime, tackling the role of an Iraqi torturer would appear to be a cakewalk.

Born to a conservative Indian family in 1969, Andrews was raised in South London where he was the elder of two brothers. Even though he was a Methodist, his Indian heritage was problematic for Andrews. "In England, the class system is about a thousand years old and it's not going to change any time soon," he explains.

Naveen Andrews has said he feels more at home in the U.S. than in his native England, where he says the class system and attitudes toward race made him feel like an outsider. (ALBERT L. ORTEGA)

As a teen he dabbled in music and acting, much to his parents' dismay. The worst was yet to come. At the age of 16 he began an affair with a teacher at his school named Geraldine Feakins. With his relationship with his parents faltering, Andrews continued the relationship with Feakins, who was married and 15 years older than her student. She had a son with Andrews (Jaisal) in 1992, but the relationship did not last. However, Andrews sees nothing wrong with the affair.

"As far as I'm concerned, that's normal in Europe, for people to have relationships with older women," he says. "It's only in America that they have an allergy about that, because when it's the other way around, nobody says a thing. I call that hypocrisy."

His attempt at acting was more successful than his relationship with Feakins.

He attended the prestigious Guildhall School of Music & Drama, where Ewan McGregor and David Thewlis were classmates, to learn his craft, and in 1993 he won accolades for his role in *The Buddha of Suburbia*. However, his personal life was deteriorating in a haze of drugs and alcohol.

His habits forced him to relocate to the U.S., where his substance abuse issues were not known. "I'd basically, virtually, killed my career in England. I used to drink and do drugs and whatever, and in all fairness they [British producers] had to deal with that," he said.

Despite his drug problem, the move to the U.S. coincided with a rise in his career. He had a significant role in the hit *The English Patient*, and played a whacked-out sixteenth-century king in *Kama Sutra: A Tale of Love*, which he calls "my Rolling Stones 1972 tour. I was on everything. In India, the heroin is pure."

Despite his success, his reputation for being unstable had caught up with him and forced him to address his issues. "I had no choice. It was either get sober or go down the toilet very quickly. It wasn't like I wanted to save my career or do this or do that; it was basically, 'Save your life.'"

After cleaning up, Andrews spent almost 10 years bouncing around in small and large parts in unheralded films that were mostly ignored. He could be found in such throwaway trash as *The Chippendales Murder* and *Rollerball*, though he also appeared in the acclaimed *Bride & Prejudice* in 2004.

Needless to say, the chance to audition for *Lost* and the role of Sayid, the former Iraqi intelligence officer, offered a break from lackluster roles that didn't tap Andrews' talent. However, there was some genuine concern on the part of the producers of *Lost* about how Sayid would be perceived. It was important that Andrews bring a mix of mystery and charisma to the role, allowing viewers to get beyond any prejudices they might hold about the people of Iraq and Muslims in general. The reaction to Andrews' portrayal of Sayid went beyond expectations.

"In [Sayid], we were all pretty nervous, in the sense that we all felt we owed a real obligation, not just to Iraqis but the entire Arab world about how this character would be played," he says. "One of the biggest kicks was getting a letter from the Arab League saying how pleased they were about this. It was the first time they had seen an Arab character like that on TV. He's romantic, and not just to other Arab women but to white women as well, which is a big no-no in Hollywood. It's all right for a white geezer to be with a black woman or a Chinese woman, but never the other way around. And we do that on this show. That's what we need to see more of."

Though *Lost* has been one of the most critically acclaimed and popular shows on television since its debut, Andrews feels the show should flame out before it grows stale. "To me, it's always been the kind of show I couldn't imagine going as long as *Friends* — three, maybe four seasons at the very most," he says, perhaps making reference to several of the shows on the HBO network that were created for limited runs. "Surely after the third season it really will be scraping bottom."

Adapting to a recurring role has also been difficult for Andrews, who had grown accustomed to film roles that lasted a few weeks, not years. "It's a new thing for me to sustain a role for two years. The longest I played a part before was four months."

Through it all, Andrews and the character of Sayid have become among the most recognizable in the *Lost* cast. Celebrity, it turns out, has been a reward of sorts for Andrews after a decade of turmoil. In the past, his appearance assured that he'd be questioned on every flight he took over the past five years. But with his star on the rise thanks to *Lost*, that's a thing of the past. "I can't tell you how many times I've been stopped in airports all over the world. Now, it's, 'Oh, you're that guy from TV. How can we help you, sir?'"

1.22   Born to Run

Original air date: May 11, 2005
Teleplay by: Edward Kitsis, Adam Horowitz
Story by: Javier Grillo-Marxuach
Directed by: Tucker Gates
Guest cast: Mackenzie Astin (Tom), Daniel Roebuck (Arzt), Beth Broderick (Diane), Anosh Yaqoob (Sanjay), Tamara Lynch (Nurse)

Flashback: Kate

As Kate tries to figure out how to convince Michael to let her onto the raft, we finally discover the significance of her toy plane; meanwhile, Locke reveals the hatch to Jack.

"Born to Run" is an episode about discretion. Jack and Locke almost come to blows over the hatch, and it leads to an argument about how each of them is keeping secrets and deciding when it's best to tell the other. Their argument could be seen as a comment on the writers and how *Lost* unfolds week after week — *they* choose when we're going to find out something about a character, and make it very difficult for the viewers to piece together their own theories without having those hypotheses frequently shattered (which is half the fun). Up until now, the flashbacks we've seen of Kate showed her involved in a bank robbery where she shot three guys just to steal a tiny plane from a safety deposit box. It seemed logical that this was the crime that put her on the lam, and why the U.S. Marshal was accompanying her on the plane. Now we discover we were entirely wrong.

In the new flashback, we meet her childhood sweetheart, and see her interacting with her loved ones, but it raises more questions than it answers (see below). Since we see Kate and Tom digging up a time capsule that they'd buried in 1989, and it contains the plane, we know this incident must have happened before the flashback in "Whatever the Case May Be." What Kate did must have been sinister, for in this episode she becomes desperate to get onto the raft; if rescue does come to the island, she doesn't want to be caught all over again. Charlie's question to her, "Don't you want to be famous?" resonates, because he doesn't seem to realize one can be famous for all the wrong reasons (strange, since he's famous as a has-been).

Meanwhile, a more important series of events is unfolding in the jungle, as Sayid (who now knows about the hatch) and Locke show Locke's discovery to

Jack. Jack remains true to his personality and immediately takes a holier-than-thou stance, accusing Locke of withholding information from him and everyone else. Locke's retort, "All due respect, Jack, but since when do I report to you?" has been a long time coming, not just for Locke, but on behalf of everyone. Jack has always had it in for Locke, especially since he deems Locke responsible for Boone's death, and when he argues that Locke has lied, Locke explains the difference between a lie and discretion. Jack used his discretion in withholding the guns, and now Locke has used his. One simple difference: Jack hid some weapons that could help defend them against predators; Locke hid something that could be their way off the island. That said, Locke seems to have won this argument, and we applaud him for taking Jack down a peg.

When everyone finds out the truth about Kate, care of Sawyer, she turns into the island's new social pariah. It's no surprise why everyone is such a hypocrite — as long as people can keep the blame away from them, they will, even if it means joining in on any witch-hunting and finger-pointing so they stay below the radar. We've seen Kate at her very best (reminiscing with Tom; helping deliver Claire's baby; talking to Sun about her troubles with Jin) and at her worst (bringing her mother to tears; organizing a bank heist and turning on her companions), but so far, all of her actions seem to stem from innate goodness, even if the results sometimes go askew. Her involvement in Michael's illness in this episode was once again intended to help out someone, and luckily the other interested party uses her discretion to keep Kate's name out of it.

Again, in this episode, it seems to be men versus women, as Kate asks Michael if he would allow her a spot on the raft because of her vast sailing experience. He refuses, which goes against the greater good, because if he listens to her and gets the most able-bodied person he can to accompany him on the raft, the rest of the survivors might have a real chance of rescue. However, there's no chance that Walt will be staying behind, despite his initial desire to stay on the island: He's figured out what Locke is trying to do, and his instincts are telling him to get off that island, fast.

Highlight: Charlie working on music for his comeback album: "This is track two, it's called 'Monster Eats the Pilot.'"
Did You Notice?:
• Arzt talks to everyone like they're in his high school science class. "Can

anyone tell me what piece of land is south of us?" It makes him hilariously annoying.

- Walt never touches Sun or Kate, or he would have figured out what they were doing in this episode.
- Sawyer learned about karma in "Outlaws," and now he's getting some of his own: he wrongfully accused Sayid of being a terrorist, and Jin of burning the raft, and now he's been wrongfully accused of poisoning Michael.
- Sawyer keeps Kate's fake passport.
- Jack has judged Kate for the things she's done, but he doesn't judge or speak harshly to Sun when he discovers what she's done.
- It's back! The man-eating Bonneville from "Special" and "Deus Ex Machina" (see Questions in "Deus Ex Machina") is the car that Kate runs into after Tom gets shot.
- Way back in "Pilot, Part 1," when Kate is patching up Jack's wound and he tells her the story of letting the fear in for five seconds, Kate says, "I would have run." Jack replies, "You're not running now." Unlike everyone else, he sees her as someone who is brave and faces her problems head on (at least, until he gets to know her).

Nitpick: Kate is on the lam . . . as a blonde in a convertible. Not exactly staying incognito. Also, we see her go into a motel room and dye her hair brown, and when she dries it it looks *far* too natural to have been a self-dye job (there are no brown marks around her face and the dye doesn't look too dark, as most dye jobs do at first).

Oops: When Sawyer reveals Kate to be a criminal in front of everyone, Claire is clearly holding a doll; her arm is across the baby's back, yet its neck is rigid and held way upright.

4 8 15 16 23 42: Kate's license plate when she first drives up to the motel is 7-C153M (all of the numbers add up to **16**), and she changes it to DPN 924A. Arzt says they can't launch the raft for another 3 or **4** months. Kate's mother's hospital room is 208. The cassette tape was recorded on August 15, 1989 (**08/15**; 1989 was **15** years before the plane crash).

It's Just a Flesh Wound: Someone poisons Michael's water.

Any Questions?:

- Who sent Kate the letter and money?
- How long was Kate a blonde? Why don't we ever see her as a blonde in any flashbacks?

- Why does Arzt say he's a doctor? Most high school teachers don't have Ph.Ds. Does he really have one?
- Why didn't Arzt speak up sooner? They've been building the raft for weeks now.
- Did Kate really spend two summers crewing J-Boats, or is she lying?
- The last interaction that Michael and Locke had was when Locke risked his life to save Walt from the polar bear. Yet in this episode, when Jack tells Michael that he and Locke are still at odds, Michael says, "Good." Why would he still feel this way about him? Because he's sided with Jack? Why doesn't he afford Locke the benefit of the doubt here?
- How did Kate break into Tom's car without setting off his car alarm? Has he not heard about Kate's convict status; or does he know, but he just doesn't believe it?
- On the recording, a young Tom tells Katie that she always wants to run away, and she says to him, "You know why." Why?
- How old is Kate? Shannon guesses that she's 22, but if that were the case, she would have been seven when they recorded the message, and she sounds more like 11 or 12.
- Why doesn't Sawyer already know about Kate's past? Hasn't Hurley told pretty much everyone on the island by now?
- What did Walt see in his vision? He seems adamant that Locke not open the hatch. Is there something terrible in it? If Locke knows Walt's capabilities, why doesn't he heed his advice or ask him some questions?
- Kate tells her mother she's put her through a lot; what did she do to her mother?
- How did the toy plane end up in a safety deposit box if it was last seen in the back seat of Tom's car?
- In "Special," Locke touches Walt's arm; why doesn't Walt see what Locke's doing then?

A Wrinkle in Time by Madeleine L'Engle (1962)

In "Numbers," Sawyer complains of headaches while reading a copy of *A Wrinkle in Time* on the beach. This young adult sci-fi/fantasy novel is about the universal war between light and dark/good and evil, and how the only way to conquer evil in the world is through individuality and love. Meg Murry is a homely girl who is picked on at school for being different, and she wishes aloud to her mother — a beautiful scientist — that she could be like everyone else. Her five-year-old brother, Charles Wallace, speaks in a more sophisticated language than most adults and seems to be able to read Meg's mind. Their father has been missing for over a year, and while her mother holds out hope that some innocent thing has happened to him and he will return, everyone else is telling them to just accept the fact he's left the family.

On a stormy night when no one can sleep, the family is visited by a strange elderly woman named Mrs. Whatsit. She, too, seems to be able to read Meg's mind, and there's an immediate connection between her and Charles Wallace. As she leaves, she turns to Mrs. Murry and reassures her that tesseracts do exist, leaving Mrs. Murry looking shocked. The next day, Meg and her brother go to a nearby haunted house, and meet Calvin O'Keefe, a popular boy in Meg's high school. Like Charles, he has the ability to see into the heart of the matter, and the three of them enter the house. Mrs. Whatsit is in the house, along with two other beings, Mrs. Which and Mrs. Who, and they tell the trio that there is an evil about to descend upon the world, called the Dark Thing, and it has already taken over other worlds, including one where Mr. Murry is imprisoned.

That night, they leave with the three women on a quest to find their father, and they "tesser" through space and time to another place. Meg describes the sensation as violent and terrifying, as if her body is being ripped apart. Mrs. Whatsit explains that tessering is like wrinkling through space, and Mrs. Who demonstrates by holding out her skirt, showing that if an ant had to move all along her skirt, it would be a long trip for it, but if she wrinkles it, she shortens the distance considerably, and the ant could travel the distance in no time at all. They explain that tessering is the fifth dimension: The first is a straight line, the second is a square, the third is a cube, the fourth is time itself, and the fifth is a tesseract (it's also the Twilight Zone, but the women don't get into that).

Which, Who, and Whatsit are celestial beings who are appearing to the children as women because it's the most benign form they thought they could take.

Mrs. Which is barely there, and shimmers, because showing herself completely takes too much effort for her. Mrs. Whatsit reveals that she was once a star, but gave it up to fight the Dark Thing. They show them how beautiful the world can be, quoting Bible verses such as Isaiah 42 and taking them for a tour of what Meg calls the Garden of Eden. In showing them this, they show them what will be lost if the Dark Thing takes over.

They send the children to Camazotz, where Mr. Murry is being held, and instruct them to stay together. They say the planet is ruled by IT, a giant brain that controls everyone's thoughts and feelings. Once there, the children discover rows of houses full of people who act exactly the same, where children stand outside and bounce balls at exactly the same time. They get to the CENTRAL Central Intelligence building, and meet a man with red eyes who offers them a delicious-looking meal that they all begin eating — all but Charles Wallace, who has a deeper understanding than the others. He spits it out and says it tastes like sand. The man pulls Charles Wallace under a spell, and the boy begins to speak in the rhetoric of IT. He takes them to where Mr. Murry is being held, and Meg manages to get her father out of the prison despite Charles Wallace/IT trying to stop her. But no matter how much Calvin and Meg try to get Charles back, IT has a secure hold over him.

Just as IT is about to put Meg under the same spell as Charles Wallace, Mr. Murry grabs her and Calvin and tessers to another planet, Ixchel. Meg, half-possessed, feels freezing cold and numb all at the same time. Large, furry, tentacled creatures with no sight or speech tend to them, and Meg calls the one who dotes on her "Aunt Beast." They serve the children a meal that looks gray and flavorless, but is the most delicious food they've ever tasted. Meg lashes out at her father for leaving Charles Wallace behind, and then realizes her fury is part of the evil that had briefly inhabited her through the Dark Thing. The three women return, and Meg knows she is the only one who can return to Camazotz to save Charles Wallace. Mrs. Whatsit reassures Meg that she has something IT doesn't have, and if she uses it, she can get Charles Wallace back. She tessers back, and comes face to face with him, taunting her in the words of IT and telling her there's nothing she has that IT doesn't have, insisting that Mrs. Whatsit is actually an agent of IT, and that Mrs. Whatsit hates her. At that moment, Meg realizes she has love, the one thing IT doesn't, and she stands before him, concentrating all her efforts on how much she loves Charles Wallace (think Xander and Willow in the season 6 finale of *Buffy*). Charles is released, and she returns to her home, where Calvin and her father are already waiting for them.

A Wrinkle in Time is about seeing things clearly, and only when everyone can see past the obvious to find the truth that lies beneath, can darkness be conquered. How things and people are perceived versus what and who they really are become one of the central motifs of the book through various references to spectacles, sight, and blindness. Meg's two discoveries at the end are crucial: the Dark Thing, which seems to be an external evil, can also be internal when one is taken over by IT (see page 37), and only when she realizes this can she conquer it on an internal level, through love.

While Sawyer is reading *A Wrinkle in Time* in season 1, the book has a lot more to do with season 2, so I won't go into details here. One ongoing motif in the book is glasses and the importance of seeing clearly. Ironically, Sawyer begins to lose his sight while reading the book. Charlie sports a tattoo that says, "Living is easy with eyes closed," and in season 2 it will become a comment on Charlie's personality. Several fans have commented on the possibility of the show taking place in a different time than ours, or that the island itself is in a time warp that is different from the rest of the outside world. The Dark Thing in L'Engle's book resembles the monster on the island that taunts them and makes them face their deepest fears. As we will see later in season 2, love can be a very powerful thing, one that might be the ultimate salvation to everyone on the island. Just as Meg saves Charles Wallace by proving her love to him, it might be that very same thing that will save each of the survivors.

1.23   Exodus, Part 1

Original air date: May 18, 2005
Written by: Damon Lindelof, Carlton Cuse
Directed by: Jack Bender
Guest cast: Daniel Roebuck (Arzt), Michelle Rodriguez (Ana Lucia), Kevin E. West (Detective Calderwood), Wendy Braun (Gina), Chard Hayward (Australian Official), Robert Frederick (Jeff), Mark "Ruz" Rusden (Airport Cop)

Flashbacks: Walt, Jack, Sawyer, Kate, Shannon, Sayid, Sun
When Rousseau appears on the beach to inform the Lostaways that the Others are coming, Jack steps up his efforts to find a way to open the hatch; as Michael launches

the raft, we flash back to see several of the survivors at the airport, boarding Oceanic flight 815.

"Exodus, Part 1" is a beautiful episode, matched only by the one that will follow. It is an episode of revelations, finally answering many of our questions about things on the island (mostly having to do with Rousseau) and showing us what some of the survivors were doing immediately before getting on the plane. While we've already had some airport flashbacks — Sun and Jin, Jack — this episode allows us to compare the present situation to the past, with the hindsight of the last 22 episodes. It's amazing how much some of these characters have changed since they landed on the island.

Rousseau's back, and it's great to see her again. Mira Furlan plays her

Arzt (played by Daniel Roebuck) appears to have found another strange creature on the island . . . er, at a fan convention.
(ALBERT L. ORTEGA)

wonderfully, making her seem reasonable yet unhinged, kind yet volatile. Seeing someone emerge from the jungle with a rifle who looks like her brain might not be firing on all cylinders is a little unnerving to those who haven't yet encountered her, and that's what makes her bold entrance into the camp that much more exciting. Through Rousseau we discover that her child, Alex, was in fact a girl, and the Others took her one week after she was born (if this really is all an experiment and Rousseau is a test subject, it's a damn cruel one); we finally see what she means by the *Black Rock*; and the characters enter into the Dark Territory that had been listed on her maps.

Sawyer finally reveals his secret to Jack about meeting Christian in a bar. We also find out Sawyer's real full name (James Ford), and Jin's own conspiracy theory about why they ended up on the island. We can compare the way Michael and Walt relate to one another now to the way they were at each other's throats in Sydney. Shannon proves to be as manipulative and bitchy as she's been on the island, but her particular target at the airport is surprising. As mentioned before, her main fear is that she will appear useless and be unable to act, but whenever she proves she can act independently of others, she always does stupid things.

This episode has an air of finality to it. Jin, Michael, Sawyer, and Walt finally leave the island on the raft, the first major split in the group. Walt separates from Vincent, giving the dog to Shannon. As the raft pulls away from the island in a majestic scene, Walt is weeping on the raft, and it's hard to tell if he's crying because he's leaving his dog, or because he has seen the fate of the people on the island. As one boat leaves the island, the group searching for the dynamite finds another, smack dab in the middle of the jungle: the *Black Rock*.

"Exodus, Part 1" had all the makings of an amazing finale, and sped up everything that had been moving along at a steadier pace thus far. It answered some questions, and raised others. Fans of *Alias* were aware of J.J. Abrams' knack for turning a show on its head and sending it off in another direction, and the anticipation of the gang finally opening the hatch, and the group on the raft finding some sort of rescue, made the week between this episode and "Exodus, Part 2" seem like an eternity.

Highlight: Arzt's constant exasperation at Hurley calling him Arnzt, and Hurley's threat to call him by his first name. Hurley: "I remember it from the flight's manifest. I think Leslie's a bitchin' name." Arzt: "Arnzt is fine."

Did You Notice?:

- Jack agrees to let Kate come with no questions, which is a big change in his character.
- Shannon complains to Boone that she wants to be in first class so that she doesn't end up sitting next to some screaming kid the whole way. In "Do No Harm," Christian Shephard shows up the night before Jack's wedding and complains about a screaming kid in first class.
- Vincent jumps in the water and tries to swim after the raft, as if it's *Walt* he needs to protect.
- When Michael and Jin are working on the raft, Michael becomes frustrated and says to Jin, "No, no, no. This one goes there, that one goes there." This is an exact echo of a line of dialogue from *The Empire Strikes Back*, where Han gets frustrated with Chewbacca as they're working on the wing of the Millennium Falcon in the docking bay at Hoth. (Sawyer will make the connection in the next episode.)

Social Contracts and the State of Nature

The island has a Locke (see page 30) and a Rousseau (see page 62), but the third philosopher who weighed in on social contract theory in a major way was Thomas Hobbes (1588–1679). His view of man was the most negative of the three, and he will no doubt play a part in future seasons of the show. It seems to be more than a coincidence that by the end of season 2, we've encountered five different Toms (see page 334).

Hobbes: In a state of nature, man is essentially evil, without morals, and with no understanding of God, and if left in a state of nature for too long, mankind would constantly be at war and would destroy itself. He believed that a social contract had to be put in place that would require a strict government ruling over man in order to maintain constant order. People would give up their freedoms to a sovereignty that would protect them and keep them from going to war.

Locke: He believed that man was essentially good, and was written upon by experience. People should contract for a government that will protect them, but they have the right to rebel against what they perceive to be tyranny.

Rousseau: He believed that man was neither good nor evil, but that society corrupted him. Like Hobbes, he called for a sovereignty to which man would forfeit his free will; but like Locke he believed that the sovereignty should be a popular one, directed by the people, and they should be able to abolish the government if it wasn't protecting their inalienable rights.

Interesting Fact: When this episode aired, The Honorable Warren Truss (the minister Sawyer headbutted, according to the police detective) was the actual Minister of Agriculture, Fisheries, and Forestry in Australia. In July 2005, he became the Minister of Transport and Regional Services.

Nitpick: The way the police handled Sawyer's deportation is suspicious — would the police really have just handed Sawyer a plane ticket, which was paid for by the Australian taxpayers, and forced him out of the country without due process? When asked if this was a likely scenario, the director of the National Association of Community Legal Centres in Australia, Julie Bishop, replied, "Theoretically, no. It should not happen. However, if the person was an immigrant or not an Australian citizen, it may happen in unusual circumstances." She went on to describe two cases where deportation had been handled in a shoddy manner, after which the Department of Immigration had to do a ton of legwork to make things right again in answer to public outcry. She concluded, "There have also been some incidents in the past with corrupt police officers doing something like the

Lost scenario. So, the *Lost* scenario is vaguely possible but unlikely, even though there have been some movie-like scenarios that have happened."

Oops: In "Walkabout," Jack tells Rose he was sitting in 23A, but in this episode he tells Ana Lucia he's sitting in 23B. Which is correct?

4 8 15 16 23 42: In Michael and Walt's flashback, the time on the alarm clock when Walt turns on the television is 5:**23**. Ana Lucia is sitting in seat **42**F. If Tom died two years ago and his son was two, Connor would now be **4**. Rousseau has **4** scratches on her arm.

Any Questions?:

- In "Pilot, Part 1," Kate tells Jack that she saw some black smoke inland, and they follow that to the cockpit of the plane. Was the smoke really coming from the plane, or was it the same black smoke they see in this episode?
- We've seen in the previous episode that Walt can see into the heart of the person who touches him; when Locke grabbed his arm, he told him not to open the hatch. In this episode, Michael chases him down the hallway of the hotel and grabs his arm, and Walt turns and says, "You are NOT my father!" Did he see something? Is Michael actually *not* Walt's father?
- There are only about 30 people assisting with the raft. Where did everybody else go?
- What is the pillar of black smoke, and what does it represent?
- On the beach, there's not a cloud in the sky. In the jungle, it's pouring rain and there's a thunderstorm. Just another mystery of the island, or a continuity error?
- Jack tells Ana Lucia that he's not married; what happened to his marriage?
- We see Jack's drinking in "Pilot, Part 1," and in this episode, we see he was already throwing them back long before he got onto the plane. Was he on the path to becoming his father when something prevented him from destroying himself?
- Why does Hurley accompany the group to the *Black Rock*? For comic relief?
- How did Montand lose his arm?
- Rousseau tells Jack that the monster is the island's security system, but she doesn't elaborate on that. Does she mean it metaphorically, or does she mean the monster is actually a mechanical security system? It's an interesting idea, and it would make sense that someone like the pilot was killed when he was moving around, whereas the others have stood still and

Reasons for Travel

When all of the characters arrive at the airport, they could all answer the question "what is your reason for travel?" the same way: They were looking for answers. But here are some of the smaller details of what everyone was up to before and during the flight:

Were put on the plane by other people:
Sawyer (deported for hitting a ministry official)
Sayid (finished his work with the CIA and they bought him a ticket)
Claire (a psychic sends her to L.A. to give her baby to an adoptive family there)
Kate (being escorted by a U.S. marshal)

Weren't in their seats at the time of the crash:
Charlie (was snorting heroin)
Jack (he'd moved over a seat to talk to Rose)

Actually lived in Australia before the flight:
Claire
Walt
Shannon

Not sure why they were on the plane:
Sceve
Arzt

Would have caught a connecting flight in L.A.:
Michael
Charlie

Don't live in Sydney or California:
Michael (New York)
Charlie (England)
Sayid (unclear)
Sun & Jin (South Korea)

avoided death. If the monster is mechanical, it probably has a motion sensor on it. But if it can be explained away by science, how does it get to these people the way it does? Where is the howl coming from? What makes it appear? Are there different forms of the monster?

- Did Arzt actually see the beast when he disappeared in the jungle momentarily?
- In Sun's flashback, Jin seems very kind to her, yet when they land on the island, he's hostile and cruel. What happened?
- How did an old wooden ship get onto the island? How old is it? If slavery

was outlawed in the early nineteenth century, it would suggest the ship is older than that if it's carrying slaves, but there's no way the dynamite could have lasted that long in those temperatures, nor would the ship be showing so little decay in the wood. Why is the ship so far inland? Did the island emerge from the ocean in the last 200 years? Is it a man-made island?

- Since Vincent is a protector, and whoever is with him always remains safe, does Walt sense that something is going to happen to Shannon, and that's why he gives the dog to her?

1.24   Exodus, Part 2

Original air date: May 25, 2005
Written by: Damon Lindelof, Carlton Cuse
Directed by: Jack Bender
Guest cast: Daniel Roebuck (Arzt), M.C. Gainey (Mr. Friendly), John Walcutt (Hawaiian Shirt), John Dixon (J.D.), Terasa Livingstone (Lily), Suzanne Turner (Ticket Agent), Michelle Arthur (Michelle), Wendy Braun (Gina), Robert Frederick (Jeff), Glenn Cannon (Old Scooter Man), Mark "Ruz" Rusden (Airport Cop), Mark "Kiwi" Kalagher (Security Agent), Mary Ann Taheny (Gate Attendant)

Flashbacks: Sayid, Jin, Charlie, Michael, Hurley, Locke

When Rousseau takes Claire's baby, Charlie and Sayid vow to get him back; the group getting the pieces of dynamite encounter problems on the way back to the hatch; and the foursome on the raft see something on the radar, and debate whether or not to use the flare gun.

"Exodus, Part 2" opens with a closeup on Aaron's eye, which is interesting — until now, the eye closeup always pertained to the person whose flashback will be the central story of the show. Most of what happens on each episode on the island is seen from one person's perspective, and that's the person who will be changed the most by episode's end. So what does all of this say about the baby, Aaron? Several conspiracy theorist viewers of *Lost* have been suggesting from the beginning that everything on the island is happening because of Aaron. If the island is

The guys of *Lost* give the Hawaiian "shaka" greeting. (ALBERT L. ORTEGA)

a purgatory, perhaps Aaron is an angel who will help lead each person to self-discovery. If the island is an experiment, perhaps it is Aaron who is the test subject, and everyone else on the plane just has incredibly bad luck. We know the Others took Rousseau's baby, Alex, when she was one week old, and Aaron is about three days old: could he be the next kidnapping victim? Two children have been born on the island, one girl, one boy. Both were given names that begin with A (the same as Adam, the first man, according to the Bible), and both names are unisex (although the feminine Erin has a different spelling). They were born 16 years apart, which is one of Hurley's magic numbers. Is there a larger purpose for Claire's child? When Rousseau kidnaps him, it certainly seems so.

This is an episode that sums up many elements of the season and allows the theories to flourish. New theories popped up from fans after this episode, while older ones were proven to be false. Through the flashbacks in this and the previous episodes, viewers were able to look at each character again and see how much they've changed from the beginning. Arzt is very funny, talking to the others like they're schoolchildren, asking them questions while he stabilizes the nitroglycerine. The writers have made him *so* unbearably annoying that as viewers we almost hope something horrible will happen to him. The scene is filled with suspense, with him being a little reckless, and it forces viewers to the edge of their seats, wondering when the explosives are going to go boom, and when he finally gets it all wrapped up it looks like he'll be okay. Until he isn't.

The guys on the raft get to know each other a little better — Michael and Sawyer rarely spoke on the island, but now they're stuck on a small raft where neither can walk away from the other, and there's no one else to talk to except a child and a man who doesn't speak English. That said, it's clear that Jin and Michael are beginning to communicate with one another and that they've formed a friendship through the building of the raft.

Jin's backstory is one of the most interesting of all of them, because it introduces a side of him that is a complete surprise. In all of the other flashbacks in this two-parter, we are simply reminded of things we already knew about the characters. But with Jin, we know something terrible happened to him at the airport and he got on that plane with the threat of Mr. Paik hanging over his head, which finally explains his behavior toward Sun when they reach the island. He held the flower up to her at the airport, and it inspired hope in her; the kind man she married seemed to be back. After he came out of the airport bathroom, he was a different person because he realized he was always going to be under Paik's thumb. No matter what he did, no matter where he went, he'd never be able to get away from him, whereas Sun naively believed she could actually escape. The man in the bathroom says to Jin, "You are not free. You never have been, and you never will be." His words echo the famous words of Jean-Jacques Rousseau, "Man is born free and everywhere he is in chains." Yet when the scene cuts to Jin on the raft, he looks happy and free for the first time in the series. He knows that Paik probably believes everyone had died in the plane, and now he'll be able to move on with his life. But as Charlie pointed out in "Born to Run," when the raft is found, it will bring a rescue mission and the media to the island, making all of the survivors instant celebrities. How will Jin prevent Paik finding out?

On the island, Charlie and Sayid have gone off looking for Claire's child. Sayid and Charlie have had very little to do with one another in this show except for Sayid coming to talk to him after Charlie killed Ethan. Sayid's a very matter-of-fact guy, as we've seen time and again. He has tremendous patience, but he's possibly the most violent man on the island. In his past he has tortured and killed people, and in "Confidence Man" we saw he's still capable of at least the former. Charlie, still on a quest to prove that he can take care of someone, has elected himself Claire's protector, and when he does encounter Rousseau again on the other side of the island, there's a smugness to him like he's finally found someone more inept than he is. His words, "You're pathetic," are exactly the ones the girl spoke to him in the hotel room before he boarded the plane. This mean streak in Charlie will become more prominent in season 2.

The monster — which might be mechanical, might be psychological, might be animal — makes another appearance in this episode, and when it shows itself to Locke, it alters him in a way that will seriously affect him in season 2. We didn't see what Locke saw in "Walkabout," but whatever he saw then filled him with peace. In this episode, he strides out into an opening in the jungle to face it head-on again, but this time it seems to fill him with terror. What is he seeing? Does it show you something about yourself? Perhaps, the first time he saw it, it gave him hope and sent him a message of some kind about why he was able to walk, showing him positive things about his life. This time, however, it seems to have shown him something dark and terrible, perhaps about himself, maybe about the island in general, but whatever it is, it changes his character in season 2. Soon he will become sullen and not as effective as he is in season 1. Could the monster be fear itself?

The key moment of the entire episode is the conversation that Locke and Jack have in the jungle after Locke has just been "rescued" from falling into the hole. Locke confronts Jack about his lack of faith in the island, and Jack is astonished that Locke doesn't realize what Jack has just done for him. Their conversation about fate, destiny, belief, and science defines these two characters, and shows the essential belief-system split on the show. Jack insists he doesn't believe in destiny, and Locke says Jack does, he just doesn't know it yet. Does Locke know something about Jack that we don't? Locke's flashback, which follows this confrontation, allows us to compare the nervous, humiliated, and helpless Locke who boarded the plane with the competent, strong warrior he is now.

This episode was amazing, and the last 10 minutes of the show offered up the biggest cliffhanger of the summer of 2005. The raft is sabotaged, one of the rafties is kidnapped, another is shot, and they're all in the water. The hatch is open, but could the act of opening it have been a huge mistake? The performances, writing, directing, and general atmosphere of this episode were superb. Along with "Exodus, Part 1," it surpassed the suspense, humor, and drama of most feature films — not an easy accomplishment for any television show. "What's in the hatch?" became one of the favorite topics of discussion during the summer that followed this episode, and the ultimate answer was a shocker.

Highlight: There are several hilarious lines in this episode, but my favorites are Hurley's to Jack, when he slowly points and says, "You got some . . . Arnzt . . . on you"; Sawyer reading the private messages in the bottle and saying, "Who the hell is Hugo and how's he got a hundred and sixty million dollars to leave to his mom?"; and finally, Sawyer's frustration when Jin speaks Korean and Michael answers him in English, causing Sawyer to shout, "Hey Han, you and Chewie wanna slow down a second and talk to me here?"

Did You Notice?:
- Sayid's flashback appears within Shannon's and Jin's, and not on its own.
- Sawyer begins singing Bob Marley's "Redemption Song" on the raft, which is the perfect song for this show — for some people, the rescue will be their redemption (the four on the raft finally feel free) but for others, the island itself is redemption.
- Locke says whenever he played Operation as a kid, he always got nailed on the funny bone. The funny bone is located on the right arm, and is one of the hardest pieces to pull out of the board. Often players will try to get that

one last, and it usually ruins them. Maybe this is where Locke's difficulties with anger management first began.

- Charlie tells Claire that "*björn* is Dutch for baby carrier" but it's actually Swedish for bear.
- Hurley's flight meal was chicken (see "Everybody Hates Hugo").
- The island has been redemptive for Charlie, because he's learned how to take care of others, and in this episode he finally fulfills his need to do so with Claire and Aaron.
- It's a good thing Jack decided to take charge and not let Kate carry one of the nitro sticks, because when the monster comes she doesn't heed his advice and put down her backpack. Instead she runs recklessly through the jungle, bouncing the pack up and down the whole way.
- As soon as Walt and Vincent are parted, Walt is no longer safe.
- Throughout the season, we never see Walt and Claire talking to each other. If he had talked to her, would he have discovered that Aaron is significant in some way?
- This episode ended with that same weird, throbbing noise in the hatch that we could hear in the beginning of "Pilot, Part 1," only this time it's much louder.

Nitpick: After everything that's happened to Claire, why was she completely alone on the beach? You'd think everyone would wait until she and Charlie were prepared so that she'd never be vulnerable, but instead Sayid was already taking everyone else through the jungle to the caves, leaving Claire behind. Also, Hurley is *so* attuned to the curse of the numbers that there's no way he would ever have stayed in hotel room 2342. He would have gone to another hotel before doing that.

Oops: When the guy confronts Jin in the airport bathroom, in the closeup you can see his eyes darting back and forth as if he's reading phonetic Korean to deliver the lines into the camera. Also, how does Hurley run down 23 flights of stairs and not end up with a single bead of perspiration on him? Finally, as the episode comes to a close and we flash back to see all of them boarding the plane, you can see on the side of Walt and Michael's seats that they have B and C written on them, but they're clearly sitting in E and F.

4 8 15 16 23 42: Hurley's flashback is *full* of them, and they're all hilarious. Hurley is in hotel room **2342**. He drives a car with the license plate TX 327 (if you assign numbers to the letters, they add up to **44** — two **4**s, or an **8** — and the 32 is a reverse **23**; the numbers also all add up to 12, which is **4** + **8**). When he blows the tire, the odometer is **42** km, the engine temperature is **23**°C, and the speed drops from **16** to **15**, **8**, and finally **4**. (It's the numbers, man!) In the airport, the flight's departure time flashes on the screen as 14:**15**. When Hurley needs to get to his gate on time, he approaches an elderly man with a ball cap that says Crazy **8**s on it, and he eventually offers him $**1,600** to use his scooter. The best use of the numbers is when, on the little scooter, Hurley zips by a sports team of girls, and in order they're wearing jerseys with the numbers **4**, **8**, **15**, **16**, **23**, and **42**. He stops at gate **23** . . . and the flight attendant tells him it's his lucky day. Which should have set off a warning bell to him that it would be everyone else's very *un*lucky day. Also, in the present, the guys on the raft are **15** miles out when they spot the boat on their radar screen.

It's Just a Flesh Wound: Charlie gets hit in the head and suffers a major gash that Sayid cauterizes with gunpowder and a match. Locke probably incurs some scratches from being pulled through the jungle by the "security system." Arzt gets blowed up real good. Sawyer is shot in the shoulder.

Any Questions?:

- Is there any significance to the fact the season opened on Jack's eye, and ends on Aaron's?
- Why doesn't Claire get a flashback of her own? She's simply seen in the final group flashback handing her bags to Arzt. Is there some significance to the fact we never see her in the airport at all?
- Was the guy who confronts Jin in the bathroom also on the plane?
- As the group goes onto the slave ship, Locke comments that it looks like it was setting out for a mining colony, probably leaving Mozambique. How would he know such a thing? He's like the Cliff Clavin of *Lost*. Mozambique's slave trade happened during the early nineteenth century, and the slaves were mostly shipped from Mozambique to Mauritius and Réunion, which are both islands off the coast of Mozambique. Why has the wood of the ship stood up over time? How would the ship have ended up *so* far off course, to the southeast of Australia?
- The opening verse of "Redemption Song" is Bob Marley singing about how pirates sold him into slavery, an interesting comment on the *Black Rock*. Is the ship more symbolic than real? Is it a sign that on the island they are slaves to things like the hatch? Or is it a reminder that the outside world, where the ship originated, contains the real chains that bind them?

- Why does Locke lift the nitroglycerine sticks out of the box instead of Jack? Jack's a surgeon, and if anyone has steady hands, he does.
- How would Charlie know what a "Baby Bjorn" baby carrier is?
- What are the wisps of black smoke on the island? Could those have been what Locke saw previously and again in this episode? We'll see it again up close in season 2, but it definitely appears to be alive in some way. As noted in "Pilot, Part 1," in the first few minutes when Jack walks onto the beach and we see the full extent of the crash, look closely around the jet engine and the plane: what appeared to be just black smoke, upon closer inspection looks a *lot* like the wisps we see in the jungle here. Could this entity have been on the plane and brought them here? Might those black wisps coming off the plane have been the exiting souls of the people who died in the crash? If the latter, are they inhabiting the island now in some way?
- What really happened to Rousseau's arm? When did Claire scratch her? Did Rousseau have anything to do with her abduction?
- Did Rousseau light the fire on the beach? Why are there no footprints around the fire? Who kept it going all day? Was there some reason to remove Charlie and Sayid from the other people on the beach? Or did Rousseau sincerely believe she could get her daughter back by doing this? Is Aaron controlling this situation in any way?
- When Michael calls his mother from the airport, he tells her Walt wasn't supposed to be his, and it wasn't part of the plan. What does he mean by that?
- The rudder breaks off after Michael and Walt have a touching father/son moment, and Walt is steering the raft. Did the rudder break off because of Walt? Did he suddenly think that he'd love to just stay on the raft with his dad forever, and then something happened that might have made that a reality?
- Why doesn't Sayid know about Charlie's heroin addiction? Hurley knew about it (Charlie confessed it to him at a fireside chat in "Numbers") and as Arzt said in the previous episode, if you want to keep a secret, don't tell the fat guy. So why didn't everyone know about it?
- If Hurley is really worth $160 million, why doesn't he sit in first class on the flight?
- If Walt is intent on finding rescue, why doesn't he simply visualize a plane flying over the island that would rescue them?

Seating Arrangements

Ah, the seating chart. It's a hotly debated topic, because it's hard to tell exactly where everyone is sitting (and the Oceanic Web site www.oceanicflight815.com, that lists the seat numbers is incorrect in many of them, according to this final episode), but in "Exodus, Part 2," we can find approximately where most of them are. The seat letters go backward if you're facing the back of the plane, from right to left, ABC, then an aisle, DEFG, another aisle, and HIJ. We know that Arzt is in a D seat, sitting near Claire because he helps her with her bags, and though we don't see her sit down, he appears to step out of the way as if she were sitting in his row. Kate is in an I, the Marshal is in an H. Hurley is in an H seat and he also purchased the I seat — it's a mistaken assumption that he's in seat 20G, because the ticket agent was going to put him there until she realized he needed two seats together, and then she had to search for two seats, putting him in a different location. Hurley sits a few rows behind Walt and Michael, who are in F and G seats respectively. Shannon and Boone are sitting in F and G seats in business class, one row from the back row in the section. Jack was assigned seat 23B (in "Exodus, Part 1" he looks at the ticket and reads it off) but he actually sits in 23A (the seat he told Rose he was in in "Walkabout"); maybe the seat was empty and he wanted to look out the window. He moves to 23C right before the crash. Locke is in 24D behind Rose, who is in 23D, and that means her husband would have been in 23E if he hadn't moved to the back of the plane. Jin's in a D seat, with Sun in an E. Sayid is in a G seat near the aisle. Charlie is in 27C (he's four rows behind Jack). We don't see where Sawyer is sitting, although he appears to go to the back of the plane, which is interesting; was he using a bathroom in economy when the crash happened?

- How did the Others get a motorboat? If they've been on the island so long, how do they fuel it? Why haven't they tried using it to get off the island?
- Why doesn't Walt defend himself in some way by imagining something happening to the Others? Can't he will them all to spontaneously combust? Or is he too confused and upset to concentrate properly?
- Why do the Others take Walt? Do they think his psychic powers are useful? Are they trying to separate him from the rest of the Lostaways? Are they conducting a social experiment of some kind on the island and think he might thwart it? Or is there a reason they keep kidnapping children?
- As we've seen in the past, strange things happen when Walt is upset, so what sort of time bomb will the Others have on their hands now?
- In "Pilot, Part 2," Sawyer fights with Sayid, calls him a terrorist, and then announces to everyone that he saw him sitting in the back row of business class the entire flight, with his hands hidden under a blanket. But in this

episode, we see him sitting in economy (economy has the blue seats), *not* behind Shannon and Boone, who are in business class with empty seats behind them. Why did Sawyer lie? Is it an inconsistency in the writing? Did Sayid move?

- We *finally* figure out where the *Flash* comic came from and why it's in Spanish, but if Hurley is fluent in Spanish, why didn't Sayid recruit him to try to make sense of Rousseau's writings? Spanish and French are similar languages, and while they're obviously not the same, Hurley might have been able to help. Why didn't he ever notice Walt reading the comic, especially when they played backgammon so often? He could have read it to him.
- What's in the hatch?

Ashes to Ashes: Leslie Arzt, known as Arnzt among his friends. A high school teacher, he died giving an important lesson on the dangers of mishandling nitroglycerine. His reasons for being in Australia are unknown.

Hello to New Faces, Good-Bye to Old: Season 2

Lost closed its first season with a bang, easily becoming the most talked about new program on television (along with *Desperate Housewives*, capping off an ace year for ABC). But it wasn't just North America that was crazy for *Lost*. When the show's first season appeared in the United Kingdom (though episodes had almost regularly been downloaded by fans over the Internet), overnight ratings were a sensation, making it one of the most successful debuts for an American show, with 6.1 million tuning in for the first hour of the pilot, outpacing the likes of *ER*.

The accolades didn't take long to come rolling in. Only months after the first season ended, *Lost* was nominated in 12 categories for the Emmy Awards, television's highest honor. Naveen Andrews got a nod, as did Terry O'Quinn. "It's very nice to get some kind of acknowledgment for your work. It's bloody good for the show," Andrews said. "We're all pretty proud of it. It's a great thing to be involved in."

Just before the second season began, *Lost* took home the Emmy award for Best Television Drama. Abrams could only conclude the whole affair was "weird." But

The cast of *Lost* holds up their Emmys for Outstanding Drama Series at the 2005 Emmy Awards. (ALBERT L. ORTEGA)

the Emmys were a clear indication that *Lost* was a mainstream hit. That notion was reinforced by the fact that the DVD release of the first season sold 400,000 copies in its first week. *Lost* was ready for a new array of fans.

It also didn't take long for someone other than Lindelof and Abrams to take credit for having a successful vision for *Lost*. In a strange case, a Los Angeles writer named Anthony Spinner filed a suit claiming Touchstone Television had stolen his idea for *Lost* from a pitch he had made in 1977. The case gathered little media attention.

As the second season approached, one other factor was having an impact on the cast. With Boone's demise at the end of the first season, every actor and actress on the set in Hawaii knew they could be next. "It's painful and nerve-racking," said Josh Holloway of the producers' secret hit list. It turns out Holloway was preparing to buy a boat with Ian Somerhalder before Boone met his untimely demise. Holloway said the cast was suddenly aware that no one should make plans. "It has changed the dynamic, and to say it hasn't is a lie. Before, it was all love and family, and now there's fear. It created a negative thing that wasn't there before. We're all watching our backs now."

This became problematic for some actors. Daniel Dae Kim could not get a commitment from producers about his character's future, something he was hoping for prior to purchasing a house in Hawaii. Still, the actor said he understood the motivations of the show's creators. "They have to be true to what they do," Kim said.

However, others were more certain of their chances of staying around, especially given the show's success. "England, Australia, New Zealand, everywhere I lived, the show's huge," said Dominic Monaghan. "It's the biggest (U.S. import) show ever on England's Channel 4. Our agents can argue what we each bring to this show."

While every individual on the *Lost* set was worried about the potential of a character's death, the producers determined it was time to shake things up, adding additional cast members, characters who also survived the plane disaster. Among those was film actress Michelle Rodriguez. Though the

Daniel Dae Kim jokes around with Dominic Monaghan. (STHANLEE MIRADOR/SHOOTING STAR)

actress' role on the show was supposed to be a big secret, news that she was signing on as a cast member leaked far before the premiere of season 2.

Lindelof had to deal with numerous rumors of new actors joining the cast. "I can categorically deny that Sam Jackson is joining the cast," he stated, nixing another rumor. "Michelle Rodriguez is joining the cast, though. We saw her meet Jack in the airport before the plane took off [in 'Exodus, Part 2']. We know that she was on the plane, but she can only be somewhere else on the island other than where the other people have been."

With Abrams off directing *Mission Impossible III*, most of the creative decisions were left to Lindelof and executive producer Carlton Cuse. While Abrams sat in on planning for the second season, both Lindelof and Cuse acknowledged that he had little input into the continually developing story line. That left many to attribute *Lost*'s success to Lindelof. Pundits were now referring to the producer and cocreator as a "genius." It turned out that his influence on the characters had extended farther than most had anticipated.

Season 1 set up the characters of Shannon and Hurley, and season 2 will completely change both of them. (ALBERT L. ORTEGA)

"There are different facets of my personality that are reflected in different characters," he explained. "The character that I identified with most last year was Jack, because he was thrust into a leadership role that he wasn't fully ready to take on. He had to make a series of hard decisions that weren't necessarily popular decisions. Entering the fray of being the executive producer of a television show, I could identify with his life situation more than I could with any of the other characters' life situations. But I also feel that I have a cynical sense of humor that is reflected in Sawyer's dialogue, and I have a vulnerable side that I always think about when I'm writing Kate. I have a happier, hippier, dippier side that is reflected when I'm writing Hurley."

With the show drawing huge ratings around the world, and accolades and awards in North America, bold decisions were made for the upcoming season. Instead of sending out the traditional DVDs that provide reporters with a sneak peek of the upcoming season, the producers at *Lost* determined to keep their cards close to their respective chests. No one would get to see what was envisioned after the boat with Sawyer, Michael, and Jin was blown up and Walt was taken, or what was underneath the hatch that Locke so wanted to find.

It was a brave decision. But it was also clear that the show's ongoing success would be determined by titillated fans who wanted answers to the show's "15 head-scratchers," as one writer put it. The actors were aware that the show had to deliver some answers to questions that had started as early as the pilot episode. O'Quinn admitted he was worried about exhausting the patience of viewers. "I've gone inside [the hatch] now, and I know to some extent what it's about," he said.

"I'm afraid that people are going to be like, 'How can you possibly deliver on such a big promise?'"

As to what was in the hatch, and the numerous other questions that popped up throughout *Lost*, fans would receive some answers in the season premiere. But the maddening riddles of *Lost* would continue to propel the show's second year.

SEASON 2 (September 2005 – May 2006)

Recurring characters in season 2: L. Scott Caldwell (Rose), Sam Anderson (Bernard), Henry Ian Cusick (Desmond), Kimberley Joseph (Cindy), Mira Furlan (Danielle Rousseau), M.C. Gainey ("Mr. Friendly"), Michael Emerson (Henry Gale), John Terry (Christian Shephard)

2.1   Man of Science, Man of Faith

Original air date: September 21, 2005
Written by: Damon Lindelof
Directed by: Jack Bender
Guest cast: Julie Bowen (Sarah), Anson Mount (Kevin), Katie Doyle (EMT), David Ely (Intern), Masayo Ford (Nurse), Julius Ledda (EMT #2), Ivana Michele Smith (Survivor), Larry Wiss (Anesthesiologist)

Flashback: Jack

While the people on the beach continue to worry about the Others coming, Locke, Kate, and Jack discover what's inside the hatch.

Almost exactly four months after the cliffhanger of "Exodus, Part 2," and after fan speculation all that time about what could possibly be inside the hatch, it was time for the season premiere. Season 1 ended with the hatch door blown off, which leads into a very long shaft going underground; Charlie and Sayid had just gotten the baby back from Rousseau; there's black smoke coming from one side of the island; Rousseau has warned the Lostaways that the Others are coming;

In season 2, the camp moves to a new beach, which is rockier than the original one.
(RYAN OZAWA)

and Sawyer's been shot, Michael and Jin are in the water, the raft has been blown up, and Walt's been kidnapped. (And as if that isn't enough, don't expect that last bunch of incidents to be addressed in this episode.) "Man of Science, Man of Faith" begins a few minutes before "Exodus, Part 2" ends, with one of the most confusing opening sequences we've seen yet. Not only do we appear to be in a flashback sequence or back on the mainland, but it seems like we've gone back in time to a sort of retro existence. That is, until something happens that brings us right back to the island.

"Man of Science, Man of Faith" has several parallels to the original pilot episode. In each case, the episode begins with someone waking up in a place that's strange to us, although in the season 2 premiere, the guy we see seems to be perfectly acquainted with his surroundings, unlike Jack was in the pilot. In the series premiere, everyone was frightened, thrown into a situation that was completely unknown and terrifying. In the case of this episode, Kate, Jack, and Locke discover this new world of the hatch, and it's certainly not what any of them

Jack is a man who must see actual proof of something before he believes it. (YORAM KAHANA/SHOOTING STAR)

Before appearing as Jack's wife Sarah on *Lost*, Julie Bowen was best known as Carol on *Ed*. (YORAM KAHANA/SHOOTING STAR)

expected it to be. In "Pilot, Part 1," no one knew who to trust, and they saw everyone around them as strangers. In this episode, the Others have caused paranoia throughout the camp: Shannon is seeing things, Charlie's ranting about Rousseau's sanity, Locke and Jack are at loggerheads, and Hurley's starting to get ticked off that no one is telling him anything. Kate uses Jack's advice about letting the fear in for only five seconds when Locke is lowering her into the bunker. Watch for several more season 1 references throughout this episode and the ones to follow it.

In another Jack-centric episode, we get the backstory to what we saw in "Do No Harm." We see the circumstances surrounding the surgery Jack performed to make Sarah walk again, but this time we see his crisis of faith (or lack of faith) throughout the situation. This is a man who refused to believe in hope or miracles, and who saw things as black and white. Even the rather cold Christian Shephard had to have a talk to his son to explain what proper bedside manner should be. Yet, even when Jack not only witnesses a miracle, he *performs* it, he seems almost offended by the idea that such a thing could exist. He's a man of science, and doesn't believe in things that can't be proven scientifically. When he goes running in the stadium and meets a man who asks him why he runs like the devil's after him, Jack merely scoffs at the notion, even though it's an apt question.

The man of faith, as we know, is Locke, and this episode expands on the important conversation Jack had with Locke in "Exodus, Part 2," in which they argued about destiny and fate. "Man of Science, Man of Faith" marks the true beginning of the philosophical argument that will change these two men during the second season. Not only will they fight about faith versus blind faith, but they will struggle through leadership issues — Jack may be the leader of the group, but why does he take over the hatch when Locke was the one who found it? (It's interesting what these characters were named: Jack is the diminutive of John, insinuating that Locke is more important.) *Lost* viewers (and Terry O'Quinn himself) have commented on the fact that Locke's character will change quite dramatically in season 2, yet despite this character becoming meeker than the warrior we knew in the first season, the alteration of his character seems entirely in keeping with what has happened. Throughout the first season, he gained his strength from the hope of what could possibly be in the hatch, and he spent his days trying to get into it. Now that it's opened, the only thing left is reality — and once hope is fulfilled, it stops being hope. It's interesting that in the flashback, Christian Shephard scolds Jack for not giving a patient false hope, because, he explains, it's what they need; Jack argues that giving people false hope is wrong. Locke lived with a false hope of what was in the hatch for several weeks, and when that hope is dashed, it slowly destroys him. Maybe Jack was right.

Highlight: Hurley being jokingly optimistic about everyone's fate on the island: "Life's not so bad, right? I mean, sure, the Others are coming to, like, eat us all, and every once in a while someone blows up all over you, but you do get to sleep in every morning."

Did You Notice?:

- Desmond uses an eerie hall of mirrors to see up the hatch tunnel, which symbolizes how distanced he is from reality, and that what he sees is 10 times removed from the original.
- Hurley seems to have been closer in his guess about what was in the hatch than anyone else. In the previous episode, Hurley says he thinks they'll find

TV dinners from the '50s, TV with cable, clean socks, and Twinkies. Earlier, in "Numbers," he tells Charlie that if he ever finds a Laundromat on the beach, to let him know.

- When Sarah is first rushed into the emergency room, she keeps saying she must dance at her wedding, and in "Do No Harm," at the rehearsal dinner, she'd said in her speech that she would.

- When Kate tells Jack that she's going to follow Locke back to the hatch, she says, "Live together, die alone, right?" which is an echo of Jack's words to the group in "White Rabbit" when, in an effort to get them to move to the caves, he tells them if they don't all live together, they will die alone.

- As mentioned in the episode guide to "Deus Ex Machina," the term *deus ex machina* refers to an event where a god suddenly enters a play, usually in the form of a crane. There's a swan in the middle of the Dharma symbol, suggesting that the hatch itself is a deus ex machina.

- Jack pokes Sarah's legs exactly the way Locke pokes his legs with a pin in "Deus Ex Machina"; Jack stops short of putting a burning stick on her foot, thankfully.

- There's a very strong magnetic field in the bunker, which finally explains why Sayid noticed the compass wasn't working properly.

- Jack says to Desmond at the stadium that it's a small world, which could be an apt epigram to this show.

- The discussion between Jack and Desmond about miracles is very similar to the chat Jack and Locke have in "White Rabbit," when Jack stumbles upon Locke collecting water while Jack's following an image of his father through the jungle. Jack tells Locke in that scene that he thought he saw someone who's not there, and Locke asks, what if he is there? Jack says that would be impossible, and Locke responds, "Even if it is, let's say it's not." Similarly, in this scene, Desmond asks Jack what if he's actually fixed Sarah, and Jack says that would be a miracle. Desmond repeats, "What if you did?" There's clearly a link between Desmond and Locke and their faith, one that will become clear in the season finale.

- The mural on the wall of the hatch is absolutely chock-full of hints and items that have already been seen on the island, and probably will be seen later. There are small fish all over, like Jesus symbols; we see the number **108** with a sun drawn around it (could it be referring to Sun?); there's also a number **16** and a **42**; there are drawings of a woman and a dark-skinned man; arrows; little people who appear to be falling out of the sky (from an airplane, perhaps?); small houses along the bottom; and what appears to be I M SICK written in one section (instead of an I there is a drawing of an eye).

- The mural on the wall has a similar artistic quality to two previous paintings we've seen on the show: in "Special," during the scene where Susan first tells Michael she's taking Walt away, you can see a large painting on the wall that has several heads and little fish that are similar to the mural in the hatch. In "Raised by Another," in Claire's apartment you can see several of Thomas's paintings in the background, and in one of them there's a series of heads with mouths open that are very similar to the heads on the mural, as well.
- There appears to be a board game on the table with black-and-white pieces (probably the Japanese game Go).
- Though a lot of the things in the hatch look like they're from the 1970s, the washer and dryer look a lot newer.

Interesting Fact: Jack tells Sarah that he ran a Tour de Stade. This is a grueling run usually associated with Harvard Stadium, where runners actually run up the actual seats, rather than the stairs. In an article in the *Boston Globe*, the writer describes how brutal the run is: "As the runners stride from row to row, they look almost like speed skaters in the way in which they slowly pump their arms. It's not uncommon to see runners spring up the first few rows but use their hands to pull their knees up by the time they get to the top. Their leg muscles just stop working. Then when they touch the back wall at row PP and head back down, runners say, their heart rate jumps up a few more beats per minute before slowing down until the next run up."

Jack works at St. Sebastian hospital. St. Sebastian is the patron saint of athletes and soldiers. According to his legend, he was a Roman soldier who aided Christians during the Roman Emperor Diocletian's persecution of the Christians. When he was discovered to be a Christian, Sebastian was tied to a tree and shot with arrows (a common depiction of him in Renaissance paintings) and left for dead. St. Irene found him and nursed him back to health, after which he confronted the emperor and was beaten to death. He was declared the patron saint of people suffering from the plague, since at the time people were looking for a saint associated with archery (the plague was often likened to an arrow shooting through a village). It is perhaps this last point that caused the writers of *Lost* to name the hospital after him.

Nitpick: A hatch is a door, yet throughout this season, people will refer to the underground bunker as the hatch (for the most part I will, too, for the sake of clarity). Also, Christian tells Jack he has to give patients hope, and lectures him about what he said to Sarah. Yet Jack talked to her behind a closed door, and Christian couldn't possibly have heard him. Is he a lip-reader?

Oops: In "Hearts and Minds," Locke says the hatch is four miles from the camp on the beach. In "House of the Rising Sun," Jack says the caves are one mile inland. But in this episode, they say the hatch is half a mile away from the caves. Which is it? Also, all those other computers on the wall in the bunker are whirring and beeping when Jack first walks in, yet we never hear them again after this episode. Did the production team just decide they were far too loud?

4 8 15 16 23 42: In the opening sequence, when Desmond is on the exercise bike, he's riding at **16** km/hr. Then he injects some medicine into his arm, and you can see the full set of numbers on the medicine vial. When the explosion happens, he runs to the safe; the last combination number is **42**. When he grabs his shirt, there are **4** identical ones hanging in the closet. After the explosion, Hurley begins repeating the numbers like Leonard did in "Numbers." Jack says the shaft looks like it's **40** feet deep, and says it would be impossible to lower **40** people down into it. Adam Rutherford's time of death is at **8:15** AM. Sarah's blood pressure lowers to **80** over 60, then **88** over 52. Jack tells Sarah's fiancé that the surgery could take 12 hours (**8 + 4**) and the fiancé says their wedding is going to happen in **8** months. Jack reassures Shannon that they still have **4** guns.

It's Just a Flesh Wound: Locke's hands bleed as he holds the rope to lower Kate down into the hatch.

Lost in Translation: Clever fans have recorded the sound of Walt speaking to Shannon, and played it backwards. Walt whispers something that has been purposely garbled. He's saying either, "Don't press the button, the button's bad," or "Press the button, no button's bad." Is he warning her not to press the button, or telling her to press it?

Any Questions?:

- Why does Desmond sleep on the top bunk?
- What is Desmond injecting into himself? Is it similar to what Rousseau injected into Sayid?
- The other person involved in the suv accident is a 57-year-old man named Adam Rutherford, the same last name as Shannon. Could it be her father?
- Hurley begins repeating the numbers just like Lenny had done, and begins

to look a little psychotic. Was he completely cured when he left the mental institution? Is he just making this stuff up, or did he really win the lottery?

- Why is the word Quarantine written inside the hatch door? Is the person inside in a quarantine, or has it been put there to scare the person inside into thinking he is?
- What was the glowing light that Locke saw at the end of "Deux Ex Machina"? Was it Desmond simply turning on a light in the hatch?
- Why couldn't Desmond hear any of the noises of the trebuchet smashing against the hatch window, or the banging and digging going on around it?
- Desmond tells Jack that he's in training for a race around the world. What sort of race? (It doesn't involve a million dollars and a guy named Phil, does it?) Did he crash on the island as part of that race?
- When Desmond tells Jack, "You have to lift it up," he's referring to his ankle, but was it also a cryptic comment referring to something else? He makes a long pause after his comment as if it does.
- Sarah makes a big deal about the way Jack smells, and we saw him drink from Desmond's water bottle. Was there something funny in the water? Or was his smell just the body odor of someone who'd just been running through a stadium?
- Jack worried that Sarah was going to be paralyzed from the waist down, which was Locke's affliction when he boarded the plane. Is there any chance that Locke approached Jack's hospital to look into getting the surgery, but wasn't granted the opportunity, either for lack of money or another reason?
- In "All the Best Cowboys Have Daddy Issues," just before Locke and Boone discover the hatch, Locke says to Boone, "Do you feel it?" Was he referring to the magnetic force from the bunker? Did the magnetic pull have anything to do with the plane crashing (did it throw off the plane's instruments)?
- The Dharma hexagon symbol that we see as Jack enters the hatch is the same one that was on the side of the plane, as noted in the episode guide for "Tabula Rasa." Was the plane brought to the island on purpose by whatever organization has built the underground bunker?
- What's happened to the people on the raft?!

Music/Bands: In the opening sequence, and again as Jack's making his way into the hatch, we hear Mama Cass Elliot's "Make Your Own Kind of Music" (*Dream a Little Dream of Me: The Music of Mama Cass Elliot*).

What's in the Hatch?

During the summer break between seasons 1 and 2, the fans had a great time coming up with weird and wonderful theories on what could be in Locke's hatch. They ranged from the existential (another hatch) to the hilarious (an old Coca-Cola bottle, which would afford Locke and Jack the opportunity to do their own commercial spot). The following were the most popular theories:

- Controls for the "security system" on the island (one fan speculated that it was an old computer from the 1970s!)
- Dead bodies
- An army of some kind waiting to attack
- Military equipment
- A storage facility
- More ladders/doors/tunnels leading them through an underground passageway, which would explain how Ethan and the Others move around the island
- The Others use it as a hideout
- The hatch is a metaphor for Pandora's box, opening all of the evil on the island
- Photos of everyone on the island
- Nothing: At the bottom, it's just solid metal, going absolutely nowhere
- Aliens
- If the island is purgatory, the hatch could be a pathway to heaven . . . or hell
- The Wizard of Oz

2.2   Adrift

Original air date: September 28, 2005
Written by: Steven Maeda, Leonard Dick
Directed by: Stephen Williams
Guest cast: Tamara Taylor (Susan), Saul Rubinek (Michael's Attorney), Jeanetta Arnette (Lizzy)

Flashback: Michael

Michael and Sawyer float on pieces of the raft, while Michael remembers the last time someone took his son away from him. Meanwhile, we see a repeat of the events of last week, from Locke's and Kate's perspectives.

If "Special" didn't break the heart of every parent watching the episode, "Adrift" certainly will. After a week of exploring the insane world that exists in the hatch, the writers turn at least partly to the guys who were on the raft, and the aftermath of Walt's kidnapping. Sawyer is in serious trouble, with a bullet in his shoulder; Michael's voice is becoming hoarse from screaming for his son; and Jin, who dived into the water to save Sawyer, is nowhere to be seen. "Adrift" reminds us that the Others weren't the first ones to take Walt away from Michael. Eight years after his wife fought for sole custody, cutting Michael out of Walt's life completely, Michael thought he was being given a second chance to be Walt's father. And then his son was taken from him again.

Unfortunately, apart from drawing a parallel between the past and the present, "Adrift" doesn't offer much new information about Michael or Walt, and just serves to delay more revelations about the hatch and what's happening back on the island. We see Susan acting like a selfish woman once again, we see Michael fighting to have Walt in his life, and we see him ultimately giving in, all things we knew about before this episode. It's well written and beautifully acted (with a painfully adorable child playing a young Walt), but it's too bad we don't get more insight into Michael's life.

We watch Michael and Sawyer acting like children, arguing and refusing to "share" their pieces of raft. Michael is hostile (though understandably distraught), despite the fact Sawyer is the one who saves his life. Michael's behavior in this episode points to an alarming personality trait he's shown throughout the series: He tends to develop a gut instinct about people, and then refuses to trust those who gave him a bad feeling early on, no matter what they do. He didn't like Walt hanging around with Locke, so he declared a personal war against him, and even when Locke saved his life, Michael didn't forgive him. In this episode, he blames Sawyer for the fact he lost Walt, and even though Sawyer argues he was shot trying to save Walt, and that he'd pulled Michael out of the water after the incident, Michael refuses to listen to him and maintains a surly attitude toward him for a few episodes to come. Michael seems to need to blame people for his problems with Walt. For years, Susan had been the obvious and rightful target of his blame for the fact Walt wasn't in his life. Then when Walt didn't respect Michael upon their reunion, he blamed Locke for turning Walt against him. Now that he's lost Walt again, he needs to blame Sawyer for allowing it to happen. Harold Perrineau is amazing in the scene where he simply sits on the raft and sobs, out of sheer exhaustion. Michael has let someone take Walt away from him again, but he couldn't do anything to stop it. It's like the island is haunting him with the worst thing that has ever happened to him. Until he learns to take responsibility

"Tent City" on the beach (Sawyer's tent is on the right) is located on a remote beach in Oahu called Papailoa, and known as Police Beach. (RYAN OZAWA)

for things, his worst nightmare will continue to haunt him like some evil *Groundhog Day*.

Meanwhile, back on the island, we see last week's discovery of the hatch from Locke's point of view, and it only serves to create more questions, rather than give us any answers. The hatch appears to contain a weird bachelor pad with a 1970ish vibe, and a crazy Scottish guy who pushes a series of six familiar numbers and a button every 108 minutes. Is he completely insane, or is he fulfilling an important job? The questions about this new scenario are endless, but because this episode simply reiterates what happened last week, it makes us anticipate next week's episode a lot more.

At the end of the episode, Sawyer sees the island and says, "We're home." It's an important line in the series, because where season 1 was all about trying to get off the island, season 2 will be about learning to adapt to life on the island, and making the best of it. They'll stop looking for rescue planes, and begin to focus on the island itself.

Highlight: Kate scarfing down the Apollo chocolate bars and stuffing more in her pants before making her escape.

Did You Notice?:
- When the camera shoots the shark from below, you can see the Dharma symbol on its belly.
- Charlie hands off Aaron to take the Mary statue instead, a move that will

The Real "Dharma Initiative"

Dharmic religions all originate from India, and they are Hinduism, Buddhism, Jainism, and Sikhism. In Hinduism, dharma refers to the religious, moral, and ethical duties of each person, and how they exist within the world. Sanatana Dharma (The Eternal Dharma) is the traditional name of Hinduism. Dharma is often translated as "a way of life," and following dharma will help align the self with the outside world. The basic concept of Hinduism is that Brahman (the divine in the universe) exists around us and within us, and we must connect our inner divinity to the outer one in nature. The Natchintanai Scripture states, "By the laws of dharma that govern body and mind, you must fear sin and act righteously. Wise men by thinking and behaving in this way become worthy to gain bliss both here and hereafter." (Perhaps the Dharma Initiative uses outside experiments to force its subjects and researchers to look within and find the real answers.)

In Buddhism, dharma refers to the highest truth (one who attains it has achieved nirvana), and also is used to describe the teachings of Buddha and the interpretation of his words. It shares some of the same interpretations of the term "dharma" with Hinduism, in that dharma offers protection from suffering. If one follows dharma by exercising moral responsibility and showing purity in thought and action, one can achieve inner happiness. Many people believe that happiness can be found in things and other people and in our surroundings (many of the characters are looking for their parents' approval; Charlie found it in screaming fans), but it can only be found by achieving inner peace, which can happen only if the laws of dharma are followed.

be more important later, and will show where his priorities are.

- Michael gives Walt a stuffed polar bear.
- Arzt was right: the current ended up carrying them right back to where they started.

Interesting Facts: There are two common answers to the riddle that Desmond poses to Locke (What did one snowman say to the other snowman?): the first is "Freeze" and the second is, "Do you smell carrots?" Not exactly ROTFLMAO, but cute. Also, a Buddhist mala, or rosary, contains **108** beads.

Nitpick: When Michael first goes to his lawyer and finds out that Brian wants to adopt Walt, he acts surprised, but that's why he was there to see him in the first place, and Susan told him that Brian wanted to adopt Walt in "Special." Also, Sawyer performs CPR on Michael after Michael was underwater for about three seconds. How could he possibly have stopped breathing in such a short amount of time?

4 8 15 16 23 42: Desmond enters these numbers into a computer, and then a countdown clock on the wall resets to **108**, which is the sum total of the numbers. Locke tells Desmond they've been on the island for **44** days.

It's Just a Flesh Wound: Kate is knocked unconscious by Desmond in the previous episode (we discover it in this one). Sawyer aggravates his bullet wound by digging the bullet out with his fingers (*shudder*). Jin has a bruise on his cheek and a cut on his forehead, presumably from the people who show up at the very end, or from when he washed up on the island rocks.

Any Questions?:

- What did Desmond mean when he said to Locke, "Are you him?" Does he assume Locke is his long-awaited replacement?
- The law office where Michael and Susan are sitting is the exact same place where Claire almost signed away the rights to Aaron before he was born. Does that mean Susan and Michael were in Australia? Or is there somehow an identical law firm in the U.S.? It's interesting that the office is a setting where parents lose their children.
- Why does Charlie tell Claire he's not religious, when we know that he is?
- Is the shark real or mechanical? It bears the same symbol we can see throughout the hatch; what does that mean?
- How did Jin end up on the island? Who are the five people who appear at the very end?
- In "Numbers," Sam Toomey's wife says that Sam and Lenny were stationed on a Pacific listening post. Is that the case, or did they serve time in the hatch, entering the numbers over and over again?

Harold Perrineau (Michael Dawson)

Until *Lost* came about, Harold Perrineau was best known for playing transvestites and a physically challenged inmate who is continually brutalized. He was recognizable to those who followed art films or HBO's often brutal series *Oz*, but despite a small role in the *Matrix* series of movies, Perrineau was far from being a star.

Which is probably why he downplayed the invitation to appear in *Lost* when the show was cast in 2004. "My first thought was blah blah blah blah, like Hollywood speak. They love you, you're great, and so, I just didn't pay any attention until the day I walked into

Harold Perrineau with his wife, Brittany, who has appeared twice on *Lost*. (ALBERT L. ORTEGA)

the room," he said. "Suddenly I was two feet taller and like, yes, I'm great, that's right, you're right. . . . We should be in business together."

In fact, Perrineau had initially turned down the audition because of a conflict with a play he was doing. Unlike other characters in the show, Perrineau was handpicked by J.J. Abrams and Damon Lindelof. "Harold was the only actor we brought to the network for Michael," says Lindelof. "He brings such intense dignity to everything he does. We thought that trait — a sense of honor — was needed since Michael was such a terrible father at first."

In what became a common occurrence during the early days of casting for *Lost*, while the producers and writers struggled to firm up a story arc, the character of Michael became clearer after Perrineau was cast. "Once I got the role the creators were like, 'Great. Now that we know you're doing it, we know where we want to go with the character.' So that's how it worked out," Perrineau explains.

Landing a role on what would become television's most popular hour was a long way removed from Perrineau's initial aspirations. He had grown up in Brooklyn (he was born in 1963) and studied music and theater. He grew up using the last name Williams, the family name of his father (his parents never married). However, when he joined the Screen Actors Guild, he found there was already a Harold Williams, so he began using his mother's surname instead.

Like many actors, Perrineau struggled to find any degree of success in his early days. That led to a series of menial jobs that covered his bills, though he remained focused on following his dream. "I've had a lot of jobs. I sold books over the phone. I was a soda jerk. I was a messenger, a busboy, a singing waiter, a shoe salesman. And they're all strange to me because all I ever wanted to do was act. They're not strange jobs, just strange to me."

Even when he finally landed a paid acting gig, the situation was far from perfect. In San Francisco, where he was performing a play, the view from his apartment was that of prostitutes plying their trade. "I was put up in an apartment-style hotel that wasn't in the best neighborhood," he says. "I'd look out the window and go, 'Look at all those hookers!'"

Among his first breaks in Hollywood was playing the freaky, cross-dressing Mercutio in Baz Luhrmann's production of *Romeo + Juliet*. Perrineau enjoyed the role and played the crazed Mercutio with fun and zest. "Mercutio was just buggin' out, you know what I mean? He was just high, crazy, stoned. In a society where macho is the thing, for Mercutio to come out in a dress, that's ballsy. Mercutio is just off his fuckin' rocker and doesn't care. Then there was that thing about him maybe loving Romeo or not, well I guess that changes things."

It wasn't the last time Perrineau would play a cross-dresser. He'd try again while playing opposite Penelope Cruz in the 2000 film *Woman on Top*. Though he admits to pre-ferring theater, by the late 1990s Perrineau was increasingly finding television work. Most notably, he was cast as Augustus Hill, the paraplegic inmate in the harsh prison drama *Oz*. As Hill, Perrineau was taking big risks as an actor in an uncompromising show. He understood that if the role was not successful, he could face difficulty getting other work. "I was scared to death to take the role of the wheelchair-bound narrator. I knew this could just end my career right here," he says.

It was while finishing the *Matrix* series of films that *Lost*'s producers cast him for the role of Michael Dawson. Used to living in big cities, the transition to Hawaii was difficult for Perrineau and his family, which includes wife Brittany and daughter Aurora. "In New York, living is hard," he explains. "In Hawaii, things are really laid-back. Sometimes it's really frustrating getting things done or finding what I want. Sometimes I'm still on my New York time, so I look pushy [laughs]. There were a lot of nights in the beginning when my wife, my daughter, and me were all in the house walking in circles asking, 'What are we doing here? There is nothing to do!' [laughs]. So the transition's been a little weird, but it's cool. It's an adventure."

As for his character, Michael, who, like Job, seems to be continually tested, Perrineau is not convinced the character's situation is likely to improve. "A lot of what happens to

Michael Dawson is that he's had a lot of bad luck," the actor says. "Bad things keep happening over and over and over. So, there's a part of me that hopes he has some good luck, that some good things happen to him. Then there's that other part of me that wants to explore what happens to people who have bad luck like that all the time. Like, what kind of person does that make them — and then . . . what kind of person does that make them on the island? Because none of the rules apply anymore.

"The only rule that applies to Michael is that his bad luck will continue."

2.3   Orientation

Original air date: October 5, 2005
Written by: Javier Grillo-Marxuach, Craig Wright
Directed by: Jack Bender
Guest cast: Kevin Tighe (Anthony Cooper), Katey Sagal (Helen), Curtis Jackson (Security Guard), Michael Lanzo (Waiter), Jean Rogers (Moderator), Roxie Sarhangi (Francine)

Flashback: Locke
Desmond tells Jack and Locke why he is in the hatch, while Michael, Sawyer, and Jin deal with their imprisonment.

Because season 1's flashbacks were full of revelations (Locke used to be paralyzed! Walt has a weird psychic ability! Hurley won the lottery! Jack's a . . . doctor . . .) this season's flashbacks serve to beef up the stories we already know. However, Locke flashbacks are always particularly fun. In "Deus Ex Machina" we saw the way Locke's father tricked him out of a kidney, and in this flashback, we see what happened immediately afterward. Locke's turn in an anger management class is not only understandable (would anyone have been able to handle that situation with grace?) but explains the weird outbursts he has every once in a while that are very un-Locke-like. In this flashback, we see that as well as having no conscience, Anthony Cooper appears to have no soul, either, and he continues to be a horrible person to his son. Locke, on the other hand, cannot let go. It's when a woman comes along that we see where his faith began — she taught him how to reach out and believe in something, even if he didn't think it possible. Until she told him that, he was a lot like Jack, needing to know the "why" of everything.

As usual, Terry O'Quinn gives an outstanding performance in these flashback scenes, proving himself as the real acting heavyweight on the show.

Jack has shown little patience with Locke's faith, but he has absolutely no time for Desmond's. Desmond seems to proceed on a blind faith to survive the situation he is in, believing that what he was told was true. In this episode, he reveals to them why he's here, that in his race around the world (which he'd mentioned to Jack a few years ago, see "Man of Science, Man of Faith") he landed here, and another man who was in the hatch nabbed him and convinced him that he had to push a button every 108 minutes. Because this episode also looks into the way Locke had been used, we can't help but wonder if Desmond, too, has been conned. Is his belief foolish? As he points out, while it might look like he's been stuck in a box to press a button as part of a weird psychological experiment, there's an undeniably strong electromagnetic force on one side of the bunker, suggesting that the station really was used for something scientific at one time.

Jack sees Desmond's and Locke's respective faiths as being blind, but they don't see themselves this way. These are not stupid men: they have both considered the possibility that they are wrong, but neither one wants to find out what happens if he's not. How is Desmond's existence any different from anyone else's? Many people live good lives because good behavior makes them happy, but also because they want to get into a Heaven of some kind that they believe exists in the afterlife. They have no evidence that such a place exists, or that there's even a god, but they don't want to take a chance, just in case.

Desmond madly raves about his mission, then leaves the hatch in a deranged panic when he thinks the world is about to end, leaving Locke to take over as the Guy Who Believes in the Button. Jack stands back and chortles disparagingly at both of them. Where his disgruntlement with Locke was based on something tangible — Locke thwarted Sayid's attempts to rescue them and sabotaged Jack's chances to save Boone — Jack becomes so angry at Desmond that his rage about the situation seems to outweigh what's actually going on. Why does Jack take Desmond's faith so personally? He seems to take personal offence at what Desmond and Locke are doing, rather than considering the predicament they've found themselves in. Yet he shows some doubt that both Desmond and Locke are genuinely out of their trees, when Locke challenges him to press the button himself and he's not sure what to do. Did Jack have faith in something once?

The orientation film that Desmond gives Locke will, again, generate more questions than answers them, but the information contained in it had fans discussing

Katey Sagal, who found fame on *Married With Children* and coolness on *Futurama*, appears as Locke's girlfriend Helen. (MARK SENNET/SHOOTING STAR)

more possibilities and directions in which this show could be going than ever before. Who is this Hanso Corporation? Or Marvin Candle? The possibilities are endless; and just when you thought we'd almost figured out the island by the end of season 1, we'll be spending at least one more season trying to figure out what this whole hatch thing is about.

Speaking of confusing, the rafties have been imprisoned in a pit by a mysterious group of people, and just as Locke's father had played him, they get played by one of the people who comes down into the hole to talk to them. Unfortunately, the two story lines are not quite happening in synch anymore (Jack enters the hatch at night, whereas the guys on the raft are in full daylight) but both make us excited to see what's going to happen next, simply because both groups are in such strange situations, at nearly the same time. Were these situations arranged by some higher power to happen in tandem like this?

Highlight: The look on Hurley's face when he discovers the food storage room.
Did You Notice?:

- Locke's hairline has receded quite dramatically from "Deus Ex Machina," showing that the stress of what his father had done to him two years earlier has really weighed on him.
- Locke's girlfriend, Helen, shares the same name as the dial-a-date operator he was talking to in "Walkabout."
- During the orientation film, there are several splices we can see thanks to the jumps in the movie and missing words, but the most obvious one hap-

pens after he says they cannot use the computer "for anything . . ."

- Candle says that one of the fields the Dharma Initiative studied was zoology, and they show a shot of polar bears.
- The copyright of the film is 1980, which means the Dharma program had to start very soon after.
- Candle never moves his left arm throughout the film (Damon Lindelof has since confirmed that the arm is indeed a prosthetic).
- During the exchange with Ana Lucia, the number 40 comes up a lot — Sawyer says 40 people survived the plane crash (it was actually 48) and Ana Lucia says she was alone for 40 days when they took her (it's Day 45 now). The number 40 is significant from a Christian perspective, because it's the number of days that Jesus spent in the wilderness, fasting. The devil visited him in several forms, tempting him, and he resisted all the temptations. It is also the number of days it rained when Noah was on his ark.
- In the photo of Desmond with a woman, it looks like Sydney Harbour in the background.
- In "Whatever the Case May Be," Shannon was singing "La Mer," and in that song, the singer sings of a white bird (which could indicate the swan) and rusty houses (which could mean the hatch itself, or the row of run-down houses you see on the mural drawing).

Interesting Fact: Kate finds some Apollo chocolate bars in the previous episode, and in this one, Hurley comments that he's never heard of them before. The writers have chosen that name carefully. Apollo was the Roman sun god, and the god of light, prophecy, the arts (especially music), archery, flocks and herds, and, possibly most importantly to Desmond, the god of plague, medicine, and healing. His relation to medicine and his being a shepherd no doubt aligns him with Jack, as well. He represents the realm of rational consciousness, which plays an important part in the ongoing debates between Locke and Jack. He was the son of Zeus, by Leto (not to be confused with Leda, who was raped by Zeus when he was in the form of a swan), and Apollo's twin sister was Artemis. When Hera, Zeus's wife, discovered her husband was the father of Leto's unborn children, she forced all of the land to rebuke Leto when she went into labor, so she would be unable to deliver her children on *terra firma*, or land. Leto discovered the floating island of Delos, which could not be considered a mainland or an actual island, and she gave birth there. Delos was surrounded by swans, which became sacred to Apollo, and it was said that every year he would travel on the back of a swan to a land where he would spend the winter. Could this be the reason this particular station is the Swan station?

Desmond first came to the bunker when he crashed into the island and someone named Kelvin emerged from the hatch. A kelvin is a unit used to measure thermodynamic temperature. One kelvin is 1/273.16 of the thermodynamic temperature of the triple point of water (triple point meaning the point at which gas, liquid, and solid forms of water exist at an equilibrium thermodynamically). To convert kelvins to Celsius, one subtracts 273.15 from the kelvin amount. (Notice in the fraction and in the conversion, two of Hurley's numbers are used.) Clearly Kelvin has been so named for a reason, but it's not immediately clear why.

The most famous solo race around the world was that of Yuri Gagarin, the first man in space. He finished his April 1961 orbit in . . . 108 minutes. (Cue *Twilight Zone* music.)

Nitpick: When the timer is at 24 minutes, Kate and Hurley are looking for the breaker box, but Kate doesn't turn the power back on until the clock is at five minutes. Why didn't Sayid just go and find it himself?

Oops: Jack says Desmond seems very calm for someone who thinks the world is going to end in 45 minutes, but we just saw the ticker moments earlier and it was at 84 minutes.

4 8 15 16 23 42: When Desmond is telling his story to everyone, the countdown clock is at 84 minutes (**8** & **4**). Candle says they have **4** minutes to press the button after the alarm begins to sound. He says they will be in charge of the lab for 540 days, and if you divide that number by five, you get **108**. Sawyer tells Ana Lucia that **40** of them made it. Jack tells Desmond they've been on the island for **40** days and no one has been sick. When Desmond's computer blows out and he begins freaking out that "it's over," the ticker is at 48 (**4** & **8**). When Sayid comes into the hatch, the ticker is at 24 (a reverse **42**). When Desmond leaves and Jack follows him through the jungle and tells him that it's crazy to push a button if you don't know what it does, Desmond says that in **15** minutes he'll either be right, or very, very wrong.

It's Just a Flesh Wound: Desmond gets whacked in the head with the butt of a gun.

Any Questions?:

- What happened to Helen to make her end up in anger management classes? Is she the same Helen Locke was talking to in "Walkabout"?

- Anthony Cooper says to Locke, "You think you're the first person that ever got conned?" immediately making us think of Sawyer. Is Anthony Cooper the *real* Sawyer who conned James "Sawyer" Ford's parents and caused their deaths?
- Kate finds an alternate exit out of the hatch, and it's very large. After all that time out in the jungle, didn't Locke once think to cast a wide net and look *everywhere* for another possible way of getting into the hatch?
- Why did Kate grab a shotgun when she had the option of a pistol?
- What kind of solo race around the world was Desmond involved in? Was it on land? On water? In the air? He mentions how he has to be physically fit, which wouldn't necessarily be the case for a plane ride, but it would be for a nautical race.
- How did Kelvin die? Why was Kelvin there in the first place? Didn't he ever tell Desmond how he came to be there?
- The orientation film creates endless questions, so here we go: It says the Swan station is number 3 of 6, so are the other five stations somewhere else on the island, or scattered around the world? What does the swan stand for? The DeGroots imagined a communal research center to look into various things, so why doesn't Desmond know what he's supposed to be researching? Is Desmond, in fact, the experiment, and not the person conducting it? One of the things they wanted to study was "utopian socialism," and wouldn't a deserted island be a form of utopia if one lived on it a certain way? What better way to study it than watching what is happening on the island right now? Why are there splices in the film? Did someone remove sections of it for a reason? Why did they call their mission the Dharma Initiative? Who is the Hanso Corporation, and how did they get involved with all of this? In "…In Translation," we see Jin beat up a man named Byung **Han**. Does he have anything to do with Hanso?
- When the ticker resets itself, the last two digits flip through a sequence as well. Why do they do that, when they're always at 00?

The Turn of the Screw by Henry James (1898)

Like *Heart of Darkness*, *The Turn of the Screw* is written using a framing story with multiple narrators. At a society party, the narrator listens to several people tell ghost stories about spirits appearing to children. Finally, one man, Douglas, says his sister's governess wrote about a ghost story that happened to her in a manuscript that she entrusted to him (there's a suggestion that Douglas was in love with the governess) and he calls for someone to retrieve it. When he begins reading, the governess (who is never named) becomes the narrating voice. She is in love with her employer and is in charge of two children, Flora, 8, and Miles, 10. The housekeeper, Mrs. Grose, becomes her confidante.

Miles has been kicked out of school, for what reasons the headmaster didn't say, and we never truly find out why. The governess sees an image of a man with red hair and a white face, and Mrs. Grose says it's Peter Quint, the valet who died the previous year. She sees him again staring into the dining room and she runs outside and looks in herself, scaring the bejesus out of Mrs. Grose, who comes into the dining room and sees the governess outside looking in. Mrs. Grose eventually says Peter liked his women young and good-looking, suggesting he was rather predatory. She also says that he and the previous governess, Miss Jessel, had had an affair, and Quint was "too free" with the boy Miles, insinuating something sexually sinister there as well. When the governess sees the ghost of Miss Jessel, Mrs. Grose tells her that Miss Jessel had had some sort of power over Flora. The more she hears about these people, the more the governess begins to suspect the children are also aware of the ghosts, and she begins to think that the ghosts have possessed the children and are reenacting their love from beyond the grave by using these two young bodies. She begins to fantasize about saving the children from these terrible ghosts. And like Jane Eyre, she thinks if she can do something to get her master's attention, he will fall in love with her and marry her.

The governess ramps up her surveillance of the children, looking for strange behaviors that might back up her theory that they've been possessed in some way. One night she finds Flora out of her bed and standing behind her curtains. She finds a way to look outside and see what Flora was looking at, assuming it's the ghosts, but it's Miles. The governess decides the children are more under the influence of the ghosts than previously thought, and she begins to stay up at night so she can watch them 24/7, and her behavior becomes increasingly paranoid and erratic. She tells Mrs. Grose what happened with the kids and tells her what her theory is, and Mrs. Grose suggests contacting the uncle, but the governess stops her from doing so. Mrs. Grose begins to wonder if the governess is to be trusted.

The children are good when they're around her, and she's careful not to let on that she knows anything about the ghosts around them. She walks to church one Sunday morning with Miles, who says he wants to go back to school to be around his "own sort," and he suggests that maybe he should contact his uncle and tell him what's going on. This unnerves the governess because she thinks Quint is making him say this. She returns home instead of going to church and sees Miss Jessel again and begins shouting at her, telling her she's a "terrible, miserable woman." The ghost disappears. When Mrs. Grose and the children return home, she tells Mrs. Grose what happened. She says that the children are working against her and the ghosts are making them evil, and Mrs. Grose, believing otherwise, sticks up for the children, but does admit that they told her things and asked her to keep quiet.

The governess goes to Miles' room. He knows that she is aware something happened to him at school, and wonders why she never said anything. He says he really wants to go back, and yells, "You know what a boy wants!" at which point the governess falls on him, hugging him and kissing him madly, until he pushes her away. The governess finally agrees to write to the uncle, and she leaves the letter for a servant named Luke to deliver. While Miles plays piano for the governess, she realizes Flora is missing. She and Mrs. Grose go outside to find Flora, and see her by the lake. Flora asks where Miles is, and the governess says she'll tell her where Miles is if Flora will tell her where Miss Jessel is (whenever the children go missing the governess assumes they are with the ghosts). Flora is infuriated, and then the governess looks across the lake, sees Jessel, and points and yells. But no one else can see her. Flora yells at the governess that she's never seen any ghosts, that she hates her, and she thinks she's cruel. She begs Mrs. Grose to take her away, which shocks the governess. Very early the following morning, Mrs. Grose tells the governess that Flora has come down with a high fever, and they agree she must be taken to London. Mrs. Grose tells the governess that Miles took the letter, but it was never sent, and that Flora is using shocking words — the governess scoffs and says clearly she got them from Miss Jessel. She sees Flora's behavior as proof of her possession.

Miles and the governess have dinner together, and they finally discuss what has been happening. She says that she only stayed there to be with him, which makes Miles visibly uncomfortable, and he says he will tell her everything soon, but first must go see Luke. Suddenly the governess sees Quint looking through the window and she grabs Miles and holds him tightly, as if to protect him, and continues the conversation with his back to the window so he can't see what's outside. Miles tells her that he took the letter and burned it, and that at school he was expelled because he said some things to certain boys he liked that were deemed inappropriate. The governess embraces him, delighted that he's finally been honest with her, and her hold tightens as she stares at Quint. Miles, knowing something has happened, asks suspiciously if she's looking at Miss Jessel, proving that he's talked to Flora and assumes the governess's erratic behavior made her ill. The governess says no, the "coward horror" is there, and Miles tries to look toward the window, and moans, "Peter Quint — you devil!" and dies.

Despite the shortness of the book (it's a 50,000-word novella) *The Turn of the Screw* has generated a plethora of critical reaction, and it has sparked some heated debates among literary critics over the past 100 years. On the one side stand the critics who read the book on the surface level and accept what the governess says as truth. As proof that the ghosts are real, they point to the fact that she is able to describe the ghost of Peter Quint to Mrs. Grose before even knowing he existed. They state that the children are possessed, and at the end Miles dies because, as the governess says in the last line of the book, he is "dispossessed." On the other end of the spectrum are the critics who believe that the governess is insane, and she is the only one seeing these ghosts. They claim the children are never possessed, but are increasingly frightened of a governess who is behaving in an erratic and scary manner, a woman who seems to be putting them in danger, rather than protecting them from it. They suggest that Miles dies at the end because the governess squeezes him so tightly it suffocates him, and that his final words are directed at her, not at Quint.

The book, if read from a point of view of most later twentieth-century critics, is highly sexualized. Many readers assume that Miles made sexual comments in school about masturbation or sexuality or homosexuality, to other boys "that [he] liked," and that's what got him expelled. Because the subject was taboo in 1898, James uses very careful language throughout the novel. There is a suggestion that Quint had an inappropriate relationship with Miles. The governess herself seems to be unnaturally affectionate toward Miles, and often describes his face as lovely or beautiful. In the final scene of the novella, she calls him "my own." When he admits to having stolen the letter, she lets out a "moan of joy" and holds him tightly to her breast, commenting in her narrative that she could feel his pulse quicken as if he were excited by her (when in fact he was probably terrified). This is a book with so many interpretations that James himself commented that how you interpret his novel says more about you than the words themselves.

So why is the orientation film tucked behind it? Perhaps because like James' novella, the video could have many interpretations, depending on who's watching it. And certainly the characters themselves have been interpreted differently by viewers. If you don't like Locke, you see him as the villain of the show, stupidly keeping them on the island and blindly pushing his button. Jack becomes the hero, the one you root for week after week hoping he can finally wrench Locke away from what he's doing and get them back on track. But if you see Locke as the key to everything on the island, you'll watch him sympathetically, and believe there really is an importance to the hatch and the button itself. You'll glower at Jack and wish he'd just leave Locke alone. Your preference will also change how you see every other character's interaction with Locke.

Perhaps the writers will eventually end the show as abruptly as James ended his novella, leaving the real ending and interpretation for the audience to decide. But if they do, they'd better not be walking down any dark alleys near fan conventions afterward. . . .

Rats in a Cage: B.F. Skinner

In the orientation film, Marvin Candle says that the DeGroots based their research on the principles established by B.F. Skinner (1904–1990). Skinner was an American psychologist whose primary research was on modes of behavior modification through operant conditioning. Where Pavlov's experiments involved negative reinforcement (dangle food in front of a rat, and when the rat steps forward to take the food he gets a small zap of electricity, causing the rat to eventually be afraid of the food), Skinner believed positive reinforcement was the only way to modify behavior in an affirmative way. He thought punishments didn't work to actually make society better. After all, criminals are aware of impending punishment if they break the law, but they do it anyway; they just try to avoid getting caught.

Instead, Skinner believed that if you gave the subject some sort of positive reinforcement, they would repeat the good behavior, and learn quickly how to avoid anything bad happening to them. He developed what is known as the Skinner box, where a rat was placed inside, and allowed to run about. Eventually, by accident, the rat would hit a lever on the side of the box that would release a food pellet. The rat would quickly ascertain that one thing led to another, and would continue to bat at the lever, releasing several pellets into the box. Skinner could then modify the experiments, and make it so a rat had to hit the lever 20 times to release one pellet. Again, the rat would catch on, the pellet would drop, and it would begin to repeatedly hit the lever. As it got closer to push number 20, the rat would bat the lever more and more quickly, anticipating the pellet that was about to drop.

Skinner also trained pigeons to do similar things (he even taught pigeons how to bowl). In one of his most famous pigeon experiments, he placed the birds into a box, and sent food through a hopper. When the food first appeared, if a pigeon was holding its head a certain way, it came to believe that it had to always hold its head that way to get more food, and in this way, Skinner claimed he created "superstition" in pigeons.

Using this and other experiments, Skinner declared that people could be trained to do something over and over if they thought there was a reward at the end. They would quit doing things that don't produce the reward, and would focus on only that which would cause a positive outcome for them and society.

Skinner's critics are many, and vocal. One of his inventions was the "baby tender," a heated crib, effectively, where his daughter slept for the first two and a half years of her life, in a controlled-temperature environment, where she would not require blankets or clothing at night. He claimed that it kept her happy, and reduced both the laundry and his daughter's chances of getting a rash from the blankets. Unfortunately, *Ladies Home Journal* published a story in 1945 about his baby tender (which was later marketed under the names "Heir Conditioner" and "Aircrib," but failed in the marketplace) and the public was aghast at this heartless scientist who kept his baby in a box. Despite the fact Deborah Skinner grew up to be a successful and happy artist living in England, urban legends reported that she suffered from a mental illness, sued her father for abuse, and committed suicide. Every few years Skinner has to make another comment in the media, just to prove she's still alive, and not psychotic.

Several Skinner detractors take offense to the idea that his experiments with rats and pigeons have any sort of connection with human beings. His controversial book, *Walden Two*, about how a utopian society of people living under his operant principles thrives in the 1940s, came under particular attack, especially by the religious right, claiming that his conclusions preclude human choice or freedom. He's been accused of championing totalitarianism, even though he claimed his book was rhetorical and fictional. Despite his detractors, Skinner remains probably the most popular psychologist since Freud, and he was a tenured professor at Harvard for most of his life.

And apparently, the DeGroots were not among his detractors. The reference to B.F. Skinner in Candle's monologue immediately conjures up images of the Skinner Box, and lends credence to Jack's theory that the Swan station is nothing more than a social experiment. However, Desmond's situation is not exactly analogous to Skinner's experiment on operant behavior in rats. Where the rat was trained essentially to press a button so something good would happen, Desmond has not learned through his environment to press the button; he's been instructed to do so. He doesn't receive any positive reinforcement by hitting the button; he does so out of fear that if he *doesn't* hit the button, something bad might happen to him. If it *is* an experiment the Hanso Corporation is putting Desmond through, it's definitely based in Skinner's research, but it departs from it a lot, as well.

2.4   Everybody Hates Hugo

Original air date: October 12, 2005
Written by: Edward Kitsis, Adam Horowitz
Directed by: Alan Taylor
Guest cast: DJ Qualls (Johnny), Lillian Hurst (Carmen Reyes), Marguerite Moreau (Starla), Billy Ray Gallion (Randy), Raj K. Bose (Pakistani Store Clerk)

Flashback: Hurley
Hurley panics when Jack puts him in charge of the new batch of food, and through a flashback, we see why.

Where "Numbers" showed us the humorous and fantastical downside to Hurley's big lottery win (super bad luck), "Everybody Hates Hugo" is about the more realistic pitfall of winning a lot of money at once. Suddenly coming into

The set of Mr. Cluck's Chicken Shack is actually a Popeye's Chicken in Oahu. (RYAN OZAWA)

money when you've never had any can be a dangerous and unhappy place to be, and Hurley's flashback takes us back to the moment when it became known that he was officially rich. As has been documented in countless cases, lottery winners often find their lives changing in negative ways, not positive ones. Family members expect a cut of the winnings, and friends wonder why the winner isn't picking up the check every time they go out. More importantly, they feel like they no longer have anything in common with the winner, and the relationship becomes uneasy. Before Hurley's lottery win he spent his time in record stores, worked at a fast food chicken hut, and hung out with his friend Johnny. He was a regular guy. But after the win, he's no longer just trying to make ends meet like all the other regular guys. Money is no longer an issue. If winners can suddenly afford new cars, large mansions, and basically anything they want, what do they have in common with their friends who rent apartments, work at part-time jobs, and struggle to make ends meet every month? Eventually, friends distance themselves, preferring to hang around with people who understand what it's like not to have money.

So now Hurley finds himself in a similar situation, when Jack makes the inexplicable decision to put him — the one guy the others have suspected of hoarding food because of his size — in charge of the food storage area. Hurley finds himself faced with this new "windfall" of food, and worries that the others will take a

DJ Qualls, who plays Hurley's friend Johnny, waits between takes of the episode. (RYAN OZAWA)

similar view of him that his friend Johnny did: that Hurley thinks he is too good for everyone else. Like so many other people on the island, Hurley worries that what happened to him before will repeat itself on the island, just like Sayid was forced to torture someone, or Michael had Walt taken from him, or Locke almost lost the use of his legs. However, his "solution" of how to deal with it is so off the wall, it makes one wonder if he was let out of the psych ward a little too early.

Meanwhile, the rafties find themselves in a compromising position, being thrown into a pit, held at gunpoint, and questioned. They soon discover that their prison wardens are not the mysterious Others, after all, but the people in the tail section of the plane who crashed on the other side of the island. Ana Lucia is the leader of the group, and comes off as a hard-core bitch. The writers (and Michelle Rodriguez herself) have almost made her too over-the-top offensive, especially after we saw her being so nice to Jack in his flashback. Libby is quiet but kind, Eko is mysterious, and Bernard is . . . *the* Bernard. The ending of this episode is wonderful, and answers a mystery that has quietly sat in the background of the show since the first episode.

The fate of the guys on the raft is no longer a secret, when Claire discovers evidence that their raft didn't make it very far. When she carries her find over to Sun, the result has the opposite effect as the revelation on the other side of the island — while we anticipate the reunion of one married couple, Sun believes she'll never see her husband again. Like Locke, however, she believes the most important thing everyone has is hope, and she refuses to take that away from anyone, taking measures to keep her discovery from anyone else.

A well-written episode, with a lot of humorous dialogue and roller-coaster emotion.

Highlight: Hurley and Johnny singing strange lyrics to "You All Everybody" by *Suck* Shaft.

Did You Notice?:

- This is the first episode where Adewale Akinnuoye-Agbaje is listed not as a guest star, but a cast member.
- During the opening dream sequence, Walt's face is on the side of the milk carton. It's interesting that even though he doesn't know Walt is missing, that little detail ended up in Hurley's dream. Also, Jin has the bruise on his cheek from where he's been hurt on the other side of the island, even though Hurley couldn't have known that, either.
- Hurley's irritating boss Randy was Locke's irritating boss Randy in "Walkabout," the guy who made fun of Locke for booking the walkabout tour in Australia.
- Watch how many times Jorge Garcia looks like he's trying not to laugh in his scenes with DJ Qualls.
- In the record store, Drive Shaft's CDs are found under "One Hit Wonders."
- This is the first time a flashback is structured to jump-cut back and forth between the present and the past, with a voiceover from one appearing in the other.
- Charlie and Claire eat the real peanut butter exactly the same way they ate the imaginary peanut butter.

Interesting Fact: Johnny's comment, "Not only will I stay gold, Ponyboy," is a reference from the 1983 film, *The Outsiders*, and the book by S.E. Hinton by the same name, where the character Johnny tells Ponyboy to "Stay gold." The comment is in response to a Robert Frost poem that Ponyboy quotes to him, "Nothing Gold Can Stay." Also, a lot of fans complained near the end of the first season that Jorge Garcia wasn't losing any weight, but if the actor lost a lot of weight, how could he still do the flashback episodes?

Nitpick: How did Claire find such perfectly fitting non-maternity clothes? She wouldn't have packed them herself, because she probably would have expected to be using maternity clothes for a few weeks beyond the baby's birth, and she wouldn't have been staying in L.A. very long. That said, she only gave birth to Aaron five days ago, yet she's down to a perfectly flat, toned stomach, and walking around with no after-effects of the birth, so maybe she did pack them herself, relying on the magic of television to help her through it.

Oops: The island humidity is doing a number on Jorge Garcia's hair. Watch how from scene to scene it's alternately long and flat-looking, but in the next shot it'll be shorter and curlier, then long and flat, short and curly. Also, considering Hurley was so terrified of the dynamite that he kept at a safe distance during the excavation and that he wouldn't volunteer to bring any back, it seems highly unlikely, and far too convenient, that he went back to get some. When would he have had the time? In the actual timeline, they made their trek to the *Black Rock* only the day before, and Hurley followed everyone back to the caves afterwards. He was on the beach with Sayid when Jack came to show him the hatch, and that was only a few hours earlier than the opening of this episode. So when could he have possibly gotten any dynamite?

4 8 15 16 23 42: When Kate wakes up Hurley from his dream, the timer is at 3:44. The lottery announcer says this is the **16**th week with no winner. Randy accuses Hurley of eating **8** pieces of chicken while on the job. Sayid says the wall between the hatch and the magnetic anomaly is **8** to 10 feet thick. Libby says there were **23** survivors in their group.

It's Just a Flesh Wound: To add to Sawyer's worsening gunshot wound, Ana Lucia throws a rock at Sawyer's head, punches him, and steps on his wound.

Any Questions?:
- Was Hurley in the psych ward for some sort of paranoia?
- Why did Claire and Shannon think Sun should decide what to do with the bottle? If they think it means the rafties are dead, that puts a lot of pressure on a widow.
- How did Randy go from a Mr. Cluck's to a box company in Tustin? We know that a meteorite hit the restaurant, and that Hurley is the owner of Locke's box company. Did he offer him a job at the company? Why? Because he took pity on him, or because he wanted him far away?

Music/Bands: When Hurley is imagining himself eating everything in the bunker, we hear Slim Smith's "My Conversation" (*Rain from the Skies*). As Hurley and Rose take inventory, you can hear The Drifters' "Up on the Roof" (*The Very Best of the Drifters*). The song playing in Johnny's van is Billy Joel's "Easy Money" (*An Innocent Man*).

Jorge Garcia (Hugo "Hurley" Reyes)

He wanted the part of Sawyer, but as the affable, slightly bumbling Hurley, Jorge (pronounced Hor-hey) Garcia landed the role that has come to be a favorite of *Lost* fans and helped make him a star.

Garcia came to the attention of J.J. Abrams through a role he played on the HBO comedy series *Curb Your Enthusiasm* in which he played a drug dealer who completely stole the show. But beyond landing an audition, it wasn't clear where Garcia might fit in to the nascent show. Like several cast members, Garcia auditioned for a role that did not exist — initially the role of Hurley was envisioned as a redneck much older than Garcia. Despite the confusion over what he might do on the new drama, Garcia was thrilled with the chance to appear on *Lost*.

"It was pretty exciting. When I got cast there was no script yet, but I knew it was a J.J. Abrams and that it was being filmed in Hawaii and that's really all I needed to hear," he said while the first season was filming.

Garcia was born in 1973 in Nebraska, and is of Chilean descent. He was raised in the Orange County suburb of San Juan Capistrano. A huge music fan (which the writers worked into his character by giving him the CD player), Garcia began taking acting lessons in 1997. It didn't take him long to begin finding work in commercials, some of which garnered the new actor some attention.

"I had a commercial for Jack in the Box, which got some attention because they ran it all the time on local television," Garcia says. "I was the guy with the paper hat that said 'jack' on it who got free curly fries because everyone thought he was Jack. It was cool — that was, like, my first taste of street recognition."

Movies followed, including parts in *Good Humor Man* and *Little Athens*, as well as work on 13 episodes of the comedy *Becker*. But after bouncing around on several bit parts, Garcia's star has risen with *Lost*. His large size makes him one of the most recognizable *Lost* actors away from the set.

Responding to criticism that Hurley wasn't dropping enough weight despite being stranded on an island, Garcia has lost 30 pounds for the second season. He chalks up the weight loss more to his ability now to eat healthier. "I can afford to not live on rum and burritos and take better care of myself. It's not like I'm doing a specific regimen. Besides, there were enough people who were waiting for my character to lose weight as a result of being stranded on a desert island."

Garcia developed friendships with other cast members, including Dominic Monaghan and Matthew Fox. Famously, Garcia has participated in Fox's ritual of skinny-dipping. "I was still taking my clothes off and Jorge went right by me. A bolt of naked lightning," Fox says.

In the end, it is Garcia's heavyset, average Joe appearance that makes him work as Hurley, says executive producer Damon Lindelof. "The thing that Jorge brought to Hurley is something we could never have written," Lindelof says. "He's the everyman. He's funny without trying to be funny. On an island full of people with dark secrets, Jorge just brought a sense of fun and lightness that created real balance not just in the cast, but in the show. More importantly, he's such a genuinely sweet guy that it oozes into his performance and has the effect of everyone rooting for him."

Everybody loves Hurley. How could you not?

(ALBERT L. ORTEGA)

As for Garcia, he appreciates Hurley's secondary status among the cast and the way the character fits into *Lost*'s intricate plotlines. "I think there's a cool aspect to the fact that Hurley isn't being a villain or a hero. He's just a regular guy. I think that has an appeal to it."

The I-Ching and the Dharma Symbol

The Dharma symbol is comprised of an octagon with eight variations of three lines. The ancient Chinese text, the *I Ching*, is comprised of 64 hexagrams, which are various combinations of the basic eight symbols that are all used in the Dharma symbol:

≡ Three unbroken lines represents Heaven
☷ Three broken lines represents Earth
☲ Broken flanked by unbroken represents Fire
☵ Unbroken flanked by broken represents Water
☶ Unbroken and two broken represents Mountain
☴ Broken and two unbroken represents Wind
☳ Two broken and an unbroken represents Thunder
☱ Two unbroken and one broken represents Lake

When the sections are put together to form a hexagram, the combinations take on a greater meaning and give warnings and advice to the "seeker" who is looking for guidance from them. To read them, you start at the top and read down through all six lines. Then imagine turning the octagon so the next group to the right of the first comes up on top, and you read that hexagram down, until you've gone all the way around and have read eight hexagrams. In the Dharma Initiative symbol, we could assume that the hexagrams are all messages to the people working within the Dharma Initiative, starting with the first hexagram at the top:

(☲☵) Fire above, Water on the bottom, which is interesting, because an upcoming episode is called "Fire + Water." This combination (hexagram 64, the last in the *I Ching*) is called "Transition (Before Completion)." It warns the seeker to be patient and to stay on the right path without dispute (a possible warning to Locke).

(☷☶) Earth above, Mountain on the bottom. This is hexagram 15, and it means Modesty or Humbling, and urges the seeker to join in equal partnerships with people (Locke and Jack should have paid more attention to this hexagram).

(☱☳) Lake above, Thunder below, which is hexagram 17, Following. At this stage, things are going well, and the seeker is told to enjoy the present without trying to change anything.

(≡☱) Heaven above, Lake on the bottom, which is hexagram 10, Treading (Conduct). The seeker is told to tread carefully and to act with humility.

(☵☲) Water above, Fire below, which is hexagram 63 Order (After

Completion). There is good fortune, it says, and it's now time to add up what is good and what is bad and maintain that balance.

(⚏) Thunder above, Earth below, which is hexagram 16, Enthusiasm. This one celebrates that everything is the way it should be, but that the seeker shouldn't become arrogant about their good fortune.

(⚏) Mountain above, Wind below, which is hexagram 18, Corruption (Decay). It warns that an important decision must be made, and the seeker must take care before making his/her decision, or they will fail.

(⚏) Wind above, Heaven on the bottom, which is "The Taming Power of the Small," hexagram 9. It urges the seeker to preserve his/her energy, and to show patience and flexibility.

The *I Ching* is not an easy book to explain, and these hexagrams might seem confusing, but understanding what they are gives us a tiny insight into the warnings and messages that the Dharma Initiative supposedly follow — and how often the survivors ignore these warnings and do the opposite. It's also interesting to note that there are four trigrams on the flag of South Korea, where Sun and Jin are from.

2.5   . . . And Found

Original air date: October 19, 2005
Written by: Carlton Cuse, Damon Lindelof
Directed by: Stephen Williams
Guest cast: Tony Lee (Jae Lee), June Kyoko Lu (Mrs. Paik), Kimberley Joseph (Cindy), Rain Chung (Mr. Kim), Kim Kim (Mrs. Shin), Robert Dahey (Poor Man), Josiah D. Lee (Tai Soo), Tomiko Okhee Lee (Mrs. Lee)

Flashback: Sun and Jin
When Sun loses her wedding ring, she fears it might be a sign that something has happened to Jin, and she and Jin both remember when they first met.

In both "House of the Rising Sun" and ". . . In Translation," we receive a glimpse of Sun and Jin's marriage, but their very different backgrounds were never explained. How did they meet? Why was this wealthy daughter of a powerful and dangerous man coupled with a poor son of an even poorer fisherman? In this

In "…And Found," we finally find out how Jin and Sun first met. (CHRISTINA RADISH)

episode, we get another glimpse into their lives before they met, although how they ended up becoming a couple will remain a mystery for now. In Jin's previous flashback, we saw his immense guilt for denying his father's existence, and in this episode, we see that even when he was in the midst of doing it, he still felt terrible about it. The irony is, the more Jin tries to reject his origins, the more they come back to haunt him. As he stands before his potential employer, pretending to be sophisticated, he is instead subjected to ridicule, shame, and humiliation, and reminded that no matter how much he wants to deny who he is and where he came from, he'll never escape it.

Sun, on the other hand, is from a life of privilege. She rolls her eyes as her mother sets her up on another matchmaking date, but Sun never comes off as a rich spoiled brat. Instead, she's far more interested in the intellectual whom she meets and who has a university background like herself. But just as Jin feels limited by where he came from, so does Sun feel trapped by her life, as she sees her future unfolding before her: marriage, babies, death. She'll never be able to use that art history degree, because her father would rather see her dead than working for an art gallery. Jin longs for the same freedoms that Sun desires, but he is restricted by lack of money. A poor man and a wealthy woman amount to the same trapped animal.

While Sun frantically searches for the wedding ring she has lost, Jin joins Eko in a search for Michael, who has suddenly disappeared on a desperate search for his son. Although one of the first encounters Jin and Eko have involves hitting each other in the face, Eko ultimately has an immense amount of respect for Jin. On the island, money means nothing, but integrity means a lot, and Jin abandoning the group out of a loyalty to his friend resonates with Eko. Jin's background growing up in a fishing village has made him one of the most valuable survivors on the island, whereas in Korea, it was something he was ashamed of. Notice also how the Tailies treat Jin better than the rest of the Lostaways ever did.

The first season of *Lost* was a perfect depiction of the title — everyone was lost, thrown terrifyingly free of their homes, their friends and family, and most importantly, themselves. But in the second season, more and more people are starting to settle in to the island as if they're here for the long-term, and they look to each other as friends. For Jin, Sawyer, and Michael, returning to their original landing spot is akin to coming "home." This season has more of a personal edge, with survivors finding themselves, and each other. And in this episode, we see how Jin and Sun originally found each other, at the very moment both had given up. Jin was leaving behind his chance to become more than the son of a fisherman, and Sun had just lost the man whose presence promised her a way out of the stifling life she saw before her. Just as Locke tells Sun she'll find her ring when she stops looking for it, so too do Jin and Sun find each other when they least expected to. Perhaps this message is one for Michael, too — maybe the only way to find Walt is to stop looking for him.

Highlight: The look on Yunjin Kim's and Jorge Garcia's faces when he tells Sun that his dog once "crapped out" $1.35 in nickels. It looks like they're both trying not to laugh.

Did You Notice?:

- Ana Lucia splits up everyone to go out into the jungle, and she joins up Eko and Cindy; Libby and Michael; and Jin, Ana, and Bernard; but she doesn't mention who Sawyer will be going with.
- Jin's previous job was at the Asiana, which, spoken quickly, sounds like Oceanic.
- His new interview is for the Seoul Gateway Hotel, which sounds like "Soul" Gateway.
- The conversation between Locke and Sun is one of the few times we see the old "Locke as philosopher" from season 1 again.
- Poor Daniel Dae Kim. He's been wearing that handcuff since the beginning of the first season. That's got to be annoying as an actor, especially in the hot temperatures of Hawaii.
- The final flashback is the first time two characters have the same memory.
- If you go back to "Everybody Hates Hugo" to the scene where Sun buries

the bottle, she has her ring on when she sets the bottle in the hole, and after she covers it with sand the ring is noticeably gone.

Interesting Fact: The current population of Namhae, the area where Jin grew up, is roughly 54,000 people. However, 40 years ago the population was more than double that, indicating people are leaving or growing old and dying.

Oops: The information on Jin's resumé is wrong. It states his last name is Kwan (it's Kwon), he's 30 years old, and born in 1974. If that were the case, then this scene would be set in 2004, but he was getting on the plane with Sun in 2004, and they were married four years before the plane crash, according to Sun in an upcoming episode ("The Hunting Party"). The mistake caused some fans to speculate that the crash happened in 2009, but the writers have admitted the resumé was a production error.

4 8 15 16 23 42: Sun tells Claire it's been **4** days since the raft left. Hurley tells a story involving $1.35 in nickels, which is 27 nickels (**23** + **4**). The matchmaker tells Sun that Jae's family owns 12 other hotels (**8** + **4**).

It's Just a Flesh Wound: Jin punches Eko in the mouth, and Eko headbutts him in return. Jin is gored in the leg by a boar and knocked down a hill.

Lost in Translation: Ana Lucia and Bernard are fishing, and Ana tells Jin that if he wants to eat, he should help them. He snorts, "Fishing style," as if to make fun of what they're doing, and says, "Doing it your way, we'll all end up starving to death."

Any Questions?:

- How is the Laundromat schedule being worked out? Why are Claire and Sun washing the clothes on the beach?
- When Jin asks Eko if he has a wife, Eko replies, "Worse." What does he mean by that?
- Who was Goodwin?

 The Third Policeman by Flann O'Brien (1967)

"'Your talk,'" I said, "'is surely the handiwork of wisdom because not one word of it do I understand.'" This line, uttered by the narrator of *The Third Policeman* to one of the policemen, in many ways sums up *Lost* itself.

In a September article in the *Chicago Tribune*, Craig Wright, who cowrote "Orientation" with Javier Grillo-Marxuach, told fans that in an upcoming episode a copy of *The Third Policeman* would figure prominently, and hinted that "whoever goes out and buys the book will have a lot more ammunition in their back pocket as they theorize about the show. They will have a lot more to speculate about — and, no small thing, they will have read a great book." Was Wright telling the truth or was he just trying to give kudos to one of his favorite reads? He certainly wasn't lying about one thing: *The Third Policeman* is a great book.

The book opens with the sinister line, "Not everybody knows how I killed old Phillip Mathers, smashing his jaw in with my spade . . ." The story is about the unnamed narrator, whose parents died when he was young, and who discovers the ramblings of an insane philosopher named de Selby. He devours everything he can find about de Selby, who believed in some ridiculous notions, such as that the world is sausage-shaped; that night is just a result of the dirt in the air that had accumulated through invisible volcanic eruptions; that houses and our desire for "interiors" are to blame for the degeneration of human culture; that sleep is simply a series of fits and heart attacks. The narrator meets a man named John Divney, who runs a bar, and together they run it for four years in the hopes that eventually they'll make enough money that the narrator can fund the publication of his own critical book on de Selby, which he believes will blow all the others out of the water. Unfortunately, the bar is a money-loser, so after four years, they come up with the quicker solution of killing Phillip Mathers, a local man, and stealing his money. They meet him in the road, kill him, and while the narrator disposes of the body, Divney disappears, and reappears later to say that he's hidden the box in a very safe place. For the next three years the narrator never lets Divney out of his sight for a minute, until Divney finally takes him to the place where he's hidden the box. Divney says he'll wait out by the road so the narrator can go into the house to retrieve it. When the narrator is in the house, a strange feeling comes over him, he discovers the box is missing, and there is Mathers, sitting in the very room with him. Suddenly the narrator's soul, whom he calls Joe, appears, and begins having conversations with him while Mathers talks to him.

The narrator, obviously discomfited, leaves and goes to a nearby parish, where he sees a very strange-looking building. There's a badge on it denoting it a police station, but he thinks it's the strangest one he's seen. He goes in to report his watch missing, and the sergeant behind the desk keeps asking him over and over if it's really a watch he's missing, and is he sure it's not a bicycle? From this point on, the conversations between the narrator and the two policemen at the station become curiouser and curiouser, as he descends into their strange little Wonderland where bicycles take on the personalities of their riders (and vice versa); where the unseen third policeman only leaves notes about lever settings on their desks the next morning; where the one policeman, MacCruiskeen, creates divine little music boxes that get tinier and tinier until one is no longer sure they're even there; and where the policeman speak in strange idioms. In other words, he seems to have entered a walking world of de Selby, without realizing that the man he revered so much expounded the same theories that are now making him so uncomfortable.

Eventually, the policemen suspect the narrator of the murder of Mathers, and hold him at the police station until his execution (the preparation for which is its own comedy of errors). MacCruiskeen and the sergeant tell the narrator about eternity, and they take him there. After stepping through a hatch and descending into the earth via elevator, they open a door and he finds a series of tunnels. At first he doesn't believe he's in eternity, but they tell him to go to the end of a tunnel and walk through the doorway, and when he does, they're standing right there, proving it's the same tunnel over and over. They explain to him that it's called eternity because no one ever grows older here. They also show him a receptacle of "omnium" where he can have any of his earthly desires, such as gold, money, a gun. He asks for all of the above, and, assuming he's just figured his way out of being executed, he makes his way to the lift, until they explain that he cannot actually enter the lift unless he's the same weight as when he got out. Devastated, he watches as they throw his riches into the fire, and he gloomily rides back up to the surface.

On the day of his execution, the policemen are suddenly called away when the lever in eternity misfires, and to his astonishment, he discovers they've left the cell open, with a bicycle near it. He finds a house with a light on, and discovers the third policeman living in it, and the policeman unmistakably has Mathers' face. He calls himself Policeman Fox, and he seems nice enough that the narrator finally gets up the nerve to ask him if he knows where the black cashbox went. Fox explains that the box contains omnium, and the narrator's wildest wishes have come true. He rushes to his house, and once there he sees Divney looking much older, balder, and fatter, and he has a wife and children. The narrator, perplexed, enters the house, and Divney falls onto the floor in a panic, begging the narrator to get away from him and sputtering that the narrator is dead. He confesses that 16 years ago, when the narrator went into the house to find the cashbox and reached under the floorboards to find it, Divney had planted a bomb that had instantly killed him. The narrator thought he'd been walking through a police station for a few days, but he'd actually been in hell for 16 years. Divney suddenly dies of a heart attack, the narrator steps outside, Divney joins him, and they begin walking up the path. They come upon a strange-looking house that appears to be a police station, and they walk in. The narrator has no recollection of any of this happening before, and we realize he's doomed to repeat this same mad play for eternity.

The Third Policeman is a brilliant book (I urge you to read it, because there is far more going on in it than I've outlined here) and it actually has a lot to do with *Lost*. Hurley's numbers are rampant in the book, and show up at prominent moments. For example, the narrator was 16 when he discovered de Selby; he tended the bar with Divney for 4 years before killing Mathers; the Sergeant tells the narrator that Fox went crazy after spending the 23rd of June with MacCruiskeen; Fox tells him he has 4 ounces of omnium; he's been dead for 16 years. The narrator has a wooden leg, and coincidentally seems to keep coming across other people with wooden legs, the same way the paths of the characters on *Lost* kept crossing before they boarded Oceanic Flight 815. Also, the curious scene where MacCruiskeen begins laying out his music boxes on the table for the narrator, with each getting progressively tinier and tinier until they are no longer visible, echoes the scene at the beginning of "Man of Science, Man of Faith," where Desmond sets up the hall of mirrors to see the events happening several feet away from him. It could also symbolize the vast overlapping that happens in the characters lives. Some are obvious (Sawyer talked to Jack's father), others are less obvious (Locke's mother may have known Hurley), and still others are invisible to us as of yet, but could become more prominent later on. The narrator is a bit of a con artist, like Sawyer, but in the end he's the one who gets conned (much like Sawyer). The sergeant's lesson on atomic theory basically suggests that atoms can move from one being to another, and that's how people become part bicycle and bicycles become part people. While the sergeant is as whacked as de Selby, in many ways the island *has* come to life, and one wonders if it's because of the people on it.

More importantly, the book makes references that could apply to the hatch. De Selby states that life is a series of brief experiences with breaks in between, and life in the hatch is broken into 108-minute segments. Every day the third policeman goes out to "eternity" and takes readings from a lever, and enters them into a notebook. His actions seem as futile as Locke's were for most of the season, and the policeman's silly little "daily readings" that don't seem to get him any closer to eternity can be interpreted as a satire on religion. When the readings begin to go haywire, the policemen fear there's going to be an explosion of some kind, just like Locke fears something terrible could happen if he doesn't enter the numbers faithfully. The whole idea of omnium being something that "some people call God," and being inside every single thing, again ties to the beliefs of the island: that everything is interconnected and that there's some higher being running things, or so Locke believes. At one point in the novel, the sergeant takes the narrator to MacCruiskeen's room and they discover a large map on the ceiling — a similar thing will happen later this season on *Lost*. When the policemen take the narrator to see "eternity," it's a doorway that is set far off in the jungle, and when they open it they peer down into a long tunnel, just as Locke did in "Man of Science, Man of Faith." The sergeant tells the narrator a strange story about a man who went up in a balloon and came back completely mad, a story that has some significance later this season as well. The narrator keeps mentioning his missing gold watch, which his "soul" reminds him he doesn't actually have, a hint that he's either lost it, or when you're dead, you don't need it. Not only does Michael say a couple of times in the show that he doesn't need a watch, but all of the characters have a feeling of loss when they arrive on the island, only to discover they aren't really missing anything.

The tiny little flash of this book on the show — in "Orientation," Desmond grabs it off his bed and stuffs it into a backpack before leaving the hatch — has been a massive boon to its small publisher. Says Chad Post, the associate director of *Third Policeman* publisher Dalkey Archive, in an e-mail in June 2006, "Since we published *The Third Policeman* in 1999 we've sold 35,000 copies — 20,000 of them in the last seven months. We did find out that *TTP* was going to be on the show about six weeks ahead of time, so we printed 10,000 copies in hopes of selling 8,000 just because of the show. When we sold those 8,000 in less than a week, we rushed it back to press and did another 12,000 or so. Luckily there was never a point when the book was out of stock, and we still have a decent number of copies in our warehouse.

"We sold just over 15,000 copies in the weeks surrounding the initial airing of 'Orientation.' When it aired in Ireland and the UK, we saw another spike in sales, bringing our total sales of *TTP* to 19,368 since the time we learned that the book was going to be on *Lost*. Even for a commercial press this would be a pretty impressive spike for a backlist title, especially a literary book by a dead author."

2.6   Abandoned

Original air date: November 9, 2005
Written by: Elizabeth Sarnoff
Directed by: Adam Davidson
Guest cast: Lindsay Frost (Sabrina), François Guétary (Philippe), Ian Somerhalder (Boone)

Flashback: Shannon

Shannon sees Walt in her tent, but no one will believe her, and she recalls a time when she was a completely different person than she is now.

Shannon Rutherford has been portrayed as a prima donna from the beginning of season 1, refusing to help out, whining and crying constantly, clinging to Boone and Sayid, and somehow painting her toenails on a sandy beach, the skillfulness of which appears to go unnoticed by everyone else. (That was only partly sarcasm.) She's a major character, and Maggie Grace is a full-fledged cast member, yet she's the only one yet to have a flashback. When we finally see that flashback in "Abandoned," it's like watching a different person entirely. Shannon used to be an aspiring ballerina who was good with kids and had a close relationship with her father, until he died. Her witch of a stepmother is worse than Shannon's ever been on the show, and we finally realize why she's been acting the way she has. That said, her behavior still seems a little out of line with what we're seeing, which only happened about two years before the crash (she says she's 18 in the flashback, and 20 on the island).

This was an episode about trust and fear of abandonment. Shannon has lost a lot in her life — her father, Boone (when he went to work for his mother), her dreams, her money, and ultimately, her self-respect. Now that she's seen Walt standing before her and Sayid refuses to believe her, she's worried she's going to lose him, too. Just as she needed her stepmother to believe in her desire to become a dancer, she needs Sayid to believe in her. With him not trusting her, she feels alone again.

Speaking of not trusting, Charlie is completely strange and out of character in this episode, as he blathers on to Locke about what a useless mother he thinks Claire is. Aaron is exactly one week old, and Charlie somehow thinks Claire should be an old hand at this. Considering she's cutting Charlie's hair, nursing Aaron with no problems, finding time to go out for walks, and seems relatively

In "Abandoned," Shannon's flashback shows us a different side of the character . . . a likeable one. (ALBERT L. ORTEGA)

stable, she's doing a pretty damn good job. Her frustration with other people seeming to know more about parenting than she does is understandable and common, but it's certainly not Charlie's place to be telling someone else that she was going to give Aaron up for adoption, essentially questioning her devotion to the baby. Locke, on the other hand, shows a surprising amount of knowledge about babies, and he is kind and patient with Claire. But when he discovers Charlie's secret, he can no longer trust the person he thought he'd saved.

Finally, Ana Lucia finally opens up about why the Tailies are so scared of the jungle, and suddenly the Others sound even creepier than we already thought they were. After losing so many of the original 23 survivors (there are only five Tailies left), they are also dealing with fear of abandonment. As they move through the jungle, the unthinkable happens without warning, and viewers realize how quick and dangerous the Others really are. They're not always a bunch of goons loudly pulling up in a motorboat. The Tailies are dealing with trust issues of their own, and the two camps have to work together to make it through the jungle to the other side of the island.

However, any trust that might have built up is suddenly shattered in the final, horrific moments of the episode. As the rain beats down on them, Ana Lucia makes a deadly mistake, and she makes an instant enemy of the one who faces her.

Highlight: Getting to see Boone again, however momentarily.
Did You Notice?:
- At the beginning of the episode, Sayid sees a gun as something that will protect Shannon.

- Cindy, the Australian Tailie, was the flight attendant who gave Jack the extra liquor on the plane.
- Shannon's father was the person killed in the accident that temporarily paralyzed Jack's future wife, Sarah.
- As the doctor is giving the grim news to Shannon and her stepmother, Jack walks behind them.
- Locke's comment to Claire is an interesting one: "Babies like the feeling of being constricted. It's not until we're older that we develop the desire to be free." He could be commenting on the hatch and how constrictive that is, or on the island itself. Yet at the same time, on the island, away from civilization, they are finally free, but no one likes it. More importantly, the Bible states that Jesus was swaddled. As Locke hands Aaron back to Claire, the mise-en-scène looks like a nativity scene, with three castaways in the background like shepherds or Wise Men.
- In "Confidence Man," as Jack is putting pressure on the artery that Sayid just ruptured, Sawyer tells Jack that if the tables were turned, he'd watch him die. Sawyer says the same thing to Michael when he tells him he would have left him behind. It's clearly a tactic he uses to make people hate him.
- As the Tailies climb the hill while passing the stretcher with Sawyer from person to person, we hear the exact music that played in "Pilot, Part 2," when Boone, Shannon, Kate, Sayid, Sawyer, and Charlie are climbing the hill looking for a place to test the radio. Just as that scene depicted a group of strangers working together to an end, so does this scene.

Interesting Fact: The previous week, the preview for this episode said someone would die, and that this would be the episode everyone would talk about for the rest of the season, leading many fans to think it would be Sawyer, especially when he passes out in Michael's arms. Naveen Andrews wasn't thrilled with the turn of events from the end of this episode, calling Shannon's death "brutal and completely unnecessary. I fail to understand, actually, why they feel this need to get rid of people."

Nitpick: There are some pretty big inconsistencies between Shannon's backstory and the story we saw in "Man of Science, Man of Faith." In the first episode of the season, Jack rushes into the emergency room and is told that Sarah's tire blew out, and she jumped the divider and went head-on with an SUV. The driver of the SUV, Shannon's father, needs to be intubated and his breathing is becoming shallow, but Jack chooses to work on Sarah instead, and Shannon's father dies. In

Abandoned Whisper Transcript

When the Tailies get to the top of the cliff and lose Cindy, they hear whispering:

Who's this in the woods?
Sawyer
Ana
I'm in someone's dream
Ich Weiss Nicht (*German for "I don't know"*)
She's heavy
Black Rock
Bring the boy
I'm in someone's dream

Look in the eyes, right?
Do you see her? (*or possibly "Lucia"*)
It's the brothers that help us
I can see eye to eye
Sawyer
Did she see?
Bossy, eh missy?
I'm in someone's dream
I know it all, I know it all
It's the eyes (*or possibly "Lucia"*)
I can see eye to eye
I'm in someone's dream

I know it all, I know it all
Do you see her? (*or possibly "Lucia"*)
I can see eye to eye
Did she see?
Shannon
Hide behind me
Bossy, eh missy?
I'm in someone's dream
I know it all (*repeated in background*)
Under the eye (*or possibly "Eye to eye"*)
It's the eyes (*or possibly "Lucia"*)
I can see eye to eye
She's bossy
I'm in someone's dream

The whispering starts in the jungle as Shannon and Sayid see Walt, and continues as Shannon runs toward Ana Lucia:

Relax dude
She likes the guy
She's coming

I don't know if I can run, but I can (*or can't*) yell
Shannon sighs (*Scream*)
Dying sucks
Hurry up
Shh

She likes this guy
Dying sucks
Hi sis
Here she comes, here she comes
His mouth
She drives me crazy
Hurry up
I see eye to eye
I see . . .

Relax dude
She likes the guy
What do you think we should do?
She's coming
We should hide, we should run
Heard some voice
See ya (*or possibly "Lucia"*)
Hide the scope
Hurry up

this episode, when Shannon and her stepmother arrive at the hospital, the doctor explains that it was *Rutherford* who hit the SUV (meaning Sarah would have been the one driving it), and that he stopped breathing at the site of the accident, which isn't true. Are the doctors lying to cover up the fact Jack refused to save Rutherford, choosing the pretty blonde instead? Or did the writers on the show mix that up, in the same way they forgot who was supposed to be driving the SUV?

Oops: Claire marvels at the way Aaron has been sleeping while swaddled, yet when the camera shows his face moments after she's said he's still asleep, he's wide awake and looking at Locke.

4 8 15 16 23 42: Claire tells Locke the baby's been up for **8** hours straight. Shannon is **18** in the flashback. The Others took **12** of the Tailies (**8 + 4**). Shannon tells her stepmother that she'll be working **16**-hour days in New York. Eko tells Bernard he needs **4** sturdy sticks to make the stretcher for Sawyer.

It's Just a Flesh Wound: Shannon is shot in the chest.

Lost in Translation: Again in backwards speak, Walt says to Shannon, "They're coming, and they're close."

Any Questions?:

- A couple of episodes ago, Shannon was a ball of craziness, yet now she's totally stable. What's happened?
- If Sayid thought Shannon needed protection, why did he build her a shelter in an isolated spot away from everyone else?
- Were Sayid and Shannon able to find some kind of birth control among the wreckage?
- When Walt hugged Shannon at the end of "Exodus, Part 1," before boarding the raft, he didn't seem to see this incident in her future. Or did he? Is this why he gave Shannon the dog as protection?

Ashes to Ashes: Shannon Rutherford, 20, who had recently lost her step-brother, Boone Carlyle. Shannon was an aspiring dancer who had hit upon hard times. She is survived by her evil stepmother.

Music/Bands: When Nora comes to Shannon's apartment, the song playing is "Stay (Wasting Time)" by the Dave Matthews Band (*Before These Crowded Streets*).

Maggie Grace (Shannon Rutherford)

Few people knew Maggie Grace when she was cast as the damaged socialite Shannon Rutherford on *Lost*. But it was a role that she had been planning for all her life.

Grace was so certain of her ability to crack Hollywood's notoriously difficult exterior that she dropped out of high school and relocated to the city at the age of 16. "Ever since I was tiny, I knew I wanted to be an actress," she says. "I used to do as much theater as I could."

Luckily for her, some degree of success came quickly. She located an agent and never had to work second jobs to support herself. Some breaks in little-known movies followed. Grace managed to gain a role in the USA Network's *Murder in Greenwich* in 2002, followed by a second role in *Shop Club* the same year. A recurring role on the short-lived *Oliver Beene* followed before she was given the opportunity to audition for *Lost*. But when she arrived to read for the role of Shannon, she had little sense of the character or her background. "All [the casting agents] sent out to agencies was that she was a 20-something spoiled socialite, and that was it," says Grace. "I was always [cast] as the girl next door, so I am happy to be playing something else."

With Shannon, Grace found herself playing a dislikable character who was despised by many fans of the show. But, as is the case with each of *Lost*'s castaways, there was more to Shannon than immediately was apparent. "I think there are good reasons for her to act the way she acts," Grace says. "Once we dig into those issues, she becomes a little bit more sympathetic."

The difficult position of playing an unlikable character, as well as Grace's ability to add nuances to the role of Shannon, was recognized by those who were developing the show's characters. "Maggie has had the difficult task of playing the [mean character], which has

The beautiful Maggie Grace moved to Hollywood at age 16 to become a star.

(CHRISTINA RADISH)

sometimes been at the cost of the audience's sympathy," *Lost* executive producer Carlton Cuse says. "But her popularity is on a major upswing. We're going to see the event that made her the kind of person she is. I think the audience will find a new level of sympathy for her."

However, just as *Lost*'s audience glimpsed more of Shannon's back story, the character was killed in a jungle mix-up. Grace, who is now pursuing a career on the big screen, was "really awesome," about being written off of the show, says Cuse. Though she was aware of Shannon's fate heading into the season, she never let on to anyone that the character would meet an untimely end. "We had to negotiate her contract for this season, so she's known for a long time this was coming," Cuse said. "But she was nothing but absolutely professional and completely tight-lipped and completely a team player in terms of going to events, doing interviews, and participating as a full member of the cast without giving any indication that she was dying."

Still, there have been perks for playing the initially nasty blonde on TV's hottest show. "I get a lot of attention from teenage boys. A lot of stock boys are happy to see me," says Grace. "They get really nervous. I've never experienced that before."

2.7   The Other 48 Days

Original air date: November 16, 2005
Written by: Damon Lindelof, Carlton Cuse
Directed by: Eric Laneuville
Guest cast: Brett Cullen (Goodwin), Josh Randall (Nathan)

Flashback: The Tailies

We return to the day of the plane crash and see how the Tailies have fared throughout their 48 days on the island.

"Abandoned" left viewers with a brutal cliffhanger, and to make matters worse, the writers delay the conclusion of that story line to show us what the people on the other side of the island (the Tailies) have been up to while we've been focusing on our beloved castaways (the Losties). Yet despite making us wait for one more week to find out what Sayid is going to do, this episode is amazing, and worth the delayed satisfaction.

What makes this episode so remarkable is the stark contrast between these 48 days and the 48 days we've seen in detail on the Losties' side of the island. The writers have cleverly drawn parallels with each day, each major event, so we can see how differently the tail-section survivors have had to exist. Ana Lucia is the leader of this small tribe. She's bitter, angry, and tough, but has a soft spot for the children. The rest of the group follows her and rarely questions her leadership. Compare that to Jack, who also has his angry and bitter moments, but seems a little more in control of his emotions (while at times looking like he's a bomb about to explode), but whose leadership is called into question constantly. Ana is more cutthroat than Jack, but because their number is so small, perhaps her "followers" don't object to her ideas because they're scared of her. Also, their situation is more dire, and they desperately need a leader, and no one else has stepped up to offer. Jack woke up in the jungle when the plane crashed, and Ana emerged from the ocean.

Similarly, Eko is very much like Locke. In the second part of the pilot, Locke says to Walt, "Two sides, one light, one dark." Perhaps Eko is the dark-skinned side of Locke. He is a priest, and acts in a religious manner — after doing something that seems to cause him shame, he stops speaking for 40 days, just as Christ fasted in the desert for 40 days while being tempted by the devil.

The Losties have plenty of water in the beginning, and when it finally runs out they ultimately find a source of fresh water. They were blessed with being near the fuselage, which housed the food and drink cart and most of the overhead compartments, and they find the majority of the luggage that was in cargo. The Tailies have nothing. As we watch Ana's group deal with landing on the island, we realize this is *Survivor* without any rewards. Where the front section people had everything to survive quite comfortably in the short term, the tail section people are using every survival skill they've ever known and they're all wearing the same clothes they boarded the plane in. No one's giving themselves a pedicure over on this side.

Faced with a dire situation, people will often resort to the same basic solutions, and we see both sides doing similar things. Ana suggests they get off the beach, as Jack had. Nathan says they need to stay on the beach, like Sayid had said. Ana counters that there are satellites and the plane's black box, which were also mentioned on the other side (Shannon mentioned the black box, Charlie the satellites) but Sayid, the electronics expert, had debunked them both. There is no communications officer/electronics whiz/torturer over here.

There is also no doctor, and we see what happens when someone is seriously hurt and there's no one to give medical attention, illustrating just how lucky the other survivors were to have Jack. This instance shows again the contrast between Ana's leadership, which is often helpless and desperate, and Jack's, where he truly can be the hero everyone looks up to. He tries to save the marshal, whereas Ana caustically states there's nothing she can do, and they just wait for the poor guy to die. On this side of the island, they have no medical supplies, no doctor . . . and no gun.

They are also missing the "400 knives" and the hunter who goes with them, and no one in their group has the skills or the weaponry to go hunting for boar. Soon after crashing, however, the lack of food becomes the least of their problems. The Tailies encounter the Others the first night in, and keep losing people from their group. On the other side of the island, we haven't even heard the whispers of the Others at this point. Ana's realization that the enemy is among them sparks the paranoia that the Losties only feel when Hurley can't find Ethan's name on the manifest. Hurley had decided to do a census, a very civilized thing to do, but the Tailies don't have the luxury of doing something like that, and have to ground their worries in primitive gut feelings. The scenes where Ana puts Nathan in the hole and interrogates him (too bad they didn't have Sayid with them) are interesting in that they draw the viewer into the action. Is he really an Other? Or are the women being unnecessarily suspicious?

In only one instance does life seem easier for the tail section people than it does for the front, and that's when they discover their bunker. Locke finds his on the 17th day, and spends about 25 days trying to get into it, with axes, a trebuchet, and dynamite. The Tailies simply open a door and walk in. That said, even the front section survivors' *bunker* is far nicer than the one these people find, which is abandoned, dirty, cold, and has no amenities. A few days later, Bernard picks up the distress call that Boone had sent out, and we *finally* discover who the person was who answered him. Where Boone saw the answer as some ray of hope, Ana believes it's all a trick, and her pessimism makes them forge onward. When they discover Jin, the rest, as they say, is history, and the episode hurtles toward the same fateful conclusion of "Abandoned."

For the entire first season, we thought the Losties were living in hell, but they were in a paradise compared to these poor souls. This episode also sheds some light on the personalities of the individual characters, and we see Ana has a tough exterior, but she's vulnerable and scared when alone; Eko has a quiet but menacing exterior, yet can be very sympathetic and sincere. A terrific episode.

Highlight: The way the writers handle the scenes we've already seen at the end, by showing them as montage sequences flashing by us.

Did You Notice?:

- There are a lot of unkept promises on this island: Charlie told Claire he wouldn't let anything happen to Aaron just before Aaron was taken; Jack promised Boone he wouldn't die; and now Ana promises Emma she'll get her home soon.
- Goodwin sounds like "Good One."
- If you go back and watch "Deus Ex Machina," it's obviously not Sam Holland's voice on the radio, but that would be just a casting necessity, and not an error.
- You can always tell when someone is lying — they use a Canadian reference. Kate tells Ray she's from Canada in "Tabula Rasa"; Sawyer tells Jess he has an investor from Toronto in "Confidence Man"; Ethan tells Hurley he's from Ontario in "Solitary"; and Nathan tells Ana Lucia he's from Canada in this episode . . . but he's actually telling the truth.

Interesting Fact: Buddhists believe we spend 49 days in the "Bardo," or the time between reincarnations.

Nitpick: Ana Lucia fingers Goodwin as the culprit when she says he emerged from the jungle and wasn't even wet. Yet Bernard was also in the jungle, and he wasn't wet. Wouldn't it stand to reason that some of the survivors landed in the jungle if Bernard did?

Oops: On Day 7, Eko is still clean-shaven, yet he didn't have a razor. A month later, he'll have a full beard. In "Abandoned," Ana Lucia says that the Others took three people, and then took nine more of them three weeks later. Yet in this episode, we see they took the other nine less than two weeks later. You'd think that would be something that would be fresh in her mind.

4 8 15 16 23 42: Libby says if Donald dies, he'll be the **4**th to go. When they bury Donald, there are **8** graves. When Goodwin comes to talk to Ana he says he's worried about her, and she's had Nathan in the pit for **4** days. The only days we see that correspond with the numbers are days **15** and **23**.

It's Just a Flesh Wound: After the crash, Libby's shoulders look burned and scraped; Bernard has a head wound; Eko is barely scratched; Ana Lucia has a wound on her forehead from where a hard-shell case hit her in the head; Cindy doesn't appear to be hurt. Later, Eko hits Ana Lucia to trick Sawyer, Michael, and Jin.

Any Questions?:

- The little boy on the beach is holding a teddy bear that looks remarkably like the one Jin and Eko saw the boy from the Others dragging through the jungle on a rope. Were those two children we saw then the two children the Others took from the Tailies?

- Why doesn't anyone wonder where the chicken came from? Isn't it a little odd that on a deserted island there's a chicken running around?

- Was Goodwin really the one who made the list? Ana states that no one knew anyone's names the first night, so how could the names have been on there?

- Why was there a glass eye in the Arrow bunker?

- We know the Swan station was originally intended to study electromagnetic waves and now it's being used to hit a button on a computer. What was the Arrow station originally for? Why has it been abandoned? Who left behind this stuff?

- Ana asks an interesting question: Why does one of the Others have a military knife that's almost 20 years old? Was Goodwin really part of the Peace Corps? How did he get onto the island?

- What did Goodwin mean when he said only the good people were on the

Both 48 Days

	Tailies	Losties
Day 1	Libby can't find water, they don't know what they'll do for food, Goodwin tries to start a fire with a stick Ana saves a girl using CPR	They have food, drinks, water, matches, and lighters from the plane, and don't run out of water until Day 6 Jack saves Rose using cpr
Day 2	Cindy the flight attendant tells everyone they were two days off course	Kate, Jack, and Charlie find a pilot that tells them exactly the same thing
Day 3	Donald howls in pain from his infected leg, and dies two days later	The marshal howls in pain from his shrapnel wound, and Sawyer and Jack put him out of his misery
Day 7	The group finds a wild chicken and catch it for food	Locke had caught a boar two days earlier
Day 12	The Others have officially taken 12 people from their camp	There have been no encounters with the Others, to their knowledge
Day 15	They have been out in the jungle walking for two days, scared of what the Others might do to them	The day before, Hurley hosted the Island Open golf tournament
Day 19	Ana throws Nathan into the pit; he's Canadian and creepy	Two days earlier, the similarly named Ethan kidnapped Claire and Charlie; he's Canadian and creepy
Day 23	Ana continues to interrogate Nathan, desperate to find out where the children are	Jack and Kate open the gun case while he plays the feelings game and admonishes her to be more truthful with him
Day 27	The group discovers a bunker, and they walk in Ana discovers who the real imposter is, and kills him	Locke finds his hatch 10 days earlier, but it takes him almost a month to get into it Claire returns to the group, and Ethan is killed two days later
Day 41	Bernard picks up Boone's radio signal and answers it, Eko looms in the shadows Eko's speech is restored	Boone sends out a radio signal before falling to his death, Locke looms in the shadows Locke's faith is restored
Day 45	Jin washes up on shore, and Libby and Cindy pull him out, unsure whether or not they can trust him	Jack, Kate, and Locke encounter Desmond holding a gun on them, and don't know who he is or if they can trust him

"The Other 48 Days" Whisper Transcript

This is the whispering that we hear when Shannon gets shot, but in this episode it's different than it was in "Abandoned," which is either a production error, or a deliberate move to make it seem like there are more Others out there than we thought.

Relax Dude, I think she likes the guy
Your life
Ich Weiss Nicht (*German for "I don't know"*)
Look out
Ana's the trigger
You're gonna kill her
Move on (*Gun shot*)
See ya (*Like a chorus singing just after the gunshot*)

Shannon
She likes the guy, she likes the guy
Shannon
Your life and time is up
Help me
Shannon, meet me on the other side
Her song (*"Ana Lucia" when reversed*)
(*Gun shot*)

Relax dude, she likes the guy, she likes the guy
Shannon (*In the background*)
I know it all, I know it all . . . (*In the background*)
Dying sucks
Shannon
I don't think you should tell her when she comes
Obviously she likes you
Who's the guy?
I want to see Shannon
Eye to eye (*In the background*)
Who's the guy?
Fire Lucia
The brothers that help us
Are you done with it?
Her song (*"Ana Lucia" when reversed*)
(*Gun shot*)
Fire

list? Does that mean that Claire and Walt are the only two good people on the other side of the island, since they're the only ones the Others have taken?

Ashes to Ashes: Three Tailies died soon after the crash, followed by Donald, who died of an infection in his leg. Then Goodwin killed Nathan, and Ana Lucia killed Goodwin.

2.8   Collision

Original air date: November 23, 2005
Written by: Javier Grillo-Marxuach, Leonard Dick
Directed by: Stephen Williams
Guest cast: Rachel Ticotin (Captain Cortez), Michael Cudlitz (Big Mike), Rick Overton (Matthew Reed), Jeanna Garcia (Shawna), Mark Gilbert (Detective Raggs), Aaron Gold (Jason McCormick), Matt Moore (Travis), Rand Wilson (Assistant D.A.)

Flashback: Ana Lucia

Worried that Sayid will take revenge on her for killing Shannon, Ana Lucia has him tied to a tree, and holds everyone captive out of desperation.

For a brief moment in this episode, we see Locke completing a crossword puzzle, filling in "GILGAMESH" as the answer to the clue "Enkidu's friend." As is often the case with *Lost*, this moment flashes past us quickly, but contains very important hints for what is to come. The Babylonian *Epic of Gilgamesh*, believed to have been written around 2500 BC, chronicles the life of Gilgamesh, who was a king 400 years earlier. Gilgamesh was believed to be one part human, two parts god, but he was a nasty ruler, so the people complained to the gods to send someone who could keep him in check. The gods sent Enkidu, who was a wild man who lived in the jungle and had been raised by animals. Through interference by Gilgamesh, Enkidu becomes mistrusted by the animals, and begins hunting them. He ultimately challenges Gilgamesh, and they do battle. For most of it, Enkidu has the upper hand, until Gilgamesh suddenly turns the tables and as he's about to be defeated, Enkidu praises Gilgamesh, who spares his life. For the rest of the book, Enkidu becomes the Gabrielle to Gilgamesh's Xena (right

While Michelle Rodriguez and Naveen Andrews are pals off camera, the characters they play become enemies. (ALBERT L. ORTEGA)

down to the widespread belief they were lovers). They fight side by side, and eventually slay the Bull of Heaven. The gods punish Enkidu for doing so, and he dies, leaving Gilgamesh distraught.

The *Lost* writers are far too careful with their allusions to simply drop something like that into a scene without a greater meaning. The question is, who is the Gilgamesh of this island, and who is Enkidu?

The flashback of this episode belongs to Ana Lucia, who was an emotionally damaged person long before she got on the plane. Tough and cocky, she lets her emotions get the better of her in pressure situations, and doesn't adhere to rules or order. Michelle Rodriguez does a brilliant job in playing her, making Ana Lucia one of the most hated characters on the show, yet still imbuing her with enough sadness that fans are forced to look at this character seriously. We wonder what Ana would have been like before she was injured on duty.

In many ways, with her wildness, she could be the Enkidu character. Sayid, who glares at her as if he's her mortal enemy, is like Gilgamesh. Gilgamesh ruled over Uruk, an ancient city whose modern-day spelling is Iraq. For most of this episode, Ana Lucia holds all the cards, and could kill Sayid at any time, but when he's able to turn her words against her, she relents, and in a reversal of the myth, Enkidu does not kill her Gilgamesh. There's no way they could ever become friends, but Ana Lucia does see a connection between herself and Sayid, which is why she ultimately relents. Someone killed a person she loved, and she took bloody revenge on them. Now she's faced with someone whose expression is suddenly deadly because of what she's done, and she fears he wants to do the same.

Or is it Jack? He's the leader of the other side of the island, and the people are often complaining that he's an unfair ruler, so to speak. Will he and Ana become friends? Or perhaps Ana is Gilgamesh, the ruler with too much power, who needs to be taken down a peg or two. Eko has a wild way about him, carrying his stick and grunting, and in many ways he's her quieter sidekick. We saw in "The Other 48 Days" that they shared a moment of mutual understanding and respect, and maybe it was this that changed them.

The person filling out the crossword, however, is Locke. When he and Eko finally come face to face, it's like the two men with faith square off. Locke has been a powerful presence on this side of the island, but he disconcerts a lot of people, especially Jack. Suddenly Eko emerges from the jungle like a wild man, and his apparently gentler nature contrasts with Locke's sudden temper tantrums and the "tests" he puts people through. Their relationship can go one of two ways: either Locke will be excited by this man who has an immense amount of faith in his surroundings and his fate, or he will resent Eko for having the faith that Locke no longer seems to have. Every time Locke presses that button, he questions why he's doing so. He never pushes it blindly, and that's why this season his faith seems to dissipate episode by episode. Every 108 minutes, he's forced to question himself, the island, and his beliefs, and over time, it grates on him. Will Eko be able to lead him back to his faith, and make him a more effective man, the way Enkidu did for Gilgamesh, or will he lose his hope — the one thing that sustains him?

Meanwhile, we finally see Jack and Kate being laid-back and completely at ease with one another. They play golf, which, as mentioned in "Solitary," is seen as a sport of isolation, but when they play it, it becomes a competition. Jack insists that hitting the ball isn't about distance, it's about accuracy. He sees golf as a civilized sport, and doesn't recognize the irony of playing it on a wild island. To his surprise (and our amusement), Kate's shot is far more accurate than his, sending him into the wild jungle to play it through, despite Kate's insistence that he just take a drop. But what he finds in the jungle will remind him that the fun and games are brief on this island, and all too quickly he must return to duty.

Michelle Rodriguez on the set of "Collision." (RYAN OZAWA)

Golf courses are one of man's ways of taming nature, but on the island, nature fights back. As soon as Sawyer returns to the camp, we realize the only reason Kate and Jack were finally having fun together was because Sawyer wasn't there to create the tension.

The final moments of this episode provide an emotional roller coaster. Sayid is finally able to carry Shannon back to the camp, and Ana has admitted that she's dead inside. We see many happy, teary reunions on the beach, but more importantly, the reunion of Jack and Ana Lucia, whom he'd only met briefly before getting onto the plane. She seemed happy then and tried to cheer him up, while he was slowly getting drunk the way his father had done. Now, 48 days and several lifetimes later, they meet again as two very different people. Ana Lucia is damaged beyond repair, while Jack is on the mend. The two leaders of their tribes finally come together, but Ana has been the far less successful one, losing 19 of her people along the way. How will they deal with each other?

Highlight: The long-awaited reunions of Bernard and Rose, and Sun and Jin.

Did You Notice?:

- This episode doesn't open on Ana Lucia's eye, but on the barrel of a gun, suggesting she sees the world through one.
- Ana Lucia's police car ID is 8-Adam-16. It's interesting the word Adam is in there.
- Notice the fury in Sayid when Michael tells him the Others took Walt — it's as if he immediately pieces together that he and Charlie were saving the wrong child, and the Others never intended to hurt Aaron.
- The police catch Jason McCormick near Echo Park, which sounds like Eko.
- Jack says Sawyer needs antibiotics to live, yet back in "Tabula Rasa," Sawyer was the one who told Jack to just let the marshal die because there weren't enough antibiotics to treat him.
- When Shannon dies, Sayid lovingly carries her body back to camp, and buries it, heartbroken. But when she "died" in "Hearts and Minds," Boone just left her body in the jungle and returned to camp alone.

Nitpick: Again, Kate just stands there when Jack asks her to get something. When is the guy going to give up and choose another gofer? Also, Libby tells Ana that she's not a good judge of character because she put Nathan in a pit, but it was Libby who encouraged her to do so.

4 8 15 16 23 42: Ana Lucia has been seeing her therapist for **4** months. Ana's badge number is **68631**, which adds up to **24** (a reverse **42**). A call comes over the police radio for car **809** and Ana's car number is **8-Adam-16**. The crossword question about Enkidu is **42**-Down. Ana Lucia was shot **4** times. Eko tells Locke that there were **4** survivors from the tail section of the plane.

It's Just a Flesh Wound: Eko and Sayid have a fight, and Eko knocks him unconscious.

Any Questions?:

- Something seems to be wrong with Ana Lucia mentally, because in crisis situations she zones out and stops thinking, working on her gut instinct only. We see her with a therapist, as well. How many people on this island have been in mental institutions, know someone who's been in one, or have had mental problems of some kind?
- Ana Lucia's mother is a strange character: on the one hand, she comes across as a harsh but caring mother who worries about her daughter; on the other, she gives in to Ana's demands immediately. When one of the detectives calls Ana into another room, her mother ruins the party by telling Ana

they have a cake for her and to look surprised. Why would she do something so meanspirited to her?

- When Locke fills in GILGAMESH, it renders all of the other words complete nonsense. "Gilgamesh" is the correct answer, so . . . were all of the other answers incorrect?
- One of the most disappointing things that has happened this season is Locke's apparent senility when it comes to Walt. They were very close, and Locke saw Walt's potential and knew he was special. He was visibly saddened when Walt left, and Walt gave him one final warning before he left about the hatch. Wouldn't Locke want to know what he meant, now that he knows what's in there? Yet when Eko shows up in the hatch with Sawyer, Locke asks about Michael and Jin. What about Walt? Does he already know Walt's been kidnapped? How? Why isn't he upset when the rest of them show up and Walt is gone?
- Why was Ana Lucia in Sydney?

Music/Bands: As Jason comes out of the bar, you can hear Staind's "Outside" (*Break the Cycle*).

Michelle Rodriguez (Ana Lucia Cortez)

Michelle Rodriguez was a bad girl before she joined the cast of *Lost* to play one. On the show, Rodriguez, who joined for the second season, plays Ana Lucia, a cop with a history and a propensity for violence. It was a character that Rodriguez, who was raised on the proverbial wrong side of the tracks, could relate to. "I see Ana Lucia as a good girl but willing to be a bad girl if it involves survival. She's not your martyr type," the actress said.

Born in Bexar County, Texas, on July 12, 1978, Rodriguez has both Puerto Rican and Dominican heritage, and lived in the U.S. until the age of eight, when her family moved to the Dominican Republic, and then Puerto Rico soon afterward. All of the geographical changes made Rodriguez resentful of her mother. "I hated my mother for a while," she says. "I didn't know why I had to be here and follow all these rules and live life the way people wanted me to."

Growing up as part of a family of Jehovah's Witnesses made her even more angry and confused. She was afraid schoolmates would see her going door to door, and was already

The striking Michelle Rodriguez first found fame in her critically acclaimed role in *Girlfight*. (ALBERT L. ORTEGA)

having difficulty at school, which often resulted in violence. "I was scared that the next door I knocked on would be a friend from school and I'd have to get into yet another fight. I got into lots of fights in school."

By the time she was 14 she had already dropped out of high school and was hanging out with a tough crowd. She had also been kicked out of six different schools. "I spent the rest of my growing up years playing Dungeons and Dragons with geeks, riding around on rollerblades, and hanging out with a bunch of drug dealers on the corner," she explains. "I was exposed to a lot of things."

Though she eventually graduated with a high school equivalency, business school didn't suit her lifestyle or ambitions. Living in New York, she answered a casting call for an indie film called *Girlfight*. Despite having no acting experience, Rodriguez was given the lead role in the film. Her portrayal of Diana Guzman drew critical raves. "At that time in my life, I actually was way more aggressive than that character," she said later. "I had to down-tone myself. I was in a very angry stage, didn't like anyone telling me what to do. I hated that I had been spat out into a system where I had to follow rules and guidelines. My teenage years, my misery of existence, lasted a lot longer than it does for most teens. Growing up, I was, 'Why am I here, and why are all these people trying to tell me what to do?' It was anger all the time, like one of those punk-rock kids you see on TV."

Her string of good luck continued when her second audition led to a role in the megahit *The Fast and the Furious* alongside Vin Diesel. Interestingly, since the film was about street racing, Rodriguez didn't have a driver's license leading up to the shooting and had to quickly learn to drive.

With two clear successes in her past, Rodriguez appeared on the big screen in other high profile roles, including lead parts in *S.W.A.T.* and *Blue Crush*. She also turned down a role on the hit *Desperate Housewives*. She had been offered the part of the girlfriend of the philandering lawn boy, but it was not to her liking. "You think I'm going to be the girl to get cheated on?" she questioned. "Give me a break!"

Fed up with Hollywood, Rodriguez retreated to her rural home until an offer came to join the cast of *Lost* in Hawaii. It was a concept that caught Rodriguez's imagination. "I told these guys, the producers, that I want to be part of this world, this show in Hawaii, because Hollywood wasn't my thing at the moment," she said. "I was tired of the monotony of it all. I don't how long it will last, because with these guys everyone is expendable."

Many fans disliked her character, Ana Lucia. Despite that, Rodriguez found comfort in *Lost*'s philosophical story line and the fast pace of the show's writing and production team. "I like that the show focuses on Earth's unsolved and undiscovered mysteries. I am so used to being pampered — like being picked up, someone coming to my house, knocking on my door, waking me up," Rodriguez said. "Here, they tell you to make sure you have a computer so they can email you about changes and be on time."

However, Rodriguez's history of stumbling into trouble with the law followed her to Hawaii where she was charged with drunk driving. Accounts of Rodriguez's arrest also indicated the actress was abusive to the officers who pulled her over. Despite the setback, Rodriguez found solace in her role on *Lost* and the distance it placed between her and Hollywood. "I've been in this business six years, and now I like being at peace and happy. I've learned more about myself and to be myself."

2.9   What Kate Did

Original air date: November 30, 2005
Written by: Steven Maeda, Craig Wright
Directed by: Paul Edwards
Guest cast: Fredric Lane (Marshal), Beth Broderick (Diane), Lindsey Ginter (Sgt. Sam Austen), James Horan (Wayne), J. Edward Sclafani (Ticket Agent)

Flashback: Kate

We finally see why Kate's been on the run all this time, and Eko gives Locke something he'd been missing.

"What Kate Did," beyond the obvious title, is about ghosts, and being haunted by things that have happened in your past. Kate's transgression is

Lilly unveils her ad campaign for fashion company michelle-K in June 2006

(ALBERT L. ORTEGA)

sparked by her seeing what she thinks is a ghost — a large black horse standing in the middle of the jungle. Before viewers could think they were watching a different "stranded on an island" show about a young boy and his black stallion, it is explained that the horse played a pivotal role in Kate's past, and was her savior of sorts. The horse is usually a symbol of intelligence, maternal instinct, and impulsiveness. In her book, *The Mammoth Dictionary of Symbols*, Nadia Julien writes that a "black horse of death and destruction is synonymous with misery." Kate is certainly intelligent, and her crime was committed out of love for her mother, but while we've seen her do several impulsive things, "what she did" wasn't one of them. She caused death and destruction, but she did what she did to end her mother's misery, not to make it worse. Unfortunately, her mother seemed committed to her abusive relationship, and didn't appreciate her daughter meddling.

More important than the ghost of the horse is the ghost of Wayne, who seems to be speaking through Sawyer. Kate reveals in this episode that every time she looks at Sawyer or has any feelings for him, she's reminded of the man she hates, and it disgusts her. Her surprising confession actually aligns her more with Sawyer than she might think. In both cases, their self-loathing is caused by their hatred for someone else, and rather than deal with it, they keep putting themselves into situations that will make them hate themselves even more. Kate kisses Jack in the jungle, but it seems to be some kind of personal test for her — if it feels right, then maybe she's not a bad person. But the way she walks away from him suggests that it didn't feel right, and she believes she'll never deserve someone like him.

Sayid is haunted by his love for Shannon, and he will quietly mourn her over the next few episodes, alone. As Sun and Jin emerge from their tent, she looks in the direction of Sayid, and realizes that only 48 hours earlier, he was feeling what she is feeling right now. Sayid has done a lot of work on behalf of the survivors and their quest to get off the island, but if you think of his actual relationships with any of them, they're limited at best. Hurley tried to strike up a conversation with him in the beginning, but when he discovered Sayid was Iraqi, he barely spoke to him again. Charlie blamed Sayid for letting Rousseau near Aaron; several people joined Jack in the caves and left Sayid on the beach; and while Kate sided with Sayid, her heart was with Jack. People tend to talk to Sayid only when he can be of immediate use to them, and otherwise they leave him alone. It's too bad no one could sympathize with him enough to help him actually dig Shannon's grave, rather than standing back and watching him do it alone.

Eko reveals a ghost of sorts when he presents Locke with something he'd found on the other side of the island. The look on Locke's face is priceless when he sees it, and the significance of the find is raised by Eko's lofty introduction to it. As he sits across from Locke and begins his sermon, we see the similarity between the two men, but also the difference. Locke tells these grandiose stories all the time, too, though he does so in the conversational style of a man who just sat down next to you on the bus and wants to tell you something, as you shift awkwardly away. Eko, on the other hand, sounds like a priest, like a believer, and his language (the most we've ever heard him say in a single shot) is such that we know whatever he hands over is going to be extremely important. When it's ultimately shown, however, it's a tad anticlimactic.

What is more interesting about their conversation is a very subtle moment, where Eko begins the well-known story of Josiah and then pauses and asks Locke if he knows the story. Locke says no. This is a guy who can tell parables about obscure moments in history at the drop of a hat, yet he's unfamiliar with this story. Locke is a man of faith, but this moment reveals that his is not a biblical faith, it's a pagan one, which is consistent with his worship of the island. When he keeps looking up and appealing to some entity, asking what they want from him, it seemed before he was talking to God. But maybe he's appealing to the elements and to the jungle. His beliefs will clash with Eko's later this season, perhaps because they believe in different things.

The one person whose ghost will change him forever is Michael. As he sits down to the computer to acclimatize himself to this new place everyone's found, he does the very thing Eko and Locke are in the next room being warned against doing. And when he does it, the result will send him on a search that will affect everyone.

Highlight: The final minute of the episode.

Did You Notice?:

- In three of the four Kate flashbacks, she is involved in a car accident.
- After the car accident with the marshal, Kate gets the key to free herself (just like she did on the plane after he'd been knocked unconscious), and he tries to strangle her (like he did in "Tabula Rasa").
- Hurley's views on race seem very narrow: in "... In Translation," when Sun suddenly spoke English, he said, "Didn't see that coming." He repeats that line in this episode when he discovers Rose's husband is white.
- When Kate walks into Sgt. Sam Austen's recruiting office, look over her right shoulder, and you'll see Sayid on the television screen behind her.
- As if to distance herself from her parents, Kate goes by "Kate" now, not "Katie," which is her father's name for her, or "Katherine," which is what her mother calls her.
- In "Born to Run" Diane began screaming for help when she saw Kate, and now we realize it's because, despite everything Wayne did to her (and to Kate), she loved him, and blamed Kate for killing him. It's still baffling that she thought Kate might hurt her, though.

Interesting Fact: The story that Eko tells is in 2 Kings 22, and 2 Chronicles 34.

Nitpick: Jack has the world's most amazing memory. A few years ago, he met a man in a stadium and talked to him for four minutes, and then when he sees Desmond's face for half a second in "Man of Science, Man of Faith," he instantly recognizes him. In "Collision," when Eko mentions "Ana Lucia," again Jack immediately knows who he's talking about, after having chatted with her in an airport bar for a couple of minutes when he was half drunk. In this episode, he remembers the *drink* Ana Lucia ordered. Also, if Kate had already doused the house in gasoline before Wayne got there (he mentions that he can smell it), I doubt she'd be sitting on the front porch flicking her lighter on and off while waiting for him to come home. Finally, when Jack asks Charlie where Kate is, he says she's on her way "back" to the caves, as if she'd come from there. But since the hatch was found, no one lives at the caves any longer, so wouldn't Jack find that odd?

4 8 15 16 23 42: Jack tells Sawyer that Kate has been watching him for 24

In "Tabula Rasa," Jack comes off as accusatory to both Kate and Sawyer, and asks each of them, "What did you do?" in a tone that suggests he already thinks they're guilty. But Jack's not the only one accusing other people of doing something (I'll only include the instances up to "What Kate Did" to avoid spoilers):

Tabula Rasa: Jack says it to Kate after the marshal tries to choke her, and again to Sawyer after he hears the gunshot.

House of the Rising Sun: After Jin attacks Michael, he looks over at Walt, causing Michael to grab Walt and say to Jin, "What did you do to him?"

Hearts and Minds: Shannon asks Boone, "What did you do to him?" after Locke has tied both of them up in the jungle.

Homecoming: When Ethan comes back to get Claire, Charlie asks, "What did you do to her?"

The Greater Good: When Locke reappears after Boone's death, Jack runs at him, yelling, "What did you do to him?"

Orientation: When the computer gets shot, Desmond screams, "What did you do? We're all going to die!"

What Kate Did: When Kate hands the insurance papers over to her mother, her mother asks, "What did you do?"

hours straight, and she was 24 years old when she killed Wayne (both a reverse **42**). When Michael asks Locke why they can't just punch in the numbers at any time, the countdown clock is at **23**. Kate's father was in Korea until **4** months before she was born.

Any Questions?:

- Does Sayid think Walt is dead? Kate asks him if he believes in ghosts, and he says he saw Walt in the jungle.
- Why was the one section taken out of the film? How did it end up in a book on the other side of the island?
- Was that really Walt talking to Michael at the end, or someone just playing with Michael's head? Is the bunker under surveillance of some kind — how else would anyone know that it was Michael sitting in front of the computer? Someone had to know he was sitting there even before he typed his name, or else they wouldn't have contacted him.
- How did the horse make it onto the island? Is it the same horse Kate saw years earlier?

- In "Born to Run," Kate checks in to a motel and there's a letter and money waiting for her. Was it her father who kept in touch with her?

Music/Bands: Kate listens to Patsy Cline's "Walkin' After Midnight" in the bunker. When Kate comes to see her mother at the diner, you can hear Skeeter Davis' "The End of the World" (*The Essential Skeeter Davis*).

2.10   The 23rd Psalm

Original air date: January 11, 2006
Written by: Carlton Cuse, Damon Lindelof
Directed by: Matt Earl Beasley
Guest cast: Adetokumboh M'Cormack (Yemi), Kolawole Obileye Jr. (Young Eko), Olekan Obileye (Young Yemi), Pierre Olivier (Ulu), Ronald Revels (Goldie), John Bryan (Thug Captain), Lawrence Jones (Lead Soldier), Moumen El Hajji (Tough Moroccan), Achraf Marzouko (Moroccan #2), Ellis St. Rose (Priest), Cynthia Charles (Nigerian Woman)

Flashback: Eko

When Eko finds Charlie's Virgin Mary statue, he insists that Charlie take him to the place where he found it.

"The 23rd Psalm" is a great episode, and Eko's surprising tie to Locke's discovery of last season is handled very well by the writers. Eko has been a mysterious character over the past nine episodes. At times, he's physically terrifying, but he also has moments of quiet gentleness. Who *is* this guy?

This guy is a man who sacrificed his soul to save his brother's. His brother, in turn, held Eko's actions against him. Like Sawyer, when Eko does a terrible thing, he is given a new name to reflect his new killer status — *Mister* Eko — and he spends the rest of his life living down to that moniker. In ". . . And Found," Sawyer asks him his name, and he tells him it's Mr. Eko. By killing those two men the first night he was on the island, he believes he hasn't changed at all since he was a young boy in Nigeria with a gun forced into his hand. Now that he's had a sign from his past, he's on a quest with Charlie to face up to the consequences of who he's become. When he finally finds what he's looking for, it offers him the cathartic experience he needs to finally drop the "Mr." from his name, and become the good person he was meant to be. Until now, he's merely impersonated a priest, but when he takes the cross and puts it around his neck, he becomes the island priest.

His revelation couldn't come at a better time — Locke, the island's disciple, has lost his faith, and Eko seems to be the perfect person to bring him back. Both men believed the island gave them a sign, and both of them were led to the Beechcraft plane. They are connected by this event that happened years earlier through the wreck that commemorates it. When Locke arrived at the plane in "Deus Ex Machina," he was beginning to lose his faith as well, but Boone's accident led him to question everything he believed in, until he received the much-needed sign from the hatch. Similarly, Eko is haunted by what he's done in the past. A life of goodness was robbed from him, and instead he gave his salvation to his brother. It's only when he arrives at the plane that he realizes his brother, in turn, gave his salvation back to Eko, and it's up to Eko to fulfill the potential of goodness that both brothers possessed.

Charlie, on the other hand, was also a religious man who was dragged away from his faith by vice. Unlike Eko, however, he blames his brother for his problems, without looking at his own complicity in the matter. Charlie also made a discovery at the Beechcraft, but it was one that is going to lead him into temptation, not away from it. He has lied to Claire, and despite everything he's done for her, she has to think of her baby over anyone else. Without his faith, Charlie will end up completely alone. He gets particularly hostile when he believes Eko doesn't respect him, and he does have a point. Claire refuses to believe his story. Sawyer makes fun of him and has punched him in the face. Sayid doesn't take Charlie seriously as a man, and, like Jack and Locke, he tends to lump Charlie in with the women when it comes to performing dangerous tasks. Hurley is Charlie's friend, but in his mind Hurley is mocking him with his "phony" story about winning the lottery. Kate has also been kind to Charlie, but the fact she was chosen in "Homecoming" to accompany the guys on the Ethan hunt, and Charlie was left behind, was very telling. When he was on heroin, he was a "rock god," (again, in his mind), and now that stuff is looking pretty good to him again.

The Virgin Mary statues are symbolic of the main characters in this episode — what may seem to be good and pure on the outside is evil on the inside. Charlie might have been an altar boy, but that was a long time ago, and he's a very different person now. Eko is a priest on the outside, a killer on the inside. Only on the island can Eko's true goodness come out.

The most shocking moment in the episode is when Eko comes face to face with the monster, or at least one incarnation of it. We finally see what that black smoke was that Jack, Kate, and Locke all saw in "Exodus." Eko stares straight into the heart of the beast, and faces his demons head-on as images of his past flash through the smoke. Having one's life flash before one's eyes — especially a life like Eko's — would be terrifying for most people, but Eko is different. Perhaps this smoke is what Locke saw in "Walkabout," and it's what gave him the courage, faith, and resolve that he carried throughout season 1, because he, too, was able to face his demons: "Yea, though I walk through the valley of the shadow of death, I will fear no evil." The question is, did the black smoke show Locke something different in "Exodus, Part 2" that took all of that resolve away? If the monster on the island is the embodiment of everyone's deepest fears, then perhaps, as the old adage goes, the only thing they have to fear is fear itself. But unlike Eko, most people cannot face their fears head on without flinching.

Highlight: Charlie's response when Eko tells him to climb the tree: "What if I don't? You gonna beat me with your Jesus stick?"

Did You Notice?:

- The casting of the young Eko and Yemi is brilliant; the boys look remarkably like their older counterparts.
- Claire has given Charlie a haircut, and now Kate gives Sawyer one, as if it's a form of sexual innuendo. Or emasculation. It's reminiscent of Delilah cutting Samson's hair in the biblical story, and taking his power away.
- When the monster appears to Eko, you can see images from Eko's life flashing in the smoke: Yemi's church; Eko's face as a boy; one of the two women who were sitting in the pew during confession; the older Yemi looking at him, disappointed; the old man Eko shot as a boy; the gun Eko used to shoot him; a young Eko holding onto his brother as the men tried to grab Yemi; the woman whose confession he interrupted; the man who named him Mister Eko; Eko holding Yemi after he'd been shot; Eko watching the plane fly away; Eko on the beach after the Oceanic crash; the crucifix from the altar of Yemi's church.
- Eko doesn't blink once while these images pass before his eyes.

Interesting Fact: In "Deus Ex Machina," when Locke found the priest, he guesses by the decomposition of the clothing that the man has been dead between two and 10 years. In this episode, we see the drug dealers pay Eko in what appear to be 100 Naira notes. The 100 Naira note was introduced in 1999, so that narrows the possible timeline of events to the past five years.

Nitpick: Claire's giant island baby appears to have doubled in size since its birth nine days ago. And why exactly does Locke teach Michael to shoot by having him destroy large containers of food? They're on an island . . . can they really afford to be letting so much food go to waste?

Oops: When the military drives up to the airbase, one of Eko's guys calls him "Eeko" by accident.

4 8 15 16 23 42: Eko and Charlie recite Psalm **23**. The side of the plane reads 5Z-GW and W is the 23rd letter in the alphabet.

Any Questions?:

- Why *does* Eko's stick have dried blood on it?
- Did "Walt" type anything that Michael saw but we didn't? What did he tell him?
- Why didn't Michael tell Jack about Walt contacting him? Hasn't he ever heard of strength in numbers?
- Charlie joins Eko's recitation of the 23rd Psalm when Eko gets to the valley of the shadow of death line, yet both of them say it incorrectly as "through the shadow of the valley of death." Is it a mistake, or intentional? Could the black smoke be the shadow that resides in the valley of death?

Adewale Akinnuoye-Agbaje (Eko)

It isn't surprising that Adewale Akinnuoye-Agbaje (pronounced Add-eh-wallay Akin-yu-oh-yay Ag-bah-jay) has made bold decisions and taken interesting roles all the way to being cast in *Lost*. After all, part of his name, which comes from his Nigerian heritage, means "brave man." "I'm Nigerian of origin and from the Yoruba tribe and the way that my ancestors have named their kin is to give you a sense of purpose," he explains. "It's based on the environment that you're born into, the time, the family . . . born into chieftaincy, and then they state your purpose, so that every time they call you, you're reminded of why you're here. So for me, sometimes it can be a little daunting."

Born in 1967, Akinnuoye-Agbaje moved from London, England, to his parent's native Nigeria when he was an infant, where he was raised by friends while his parents

Adewale Akinnuoye-Agbaje was best known to audiences as Adebisi on *Oz* before taking the role of Eko. (CHRISTINA RADISH)

established careers. More than a decade later he returned. With several family members being lawyers, Akinnuoye-Agbaje pursued an education that would lead him to a career in law, though he was not personally interested in becoming a lawyer. "[Law school] was more a parental obligation than a personal goal," he says. "I was more interested in the creative fields. As soon as I finished my education, I turned to that."

Despite, "studying [his] heart out," Akinnuoye-Agbaje wanted something more. He wanted to become an actor. "My head was swollen from all that studying. I figured I needed a break." He was 27 by the time his first appearances in film and television began. Early on he made appearances in television shows like *Red Shoe Diaries*. But he also landed a role in the epic *Congo*, and he soon found himself back on television, appearing as the notorious and violent gangster Adebisi on the prison drama *Oz*.

"When I present myself to a cast and directors, I bring everything that I am," he explains, noting that his varied cultural background provided him with versatility. "I did it in different accents: English, Jamaican, American, British, Upper British, Cockney, and I gave them a plethora, and that enlightens them to the dimensions of what a black character can do. We took an African character to prison. What that did, it gave me creative license because they'd never written for a Nigerian character. They would write it in American and I would translate it, but I had free will. They didn't know, but the beautiful thing is that they trusted me and I trusted them and that's when you get something beautiful and organic."

The only side effect of his time spent on *Oz* was the propensity of some casting agents to feel that Akinnuoye-Agbaje was best suited to play evil villains. Despite the fear of typecasting, he enjoyed portraying the nefarious Adebisi. "In truth, I don't necessarily play bad guys," Akinnuoye-Agbaje says, noting he's a practicing Buddhist. "I look for characters where I can really dig into them and get into their guts and their pain. I want interesting guys that do bad things, but have a humane and compassionate and humorous [side]. That's life."

After *Oz* ended, Akinnuoye-Agbaje made appearances in several big-budget films, including *The Bourne Identity* and *Get Rich or Die Tryin'*, alongside rapper 50 Cent. Living in London at the time, Akinnuoye-Agbaje had not seen *Lost*'s debut and was skeptical about the show when it came to his attention. "People crash-land on an island," Adewale says. "It just rang out with all the clichés."

But as the second season of *Lost* was being prepared, executive producer Damon Lindelof and the show's writers were looking to flesh out the story of the plane crash and reveal additional survivors. Among those new characters was Mr. Eko, an African with a nasty past. Akinnuoye-Agbaje was immediately attracted to the possibilities of the character. "Less is more," Akinnuoye-Agbaje says. "It keeps you guessing. [Eko] could really do anything. There's a dangerous element to him."

From the producers' standpoint, Eko added to the mix of cultural backgrounds on the island. "This community is formed by characters from many different backgrounds," says Lindelof. "An African character coming from a place where the many issues would be fundamental life-and-death issues would be an interesting person to add to the mix."

Akinnuoye-Agbaje had significant input into his character, even down to choosing the name "Eko," the "Lord of Legos," a reference to a location in Nigeria that he felt was in keeping with the character.

For an actor used to a degree of anonymity, the biggest challenge for Akinnuoye-Agbaje to date has been dealing with the fame that comes from being a visible part of one of TV's most popular shows. "I had no idea that in the three months, how fast it would turn around. The first week, I was getting bags of fan mail."

Eko's Jesus Stick

On Eko's "Jesus stick" (as Charlie calls it), he etches various scripture references. In "The 23rd Psalm," four of them are very clear to us: the titular psalm; Revelation 3; Colosians [Colossians] 4 (it appears to be 14, but there are only 4 chapters in the book); and Titus 3.

Revelation 3

The Revelation to John was written during Christian persecutions, and it claims to be the words of Christ encouraging Christians not to sway from the church, even during times of persecution, explaining that come the Day of Judgment, Christians will be saved if they remain true to their church and to God. The entire book is a description of the Apocalypse, and it is one of the most controversial books in the bible.

Chapter 3 contains instructions on sending messages to the angels of three churches. To the church in Sardis, Christ says, "I know that you have the reputation of being alive, even though you are dead! So wake up, and strengthen what you still have before it dies completely. For I find that what you have done is not yet perfect in the sight of my God." He warns the listeners in Sardis that if they do not change their ways, they will be robbed of eternal life. But for those who have been good and followed the word of the Lord, "You will walk with me, clothed in white, because you are worthy to do so. Those who win the victory will be clothed like this in white, and I will not remove their names from the book of the living." (It is interesting that Christ refers to good people as being names on a list in a book, just as the Others list the names of "good people" on a piece of paper.) He assures the church in Philadelphia that they have been good people, and will be let into Heaven, because He has a key. He states that any group belonging to Satan will be forced to bow at their feet, and says He's coming soon. He tells the church in Laodicea, "I know what you have done; I know that you are neither cold nor hot. How I wish you were either one or the other! But because you are lukewarm, neither hot nor cold, I am going to spit you out of my mouth! You say, 'I am rich and well off; I have all I need.' But you do not know how miserable and pitiful you are! You are poor, naked, and blind." He tells them that only if they turn to Him to find their riches, and if they do, they will obtain their rightful place beside Him.

Colossians 4

This New Testament book is Paul's letter from prison to the church at Colossae, where he learned there were false teachers. His letter is outlining proper Christian conduct. He writes something that is obviously very important to Eko: "Be wise in the way you act toward those who are not believers, making good use of every opportunity you have. Your speech should always be pleasant and interesting, and you should know how to give the right answer to everyone."

Titus 3

Paul's letter to Titus, his young helper who was supervising the church, is about the qualities church leaders ought to exude, how to treat people in the church, and finally what good Christian conduct should be. It could be interpreted as a comment on Jack, Ana Lucia, and Locke.

"Remind your people to submit to rulers and authorities, to obey them, and to be ready to do good in every way. Tell them not to speak evil of anyone, but to be peaceful and friendly, and always to show a gentle attitude toward everyone. For we ourselves were once foolish, disobedient, and wrong. We were slaves to passions and pleasures of all kinds. We spent our lives in malice and envy; others hated us and we hated them. But when the kindness and love of God our Savior was revealed, he saved us. It was not because of any good deeds that we ourselves had done, but because of his own mercy that he saved us, through the Holy Spirit, who gives us new birth and new life by washing us. God poured out the Holy Spirit abundantly on us through Jesus Christ our Savior, so that by his grace we might be put right with God and come into possession of the eternal life we hope for. This is a true saying.

"I want you to give special emphasis to these matters, so that those who believe in God may be concerned with giving their time to doing good deeds, which are good and useful for everyone. But avoid stupid arguments, long lists of ancestors, quarrels, and fights about the Law. They are useless and worthless. Give at least two warnings to the person who causes divisions, and then have nothing more to do with him. You know that such a person is corrupt, and his sins prove that he is wrong."

2.11   The Hunting Party

Original air date: January 18, 2006
Written by: Elizabeth Sarnoff, Christina M. Kim
Directed by: Stephen Williams
Guest cast: Monica Dean (Gabriela), Ronald Guttman (Angelo)

Flashback: Jack

When Michael takes some guns and disappears to find Walt, Jack goes looking for him, accompanied by Locke and Sawyer.

M.C. Gainey plays the mysterious "Mr. Friendly," whom we first saw in "Exodus, Part 2." (ALBERT L. ORTEGA)

When it comes to flashbacks, we've seen far more of Jack's past than anyone else's. His story is beginning to feel a little redundant — he's under Christian's thumb, he doesn't believe in miracles, he didn't exactly marry Sarah for love. Christian Shephard pervades Jack's flashbacks, and haunts his memories. But just as we've seen in previous episodes, in many ways Jack has become his father. Just as Christian is constantly punishing Jack for everything he believes Jack has done wrong, Jack punishes Kate and makes her face up to everything she does.

In the most recent flashback, Christian criticized Jack's lack of bedside manner, explaining to him the importance of hope. In this episode, we see how much Jack has changed when he gives a patient false hope. He takes on a patient whom he knows he can't help, but because he saved Sarah through a miracle, he thinks he can give a repeat performance. But what makes this episode interesting is the speculation of what happened between his wedding and this moment we're seeing now. Does he take on the patient out of arrogance, believing he is some sort of Christ figure who can make the crippled walk? When Gabriela pushes Christian aside and tells Jack it's him they want, not his father, it's a moment that's been a lifetime coming, and one that was sure to make his ego flare up.

Or has he discovered faith somewhere along the way, only to have it come crashing down when his experience with Gabriela's father doesn't work out? If he actually did begin to believe in miracles, and think that maybe he could be an instrument of God in some way, it would begin to explain the outright hostility he displays toward Locke and his faith. What better person to argue against Locke's beliefs than someone who has had his own destroyed? Locke maintains his defiance of Jack, asking him pointed questions during their trek — "Where are *you* going,

Jack?" — but he's toned down a lot from the man he was at the beginning of the season. He's still up for a debate with Jack, but he lacks the passion and fervor he once had.

All that aside, what makes this episode so exciting has very little to do with Jack. After arguing for hours, Locke, Sawyer, and Jack believe they are getting nearer to Michael . . . instead they come face to face with the Others. Seeing the same bearded man from "Exodus, Part 2" (whom the writers call "Mr. Friendly") is chilling, and this time he talks to them, explaining his position on the whole matter, and calmly tells them to walk away. For Sawyer, it's a nasty reminder of what he's already been through, but for Jack and Locke, it's a new experience. Until now, the

In "The Hunting Party," Jack comes to terms with the fact that he won't always be able to fix everything. (CHRISTINA RADISH)

Others have been nothing more than bogeymen to them, but when they finally meet "Zeke," they not only discover these people are serious, but there are *far* more of them than they'd originally thought.

So why is this a Jack-centric episode? Just as Jack blamed Locke for his failure to save Boone's life in "Do No Harm," he blames Kate for his failure to find Michael in this episode. He lost Sarah because he was blind to his own situation, and now he's lost Michael. In the flashbacks, he only blames himself for his downfalls, but on the island, he finds scapegoats everywhere, the same way Christian blamed Jack for the loss of his license, rather than looking at his own failures in the matter. Now that the Others have arrived, they offer another enemy Jack can point to. The sudden appearance of this hostile group of people has allowed the Lostaways to stop looking within, and turn their gazes outward, which makes for less soul-searching, and a lot more bloodshed.

Whether Jack wants her to or not, Kate is always the first to volunteer for any trek or expedition into the jungle. The following is a list of Kate's travels (warning: the last two contain spoilers for upcoming episodes):

Pilot, Part 1: Kate accompanies Jack and Charlie to the cockpit to find the transceiver
Pilot, Part 2: Kate and Sayid, Charlie, Sawyer, Boone, and Shannon travel to a high point on the island to find a signal for the transceiver
Walkabout: Kate and Sawyer go into the jungle to help Sayid triangulate his signal
House of the Rising Sun: Kate accompanies Jack, Locke, and Charlie to the caves to get water for the first time
The Moth: Kate and Sayid go out into the jungle to triangulate Rousseau's signal
Homecoming: Kate accompanies Sayid, Locke, Jack, and Sawyer to the jungle with Claire to find Ethan
Exodus, Parts 1 & 2: Kate accompanies Rousseau, Hurley, Jack, Locke, and Arzt to find the dynamite on the *Black Rock*
Man of Science, Man of Faith: Kate follows Locke back to the hatch, and is the first person to descend into it
The Hunting Party: Kate follows Jack, Locke, and Sawyer when they search for Michael, despite Jack telling her not to
S.O.S.: Kate accompanies Jack back to the site where they last met the Others to see if they can trade Henry for Walt
Live Together, Die Alone: Kate accompanies Jack, Michael, Hurley, and Sawyer to the Others' camp, or so she believes

Highlight: Hurley's interest in one of Desmond's records when Sayid says the music they're listening to is depressing. "We can change it, dude. You ever heard of Geronimo Jackson?"

Did You Notice?:

- In "What Kate Did," Eko tells Locke the story of Josiah building the temple and how they built it using a book, which was the Old Testament. The following episode, Locke changed the combination of the armory lock, and in this episode, we find out the combination is 25-29-40. It's likely that the combination is referring to Exodus 25: 29–40, which is the original story Josiah would have been following. In this passage, God gives instructions on how to build the Ark of the Covenant.
- Jack and Kate seem to be stuck in the same rut, where he treats her like she's

three years old and she refuses to listen to him, while Jin and Sun are actually making progress in their relationship.

- The two Italian people who come to meet Jack are named Angelo and Gabriela, probably a reference to the Archangel Gabriel. Gabriel is a messenger of God, and in the New Testament, he is the angel who appears to Mary to tell her of the immaculate conception. He is often also seen as the angel of death, and is believed to be the angel in Revelation who blows the trumpet on Judgment Day.

- Locke tells Jack the path he himself is following is as straight as the interstate, and he knows where he's going, and then he asks Jack if he knows where *he* is going. Locke's obviously making a comment on their beliefs, but in his case, his metaphor is mere posturing, since he wandered from his own path long ago.

- Locke's question, "Who are we to tell anyone what they can or can't do?" is an echo of his mantra throughout season 1, "Don't tell me what I can't do."

- Mr. Friendly talks about Walt like he's still alive.

- When Kate appears, Sawyer acts like a protector, Jack like a punisher.

- Jack's relationship to Kate is very complex because of the memories she sparks for him. In season 1, she reminded him of his father. Now she reminds him of Sarah, but also of himself. Part of the reason Jack punishes Kate so often is because she reminds him of himself — in this episode, she begs his forgiveness and says she made a mistake, and in the flashback, he tells Sarah that he made a mistake.

- Now we know how Locke knew Hurley's name was Hugo, which is how he referred to him in "Exodus, Part 2."

- The two tribes are reminiscent of *Lord of the Flies* (see page 37). The novel's Jack heads up the tribe of savages like the Others, and Ralph argues for reason and order on the island.

Interesting Fact: Geronimo Jackson is not a real musical act. Also, Mr. Friendly quotes a "smart" man as saying, "Since the dawn of our species, man's been blessed with curiosity." He's quoting Alvar Hanso, from a speech he supposedly gave to the UN Security Council in 1967. Hanso is, of course, a fictional character created by the writers of *Lost*, but fans who checked out the original version of the Hanso Foundation Web site that the show mounted could see his 1967 speech weeks before Mr. Friendly quoted it.

Nitpick: Locke tells Sawyer he saw the flight manifest and that Sawyer's name was James Ford. Hurley is upset in "Raised by Another" when he realizes Ethan's name isn't on the manifest, but why didn't he get upset when he couldn't find Sawyer's name on the manifest, either?

Oops: If you look closely at Angelo's X-ray, it's dated November 16, 2005, over a year *after* the crash of Oceanic Flight 815.

4 8 15 16 23 42: When Jack and Locke are trapped in the armory, they worry that no one is scheduled to come into the bunker for another **4** hours. The last number on the safe combination is a **40**. In the flashback, Gabriela mentions it's **4**:30 in the morning. In the jungle, Jack, Locke, and Sawyer hear **7** shots, but there are only **3** shell cases on the ground, meaning **4** of them are missing. When Jin tells Sun he doesn't like being told what to do, she says that was her life for **4** years. At the end of the episode, **4** people return to the camp.

It's Just a Flesh Wound: Sawyer is grazed by a bullet when he aims his gun at Mr. Friendly.

Lost in Translation: When Charlie is singing a Kinks song to Jin, Jin turns to him and says, "Hey, because of you all the fish are running away!"

Any Questions?:

- Christian tells Jack that when it comes to Gabriela, there's a line, and he should recognize it and not cross it. Jack says, "I guess you would know." What does he mean? Did Christian cheat on Jack's mother?
- Why does Locke choose this moment to ask Sawyer about his real name?
- When Jack refuses to lay down his weapons, Mr. Friendly calls for Alex, and tells her to bring out Kate. Alex is Danielle's daughter's name. Is she still alive and now living as an Other?
- The scene where Mr. Friendly holds a gun to Kate's head and counts to three echoes the bank robbery scene in "Whatever the Case May Be." In that episode, Kate's fear is fake, but it's very real here.

Music/Bands: In the bunker, Charlie and Hurley listen to "Fall on Me" by the Pousette-Dart Band (*Amnesia*).

2.12   Fire + Water

Original air date: January 25, 2006
Written by: Edward Kitsis, Adam Horowitz

Directed by: Jack Bender

Guest cast: Neil Hopkins (Liam), Vanessa Branch (Karen), Sammi Davis (Mrs. Pace), Jeremy Shada (Young Charlie), Zack Shada (Young Liam), Craig Young (Commercial Director)

Flashback: Charlie

Charlie begins having visions that Aaron is in trouble, and he takes dangerous steps to "save" him.

No matter how good a series is, eventually a dud of an episode will come along (think "Beer Bad" on *Buffy the Vampire Slayer*). While the worst episode of *Lost* is ten times better than the best of most other shows, "Fire + Water" is still this season's low point. In the previous episode, we got another glimpse of the Others, they threatened our castaways, and Jack finally approached Ana about forming an army to go up against them, promising that this week's episode would be just as exciting. Instead, "Fire + Water" completely dumps the ongoing plot-line, focusing instead on Charlie in an ill-timed attempt to try to draw his character into a season that is far more centered on the new people and the bunker than keeping up with all of the secondary characters of season 1.

Just as Jack's flashbacks felt a wee bit redundant in the previous episode, Charlie's are starting to hit us over the head with an unchanging message. Charlie was a rock star in a mediocre one-hit-wonder rock band that rose to the top and flamed out before most of their audience could bat an eye. He was a devout Christian who was tempted by the trappings of fame, and became a heroin addict because of his brother. While his brother found help, Charlie clung to his belief that the band was actually something more than a flash in the pan, and he was unable to shake the monkey off his back. In "The Moth," we watched the triumphant victory of Charlie over his heroin addiction, which seemed to signal a new dawn for him, but when Locke found copious amounts of heroin on the island in "Deus Ex Machina," we knew it could only end badly. Now that Charlie has not only discovered the heroin, but is hoarding it inside a tree trunk "just in case," it's difficult even for Charlie's biggest fans to trust him.

In this episode, Charlie moves beyond his unfair fear that Claire might not be a good mother because she doesn't know what she's doing (as he confessed to Locke in "Abandoned") and now believes that the baby is only safe with him, and that he needs to save it somehow. He begins having dreams in which Aaron is in mortal peril, or trapped in religious iconographical paintings. But his sudden fears are

Charlie is always trying to save people, but in "Fire + Water" he ends up alienating everyone because of it. (YORAM KAHANA/SHOOTING STAR)

never quite explained. It's not tied to anything that comes before or after it, and just seems stuck in the middle of the season without actually relating to the seasonal arc. The flashbacks with Liam are interesting because we get to see the irony that Liam quit drugs to save his family, while Charlie drove his family away through his own drug use. Now that he's on the island, and possibly using again, he's driving away Claire and Aaron — his new family. Charlie thought that by sticking with Drive Shaft he could protect his brother from the evils of showbiz, even if it meant Charlie becoming an addict. Now he thinks he can save Aaron, but all he's doing is terrifying Claire and isolating himself from everyone else. The only explanation for Charlie's fears is that the appearance of the heroin on the island is tempting Charlie, and he knows he's in danger of using again. He's projecting his fears for his own safety onto Aaron, rather than realize it is *he* who needs to be saved.

Claire might seem like she's overreacting — after all, there's been no proof that Charlie's actually using again. He's been there for Claire right from the beginning, and has always helped her and stood by her side, no matter what, yet she won't give him the benefit of the doubt. He's still sporting the scar on his forehead that he got from saving Aaron, but she pushes him away. But from her point of view, Charlie has lied to her, hidden things from her, and is suddenly acting in a strange manner, all indicators that he's been using the heroin in the statues, and she cannot risk a heroin addict being around her baby . . . certainly not one who sleepwalks with her baby into the crashing waters in the middle of the night.

Locke, too, seems completely out of character when he hits Charlie repeatedly upon retrieving Aaron from him. After all, this is a man who was ostracized by the group in season 1 for causing Boone's death, and has had his faith questioned every step of the way by Jack. Now, faced with a man who just wants the baby to be baptized, he introduces his knuckles to Charlie's face, and then just leaves him there. From Locke's perspective, he spent a month trying to get into a hatch that has suddenly been taken over by everyone else, and has caused him nothing but grief. Is he punishing Charlie unnecessarily, or trying to prevent him from making the same over-the-top mistakes that he believes he himself has made? Or, is he starting to think he was doing the wrong thing in season 1? Notice how Locke becomes particularly hostile to Charlie when Charlie begins spouting Locke's season 1 rhetoric about the island saving everyone.

The day after the trauma, everyone else seems to go back to normal except for Charlie, who, hood up, resembles the man who first arrived on the island, utterly lost. Charlie wants to recapture the fame he once had, and wants the world to be watching him. He gets his way, when all of the Lostaways are staring at him as he bellows from the waves that he's doing the right thing. But just as the fans of Drive Shaft abandoned him after one hit song, the people he thought were his friends have all turned their backs on him. And we'll soon discover that Charlie isn't just a danger to himself.

Highlight: Hurley flirting with Libby.
Did You Notice?:
- Charlie's mom tells him he's special, the word Brian Porter used to describe Walt, and Emily Locke used to describe her son.
- Sawyer's nicknames for people range from playful to outright cruel, but no one seems to have harsher ones than Hurley, whose nicknames all pertain to his size.
- One of the tip-offs that the piano dream is actually a dream is that in "White Rabbit," Charlie admitted to Jack, "I don't swim!" yet he's swimming in his dream to save Aaron.

- The entrance to Charlie's apartment looks like the one in Austin Powers' bachelor pad.
- In the corners of the giant crib in the "Charlie's lowest moment" scene, you can see two stuffed polar bears.
- It's difficult to see in the episode, but before this episode aired, in a podcast for the show, Damon Lindelof told viewers to watch the London skyline for an important sign. As the commercial director storms out to his trailer, there's a large building to the right, and on the side of it is a sign for "Widmore Construction" (see page 280).
- *Locke* seems to be very obsessed with *locks*. Both of them seem to change every time we're just about to figure out what they're all about.

Interesting Fact: The first image in the episode is Verrocchio's painting *The Baptism of Christ*, which depicts John the Baptist baptizing Christ, with two angels sitting on the ground beside him holding his garments. There's a dove in the sky. This is the same image from Charlie's dream later in the episode, with Hurley as John the Baptist and Mrs. Pace and Claire as the angels holding Christ's garments, but there's no Christ (presumably it's Aaron). Also, the title of the episode refers to the fire that Charlie sets, and the water that he takes Aaron into. Both of these elements are often seen as redemptive, with water being used in baptism, and fire used in the image of a phoenix rising from the flames, ready to start life anew. Finally, the writers were originally going to start a romantic thing between Ana Lucia and Jack, but her tough exterior made them change their minds.

Nitpick: None of Charlie's nightmares are worse than the ones I'm going to have after suffering through that "You All Every Butties" scene. That was truly awful. Not only is it the most cringeworthy moment of the series, but it goes against every point the writers have been trying to make about Drive Shaft. We've been led to believe they were one-hit wonders, and it was a second-rate hit at that. Yet now they're suggesting it was a big enough hit that a large company would develop a jingle out of it, as if the song — and the band — were instantly recognizable to all consumers. Secondly, if a large company pays an advertising agency to come up with an idea for a commercial and spends thousands of dollars procuring the band, writing the stupid song, designing the set, and developing their ad campaign (which would be what, "For today's cutting-edge baby"?), there's no way they'd let some prima donna director just arbitrarily fire the band, forcing them to drop the entire idea. Also, why couldn't Locke let Claire use the bed in the hatch? If someone were at the computer monitoring it closely, then the moment the countdown clock reached four minutes they'd be ready to enter the numbers, and at most it would beep four or five times, which probably wouldn't wake up Claire or the baby.

Oops: When Charlie goes into his apartment and the piano is missing, it's missing from the wrong side; it was originally on the other side of the apartment, near the kitchen, but the chair and piano light are sitting on the other side. Also, Eko tells Claire that when the dove appeared in the sky, John the Baptist knew he'd cleansed Christ of his sins. He's wrong, though; Christ was without sin, as any good Christian believes. Rather, there are two schools of thought as to why Christ was baptized: either he was taking all of humanity's sins upon himself, or he was showing others the importance of baptism.

4 8 15 16 23 42: In the commercial shoot, the director calls to rotate on the **8** count. Charlie smashes one of the statues, and Locke sees him, and confiscates the rest of them. When we see Locke put them on the shelf in the armory, there are 7 statues, which means Charlie was hiding **8** of them, since he smashed one.

It's Just a Flesh Wound: Claire slaps Charlie's face. Locke punches Charlie three times, and Charlie gets a big cut on his left cheek that requires stitches.

Any Questions?:

- Why did Charlie believe he could save his family through his music? Why did they need saving? The first scene in the episode is a dream, not a flashback, so what were his parents really like?
- Charlie's father was a butcher, but why do we see him chopping a doll's head off? Was he an abusive man?
- Is Charlie using again, or are we just being led to think he is?
- *Does* Hurley know Libby from somewhere? She's a psychologist, so did she work at the mental hospital where Hurley was?
- Why is Eko marking off his favorite trees?
- Locke asks Charlie if he's using again, and Charlie objects to the question, prompting Locke to point out that he didn't answer what he asked. Later Jack says exactly the same thing to Charlie. Maybe Jack and Locke are more alike than they'd like to think.
- Knowing what a temptation those statues will be to Charlie, why does Locke decide to keep them rather than destroy them?

Music/Bands: The Kinks' "He's Evil" (*Preservation: Act 2*) is playing in Charlie's apartment when he gets home, an interesting choice, since it's about a guy who seems sweet and innocent on the outside, but who is evil and conniving on the inside. It's the song he sang on the beach in "The 23rd Psalm." While Hurley and Libby do their laundry, you can hear Perry Como's "Papa Loves Mambo" (*The Very Best of Perry Como*).

I've Got a Theory, Season 2

One of the characters is behind everything, and they are now running the show, unbeknownst to the others. This lesser-known theory often suggests the culprit is Locke, who couldn't walk before he got on the plane, but can walk now. What if his father is actually Alvar Hanso, and through Hanso's foundation Locke was told he would be given the ability to walk again if he just led this experiment for them? He has ties to a few of the people on the island (Hurley owned his company and stayed at the same mental hospital as Locke's mother; Jack was able to make a paralyzed woman walk again . . . did Locke go to him and get turned away?). However, this theory undercuts the moments where we see Locke all alone, like in "Deus Ex Machina," where he's beating his hands against the hatch door. If he were really play-acting, why is he doing this? It seems unlikely that Locke would have more knowledge than we know.

The Others are all scientists who are pretending to be hillbillies as part of the island experiment. This theory finds some legs later in the season, and there is a lot of evidence backing it up. They have a motorboat, and therefore have access to fuel, yet they haven't tried to leave the island. There are other hints in upcoming episodes like "Maternity Leave" that suggest the Others may not be what they seem. Are they kidnapping people as part of the experiment? In season 1, fans wondered if the island was a strange lab, and in season 2, with the discovery of the hatch and the story of the de Groots, it's certainly possible. But where do the Others fit in?

The plane broke up because it went through a wormhole of some kind, and now the survivors are in another time. In "Exodus, Part 1," the castaways found the *Black Rock*, an old pirate ship that had landed on the island probably in the nineteenth century (the skeletons on board would back up the idea of time passing) yet it had volatile dynamite on board that had somehow survived the heat. In "The Long Con," Hurley will make a joke about being in a time warp, and something that Sayid discovers could actually attest to that. The hatch seems to contain a bunch of relics from the 1970s, and nothing has been updated in 20 years. Or is it new, and the time is actually the early 1980s?

The island is a hallucination, probably Hurley's. In season 1, many fans thought Jack might be behind it, but by season 2, we knew that Hurley had spent time in a mental hospital, the numbers still seemed to have no meaning to anyone but him, yet they were recurring everywhere, and Hurley is probably the most popular guy on the island. Are the people on the island extensions of his personality, and not Jack's? (See "Dave.") Libby's explanation of Donald in "Dave," which proves people on the island know things Hurley doesn't, shows why this theory doesn't hold much water.

One person on the island is being experimented on, and everyone else is in on the joke. Again, most people look to Jack here — what if all of this is for his own redemption, and everyone on the plane is in cahoots with the possible scientists on the island? This theory has been bandied about, but it would definitely undercut all of the personal revelations that the other characters have had. If we believe they were all in on it, it renders all of the non-Jack episodes meaningless.

The parents of the castaways are behind it. We've seen Christian Shephard haunting every one of Jack's flashbacks, and he's also appeared in Sawyer's (and yet another one later in the season). Sun's father has dominated both her life and Jin's. Locke's father is wealthy and powerful. What if the wealthier, more overbearing parents were able to get the parents of other characters on board (Hurley's mom wishes he could find himself; Claire's parents have given up on her; Ana Lucia's mother knows she needs help; Kate's parents both think she's almost beyond hope) and put all of their children on a plane to teach them a little something? But what about Rose and Bernard, or the one or two characters who don't have serious parental issues? Or what about the hundreds of other people who died in the crash? It would make the parents mass murderers, so this probably isn't likely.

There's some sort of virus on the island that creates genetic mutations in people, and maybe these survivors have been specifically chosen as part of a medical experiment. We've seen Ethan's superstrength. Desmond maniacally injected himself with something that we'll soon see another character injected with because he was protecting himself against something on the island that made people "sick." Is there a virus on the island? Have the Others been exposed to it for so long that they're starting to become genetic mutants? Does this virus have the power to strengthen, rather than weaken? (It would explain Walt's sudden heightened powers, or Locke's ability to walk.) The virus could also be what is causing the prophetic dreams and hallucinations, like Claire's in "Raised by Another" or Charlie's in "Fire + Water."

2.13   The Long Con

Original air date: February 8, 2006
Written by: Leonard Dick, Steven Maeda
Directed by: Roxann Dawson
Guest cast: Kim Dickens (Cassidy), Beth Broderick (Diane), Kevin Dunn (Gordy), Finn Armstrong (Arthur), Richard Cavanna (Peter)

Flashback: Sawyer
When Sun is abducted and hurt, everyone suspects the Others, until Kate and Sawyer begin finding clues that lead them to think there's an enemy among them.

It's clear now that every character on the island has a past they're trying to escape in some way. Kate has been on the run for years, and one of her biggest fears is that people on the island will know what she's done. Jack has felt responsible for the death of his father, but despite Sawyer's reassurance that Christian didn't hate him, he won't relax, and there's clearly something else that's happened in his past that he can't let go. Hurley worries that people will think he's crazy, he's only confessed his lottery winnings to two people, and he hopes that on the island he'll stop bringing bad luck to those around him. Locke is escaping a life of futility and paralysis, and finally feels useful, though he's beginning to question why he was healed. Michael lost Walt once, and finally got him back, but it's happened again, so he's determined not to let the Others win.

Sawyer, on the other hand, stands apart from everyone else in that he is exactly the same person on the island that he was before the crash, and he's never attempted to reinvent himself in any way — he doesn't need to, because he already did so years ago. In "The Long Con," he not only remembers one of the worst things he once did, but he's able to finally bring that person he used to be and his actions to the island, once and for all. Sawyer has never tried to hide who he was; in fact, he's done quite the opposite, exaggerating his negative side and making people hate him even more. We've had glimpses of the kinder, gentler Sawyer, but he never lasts for long. If Sawyer gets the slightest whiff of betrayal, he'll act against the person before they can hurt him.

"New sheriff in town, boys! You all best get used to it." (SHOOTING STAR)

It's been a week since Sawyer has returned from his failed attempt to get off the island. He's been in a coma and he's seen death, rifts, previously popular people falling out of favor, characters losing touch with themselves and each other, and finally a bad encounter with the Others. He's spotted the vulnerability in the group, and he goes right for it. Specifically, he's found a weakness in Kate, who missed him while he was gone, nursed him back to health, and now flirts with him daily on the beach while Jack fumes from a distance. He places the kernel of doubt in Kate's head, and it allows him to weasel in and make her his unwitting sidekick.

Meanwhile, Jack and Locke make an agreement of their own, but knowing their past, it's inevitable that it's going to end badly. The previous day Locke lost his trust in Charlie — Charlie's sobriety was important to Locke. All his life Locke has felt completely useless, with one endeavor after another turning out to be worthless. By helping Charlie kick his habit, Locke felt he was finally making a difference, but now he believes Charlie will always be a heroin addict, and it's affected him deeply. As he quietly sits in the hatch, searching through books as if looking for an answer and constantly changing the lock combinations because he doesn't trust anyone, we see a man who's not yet broken, but certainly fractured. He shared the experience of the Others with Jack and Sawyer, yet instead of the three banding together to come up with a plan, they've all separated, making individual plans while Locke sits alone, wondering why no one consults him. When Sawyer finally does come to talk to him, and tells him what Locke wants to hear (that Jack can't be trusted), Locke helps Sawyer, not realizing it's just like the kidney incident all over again. And we can only imagine what this new betrayal will do to him.

The one thing that will continue to nag at everyone throughout this season is the lack of communication within this band of survivors. Instead of forming a proper army using everyone they've got (including a soldier and a hunter and a cop and a con man and a former-drug-dealer-who's-now-a-priest and a woman who can handle a gun and a rock star who makes good bait) this group runs off in different directions trying to come up with 48 different ways they could deal with the Others. It's this lack of unity and communication that will not only prove a little annoying to watch, but will be their downfall in the end.

Highlight: Sawyer sitting at the hatch computer and saying, "I'm *this close* to the high score on Donkey Kong."

Did You Notice?:

- Sawyer asks Charlie what it's like to be the most hated, for a change, and it's what he asked Boone in "White Rabbit" after Boone stole the drinking water.
- When Sawyer goes into the diner to meet with Gordy, the waitress who serves them is Kate's mom, Diane. She must have changed jobs, because this is not the same diner we saw in "What Kate Did."
- Sawyer counts to five before walking back into the house, just as Jack taught Kate to count to five and then let her fear go.
- It has clearly been established that when Charlie's hood is up, he's on drugs: In "Walkabout," Charlie's hood is up when he rejoins everyone at the memorial service after snorting heroin, and in "The Moth," Charlie's hood is up when he asks Locke for the drugs, and he puts it back down after he throws them on the fire.
- Charlie punched Boone in "White Rabbit" when Boone thought he was

doing the right thing, just as Locke punches Charlie in "Fire + Water," but Boone didn't seek revenge.

- When Sayid and Hurley pick up the radio transmission, you hear the station's call letters as WUSO. While that's actually a university radio station in Ohio, it also recalls the USO during WWII.

Interesting Facts: Locke has changed the combination on the armory lock to 7-33-18. Since his name is John, he could be remembering it as the Book of John in the Bible, chapter 18, verses 7–33, which recount Peter's denial of Christ three times (see "The Moth").

Nitpick: Hurley is reading a manuscript called *Bad Twin*, which is a real fiction tie-in to the show (see page 299). It's a great marketing ploy, but such a lame tactic at the same time to have a character commenting on it. Blech.

4 8 15 16 23 42: Sawyer tells Cassidy that 40 grand in a mutual fund isn't real money.

It's Just a Flesh Wound: Sun is hit on the forehead, leaving her with a bump and a cut.

Lost in Translation: When Vincent runs over to Sun and into her garden, she says to him, "Careful over there; don't step on it." As Jin runs up to the tent when he sees Sun lying there, he yells, "Sweetheart! Sweetheart! What happened?" After she wakes up and begins talking, Jin says, "What are you saying now? Tell me, too." Sun says to him, "I'm telling him exactly what I've already told you." Then Jin interrupts her again and says, "We can't just sit here and take it like this. We have to catch them!" Sun counters, "Honey, please," and he says forcefully, "No!" When Jack walks toward Sawyer in the bunker after Sawyer holds up the painkillers, Jin says, "No, don't pay any attention to Sawyer. Stop it."

Any Questions?:

- Why doesn't Kate get suspicious of Sawyer when he says the seam is different on the hood that was put over Sun? There's no way he could have seen the seam on Kate's hood: It was dark, and it was on her head for half a second before Mr. Friendly whipped it off.
- Ana Lucia has killed someone before coming onto the island, but she's gotten away with it. On the island, she's killed someone who was part of the camp, and she's gotten away with it. Kate killed someone in her former life, and she was caught for it. So how exactly does Jack justify treating Kate like dirt, and joining up with Ana like she's his new best friend forever? As long as you get away with it, you're still cool in Jack's book?

- Why does Ana mix up Scott and Steve? The joke worked in season 1 because the two guys looked alike, but now that Steve is dead (though everyone thinks it was Scott), how would Ana even know to mix him up with someone else? Perhaps the writers would say Scott (who is pretending to be Steve) slipped up when talking to her and introduced himself as Scott.
- Locke tells Sawyer that he's alphabetizing the books, but he looks like he's up to something more serious than that. What is he really doing? Looking for more pieces of the orientation film?
- Gordy says Sawyer owes him. For what?
- Is Hurley really kidding when he makes the comment about the sound coming from another time? Is the comment just the writers poking fun at some of the more outlandish theories fans have come up with, or was this scene actually important?
- Why doesn't Sawyer take the photo of him and Cassidy with him when he leaves her? Couldn't she take it to the police and send out a manhunt for him?
- Sawyer was conning Cassidy all along, but was she also conning him? She seemed like a natural, especially when she initially tells him she doesn't have any money, and then conveniently has some money. What really happened after Sawyer drove away that we didn't get to see in this episode? Watch the episode again, assuming that Cassidy was on to him from the beginning and was actually conning *him* and you can see certain things in her facial expressions that tell us that's exactly what she was doing.

Music/Bands: At the end of the episode, Sayid and Hurley listen to "Moonlight Serenade" by The Glenn Miller Orchestra.

"An Occurrence at Owl Creek Bridge" by Ambrose Bierce (1891)

This short story was originally written in 1886 but was published in a short story collection five years later. It opens with a man, Peyton Farquhar, standing on a bridge in Alabama, surrounded by Union soldiers, and he's about to be hanged. They walk him out on a plank over the water, with an officer standing on the other end. The officer steps off, causing the plank to tilt, and the condemned man falls to his death.

Only he doesn't. The rope catches around his neck and pulls tight before snapping, and he splashes into the water below. For a moment, it's not clear to him what's happened, but when he realizes he's still alive, he also understands the reality of his current situation — that unless he frees himself from the ropes tying his hands and feet, he'll drown. He wrestles himself free, and swims to the surface of the water, only to be met with a hail of bullets from the soldiers above. He begins madly paddling down the stream, and the soldiers continue to shoot at him, even firing cannonballs into the water around him. The man paddles for his life, determined that he's not going to cheat death twice only to meet it on the third try.

While all of this is happening, we discover through flashbacks that Farquhar is a Confederate sympathizer who somehow sabotaged the work that the soldiers were doing on the railroad over Owl Creek Bridge, which led to his current predicament. Back in the present, he swims as hard as he can and eventually gets to shore, beyond the range of bullets. He's exhausted. As he lies there, the sand, plants, and trees around him suddenly sparkle like heavenly beings. He's gained a new appreciation for life, because it was almost taken from him. But the shots continue behind him, so he begins to run.

He runs all day and into the night, and as he gets closer to his home — and his beautiful wife — his throat begins to swell, and he's finding it harder to breathe. He's convinced he needs water, and then, before he knows it, he's suddenly at his gate. He opens it, and runs up the walk to his wife, who is standing there waiting for him. Just as he's about to hold her in his arms, he suddenly feels a piercing pain around his neck, and then darkness. He is in fact back at Owl Creek Bridge, swinging from the rope, dead.

The story has been made into several films, and a 1962 French version won best short film at the Cannes film festival that year, and again at the Academy Awards the following year. The film was bought by the producers of the *Twilight Zone*, who aired it as one of their fifth season episodes. The story was the inspiration behind other movies such as *Jacob's Ladder* (1990), and has been extremely influential because of the idea of an extended dying hallucination. Farquhar imagined all of what happened to him in the split second it took to break his neck. In *Jacob's Ladder*, a similar plot leads one character (believed to be an angel) to explain that hell is really purgatory, and those who are ready to let go won't see it as a hell: "The only thing that burns in Hell is the part of you that won't let go of life, your memories, your attachments. They burn them all away. But they're not punishing you

. . . they're freeing your soul. So, if you're frightened of dying and . . . and you're holding on, you'll see devils tearing your life away. But if you've made your peace, then the devils are really angels, freeing you from the earth."

On *Lost*, as mentioned, one of the pervading theories is that the characters are really in purgatory. The writers have denied that this theory is correct, and by referencing "An Occurrence at Owl Creek Bridge," they are backing up their statement. Notice in "The Long Con," that Locke is looking for answers in the book and he picks up a copy of "An Occurrence at Owl Creek Bridge," shakes it, and tosses it aside. It's as if the writers are telling us, "Nope, no answers there. These characters are *not* in purgatory. Try again." But for the sake of argument, Bierce's story is an interesting look at how the split second of death could create a lifetime of trying to redeem oneself for the bad things one has done.

2.14   One of Them

Original air date: February 18, 2006
Written by: Damon Lindelof, Carlton Cuse
Directed by: Stephen Williams
Guest cast: Clancy Brown (Joe Inman), Lindsey Ginter (Sgt. Sam Austen), Marc Casabani (Tariq), Theo Rossi (Sgt. Tony Buccoli), Thomas Meharey (U.S. Soldier #1), Kamari Borden (U.S. Soldier #2)

Flashback: Sayid

Rousseau and Sayid find a man in the jungle, whom Sayid takes back to the hatch. The man claims his name is Henry Gale and that he crashed on the island, too.

In the previous episode, Sawyer reiterated that a tiger doesn't change its stripes. In "One of Them," we find out how the tiger got its stripes in the first place. This is an episode about loyalty — how do we know when it's right to be loyal to someone, and when does loyalty become blind faith? Who do you align yourself with: the side that you've always been on, or the side you think is right?

"One of Them" flashes back to Sayid in the Gulf War in 1991. It's amazing how much younger Naveen Andrews looks in these scenes, with a wide-eyed naiveté that Sayid lost long ago. Since he looks younger and less confident in this episode than he did in the "Solitary" flashback, and this flashback seems to be the first time he tortured someone, the events of this episode must have preceded the ones in "Solitary." In both cases, we see him working in the Republican Guard, but betraying his army to conspire with the enemy. Now, on the island, he faces someone he believes is his enemy, and the man is pleading that he's no different than Sayid or the other castaways. Sayid doesn't believe him, possibly because he sees himself in the turncoat Henry Gale. He's also learned from his many years as a torturer who is lying and who is telling the truth. And as far as he's concerned, Henry is lying.

Jack and Locke, as usual, are on opposite sides of the Henry issue. Jack worries that Sayid is going too far. Locke has decided to wait things out and see what evidence Sayid can come up with before making his decision. In their growing hatred for each other, Jack and Locke don't realize that they've actually switched places — usually Locke goes with his gut, and Jack waits to see the evidence. They both fall back to their old selves, however, when Jack threatens Locke and refuses to let him push the button. In a terrifying scene, we see the beginnings of what happens when the numbers do not get entered in time. Is it all smoke and mirrors, or could what we saw have turned into something much bigger if Locke hadn't acted so quickly?

Meanwhile, out in the jungle, Sawyer and Hurley are looking for a tree frog. In the previous episode, Sawyer shocked everyone when he stole all the guns and declared himself the Sheriff of Craphole Island, yet just as the boar became his nemesis in "Outlaws," now he thinks the irritating chirp of a tree frog is his worst enemy. The scene where Hurley and Sawyer finally find the poor thing is violent and shocking. What Sawyer does is detestable, as if the writers are trying to get the viewers to hate him as much as he wants everyone on the island to. However, the two plotlines are linked: Sawyer crushes the frog for no reason other than it was in the wrong place at the wrong time, just as Henry accidentally landed in the trap. Sawyer shows the frog no mercy: he kills it instantly and goopily. Sayid doesn't kill Henry Gale, because he believes he might be worth keeping alive, but he, too, shows no mercy.

Henry Gale is the enemy, or so Sayid believes. He thinks Gale's "one of them." If he's not a castaway, he's foreign, Other. Yet similarly, Sayid has never belonged. In the Gulf War, the U.S. was his enemy, yet he worked with them. Later, Nadia was aligned with enemy insurgents, yet he sided with her against his own people. He has come to the island with everyone else on flight 815, yet he is always subtly pushed away by everyone else come leadership time. The only time he's felt like he belonged was with Nadia or Shannon, and they're both gone. Sayid punishes Henry Gale for being an Other, but he's always been Other himself. "One of Them" is a terrific episode, and one of the highlights of season 2.

Highlight: The numbers suddenly going haywire, and the terrified look on Locke's face.

Did You Notice?:

- The sergeant — Sgt. Austen — who initially tells Sayid about the helicopter going down, and then accompanies him in the truck at the end, is the man Kate believed to be her father. He's looking at a picture of her in the end. He already knows that it's not his daughter, and yet we can tell in this scene that he adores her nonetheless.
- When Sawyer and Hurley are walking through the jungle, Hurley says this is how people die in scary movies, which is what he'd said to Charlie in "Outlaws" when they were burying Ethan.
- This is the first time Sayid has declared, "I am a torturer," as if he's accepted it, and will now become the person people have always told him he is. In the past, Sayid seems to be forced into situations, whether it's torturing Nadia, Tariq, Sawyer, or tricking Essam. But in this episode he embraces who he is and tortures Henry despite others trying to stop him.

Interesting Facts: Sayid says his birthplace is Tikrit (pop. 29,000), which is not only the birthplace of Saddam Hussein, but legendary twelfth century Kurdish leader Saladin.

When the numbers began to scroll to various weird images, it was instantly picked up by fans that the symbols were hieroglyphs of some kind. The night this episode aired, forums, chatrooms, and mailing lists lit up with theories of what the glyphs might have meant. It only took about 24 hours before one fan, who went by the screen name onehundredeight, discovered a book called *A Concise Dictionary of Middle Egyptian* by Raymond O. Faulkner, in which the author listed various groupings of hieroglyphics and their meanings. Onehundredeight determined that the one glyph we don't see is a spiral, and that the five symbols together translated to "cause to die," or, more bluntly, to kill. (Fans like onehundredeight are the very people the writers are testing in every episode.)

Henry Gale (1874–1942) was the name of an American astrophysicist and co-author of a popular physics book, *First Course in Physics*. It is also the name of

See you in the next life . . .

Solitary: Nadia writes a note to Sayid on the back of a photograph of herself that reads, "You'll find me in the next life, if not in this one."

Deus Ex Machina: Just before going into surgery, Anthony says to Locke, "See you on the other side, son."

Man of Science, Man of Faith: As Desmond leaves Jack in the stadium after Jack's twisted his ankle, he says, "See you in another life, yeah?" He says exactly the same thing to Jack as he leaves the hatch in "Orientation."

Dave: As Dave jumps off the cliff, he says, "See you in another life, Hurley."

Three Minutes: One of the Others takes Michael's blood and says, "See you in the funny pages." Which is probably a warped "Others" version of the statement.

Live Together, Die Alone: As Desmond descends into the room under the computer room at the end of the episode, he says to Locke, "I'll see you in another life, brother."

Dorothy's uncle in *The Wizard of Oz* (see page 334).

4 8 15 16 23 42: Inman shows Sayid a videotape that says it's Reel **23**108-**42**. Tariq tells Sayid that the American soldier was buried **4** kilometers from where they are. Henry says he's been on the island for **4** months. Sayid was **23** when the Americans invaded Iraq. Henry says the balloon he was in was 140 feet high by 60 feet wide: that makes it 8400 (**8** and **4**) square feet. When Locke begins to tell Jack the combination to the safe, the first number is **15**. When the timer runs to zero, **4** of the numbers turn into hieroglyphics.

It's Just a Flesh Wound: Henry Gale incurs many wounds care of Sayid.

Any Questions?:

- Tariq tells Sayid that Sayid is the son of a great hero. Who was his father?
- Is Henry telling the truth?
- Why does Sayid talk to Charlie? He appeals to his sense of anger about the Others hurting him, but Charlie is ineffective about everything, so what good is he to Sayid?

2.15   Maternity Leave

Original air date: March 1, 2006

Written by: Dawn Lambertsen Kelly, Matt Ragghianti
Directed by: Jack Bender
Guest cast: William Mapother (Ethan), Tania Raymonde (Teenage Girl)

Flashback: Claire

Claire begins to remember what happened when she was kidnapped by the Others, and she decides to return to the place where she was being held.

Claire has been a bit of a non-presence all season. Most of the action has been happening in the bunker, and she's still on the beach. She occasionally rushes in, tells Jack that her baby looks sick, he says no, Aaron's fine, and she rushes away again. We've seen her chatting to Locke and Charlie, but she's had less than 10 minutes of screen time all season. In season 1, Claire was laid-back, talked about astrology, was funny, sweet, and cheerful. This season she's worried, nitpicky, nagging, and hostile, and she's had a pretty big personality change. In other words, she's a new mom. Many women suffer extreme anxieties after the birth of a child, but poor Claire has very few people she can turn to. Apparently, the only parent on the island is Michael, and he has been absent from his son's life til now. Claire has no parenting books, no toys, no bottles, nothing to ease the strain of being a 24/7 parent to this new baby. So when she begins to have strange nightmares and visions, it's no wonder she wants to solve the problem quickly so she can get back to worrying about Aaron.

This episode contains the first flashback to an incident that happened on the island rather than before the crash. Or is it? Libby suggests that the flashbacks Claire is experiencing could actually be memories from before, and she makes a good point. Many of the things she "remembers" happened in "Raised by Another," before she was kidnapped. The mobile that she sees in the bunker in her flashback was the same mobile (complete with Oceanic planes) she saw in her dream at the beginning of that earlier episode. In "Maternity Leave," Ethan asks Claire when her last checkup was and she says she's been busy, and he tells her that traveling in her third trimester usually isn't recommended. In "Raised by Another," Jack does an examination of her and asks how her OB-GYN was in Sydney, and then wonders aloud why she allowed Claire to travel in her third trimester. He asks if her ultrasound was okay, and if she's feeling okay, and she nods her head fervently and unconvincingly, leading us to wonder if she's had any prenatal care at all while in Sydney. Did she know she was lying, and that lie manifested itself in her subconscious and created another situation where she was actually telling the truth? The mobile also played "Catch a Falling Star," the song

In "Maternity Leave," Claire begins to remember snippets of what happened when she was kidnapped. (CHRISTINA RADISH)

The beautiful Mira Furlan (Rousseau cleans up well!). (S.BAK/SHOOTING STAR)

she requested the potential adoptive couple to sing to the baby when he was born; since it would have been virtually impossible for the people on the island to have known she requested that, the mobile seems to have been more a figment of Claire's imagination than anything else.

Meanwhile, Henry Gale is starting to become the concrete version of the tension between Jack and Locke. Locke gives Gale a copy of Dostoevsky's *The Brothers Karamazov*, a novel about religious faith and doubt (see page 270). As Jack bosses Locke around and seems to have quickly taken over Locke's bunker, Henry senses the conflict and moves in to rub salt in Locke's wounds. His manipulation of Locke's vulnerability makes him seem less like a random guy who landed on the island in a balloon and more like a liar, trickster, and an Other. Sayid and Rousseau are convinced that's what he is, and when Eko enters his cell to give his "confession" to Gale, he's convinced Gale's a liar, too.

This episode is all about con games. Gale is possibly running one on the Lostaways, and in one of Claire's flashbacks, we discover that the Others are running one of their own. Kate's discovery in this new Caduceus hatch is a shocker: we haven't even nailed down who the Others are yet, and then they go and pull a switcheroo on us. Even Rousseau, who up to now has been one part lonely, crazy, but well-meaning French chick, and one part deceitful enemy, suddenly seems to move over to the well-meaning side. Claire gives Rousseau the hope she's been looking for, and we discover that while Rousseau was working against Claire in "Exodus, Part 2," she was her salvation in "Homecoming." Is she finally being sincere, or is this just another veil being pulled over our eyes to make us believe one thing before showing us another?

Highlight: When Kate tells Sawyer she needs a gun, and he doesn't get to ask why, his response is priceless. "Yes, I do. Watch: Why?"

Did You Notice?:

- The "Previously on *Lost*" segments at the beginning of episode are getting increasingly longer, because season 2 suffered severely from terrible scheduling by the networks. Flip through the episode guide and take a look at the air dates: you'll see that fans would wait three weeks for a new episode, get one, then wait another four, get two, wait another three, get one, wait another five, etc. It was a ridiculous way to treat fans of such a complex show. Luckily, ABC listened to fan complaints, and agreed that in season 3 the show would be shown in two solid blocks with no repeats.

- Kate reassures Claire that if something were wrong, Jack would know, but he ignored her in season 1 when she believed someone was trying to hurt her, and she ended up being kidnapped. So it's not likely Claire's going to have a lot of faith in Jack.

- Beside the medicine Ethan injects into Claire is another vial that says something about bacteria on it.

- The man who talks to Ethan in the hallway is Mr. Friendly from "The Hunting Party."

- The flashbacks usually begin with a closeup of the person's eye, but only when Claire is being drugged by the teenage girl does the camera zoom in on Claire's eye, as if to suggest only the events that follow are actually real.

- Cutting the beard is a sign of mourning in the Old Testament, and since Eko cut two braids in his beard, they probably signified the two people he killed. Or maybe he was just trying to get Henry to soil himself.

Interesting Facts: Henry Gale asking Locke if there was any Stephen King was a shout-out to the horror heavyweight, who writes a regular column for *Entertainment Weekly* where he has extolled the virtues of *Lost*, what he considers to be one of the best shows on television.

Henry Gale mentions that Hemingway was admirable because he fought in the Spanish Civil War, but Hemingway never actually fought in that war. He reported on the war for the North American Newspaper Alliance, and openly supported the Republican/Loyalists.

Sawyer's beach book of the week is Walker Percy's *Lancelot*. The book is about a modern-day Lancelot who is in an institution of some kind (it's never clear where) and he's lost his unfaithful wife in a house fire, which he started. The book is one long monologue that Lance delivers to his friend, whom he calls Percival, who is a religious man. The book is a difficult read, and is often misunderstood because Lance is a despicable character who believes that men and women simply need to embrace who they really are: men are rapists, and women want to be raped. He uses racial slurs for African-Americans (while explaining that he was also a supporter of the NAACP) and presumably it's his rantings that have landed him in this place. But keep reading, because the last line of the novel is worth the buildup (and no, don't go and look ahead). The final word actually forces the reader to go back and rethink everything Lance has said and consider it through a new lens (let's hope Sawyer actually made it to the end).

Nitpick: Jack and Locke seem to have suddenly switched sides on their views on whether or not Henry Gale is telling the truth. When we last left them, Jack was angry they were holding him against his will, and now he's a big proponent of it. What happened? Also, while there is the rare baby who sleeps well at night, 16-day-old babies don't typically do that (and shouldn't, since they require feedings every two to four hours), and just two episodes ago Claire was complaining that Aaron doesn't sleep at night and just cries. So why would she now be saying he "typically" sleeps through the night, when he's shown no patterns at all? And how could Aaron have caught roseola? Roseola usually affects babies that are six to 24 months old, not as young as Aaron, and it's caused by a virus. It's passed from one person to another through fluids, so someone with a cold or flu would have had to cough or sneeze on him, and no one's been sick since he was born. Finally, we know that Claire has been breastfeeding Aaron exclusively, and now she's about to go into the jungle for a few hours, leaving Aaron with Sun, who has absolutely nothing to feed him. Either Claire doesn't go far, or she's assuming it's okay for Aaron to starve a little while he's ill.

Oops: Claire tells Libby she's upset that two weeks are missing from her memory. But she was taken around day 17, and returned about 10 days later, with no memory since the plane crash, so it's more like a month is missing from her memory.

4 8 15 16 23 42: On the top of the vial of medicine that Ethan administers to Claire, it says CR **4-81516-23 42**.

It's Just a Flesh Wound: We see how Rousseau incurred the scratches on her arm, and Claire got the bump on her forehead from "Homecoming." Claire is also injected multiple times and drugged.

Any Questions?:

- Did Locke tell anyone what happened when the countdown clock went to zero?
- Why would Claire have gone *anywhere* with the woman who stole her baby?
- Claire says she has no memories of what happened to her, yet in "Do No Harm," when she's giving birth, she says to Kate that she's worried the Others have done something to her baby. Does she remember the injections?
- What did Ethan inject Claire with? Was it the same medicine Desmond was injecting into himself in "Man of Science, Man of Faith"? Why are people injecting it? What do they think it does? Are the injections making her act drunk, or is that the sedatives they're giving her?
- Why is Eko chopping trees?
- Sun's face seems to take on a strange look when Claire asks her if she's a mother. Did Sun lose a child? Is she lying to Claire?
- Is it significant that the animals that are on the wall of the baby room in Claire's flashback are African (monkey, zebra, lion, hippo, tiger)?
- Where *did* all the stuff in the room come from?
- Is Claire clairvoyant? Is that why her character is named as such?
- The man in the hallway talking to Ethan mentions a list. Is this the same sort of list that Ana Lucia found in "The Other 48 Days"?
- Who is Mr. Friendly talking about when he says, "You know what he's going to do when he finds out?"
- When Rousseau steps up to the gun and tells Kate to kill her, it's a poignant, beautifully acted moment. Is Rousseau really suicidal, or does she know Kate won't pull the trigger?
- Claire mentions that Ethan's water tastes sour. What was in it? Is it what made her lose her memory just before going back to the camp?

Do You Want to Know a Secret?

Every once in a while one character asks another if they want to know a secret, and usually what they tell them is debunked later on.

Pilot, Part 2: Locke creepily asks Walt if he wants to know a secret, and later Walt tells Michael his secret was that a miracle happened on the island.
Man of Science, Man of Faith: Sarah tells Jack to come close, and she whispers to him that she knows she won't be dancing at her wedding now.
. . . And Found: Jae Lee tells Sun his secret, that he's running away to marry an American girl he met at Harvard.
Maternity Leave: Ethan's secret is that he's going to miss Claire, and wishes she didn't have to go.

- Are the Others actors? If so, why would Ethan put himself in harm's way, risking life and limb?
- Is the teenager in the hatch really Alex? Why, after all these years, hasn't she tried to escape, if she was able to help Claire escape?
- Why does Eko confess to Henry? Does he believe he's one of the Others? Does he think he's even more powerful than that, some sort of Messiah, and the island is Judgment Day?
- Why does Locke let Henry get to him at the end like that?
- Does Locke think he's Hemingway or Dostoevsky?
- In "Exodus, Part 1," Claire sees the scratches on Rousseau's arm and Rousseau lies and says she got them from a bush. Why didn't she tell the truth to Claire? If she'd told everyone what had happened, could they have formed a group and gone back into the jungle to the hatch before the Others could vacate the premises? Does Rousseau mistrust the Lostaways the way they mistrust her?
- In "Homecoming," Ethan reappears to reclaim Claire, and he has four scratches on his face. Where did he get them? Claire didn't scratch him, and Rousseau wouldn't have been near Ethan to do it, either. Did Alex scratch his face when he possibly interrogated her? Was he cut by some of the Others for accidentally losing Claire?

2.16   The Whole Truth

Original air date: March 22, 2006
Written by: Elizabeth Sarnoff, Christina M. Kim
Directed by: Karen Gaviola
Guest cast: Tony Lee (Jae Lee), Greg Joung Paik (Dr. Je-Gyu Kim)

Flashback: Sun

Sun discovers something that will completely change her life, and Sayid and Ana Lucia go off in search of Henry's balloon.

The theme of conning and lying to others continues in this episode, from its title to its final line of dialogue. So far we've caught almost every character in a lie of some kind, and through the flashbacks we know that most of them were expert liars before they set food on the island. As I've said already, communication is a serious problem, and it's because of everyone's secrets and duplicity that they keep getting into trouble.

After wrangling a pregnancy test out of a smug Sawyer, Sun is shocked to discover that she's pregnant. But through flashbacks, we see that despite her relationship with Jae Lee appearing to be over in ". . . And Found," when she walked out of the restaurant and into Jin, it continued long after that. Jae Lee met her in secret, in a lavish hotel room, to . . . teach her English. But were they doing more than just conjugating verbs together? When the viewer becomes privy to a doctor's prognosis that renders the couple infertile, it makes Sun look even more suspicious. She's one of the few people on the island who viewers trust completely, and after the hardship she and Jin have been going through, they're the couple we're rooting for above all others. We would love to believe that Sun is telling the truth, but the looks of longing between her and Jae Lee were undeniable. As if to brace viewers for the possible infidelity and make sure people don't turn away from Sun, we get more glimpses of evil, nasty Jin — his reaction to finding out Sun is infertile is particularly repugnant.

Ana Lucia and Sayid go off to find the balloon with Charlie, and Ana finally has to face what she's done to Sayid. Ana makes an interesting comment to Charlie and Sayid that "Jack and Locke are a little too busy worrying about Locke and Jack," pointing to the major flaw between these two men in season 2. (Sawyer also mentioned in "The Long Con" that Locke and Jack were so caught up in hating each other they didn't see him coming, and they don't seem to have learned anything since then.) She's seen through Locke's attempt to drive a wedge between her and Jack, but at the same time she gives in to it, and acts independently of Jack. The main thing Locke seems to have learned from Henry Gale is how to divide and conquer, and it's fun to see a little bit of the old Locke back when he refers to the bunker as "*my* hatch."

Sun is one of the most beloved characters on the show, and fans hate the thought that she might be keeping another secret from Jin. (SUE SCHNEIDER/MOONGLOW PHOTOS)

Speaking of con artists and deceitful tricks, Henry Gale is quickly becoming one of the most entertaining characters on television. His manipulation of Locke began in the previous week, and now he begins working on Jack, but quickly finds that Jack is a tougher nut to crack. He reads out a quote from *The Brothers Karamazov* — "Men reject their prophets and slay them, but they love their martyrs and honor those whom they have slain" — showing the hypocrisy that exists in a society that can crucify a man for claiming to be a savior, and then uphold him as the Son of God after he's dead. John Locke is a prophet of sorts on the island, but Jack treats him like dirt. And we all know Jack isn't the kind of guy who would ever worship a martyr afterward. Michael Emerson plays Henry Gale with aplomb, and from his voice to his facial expressions to the way he holds his body, he reminds the viewer of Kevin Spacey in *The Usual Suspects* as Verbal Kint. In the film, a detective is determined to get to the bottom of things through questioning Kint, a squirmy, annoying little man. With Henry's final comment about Ana Lucia and Sayid's mission, he plays with Jack and Locke's minds, just like Kint toys with the detective.

Jack tells Sun in this episode that the only thing she can do is come clean with Jin and tell him the truth. Part of what he's saying is clearly directed at Kate, who is standing right there, but as soon as he says it, he turns and lies to Kate, showing his hypocrisy and lack of trust. At the end of the episode, Sun tells Jin "the truth," and he believes her wholeheartedly, saying that the baby is a miracle. No one trusts anyone on this island, except Jin, who trusts his wife. In "Hearts and Minds," Sun says to Kate, "Have you never lied to a man you loved?" and that question echoes at the end of this episode. Is she lying to Jin so his feelings won't be hurt? Or is this really a miracle baby? Sun holds her hands over her tummy and grins, and it's not clear if she's happy because she's finally pregnant, or because she's carrying Jae Lee's child.

Highlight: Sawyer reading *Are You There, God? It's Me, Margaret* and complaining that there's not enough sex in it.

Did You Notice?:

- Jin tells Sun at the very beginning that "a baby will change everything. A baby will make it better." Are those prophetic words that will have a larger meaning on the island?
- Sun believes Jin's request for her to come back to the beach is an unfair one, because she wants to be left alone in her garden. But it's not any different than her request that he stay behind while the others went off to look for Michael in "The Hunting Party"; just as Sun was worried something might happen to him in that episode, Jin worries something might happen to her now.
- Jin tears up the garden, just as Sun tore it up in ". . . And Found" when she was looking for her wedding ring. (How does anything grow there?)
- Locke tells Ana Lucia that she runs like the devil's chasing her, and that's what Desmond told Jack in "Man of Science, Man of Faith" in Jack's flashback.
- Jack always repeats Locke's name when he's really angry with him, "Really John? You have an idea, John? Well, John, why don't you enlighten the rest of us, John? Because, John, we'd all love to hear it. John."
- Locke is looking at the Geronimo Jackson record in the hatch.
- Charlie hypocritically says to Ana Lucia that the last time she was holding a gun she murdered someone. Interesting . . . the last time *Charlie* held a gun, Ethan ended up with four holes in his chest.
- When Dr. Kim tells Sun the truth, she looks horrified, as if she's had unprotected sex with someone else thinking she couldn't get pregnant.

- Suddenly many of Jin's actions when he's around children make sense. In "Pilot, Part 2," he's appalled when Claire puts his hand on her belly, but momentarily looks interested. In "House of the Rising Sun," when he's handcuffed to the plane and Walt is nearby, he just looks at him with quiet affection. In "Homecoming," when Claire is returned to the camp, Jin looks concerned and asks Sun if the baby is going to be okay. Sun looks miffed and says bluntly, "I'm sure the baby is fine." In "Do No Harm," he's the one who comforts Claire when she's in labor, and jumps up and down in glee when the baby is born. In "The Greater Good," Charlie asks Jin where Sun is, and wonders if she could help with Aaron, and Jin says, "No!" It seems at the time like he's saying he doesn't know where she is, but now it seems he was saying no, she can't/won't help with the baby because it would be too upsetting.

Interesting Facts: *Are You There, God? It's Me, Margaret* is a novel by Judy Blume about a young girl as she enters adolescence and menstruates for the first time. Written in 1970, the book made the news again in 2006 when it was discovered Blume had rewritten parts of it for a new edition (in the original, Margaret struggles with belted feminine pads, and Blume changed that to modern adhesive ones in the updated edition). Religion plays a part in the novel, because Margaret has one Christian parent and one Jewish parent, and she always feels torn between the two, and is brought up without any religion. Because of its subject matter, the book is consistently on the top 100 "most frequently challenged books," as tallied by the American Library Association.

Nitpick: At the beginning of the episode, Jin finds Sun in the garden and yells at her about how he couldn't find her and wants her to return to the beach with him. When we see her next, she's alone. Where did Jin go? Why is the word "confident" on the pregnancy test box? It doesn't make any sense in the context of the other ones — easy-to-use, convenient, and accurate. The others are adjectives to describe the actual test, and confident would apparently describe the user. Also, the doctor says he lied and told Jin and Sun that Sun was the infertile one because he was scared of Jin, but wouldn't telling the daughter of Mr. Paik that she was physically "deficient" in a way infuriate Paik even more?

Oops: One of the subtitles has a spelling error in it, when the doctor says, "You're husband, he works for your father." Also, Sun works in the garden constantly, yet never has a speck of dirt under her fingernails.

Lost in Translation: When Sawyer and Bernard are speaking and Jin can't understand them, what the director did was take the words they were speaking and run them backwards. If you reverse the audio, as many fans have done, the translation is this:

Bernard: Well, how do you know?

Sawyer: I got my sources.

Bernard: Aren't you going to tell him?

Sawyer: Not my place.

Bernard: You should tell him.

Sawyer: Hell no! Let Sunshine tell him.

Any Questions?:

- Was there a relationship between Sun and Jae Lee? How long after ". . . And Found" is this flashback supposed to be? In that one, it was before Jin and Sun met, and Jae Lee was going to leave six months later to go to America. In this one, Jin and Sun have been married for some time and Jae Lee has gone to America and come back, his heart broken.

- What are Charlie and Sayid building when Ana Lucia approaches Sayid? Charlie asks about a dining room table, but that doesn't make any sense. Is Sayid making some sort of instrument of torture? After what happened two episodes ago, he wouldn't just stop the torture of Henry Gale altogether.

- Kate becomes oddly silent after telling Sun she's taken a pregnancy test before. Was it when she was married? Was it positive or negative? Did she have an abortion? Does she have a child?

- When Jack tells Sun it's important that she tell the truth to Jin, he seems very passionate about his words. It's obvious he's directing part of his speech at Kate, but did Sarah deceive him about a pregnancy? We saw in "The Hunting Party" that Sarah told him she wasn't pregnant: was she lying?

Music/Bands: Jack and Locke are listening to The Seeds' "Pushin' Too Hard" (*The Seeds*) while Ana Lucia is interrogating Henry.

 The Brothers Karamazov by Fyodor Dostoevsky (1880)

Fyodor Pavlovich Karamazov is a womanizer and cad who marries a woman and has a son, Dmitri. Three years later, she leaves him for another man, leaving

Dmitri behind to be raised by a servant and his mother's various relatives. She dies, and Fyodor comes into her money. Meanwhile, Fyodor remarries and has two more sons, Ivan and Alyosha, but his wife dies when the boys are very young. Alyosha is as good and pure as Fyodor is corrupt, whereas Dmitri is passionate and stubborn and Ivan is restrained, an intellectual struggling to reconcile his religious beliefs. Ivan needs actual evidence to believe in something, and while he begins as a religious man, he becomes an atheist. When Dmitri is a teenager he believes Fyodor has stolen his inheritance and he begins warring with his father. Ivan goes off to school, but Alyosha stays with Fyodor and announces he's going to study at the local seminary under a monk, Zosima. Dmitri comes home to try to work out his differences with his father, and Alyosha arranges a meeting between the two with Zosima acting as the mediator.

Fyodor arrives with Ivan at the monastery, and his lack of decorum and Ivan's spouting of atheistic jargon humiliates Alyosha, who thinks they're both being disrespectful to Zosima. While they wait for Dmitri to arrive, Zosima leaves to speak with some of the women of faith who have come to ask his guidance, and it's through his goodness that the flaws of all of the other characters (including Alyosha) become magnified. When Alyosha and Zosima return to the others, Ivan is arguing with the monks. In the midst of his argument, Dmitri arrives and Fyodor accuses him of abandoning his fiancée, Katerina, for another woman, Grushenka, and then letting Ivan have the fiancée. Dmitri counters that Fyodor wants Grushenka, and that Fyodor has offered her 3,000 rubles to be with him. Zosima suddenly gets up, kneels in front of Dmitri, and leaves the room. When Alyosha follows him, Zosima tells him to leave the monastery and pursue a life outside his walls, and that he sees great things in Alyosha's future. Alyosha is devastated and talks to a fellow student Rakitin (who secretly hates him), who tells him he believes Zosima saw the end of the Karamazovs coming, with murder and bloodshed in their future, and by bowing in front of Dmitri he was acknowledging that this would happen.

The narrative moves back to the birth of Smerdyakov years earlier, whom Fyodor's servant Grigory finds outside moments after he is born, with the mentally handicapped mother dying beside him. Grigory knows that the only person who could have done this to her is Fyodor. He takes the boy and raises him as his own. Smerdyakov grows up to be epileptic and sarcastic to his brothers. Meanwhile, Dmitri tells Alyosha that he tried to seduce Katerina; she wanted to marry him when she came into money, but instead he used 3,000 rubles of her money to woo Grushenka. Now he feels terrible that he did so. He asks Alyosha to go to Katerina and tell her the wedding is off and to steal the 3,000 rubles from Fyodor that he'd originally stolen from Katerina to give it back to her. The next day, Alyosha receives a letter from Lise, a girl who has recently been healed of paralysis but is now full of religious doubt. Lise is a strange character in the book who sends Alyosha a letter saying she loves him, then tells him she was joking, then professes her love again and they become engaged, and then she breaks off the engagement. Later in the book, she purposely slams her finger in the door to convince herself that she is a cruel person.

Zosima calls his students to his bedside and tells them to love all of mankind and never judge other people. Alyosha sees a schoolboy being attacked by other boys, and when Alyosha tries to help the victim, the boy attacks him instead, which baffles Alyosha. Alyosha finds Ivan and Katerina there, and despite the two of them obviously being in love, Katerina says she will stay loyal to Dmitri, and Ivan says he believes that is the right thing to do. Ivan announces he's moving to Moscow. After Ivan leaves, Katerina tells Alyosha about a captain whom Dmitri had once beaten in front of his son, and asks him to take 200 rubles to the man to try to make up for it. When Alyosha does so, he realizes the captain's son is Ilyusha, the boy who had attacked him earlier because he knew Dmitri was Alyosha's brother. The captain refuses to take the money.

Alyosha meets with Ivan in a restaurant. The two brothers begin a frank discussion about the existence of God, and Ivan admits that in his heart he wants to believe in God, but his problem lies in the intellectualization of God — either there is no God, or there is a God who is a cruel creator, who allows death and misery to rule the world. He says he became an atheist because it was the less painful belief. He is especially upset that children are allowed to suffer.

Ivan reads and then explains a prose poem he's written, "The Grand Inquisitor," in which Christ returns in the sixteenth century to a town in Spain and is promptly arrested by the Catholic Church. The Grand Inquisitor comes to Christ's cell to talk to him, and tells him that Christ's big mistake was granting humankind free will, and by doing so, he allowed eternal suffering as a result of that free will. The Church, on the other hand, has taken free will away, and they are correcting Christ's mistake by doing the work of Satan, who believed man should not have free will, and was correct. Christ quietly listens and then wordlessly kisses the Inquisitor on the lips, who lets him go. Similarly, when Ivan finishes, Alyosha kisses Ivan. Both actions represent a love and forgiveness that is too big for words.

When Ivan returns home, Smerdyakov is there and tells him that Dmitri now knows the secret knock that Grushenka will use if she decides to come to Fyodor. He's afraid that Fyodor will use it and Dmitri will kill him. He begs Ivan to do something, but Ivan says he's leaving for Russia and cannot be responsible for another man's actions. The next morning, Fyodor asks Ivan to go to a nearby town to deal with some wood, so Ivan agrees. Meanwhile, Smerdyakov trips and falls down the stairs, which brings on a seizure and confines him to bed.

Alyosha visits Zosima again, and Zosima tells him stories of love and faith. Again Zosima tells Alyosha to love mankind and never judge. Suddenly, he reaches his arms out as if to embrace the world, and dies. Everyone at the monastery believes a miracle will occur to signal Zosima's passing, but the body instead gives off a terrible odor. The people believe that if the body can give off such a stench, it must symbolize that Zosima was evil within. Alyosha is devastated, and it causes him to momentarily doubt his faith.

Rakitin takes him to Grushenka's. We find out that Grushenka was betrayed by a lover who was an officer, and now he suddenly wants her back. She makes fun of the fact Alyosha is studying to be a monk, but when she realizes Zosima has died, she apologizes and then confesses that she is a bad person. She and Alyosha begin a deep and heartfelt discussion that angers Rakitin. She admits that she paid Rakitin to bring Alyosha there to corrupt him. At the end of the discussion Grushenka no longer feels ashamed of herself, and Alyosha begins to regain his hope. She receives the message from her lover that he is coming. She tells Alyosha to tell Dmitri that she loved him once. That night Alyosha has a dream where Zosima tells him he's restored a woman's faith, and she will have a good life now because of him. Alyosha wakes up, overjoyed with his dream, and runs outside and kisses the ground.

The action moves to Dmitri, who is desperate for money and worried he's going to lose Grushenka. After several attempts to find money, he goes to Fyodor's house, but Grushenka is not there. He's attacked by Grigory, but manages to hit the servant in the head with a pestle. In a panic, he leaves, his shirt covered in blood. The next thing we know (the narrator is a bit cagey at this point), Dmitri suddenly has a lot of money and he's throwing it around. Dmitri finds out that Grushenka has returned to her old lover. He brings them wine and food, and they all play cards. Grushenka quickly realizes she loves Dmitri. Dmitri locks the officer in another room and he and Grushenka begin to plan their future together, when the police suddenly show up and announce that Fyodor

Karamazov is dead, and Dmitri is the prime suspect. He insists he is innocent, but readers don't know if he is. When the police take his bloody clothes from him, Dmitri finally breaks down and says he's always kept 1500 rubles in a locket around his neck, and when he found out Grushenka was with the officer he was going to see her one last time and then kill himself, so he no longer needed the money. Grushenka stands by him and believes he is innocent.

Meanwhile, Alyosha has befriended a boy named Kolya. Kolya tells him Ilyusha is gravely ill. Alyosha and Kolya become friends. They realize Ilyusha is going to die, and Kolya begins to cry. This section is a response to the section where Ivan talked about an inhumane God who allows the suffering of children. Rather than indict God for it, Alyosha decides to do his part to make the suffering less, and see if he can bring some peace to the children surrounding Ilyusha.

Alyosha goes to visit Grushenka, who says she believes Ivan and Dmitri have been secretly plotting behind her back, and she worries Dmitri is back with Katerina. Alyosha confronts Dmitri, who admits that Ivan has been meeting with him, as Grushenka suspected, but it's because Ivan has plotted a way for Dmitri to escape. Alyosha reassures him that he's always believed in his innocence, which gives Dmitri hope, and he agrees not to escape.

Meanwhile, Smerdyakov has grown ill, and tells Ivan that he believes Ivan left the night of Fyodor's death because he believed Dmitri would kill Fyodor, and he wanted his inheritance, and that makes him complicit in the murder. Ivan becomes increasingly guilt-ridden, and begins to believe him, until Smerdyakov finally admits that *he* killed Fyodor. Ivan returns to his room, relieved and convinced that he can finally free Dmitri, but when he gets there he hallucinates a man claiming to be the devil. The devil taunts him until Ivan goes mad, and when Alyosha suddenly shows up to tell him that Smerdyakov has hanged himself, he finds Ivan in the midst of a nervous breakdown.

At the beginning of Dmitri's trial, almost everyone in the courtroom believes he is guilty, despite his declaration of innocence. Alyosha takes the stand and suggests that Dmitri had the money on him and is innocent, and that he believes Smerdyakov killed him. Katerina testifies that Dmitri saved her father from prison. Grushenka pleads with the jury that Dmitri is innocent. Ivan takes the stand, but he rants like a lunatic, saying that Smerdyakov did it, but Ivan was responsible for it, and that the devil meets him at night to tell him so. He's removed from the courtroom, and suddenly Katerina changes her testimony to stick up for Ivan and says that Dmitri is violent, and shows them a letter he wrote to her offering to kill Fyodor for the money he owed her. In the closing arguments the prosecution points to the letter and circumstantial evidence to prove his guilt, and the defense argues that there is no hard proof that Dmitri has killed his father, and even if he did, Fyodor was never really a father to him. By the end, the entire courtroom has been won over to Dmitri's innocence, showing that Alyosha's earlier assertion that hearts can be won by learning the truth to be correct. But when the jury returns, they give a verdict of guilty.

Katerina takes Ivan into her home to care for him, and she and Alyosha agree to try to free Dmitri. Alyosha meets with Dmitri, who has accepted his fate, but agrees to break out so he can be with Grushenka. Katerina begs his forgiveness, which he gives her, but Grushenka is not as forthcoming with hers. Dmitri agrees to flee to America. Meanwhile, Ilyusha dies, and Alyosha goes to the boy's funeral. He talks to the other boys who are all dealing with this difficult situation, and tells them they must continue to stand by each other with love and forgiveness, and the boys all cheer for him.

The Brothers Karamazov is about faith and the loss of it, and how each can affect people, which is also the central theme of season 2 of *Lost*. Ivan is like Jack, rationalizing his belief in God until he ceases to believe, because if he did, it would render so many other things in his life confusing or meaningless. Ivan's ongoing inner conflict — deep down he *does* believe in God, and his remorse and madness when he faces the devil prove that his faith is strong — is illustrated in the conflict between Jack and Locke that festers throughout the season. The famous chapter where Ivan reads "The Grand Inquisitor" also points to the second major theme of the novel: free will. Ivan believes free will is dangerous and causes suffering, and that the ideal situation is to take free will away. Similarly, Locke worries that his free will has been replaced by the service to the button, and while he faithfully presses it in the beginning, his doubt eats away at him throughout the season. Yet Jack argues that Locke has used his free will to *choose* to press the button, which disturbs Locke further. Like Lise, Locke was paralyzed, but with his healing comes religious doubt.

Dostoevsky shows in detail both sides of the argument on faith. Alyosha and Zosima represent two men who believe in God, who have faith in themselves, humanity, and their religion. Ivan, on the other hand, expresses disgust for the principles of religion, for the suffering of mankind, and for a God who allows it to happen. His doubt leaves him empty and angry, always starting philosophical arguments with the people around him. Through Ivan, Dostoevsky shows us that faith leads to light, and doubt leads to darkness and, in Ivan's case, madness. Dmitri and Fyodor represent the sensualist natures — both men love womanizing and drinking, and it leads to their downfalls.

All of the brothers suffer from the same severe parenting issues as do the characters of *Lost*. Fyodor is a terrible father. He's most like Anthony Cooper, in that he's abandoned his sons completely, yet when they're around, he uses them, steals from them, and tosses them aside again. The novel ends on the redemption of several characters, which is also what *Lost* is about. It's interesting, also, that to Ivan, the biggest injustice in the world is the suffering of children, and the Others seem to have their eyes on the children above all others.

It's important that Henry Gale is the character who reads *Brothers Karamazov*, because he will use the arguments within the book to wheedle his way into Locke's psyche, and begin to cause doubt in this man of seemingly strong faith.

2.17   Lockdown

Original air date: March 29, 2006
Written by: Carlton Cuse, Damon Lindelof
Directed by: Stephen Williams
Guest cast: Kevin Tighe (Anthony Cooper), Andrea Gabriel (Nadia), Katey Sagal (Helen), Geoffrey Rivas (Father Chuck), Theo Coumbis (Jimmy Bane)

Flashback: Locke
A sudden lockdown occurs in the hatch, bringing down the blast doors and trapping Locke in a room away from the computer.

The title of this episode not only refers to a terrifying incident that happens in the bunker, but to a lockdown on the truth. A few of the mysteries of this season are answered in this episode, but, as usual, answers simply lead to more questions. "Lockdown" is another Locke episode (the title also refers to Locke being pinned down), and as I've mentioned, his are always the best flashbacks. The flashback is a continuation of the story that began in "Orientation," where he lied to Helen, made a choice, and was forgiven. In this episode, we don't get such a happy ending.

Locke's life has been a series of bad decisions, made either by him or by other people on his behalf. In "Deus Ex Machina," he ignored the private investigator's attempts to stop his search for his parents, and befriended his father, only to be horribly betrayed. This one decision seems to have influenced all of his bad decisions that have followed, as he's either ignored Helen's pleas (in order to get answers from Cooper), or he's tried to prove that he's a big man, as if that would be a snub to his father. Everything he's done on the island was meant to prove himself, and to find the spiritual answers he's spent a lifetime searching for. He found the hatch, but in uncovering it he's opened himself up to ridicule from Jack, and it's destroyed his hope and faith on the island. Now, as we look into his past, we see he makes

Locke makes an important discovery in "Lockdown," but pays a price to do so. (CHRISTINA RADISH)

yet another bad decision and gets sucked back into the world of Anthony Cooper. He should have just gone on that picnic.

When the blast doors come crashing down in the hatch, Locke must make another difficult decision — does he let Henry out to push the button and continue saving the world? Or does he try to do it himself, since Henry might be lying anyway? His gut decision proves correct in the short term, but in trying to get the doors back open, the unthinkable happens, and we're suddenly reminded of a much earlier flashback to Locke's life.

Just as Locke reveals himself to Helen at the end of his flashback, the island reveals itself to Locke as a glorious map fleetingly appears on the wall, containing so much information it has taken fans months to just scratch the surface of what it could mean (see page 281). As Locke tries to take in as much of the map as he can, Jack and Sawyer are on the beach playing poker, the classic game of bluffing and conning. From what we know about Sawyer, he should easily outplay Jack, since Jack seems to wear his emotions and thoughts on his sleeve, while Sawyer has turned the art of the con into a living. But when Jack kicks Sawyer's cocky butt all over his stack of papayas (much to Kate and Hurley's delight) it seems there's more to the good doctor than meets the eye. Is Sawyer really the skilled con artist he thinks he is, or is his proficiency as a confidence man only in his head?

Just as Jack and Sawyer lay down their cards, and Locke discovers a new way to navigate the island, Henry Gale finally seems to be off the hook. Sayid, Ana Lucia, and Charlie have found his balloon, and it's exactly where he said it would be. He helps Locke in the hatch and does not abandon him, which he could have easily done, and he finally seems like the real deal. Until Sayid returns, and a new lockdown begins.

Highlight: Kate wondering aloud if she needs to go get a ruler during Jack and Sawyer's testosterone war.

Did You Notice?:

- Libby gets stung by a sea urchin, which is what happened to Hurley in "Hearts and Minds."
- The scripture that the priest reads at Anthony's funeral is 1 Thessalonians: "For we who are alive, who are left, will be caught up together with them in the clouds to meet the Lord in the air. And so we will live with the Lord forever." It's interesting that the priest made mention of meeting God in the air, when one of the fan conspiracy theories is that everyone on the plane actually died in the air.
- When Hurley is playing Texas Hold 'Em with Sawyer, there's a jack on the river, perhaps foreshadowing who was actually going to win the game.
- The woman whose house Locke does the home inspection on is Sayid's Nadia from "Solitary." Apparently the CIA was telling the truth when they said she lives in Irvine, California, which is about 10 minutes from Tustin, where Locke lived.
- The poker game between Jack and Sawyer is a metaphor for their ongoing macho battle on the island. No matter how important and tough Sawyer thinks he is, Jack will always win.
- As Locke gets out of his truck at the Flightline Motel, you can see Oceanic planes flying overhead.
- When Anthony is stuffing his money into the bag, there is a Chinese

takeout box on the counter behind him with a symbol similar to the Dharma logo on it.

Interesting Facts: Often, when the camera shows the countdown clock, it's sitting at 47 minutes. The number 47 was a prominent numeral on *Alias* for the first three seasons.

Nitpick: If Sayid, Ana Lucia, and Charlie were looking for a *giant* yellow-and-orange balloon that had got caught in the trees, and they were sent to a very specific area to look for it, why didn't it occur to anyone to look *up* for the three hours they were out there looking? Also, in "Everybody Hates Hugo," someone taped the numbers to the computer. Why is the piece of paper gone? Finally, didn't Helen and Locke find it strange that they were the only two people at Anthony's funeral? Didn't they wonder who must have placed the obituary?

Michael Emerson, who plays Henry Gale, won an Emmy award for his guest-starring role on *The Practice.* (CHRISTINA RADISH)

Oops: There was no shelf beneath the grate in the pantry, and Henry had to stand on tiptoe just to push the grate aside, yet when he pokes his head through, he looks like someone is pushing him up. The shelves aren't moveable, and there weren't any crates around for him to stand on.

4 8 15 16 23 42: During Hurley's game with Sawyer, there's a **4** and an **8** on the river, and Hurley's initial bet is **4** papayas. On the side of Locke's truck is the phone number of Welcome Home home inspection service, and it's 714-555-01**16**. (7 + 1 = **8**; 5 + 5 + 5 = **15**.) His license plate is 4TRI019. Cooper's safety deposit box is number **1516**. On the real Henry Gale's driver's license, his address is **815** Walnut Ridge Rd., and his zip code is 55391 (which adds up to **23**). It's hard to read, but it appears his birth date is **08**/**11**/64 (**4** x **16** = 64).

It's Just a Flesh Wound: Locke's legs are caught under the panic doors, and one of the metal rods goes into his right leg.

Any Questions?:

- This episode contains the third instance of "Widmore," which means the company must have some tie to the Dharma Initiative or to the Hanso Corporation. The first was in "Fire + Water": as Charlie and the band are heading off to their video shoot, you can see a building in the Manchester skyline that says Widmore Construction. In "The Whole Truth," the pregnancy test that Sun gets from Sawyer says Widmore Labs on it. And finally, in this episode, that same Widmore Labs logo appears on the bottom of Henry's balloon, in the purple oval underneath the caution sign. What is Widmore's connection to the island, and why are we seeing their logo everywhere?
- Anthony fakes his own death, ruins Locke's life *again*, and runs off with half a million dollars that he's stolen from two guys. If anyone is the con man of the century, it's him. Is he really Locke's father? Did he pay Emily to set up Locke in "Deus Ex Machina," knowing that she was mentally unbalanced and hard up for cash?
- When and why was Jack in Thailand?
- Did Locke take the $200,000, or had Anthony already taken it before he could return to the hotel room?
- Why didn't Henry run?
- Where did that parachute drop come from? Was it the reason the bunker went into lockdown mode? On the blast door map there are references to "P.RD: every 6–8 months" and nearby it says, "complete shutdown in effect," and "activity minimal during lockdown and restocking procedures." Does P.RD refer to some kind of parachute restocking drop and it was commenting on the lockdown that happens at the same time?
- Why would the lockdown happen so soon after the countdown clock runs down, since the occupant might be in another room? Isn't it in the Dharma Initiative's best interest to keep the computer fully accessible at all times? Or does this prove it's all a sham?

Ashes to Ashes: The real Henry Gale, an African-American male from Minnesota, was traveling the world in a hot-air balloon when he crashed on the island. He is survived by his wife Jennifer, to whom he left his final letter.

Music/Bands: While Locke is exercising in the bunker, you can hear Les McCann's "Compared to What," from *Swiss Movement*. In Locke and Helen's house, you can hear George Jones' "I'll Share My World With You," (which Locke certainly does), which can be found on the 1969 album of the same name.

The Blast Door Map

In "Lockdown," in a moment of complete panic, Locke discovers a map on the back of a blast door that can only be read under black light. The map is immensely complex, and full of Latin terms (there are several screen captures and translations of the map online, but the best one is at www.lost.cubit.net/pics/2x17/blastDoorMapOverlay.jpg; the Latin translations I've used below are from that site). We'll find out later who is responsible for drawing it, but the following are some of its features.

In the center of the map is a large question mark with "Designation unknown; purpose unknown; relation to D.I.H.G. unknown" (D.I. probably stands for Dharma Initiative). Below that is a line to the Swan station, with an arrow pointing to it and "I Am Here" written in a bubble. If we see the stations on a clock, the Swan is at 6, the Flame is at 8, the Staff is at 10, the Arrow (where the Tailies were staying) is at 1. At 2 o'clock a station is marked "C3?" and at 4 is one marked "C4?" If we can assume the person who drew the map was stuck in the hatch pressing the button every 108 minutes, he must have had a partner in order to go to the other side of the island and explore that territory, which would have taken days (there's even a comment at one point, "Estimated travel time incompatible with 108. Do not attempt to journey").

Between the stations are various tunnels drawn on, as if to either suggest an underground way of transportation, or simply to show the path of the cartographer as he moved through the jungle. Next to each station is a Latin phrase, clearly written by someone who is tired of being stuck in the hatch (and who knows their ancient poets). Starting with the center station:

Nil actum reputa si quid superest agendum: "Don't consider that anything has been done if anything is left to be done." (Roman poet Lucan, 39–65 AD)

Ut sit magna, tamen certe lenta ira deorum est: "The wrath of the gods may be great, but it certainly is slow." (Satirist Juvenal, first and second century AD, who was an influence on Jean-Jacques Rousseau)

Cogito ergo doleo: "I think, therefore I am depressed." (An obvious twist on René Descartes)

Malum consilium quod mutari non potest: "It's a bad plan that can't be changed." (Poet Publilius Syrus, first century BC)

Sursum corda / Sursum corda / Sursum corda: This means "Lift up your hearts" and is a line in the opening of the Eucharistic prayer. Sursum Corda is also the name of a Washington, D.C. low-income co-op that was built in the 1960s as an experiment, but became overrun with drugs and violence in the mid-1980s.

Credo nos in fluctu eodem esse: "I think we're on the same wavelength."

Mus uni non fidit antro: "A mouse does not rely on just one hole." (Roman poet Plautus, 254–184 BC)

Liberate te ex inferis: "Save yourself from hell."

Outside the inner station area are several formulas involving the numbers, as if the cartographer were trying to figure out what the numbers actually mean. More importantly (and confusingly), the person wrote about things that happened on the island at various times in the past. Could the cartographer have been Desmond, or his predecessor, or the one before him, or a combination of several of them? On the left-hand side, starting at the top and moving down, there are comments like, "Caduceus station believed to have been abandoned due to AH/MDG incident of 1985." Could AH stand for Alvar Hanso? What could MDG mean (does the DG stand for DeGroot?)? And why would they say the Caduceus station has been abandoned when we saw it up and running in "Maternity Leave"? There are other Latin phrases like *Aegrescit medendo*, which translates as "the disease worsens with the treatment" or "the remedy is worse than the disease." Could this be a reference to the vaccine and the "sickness" that Rousseau was talking about? There are several references to "Cerberus" and "Cerberus activity," but it's unclear what Cerberus means. In Greek mythology, Cerberus was the three-headed hound who guarded the gates of Hades and let no living person enter and no dead person leave. Perhaps Cerberus is what the cartographer has nicknamed the monster. There are also references to DharmaTel Intranet servers, which could be talking about the means of communication we saw Michael use in "What Kate Did." Apparently it shut down on April 8, 2000; August 15, 2001; and January 6, 2003.

Near the bottom, there are several other comments about D.I.H.G. The first two letters are obviously Dharma Initiative, although the H.G. is unclear (Health Group? Henry Gale?). Whatever it is, it seems to involve research of some kind, in references like, "Possible recreation area for D.I.H.G. survey teams." This area also contains comments about something happening every 6–8 months (P.RD), a "complete shutdown in effect," and references to the "incident" and the "accident."

On the right side of the map, it suggests the Arrow station is a "possible manufacturing facility with light industrial equipment." It says "suspected shutdown date 10.28.84." Was the note written before 1984 in anticipation of the end of the research, or was it written after? That side of the island contains "mountainous terrain" that is probably being used by the D.I.H.G. for meteorological research. Some of the more intriguing comments are made in this area, such as, "Geological composition most likely to cause magnetic interference/interfere with weather ?research? project" and "Interference might also prevent location from use as a listening station/cryptography research or analysis." Is this any reference to Rousseau's message? Was there interference in this part of the island that prevented her message from being transmitted properly? The cartographer also writes, "High potential for R.V.S. facility."

As we come down this side of the map (which includes the Latin phrase *Hic sunt dracones*, or "here be dragons") we appear to be entering the area where the bears have been spotted. The artist writes, "Sightings coincide with emergency shutdown of Intranet services, periods of heightened security." The artist believes this is a possible location of a zoological research facility, and in the corner, has written, "Stated goal, repatriation accelerated de-territorialization of *ursus maritimus* [polar bear] through gene therapy and climate change." Suddenly, the polar bears that the writers were making us think had been brought on by Walt in "Pilot, Part 2" and "Special" seem in fact to have been part of a genetic experiment to find out what happens to a polar bear in a tropical climate. To the northwest of this comment is the ominous message, "Known final resting place of Magnus Hanso/Blackrock." Who is Magnus Hanso? The brother or father of Alvar Hanso? Or was he one of the original sailors (or captives) on the *Black Rock*?

The blast door map is the single most absorbing prop ever used on the show, and has created more discussion and fervor among fans than any other. The more familiar we can become with the map, the more we can begin looking for possible solutions to the mysteries it presents.

2.18   Dave

Original air date: April 5, 2006
Written by: Edward Kitsis, Adam Horowitz
Directed by: Jack Bender

Guest cast: Evan Handler (Dave), Bruce Davison (Dr. Brooks), Ron Bottitta (Leonard), Grisel Toledo (Nurse)

Flashback: Hurley/Libby

When Hurley finally admits his obsession with food, he sees someone from his past on the island.

After the incredible momentum of "Lockdown," the show lags a bit with this Hurley flashback that's not much more than filler, if such a thing could exist on *Lost*. At the end of the previous episode, the Lostaways discovered a crate full of food and supplies that seems to have literally appeared out of thin air, but the very sight of it almost mocks Hurley, who has made a new resolution to stay away from foods that are bad for him. And just like that, Charlotte's husband in *Sex and the City* suddenly appears in the jungle, taunting Hurley like some deranged version of the vision Jack saw of his father in "White Rabbit." We flash back to see Hurley as a patient in a mental hospital and discover why he was there in the first place (this episode answers a few of the questions I posed at the end of "Numbers"), and while the other two Hurley episodes have shown us about his lottery win, and have offered us some comic relief, this is the first real glimpse we get of the emotional background of his character.

The problem with the episode is its inconsistencies. Why now? Dave was brought on by a serious trauma that happened to Hurley years ago when something happened that eventually caused him to be institutionalized, and he represents Hurley's tendency to overeat. But we saw in the previous flashback that when Hurley worked at Mr. Cluck's, it was nothing for him to knock back an eight-piece chicken combo as a snack. His obsession with food has never abated, so why does Dave show up now? Why didn't he show up when the hatch was first discovered full of food? The last time Dave appeared, Hurley believed his appetite had killed two people. Does he think his eating is putting people in danger now?

What seems more probable is that the writers needed something to use as a backstory to frame the Henry Gale interrogation, and they wanted to have fun debunking a popular fan theory (see page 249). Since it was first mentioned that Hurley spent time in a mental hospital, it's been widely speculated that Hurley might have been imagining everything we've seen happening on the island. This episode throws that option out there for us to ponder, and then breaks it down by the end of the episode (or so it seems). Dave uses actual criticisms of the show to convince Hurley he's crazy, listing off the oh-so-convenient coincidences that have caused some eye-rolling among viewers. Despite this episode being a bit of a let-down compared to last week's, Evan Handler is brilliantly cast as Dave.

The more interesting story line in this episode is the fallout from discovering Henry Gales' deception . . . or should I say Not-Henry Gale? When Sayid goes after Henry this time, no one holds him back the way Jack had in "One of Them." Henry comes off as flustered, telling a story about finding the real Henry already dead, before Sayid reveals that to be a lie, and Henry comes back with a new story. At this point, Henry just seems to be digging his *own* grave, and we wonder why he won't just tell the truth. He insists he is, but he's constantly discovered to be a liar. The

When Hurley first meets Libby, he thinks he knows her from somewhere; in this episode, we find out where. (ALBERT L. ORTEGA)

most revealing moment of the interrogation is when Henry shouts with passion that Mr. Friendly is nobody and that there's actually someone much higher who is a dangerous man. Sayid's rage gets out of control again as he tries to convince Henry that *he* is the dangerous man, but something in Henry's eyes tells us that no matter what Sayid has done in his life, he's no comparison to this other person.

Is this man that Henry is talking about real? Is he really as dangerous as Henry insists he is? Is he talking about God? He apparently answers to someone who could destroy him if he steps out of line. Similarly Locke believes in a button that he must push because he thinks not doing so would destroy the world. In an episode that features an imaginary person whom Hurley believes in, but turns out to be nothing but a false conviction, is it possible Locke and Henry are being similarly misled?

Highlight: Charlie's response when Hurley asks if anyone saw a man in a bathrobe running with a coconut: "No, I saw a polar bear on rollerblades with a mango."

Did You Notice?:

- In "White Rabbit," Locke tells Jack that crazy people don't know they're crazy, they just think they're getting saner, which is an interesting commentary on this episode.
- Hurley has insisted in the past two episodes with his flashbacks that he's not crazy, but we find out in this episode that he is. A hint of that was at the end of "Numbers," where the only person who agrees with him that the numbers are cursed is Rousseau, whom Sayid thinks is crazy.
- Sawyer calls Charlie Tattoo, which was his nickname for Walt in season 1.
- When Libby jokes that the island won't let Hurley lose weight, she sounds like Locke.
- The psychiatrist says Hurley's been in the hospital for two months, which is the same amount of time they've been on the island.
- In "What Kate Did," Hurley gives Jack the definition of transference, and his psychiatrist probably told him about it in relation to Dave.
- When Hurley's in the psychiatrist's office, he's sitting under a poster of a deserted island that looks remarkably like the one they're on, again fueling the idea that all of this is in Hurley's head.
- There are obvious hints throughout the episode that Dave is not real: He says "Dude" all the time, which is something Hurley would probably imagine anyone saying; when he's on the basketball court he's complaining that no one is paying attention to him or passing the ball to him; he often uses Spanish phrases; you never see anyone else speak to Dave except Dr. Brooks, who knows he's not real.
- Locke wiggles his toes as Jack's examining him, the same thing he did when he first landed on the island and realized he could walk again.
- Henry is being held in a Christ pose while being interrogated by Sayid.
- Sayid tells Henry he should have checked the real Henry's wallet, but he probably did check the wallet, which is how he knew he was from Minnesota and that his wife's name was Jennifer.
- As Hurley is beating up Sawyer, he's shouting out the terrible nicknames Sawyer's called him in past episodes, including mispronouncing "Barbar." It's about time: Sawyer's nicknames are usually biting but good-natured, except those for Sayid or Hurley, which are either racist, or just plain cruel.

Sawyer's Nicknames

Sayid: Boy, Buddy, Chief, Abdul, Al-Jazeera, Omar, Captain Falafel, Muhammad, Boss, Ali, Genius, Red Beret, Captain Arab

Hurley: Lardo, Porkpie, Stay Puff, Jabba, Jethro, Hoss, Pillsbury, Rerun, Barbar (means to say Babar), Hambone, Mutton Chops, Deep Dish, Mongo, Grape Ape

Jack: Hero, Doc, Jackass, Metro, Jacko, Saint Jack, Cowboy, Chico, Doctor Quinn, Brother, Hoss, Sheriff, El Jacko, Amarillo Slim, Cool Hand, Doctor Giggles

Kate: Sweetheart, Freckles, Baby, Girl, Woman, Boar Expert, Sassafras, Puddin', Sweet Cheeks, Sheena, Thelma, Pippi Longstocking

Shannon: Sweet Cheeks, Sticks

Jin: Mr. Miyagi, Chief, Bruce, Kato, Sulu, Boy, Chewie, Daddio, Papa-San, Jin Senior

Charlie: Sport, Reject from VH-1 Has-Beens, Amigo, Chucky, Tattoo, Baby 'Napper

Boone: Son

Walt: Tattoo, Kid, Short-round, Kazoo

Ethan: Jungle Boy

Sun: Betty, Tokyo Rose, Sunshine

Claire: Mamacita

Aaron: Baby Huey

Michael: Chief, Mickey, Boss, Mike, Han (as in Solo), Hoss, Mikey

Eko: Shaft

Ana Lucia: Cupcake, Rambina, Hot Lips, Bitch, Ponce de Leon, Ana-Lulu, Little Red Riding Hood, Lucy, Muchacha, Little Amiga

Locke: Mr. Clean, Hoss, Brutus, Gimpy McCrutch

Mr. Friendly: Zeke, Bluebeard

Libby: Moonbeam

Bernard: Bernie, Suzie, Norma Rae

Henry: The Artist Formerly Known as Henry Gale

- Someone on the show seriously has it in for ranch dressing. We watch Hurley gloop it all over the ground in this episode in an attempt to destroy it. In "Everybody Hates Hugo," it was the first item Hurley inventoried as "salad dressing, ranch composite," to which he comments sarcastically, "Sounds tasty." In "One of Them," Sawyer discovered Hurley eating ranch dressing in the jungle. And in "The 23rd Psalm," Locke taught Michael to shoot by having him aim at the massive containers of ranch dressing.

Interesting Facts: Clonazepam, the drug that Hurley was taking, is used to treat seizures and panic disorder. It's something that can become habit-forming in patients, and can cause adverse reactions in patients who suddenly go off it. Let's hope Hurley wasn't still on it when he boarded the plane.

Nitpick: Why would Sawyer throw the cookie away like he does? They're on a deserted island. Just because food occasionally drops from the sky doesn't mean it'll keep doing so forever. Similarly, why doesn't Hurley give his food to other castaways, rather than destroy it? Also, the joke Sawyer makes about Sayid working in a mini-mart is too offensive, even for Sawyer. Holloway looks noticeably uncomfortable as he delivers the line.

4 8 15 16 23 42: Lenny repeats the numbers again while playing Connect Four, and Dave comments that the worst that could happen to Hurley is that Lenny could call him a **23**. Dr. Brooks tells Hurley there were **23** people standing on a deck that was made to hold **8**.

It's Just a Flesh Wound: Dave hits Hurley throughout the episode to show he's real, including throwing a coconut at Hurley's stomach. Sayid has probably beaten Henry Gale further, though we don't see him doing it.

Any Questions?:

- Who is the big guy Henry is talking about?
- Who died when the deck collapsed? Was Hurley's father on it?
- Did the real Henry Gale actually write the letter to Jennifer, or did the Others do it and plant it on him as part of some overall plan?
- Did Henry input the numbers, or is he just screwing with Locke now that he's been revealed to be a liar?
- At the beginning of the season, Libby said she was a psychologist. *Was* Libby ever a doctor? Did she ever talk to Hurley when she was at the hospital? Did she know about his money and follow him?
- In "Maternity Leave," Mr. Friendly is talking to Ethan in the hallway and worries about what "he" is going to do when he finds out: Is it the same "he" that Henry is talking about in this one?

Cynthia Watros (Libby)

It didn't take long for news to leak out in the summer of 2005 that two new actresses would be joining the cast of *Lost*. While Michelle Rodriguez was better known from her work on the big screen, the second new member, Cynthia Watros, was an Emmy winner who had a lengthy history in television and film.

Watros, who was born in 1968, was the second child of Bruce and Nancy Watros, who divorced when Cynthia was seven. During her teen years, Watros was diagnosed with immune thrombocytopeniac purpura, an autoimmune disease of the blood that required her to have a splenectomy, as well as going for chemotherapy treatments for two years.

She recovered from her illness and attended Boston University's School of Fine Arts, where she trained in acting, including roles in plays like Ariel Dorfman's *Death and the Maiden*. She moved to New York following her graduation and began to find work in off-Broadway plays.

But her true calling turned out to be television. As a regular on the soap opera *Guiding Light*, she was named one of "Daytime Television's 50 Most Beautiful People," and won an Emmy for her portrayal of a revenge-seeking nurse. From there, she landed a notable role as a stripper on the Michael J. Fox series *Spin City* in 1997, in which she demonstrated her comedy skills. She followed that with a role on *Titus*, where she played Erin, a complex and compelling character. It was during this time that Watros became pregnant with twins. "Before the ultrasound, I had just told the *Titus* people that I was pregnant . . . They had said 'Oh, you won't get that big, it will be fine,'" She explained. "And I had to go and say, 'Well, you know about that "big" thing? I'm having twins, so I think I'm going to get kind of big!'"

When Fox killed *Titus* in 2002 after two seasons, Watros joined the cast of *The Drew Carey Show*, continuing with the series until it finished two years later.

Though she has acted in numerous films, in 2005, Watros was approached by Damon Lindelof to take on the role of Libby, a clinical therapist marooned on the island. "She is going to bring a flavor to the show that doesn't exist right now," Lindelof said. "She's not as intense as some of the other characters. She's that person you want in the trenches with you who can take lemons and make lemonade."

It was midway through the season that Watros made headlines when she was arrested and charged with drinking and driving, the same evening that Rodriguez was charged with the same offense (but in an unrelated incident). Watros currently lives in Los Angeles with her husband, real estate developer Curt Gilliland, and the couple's twin daughters, Emma Rose Marie and Sadie Anna Marie.

2.19   S.O.S.

Original air date: April 12, 2006
Written by: Steven Maeda, Leonard Dick
Directed by: Eric Laneuville
Guest cast: Wayne Pygram (Isaac), Donna Smallwood (Aussie Woman)

Flashback: Rose and Bernard

Bernard tries to recruit people on the island to help him make a giant SOS sign, and he can't figure out why Rose is reluctant to assist him.

With only five episodes left to answer countless questions, watching an episode that provided flashbacks to a couple of secondary characters (whose actors aren't even cast members) was a surprise. But this episode wasn't actually a filler: it contains some very important questions that will make us reevaluate the island, the castaways, and their hope of rescue. In Rose and Bernard's flashback, we discover that Rose was dying of cancer before she got on the plane. Bernard

The street where Bernard first met Rose is actually in downtown Honolulu. (RYAN OZAWA)

married her anyway, but then he became a man on a mission, looking for ways to heal her. Ironically, it was the plane crash that saved her, and just as Locke mysteriously regained the ability to walk, Rose is convinced her cancer is gone.

The episode raises a very important issue: why hasn't season 2 touched on any rescue attempts? In season 1 Sayid spent half his time working on a transceiver, and the other half decoding maps and looking through the jungle for a transmission source. Two rafts were built with the intention of getting off the island and sending help back. People were barely surviving, too busy watching the horizon for ships or planes. But when the hatch was uncovered, along with all of the basic amenities people were missing, suddenly scant survival turned to comfortable living, and instead of looking for rescue, people began building stronger shelters. Just when people began thinking to themselves, "You know, if we just had a regular food supply on the island, I could probably stay here," a food supply fell from the sky. In season 1, if that had happened, Sayid would have been scouring the skies for planes afterwards, trying to communicate with them by radio, Jin and Sawyer would have been building a new boat, and bonfires would have gone up all over the beach. Instead, people shrugged their shoulders, packed the food

Bernard (Sam Anderson) just wants to help his wife get off the island, but her confession to him changes his mind. (ALBERT L. ORTEGA)

away, and returned to their interrogation of a guy who was tied up in their armory. Season 1 was about getting off the island; season 2 is about learning to live on it.

Bernard comes up with the brilliant idea to build a giant sos sign, and is shocked and dismayed when Charlie and Eko are too busy building a church, most of the background characters complain that walking a half mile to get the rocks is just too much work, and Jin begins to help but can't put up with Bernard's temper tantrums or all the work it entails (this after he worked alongside Michael to build a raft). Does Bernard have a point — that people are becoming lazy and have just given up hope? Or is there something larger at work here? So many people have found redemption, peace, and happiness on the island (see page 293). Many must be wondering if life on the island is actually better than their lives before the plane crash. Claire and Sun have proven that regeneration on the island is possible, and perhaps Aaron will be the first of many island children. Bernard is the first to declare that he will never leave the island, and as time goes on, there will no doubt be more people who feel the same.

Meanwhile, Locke tries to recreate the map he saw on the wall, but he can't concentrate because he's beginning to doubt the importance of any of his discoveries.

He's losing faith in the button, the hatch, and the island, so a map involving any of those things is beginning to look worthless to him. The island doesn't hold any mystique for him anymore. Henry has been pressing Locke's psychological buttons, and enjoying every minute of it. Locke's conversation with Rose — and his discovery that he's not alone in believing the island has healed him — momentarily boosts his faith, and he begins to see the picture of the map in his head again.

Highlight: Eko refusing to help out Bernard by proselytizing instead, and Bernard responds, "I think I liked you better when you just hit people with your stick."

Did You Notice?:

- All of the Dharma goods have the same code on them: DI 9FFTR731. The DI would probably stand for Dharma Initiative, but the rest of the code is a mystery.
- This episode provided an opportunity to finally learn some more names of background characters: Neil (the frogurt guy), Jenkins (which is Steve Jenkins, i.e., Scott), Craig, and Richard.
- When we see the wall of photos and letters to Isaac of the Uluru, the camera seems to linger on one note that looks like it was written by a child, and says, "Dear Issac [sic], Thank you for making me feel all better," but it has two adult signatures. Beside it is a strange photo of the Golden Gate Bridge, upside-down (an Aussie joke, perhaps?). There is probably a ton of important information on that letter wall.
- Isaac mentioned "magnetic" energy as being something that he harnesses and gives to others.
- The look on Uluru's face when his eyes pop open and he stares at Rose was very similar to the look the psychic gave to Claire when he was holding her hands.
- Rose tells Isaac, "I'm gonna tell [Bernard] you fixed me," and repeats it. "You fixed me" is a phrase Sarah used to describe what Jack did for her.

Interesting Facts: Uluru is another name for Ayers Rock, a large red rock formation in Australia (Rose and Bernard appear to pass by it when they're driving in the Outback). The rock is **8** kilometers around at its base, and 346 meters high. The local indigenous people have ascribed a mystical quality to the formation,

Island Redemption

Lost has always been about redemption and healing, whether it's physical or spiritual. Some of the survivors have been healed by the island, some of them oscillate between redemption and defeat, and others are still looking:

Healed:
- Rose is cured of cancer; Bernard has a future with his wife
- Shannon needed someone to love her and promise to never leave her, and she found that in Sayid
- Claire has Aaron and no longer deals with the guilt associated with having to give him up, and she no longer has to raise him alone, which was her fear
- Sun gets pregnant, something that she'd been told was an impossibility; Jin finally anticipates the family he always wanted
- Eko finds his faith again, and becomes the priest he'd been falsely saying he was
- Ana Lucia realizes killing the person who deceived her isn't the way to go
- Boone discovers that his sister is an unhealthy burden to him, and he distances himself from her
- Desmond realizes that Penelope loved him

Giveth, and Taketh away:
- Locke got back his ability to walk and found faith again . . . but the island has hurt one of his legs again and he's lost his faith
- Charlie kicked his heroin habit . . . but the temptation of having it nearby cost him his friends, and his faith
- Michael got an opportunity to be a father to his son . . . but Walt was taken away from him

Not healed:
- Sawyer never found the real Sawyer, and he hasn't been able to discard his hatred for the man
- Hurley is still haunted by the numbers
- It's unclear what Libby is searching for
- Kate's captor dies, leaving her a free woman . . . but she remains haunted by her past and what she did, and if rescued, will be back in captivity
- Jack was told that his father really didn't hate him . . . but his main goal was to finally put his father to rest, and he hasn't been able to do that
- Sayid tried to put his past deeds behind him, and found love again in Shannon, but she was murdered, and he has embraced his identity as a torturer and given up on ever seeing Nadia again

and ask tourists not to climb or photograph the rock, but most of their pleas are ignored, and it's not illegal to do so. Also, Locke is drawing his map over a poem by Alfred de Musset (1810–1857) called "Sur les débuts de Mesdemoiselles Rachel et Pauline Garcia." It contains a line that would be interesting to Locke: "*Obéissez sans crainte au dieu qui vous inspire*," or "Obey without doubt the God who inspires you."

Oops: Locke says Jack told him his leg will heal in four weeks, but Jack had actually said two.

4 8 15 16 23 42: Kate and Sawyer are prying some sort of shellfish off the rocks, and he tells her she's caught **4** in the last half hour. Bernard is 56 years old, which means if you divide his age into months, you get 672, which is **42** x **16**. Bernard comments that he bunked with Eko for 48 days (**4** & **8**), and now he doesn't call or write. He tells the volunteers the letters need to be **40** feet high. He complains to Rose that he originally had **15** people helping him, and now he only has **4**. There are **15** bullets in Jack's gun. Locke tells Rose that Jack told him his leg would heal in **4** weeks.

Any Questions?:

- When the alarm begins, Jack steps in and tells Locke to push the button. If Locke had just gone back to his map, would Jack have pushed it?
- Why does Henry say to Jack, "They'll never give you Walt"?
- When Jack opens the door, Henry slowly lifts his head like a robot. What was *that* about?
- When Locke asks Ana Lucia to open the armory door, she's doing something on the floor. What is she trying to put together?
- What did Isaac feel/see that made him give up on Rose?
- Rose remembers seeing Locke in the airport, but does he remember seeing her?
- While Rose momentarily restored Locke's faith in the power of the island, did she also put a damper on him, now that he knows he's not a chosen one?

Music/Bands: When Bernard proposes to Rose, the violinists play Roger Edens' "The Right Girl for Me," a song made popular by Frank Sinatra. Locke plays Otis Redding's "These Arms of Mine" in the hatch.

L. Scott Caldwell (Rose)

As an actress who continues to gain acclaim for her work in the theater on and off Broadway, Chicago native L. Scott Caldwell had an extensive career before taking the role of Rose on *Lost*. Initially, Rose appeared to be a secondary character, with few lines in the first season. Not a regular cast member, Caldwell used the time off to continue her first love — stage acting. But the actress gained more screen time in the second season of *Lost*, including a flashback for her character.

On Broadway, Caldwell was awarded a Tony for her role in Joe Turner's *Come and Gone*, while her other theater credits include *Proposals*, *A Month of Sundays*, and *Home*. She has also appeared off-Broadway in *About Heaven & Earth*, *Colored People's Time*, and *The Imprisonment of Obatala*.

Sam Anderson (Bernard)

The role of Bernard is the most recent in the long career of character actor Sam Anderson. In fact, Anderson might have the most extensive background of any actor on *Lost*, having appeared on television programs like *WKRP in Cincinnati* in the late 1970s.

In fact, Anderson has played a gallery of characters, from the lecherous school principal in *Forrest Gump*, to the arrogant Dr. Kayson on *ER*, and Donna's racist dad in *La Bamba*. More recently, he played the evil lawyer Holland Manners on *Angel* and the tortured father on *Boomtown*, but he's also known for his guest role on *Friends*, playing the Fonzie-loving doctor who delivered Phoebe's triplets.

Like L. Scott Caldwell, Anderson also has an extensive theater background. In Los Angeles he has appeared in such wide-ranging shows as *Taking Sides*, and *Napoli Milionaria*, which won him the 2002 Ovation Award for Best Actor in a Leading Role, the category covering all of Los Angeles' live theaters. He has also been the recipient of *L.A. Weekly* and *Dramalogue Awards*, and shared a Screen Actors Guild Award for Outstanding Ensemble for his work on *ER*.

Anderson has advanced degrees in theater, American literature, and creative writing. He is an active writer and a member of the Mystery Writers of America.

2.20 Two for the Road

Original air date: May 3, 2006
Written by: Elizabeth Sarnoff, Christina M. Kim
Directed by: Paul Edwards
Guest cast: Rachel Ticotin (Captain Cortez), Gabrielle Fitzpatrick (Lindsey)

Flashback: Ana Lucia

Michael's back with some crucial information about the Others, and when Henry tries to kill Ana Lucia, she's out for revenge.

No matter how many things happen in this episode, fans will always remember it for the ending. And oh, what an ending it is. Just when we thought there weren't enough hours in a full year's television schedule to answer the questions we have so far, this episode lobs more mysteries, shocks, and questions at us. Although the ending overshadows everything else in the episode, the appearance of a particular recurring character in Ana's flashback is best summed up by Henry's reaction to Ana throwing him the knife: "Whaaaat?" Until now, we thought Sawyer had the closest tie to Christian Shephard after Jack, but now we discover Ana Lucia was far closer to him. Christian's mission in Australia is only vaguely clearer to us now than it was before, but the writers keep it shrouded in enough mystery to keep viewers guessing. Undoubtedly, it will be continued in yet another character's flashback. Christian is more interesting than some of the characters on the island.

Not-Henry continues to be an exciting and intriguing enigma.

John Terry, who plays Christian Shephard, has appeared in dozens of shows, including *24*, *ER*, and *Las Vegas*. (STHANLEE MIRADOR/SHOOTING STAR)

Nothing brings people together faster than uniting against a common enemy, and when Michael comes back with news of the Others, and Henry is unveiled as the nasty man he is, Jack and Locke finally come to a truce. It's no doubt a temporary one, however; it's not like the two of them will be hitting the bars together after they win this war. *If they win this war.*

Libby and Hurley get past their troubles from "Dave" quickly and a little too conveniently; Hurley doesn't have any of the aftershocks of what he went through so recently, and they act as if it never happened. But finally, a happy relationship on the island. The last time we saw two people get together, it was Shannon and Sayid, and after a rough start, their love was able to blossom until it was ended with a bullet. With

Ana Lucia finally finds some redemption in this episode . . . and something else.
(ALBERT L. ORTEGA)

Hurley and Libby, we get another chance to see happiness, and it's great to finally see two people come together in this way, without their love being thwarted by a . . . oh. Never mind.

Of course, as mentioned, the end of the episode was what everyone was talking about the next day. Who didn't watch that scene with their jaws sitting on the floor? What could have compelled Michael to do that? Some fans thought he'd been brainwashed by the Others. Some thought he had become a member of the Others, and was acting on orders. But the more likely scenario is that he's been offered a trade . . . if he lied to Jack and everyone, and in fact he did see Walt, perhaps they convinced him that they would give Walt to him if he could get Henry back for them. At the end of this mind-blowing scene, we can't help but look back to Michael in his early flashbacks, to the young, innocent guy who loved his son so much he'd do anything for him . . . and then fast-forward 10 years to the day when he was forced to do just that. The writers have their work cut out for them now. With the finale only three episodes away, they're going to have to work hard to top this one.

Highlight: Hurley saying to Sayid that he would hold the radio over his head to woo Libby. (The reference was far funnier before Hurley actually explained it; if he'd just left it at that, fans of *Say Anything* would have laughed, and people who didn't know what he was talking about would have forgotten about it half a minute later.)

Did You Notice?:

- Ana's mother tells her, "If you don't want my help you're going to have to get it from somewhere else." Apparently Australia is that somewhere else.
- Sawyer tells Ana to "Git!" like she's a dog.
- "Walkin' After Midnight" is playing in the car when Christian and Ana go on their mission, and it's the same song Kate is playing in the hatch when she tells an unconscious Sawyer about the horse.
- Ana Lucia pulling up to the bar is an incident that happens moments before we see Sawyer's flashback to the bar in "Outlaws."
- The last time Locke and Michael saw each other was when Michael knocked Locke unconscious and locked him in the armory. Now that they reunite, Michael just says, "Hey John," and there's no mention of it.
- At the beginning of "What Kate Did," Jin and Sun emerged from a night of lovin' and Hurley knowingly gave him the thumbs-up. Jin jokingly returns the gesture in this episode.
- Sawyer says he's the only one who will know the ending to *Bad Twin*, but Hurley already read it in "The Long Con."
- When Ana Lucia talks to Michael in the final moments of the episode, she turns the gun over and over in her hands, as if she needs it to find the nerve to say the things she needs to say. She did exactly the same thing in "Collision" when Sayid was tied to the tree and she was telling him about being a cop.
- Henry doesn't look surprised when Michael walks into the armory, so he was clearly listening through the door.

Interesting Fact: Again, Locke's combination seems to be pointing directly to a passage in the book of John. The combo is 18-1-31, and John 1:18-31 is the passage where John the Baptist denies that he is Christ, and points out the real son of God. Is this a suggestion by Locke that he is not actually the most important person here? Does he believe Jack is the real Christ, or Eko? In this passage, John the Baptist says, "A man who comes after me has surpassed me because he was before me."

Nitpick: Where exactly was Ana hiding the gun? She had on a tank top and tight jeans, and the handle of the gun wasn't sticking up out of her pants, and nothing was in her hands. And apparently just one *Bad Twin* market tie-in wasn't enough (see page 253). Double blech. Finally, it seems strange that Ana Lucia makes the airport cell phone call when she does. She's standing in the lineup, calls her mother, and the next thing you know she's sitting on a chair nearby. Did she leave the line? Did she stand there talking on the phone while the ticket agent got her boarding pass ready? (In which case, it's strange that she only mentions she's in Sydney when she's around the corner in the next scene.) Wasn't the conversation rather private? Why have it next to a ticket agent?

Oops: In "Collision" the guy who shot Ana Lucia was named Jason McCormick, but in this episode they're calling him Jason Alder. Also, we saw Ana shoot him six times in the parking lot, but here Captain Cortez says he was shot five times.

4 8 15 16 23 42: When Ana Lucia's car first pulls into the parking lot in the flashback, you can see police cars with all the numbers on them. In the middle foreground is **23**, then **16**, **15**, and **08**, on the far left side of the screen is **04** and on the right, in the foreground, is **42**. When Christian knocks on Ana Lucia's door, she says he's been sitting in his hotel room, drinking for **4** days. The first number in the safe combination is **18**. Michael shoots the gun **4** times at the end.

It's Just a Flesh Wound: Henry gives Ana a gash in the forehead and tries to strangle her. Locke whacks Henry in the back of the head with a crutch. Michael shoots Ana in the chest once and Libby in the abdomen twice, then shoots his own shoulder.

Any Questions?:

- Henry tells Ana Lucia that she's killed "two of us," two good people who were just leaving her alone. Who is he talking about? We only saw her kill one of the Others, and that was Goodwin. He's not talking about Nathan, because Goodwin told Ana Lucia that Nathan was a bad person who had to die. Is he talking about Shannon? Why would he consider her to be one of them?

Fate and Destiny

As Locke explains in "Exodus, Part 2," he believes that the island brought everyone to it, because it's their destiny. Jack, on the other hand, doesn't believe in fate or destiny, and thinks anyone who does is not accepting responsibility for their own actions. The theme crops up a lot in the series:

Walkabout: Locke tells the story of Norman Croucher, double amputee, who climbed Mt. Everest because it was his destiny. When the man at the travel agency tells Locke he can't go on the walkabout tour, Locke begins shouting that he must go, because it's his destiny.

Special: Michael tells Walt that building the raft means they are taking control of their destiny.

Outlaws: Christian tells Sawyer that some people are fated to suffer. Jack later tells Sawyer that his father never took responsibility for his actions, and put it on fate.

Deus Ex Machina: Locke tells Boone they were meant to find the hatch. In the flashback, Detective Frainey tells Locke that even if he thinks this was meant to be, it wasn't. Just before the transplant operation, Locke tells Anthony that this was meant to be.

The Greater Good: Haddad suggests that it was fate that made Sayid and Essam meet in the mosque; and later, when Sayid convinces Essam to become a martyr, Essam repeats that it was fate that brought them together.

Exodus, Part 2: Locke says they'll let fate decide on who will carry the dynamite, and they draw straws. Jack then alters the fate that was decided by putting them in his pack, despite not drawing the correct straw. Sun wonders if fate is punishing them for things they did before, and Claire says there is no such thing as fate. Locke later tells Jack that the island brought them there, and it's destiny. Jack says he doesn't believe in destiny, and Locke assures him he does.

Man of Science, Man of Faith/Adrift/Orientation: Jack mocks Locke about how opening the hatch was everyone's destiny, and then when they're inside the hatch and Desmond is holding a gun to Locke's head, Jack yells at Locke, asking him if this was his destiny.

. . . And Found: Jin's friend Tai Soo is looking through a destiny book, and tells Jin that he is fated to meet the woman he will fall in love with, and love will look orange.

What Kate Did: Eko tells Locke not to mistake coincidence for fate.

Two for the Road: Christian suggests that fate has thrown he and Ana Lucia together so they could help each other out. When he shows up at her hotel room door and says it's time to go, he says it's because fate's calling. When Ana Lucia stops the car in front of the bar, Christian says, "My, my, look what fate has delivered up this time."

Live Together, Die Alone: Sayid tells Jack that fate has given them the answer to how Sayid can get to the other side of the island ahead of Jack: he'll take Desmond's boat. Locke tells Desmond that he believed it was his destiny to get into the hatch, but now he sees that was all wrong. Desmond reminds Locke of the night Locke was banging his fists on the hatch door, which saved Desmond's life, and disagrees with him that there's no such thing as fate.

- When they choose names, why does Christian give Ana the same name as his daughter-in-law? Was he the man Sarah left Jack for?
- Is Henry telling the truth to Locke about his mission?
- When Ana Lucia takes Christian to a woman's house in the middle of the night, he's yelling about needing to see his daughter. What daughter? This woman is a dead ringer for an older version of Claire — are Jack and Claire half-brother and -sister? After all, Claire did say her father abandoned her and she no longer has anything to do with her mother.
- Not only did Locke lie about where Ana's cut had come from, but he's the one who taught Michael how to shoot. Does that make him doubly responsible for her death?
- The camera lingers on Ana Lucia's mother writing down her flight and time. She tells Ana that she will be there when she lands. Was she telling the truth? Is she on the island somewhere? Did the parents have anything to do with the crash, since so many of them were showing animosity toward their children beforehand?
- In "Exodus, Part 2," Jack encounters Ana Lucia in the airport bar, and she's interrupted by a cell phone call where she says "Hi, I'm in Sydney." It's clearly not her mother, since she already talked to her mother and told her where she was. Who is it? Also, she seems much cheerier when she talks to Jack than we ever see her for the rest of the series. Is it because she thought her life was finally going to change?

Ashes to Ashes: Ana Lucia Cortez, former LAPD officer, who was in Australia working for another man. She has murdered two people, killed another by accident, and her actions led to the death of a fourth man. She is survived by her mother, an LAPD captain.

Music/Bands: When Ana Lucia and Christian are driving in the rain, they're listening to Patsy Cline's "Walkin' After Midnight." Later, when Christian turns on the car radio, you hear Australian singer Kasey Chambers' "The Hard Way" (*The Captain*).

✍ *Bad Twin* by Gary Troup (2006)

Bad Twin isn't like the other books I've examined in *Finding Lost*. It's not on the show because it's a classic or because one of the writers loved it and wanted other people to read it. It's in here because it's a marketing tool created by the show to use other media to explore the themes of *Lost*. Unlike the other books mentioned so far, it's not very good. It's not earth-shattering or life-changing or, for the most part, that interesting; but it's a fun way to kill a couple of hours.

In the story, Paul Artisan is a small-time private detective who works for insurance companies catching people committing fraud. He gets a visit one day from a man who wants him on a much bigger job — finding his older brother. The man's name is Cliff Widmore (an important surname on *Lost*), and his brother is his mirror twin. The detective is sent on a whirlwind adventure trying to find the brother, and along the way narrowly escapes death several times, and begins to realize his goose chase is far more sordid than a simple missing persons case. *Bad Twin* was advertised right on the show when Hurley and Sawyer were each seen reading the manuscript, and the fictional story behind the book is that Gary Troup (an anagram of "purgatory") was a passenger on Flight 815 — he's rumored to be the guy from "Pilot, Part 1" who gets sucked into the jet engine when Locke tells him to move out of the way. He had been in Sydney meeting with his publisher (Walkabout Books, a reference to the first Locke flashback episode), and was on his way back home when the plane disappeared. The book opens with bogus letters from his publisher inviting him to Sydney, which offers the book's first eye roll. First of all, most publishers don't have the money to fly over an author just for a chat; though they might for a book launch or something more substantial. Secondly, who sends letters through the mail? His publisher would more likely have e-mailed him, and he would have replied by e-mail. The book is dedicated to a flight attendant named Cindy, who also appears in the book as a character (and we know her as one of the Tailies on *Lost*). There are references to various organizations, occurrences of the numbers, and thematic similarities to *Lost*. Unfortunately, there's also a glaring error in the book that several people have found. One of the characters has a theory on the case Artisan's working on, and it hinges on a law that was changed on November 28, 2004, in Scotland. A law that hadn't yet been changed when Troup would have written the book. Oops.

The big difference between the show and the book, unfortunately, is Manny Weissman. This annoying man is the best friend (and former professor) of Artisan. Where on *Lost* the writers drop in obscure literary, philosophical, and biblical references and either assume intelligence in their viewers or the ability to go and look it up, in *Bad Twin* Weissman explains even the simplest symbolism to us as if we're a bunch of idiots. As Artisan talks about how one brother is left-handed, Weissman explains the meaning of "sinister" (as if every literature student reading the book didn't see that one a mile away). He explains obvious references to the prodigal son, *King Lear*, and dozens of other allusions that most people with high school English would catch. Why would the writers assume that television viewers were far more intelligent than book readers?

I'm not going to do the same analysis here that I've done for the other books, but instead will point out some page numbers that would be of interest to those who've already read *Bad Twin* and wanted more insight into the connections with *Lost*:

12: The description of Zander is very similar to Sawyer.

13, 88, 90, 142, 177, 233: Significant uses of Hurley's numbers.

16: Troup mentions the Widmores have "investments in a wide range of scientific enterprises, both mainstream and fringe," suggesting a connection to the Dharma Initiative.

21: Argos is a chocolate Lab and is a sweet dog, which sets him up as the good twin to a certain eerie dog on the island.

23, 130, 154, 168: Weissman references literature and philosophers also referenced on *Lost*.

31: The description of the Hanso Foundation puts it in the same building as Widmore, though Hanso is on the 42nd floor of the building. (Other Hanso references are on pages 29, 32, 149.)

41: Artisan mentions Paik Heavy Industries and how Mr. Paik is a particularly hostile man. We know him as Sun's father.

52: Artisan goes to visit Moth, which is the name of an episode of *Lost*. His boat is the *Escape Hatch*.

58: Cliff's dead wife is named Shannon, and she's a total princess. It's clear she's not the Shannon we know, but it's interesting that they have the same name.

68: We find out what the word "artisan" means in Basque, which connects him to a particular character on the island.

79: Someone suggests Artisan should check out a yoga teacher whose name they can't remember, but they suggest Moonbeam, which is a nickname Sawyer gave to Libby.

81: The description of Cliff on this page could be describing Jack (it's interesting that the descriptions of the twin brothers match the guys who are warring for Kate's affection).

87: The elevator ride described here is very much like the one in *The Third Policeman*.

97–99, 224–225: Weissman analyzes purgatory for us, and one could read it as an apt analysis of *Lost*.

117: The discussion on what makes a person good or bad could be useful when trying to figure out the Others.

124: Captain Jocko could be Mr. Friendly.

157: Artisan eats at a certain chicken hut we know from a season 2 flashback.

192: Artisan feels like he's come out of a cocoon (see "The Moth").

198: The theme of light and dark is explored.

222: Arthur's revelation about an argument he had with Zander mirrors the relationship between Christian and Jack.

223: As a bit of a wink to *Lost*'s filming location, the Oceanic flight from Sydney to LAX stops in Oahu, Hawaii, to refuel.

245: A minister gives a sermon on destiny and fate that's actually rather good, and ties in to the season-long argument between Jack and Locke.

Bad Twin hit stores in May 2006, ended up on the *New York Times* bestseller list, and gave fans something to talk about as the season came to a close and the summer loomed ahead. *Daily Variety* revealed the real author of the book to be Laurence Shames, who'd authored other thrillers. What makes the book a bit of a head-scratcher is the very references to the show, however. How did Troup know about Paik, or Hanso, or the Widmores, and why don't Hurley and Sawyer find it strange that he does? *Bad Twin* is an okay read, but it's not a book you'd want to be stuck on a desert island with.

2.21   ?

Original air date: May 10, 2006

Written by: Damon Lindelof, Carlton Cuse

Directed by: Deran Serafian

Guest cast: Nick Jameson (Richard Malkin), Adetokumboh M'Cormack (Yemi), Oliver Muirhead (Monsignor), Melissa Bickerton (Joyce Malkin), Brooke Mikey Anderson (Charlotte), Peter Lawn (Caldwell), Felix Williamson (Dr. Ian McVay)

Flashback: Eko

Eko has a prophetic dream that leads him to a very familiar place in the jungle.

"?" shows us another important step on Locke's journey of faith. In this episode, Locke seems to come full circle, and returns to the angry, bitter man he was before he got on the plane. His beliefs are finally so shadowed in doubt, he can no longer see the mystical signs that are right in front of him. "?" is not only a flashback to Eko's life before the crash, but a symbolic and thematic flashback to the season 1 episode, "Deus Ex Machina." As in that episode, one character believes the island has given something to him, and he has a dream that leads him to the plane in the jungle. A cliff is climbed, and the character who had the dream believes he's found a sign on the island, but another character suffers a horrible loss as a result. In season 1, the character who followed his dream and became the believer was Locke, and Boone was the one who suffered the consequences. In this episode, Eko is the believer, and it is Locke who pays the price when his hard-earned faith is finally ripped away from him once and for all. In both episodes, Locke has trouble walking.

The orientation video in the Pearl station quotes Karen DeGroot as saying, "Careful observation is the only key to true and complete awareness." So, to get a true awareness of where Locke's mindset is at by the end of this episode, we need to go back and observe everything that has happened to him this season. In season 1, he found a hatch, and it inspired him and became his obsession. He believed the island was sending him a sign, that Boone's death was a necessary sacrifice, and that whatever was in that hatch would be of the utmost importance. Then he saw something horrifying in the jungle, and Jack taunted him for having so much blind faith. When he finally discovered what was in the hatch, it wasn't the celestial sign he had hoped it would be, but an outdated bachelor pad . . . until he found the computer, and realized *this* was what the island wanted him to do. But

In "?" Eko's faith leads him to the same spot Locke's belief led him to in "Deus Ex Machina."
(CHRISTINA RADISH)

again, Jack mocked him, saying maybe this is all a big joke. Locke began pushing the button, but was never as certain of what he was doing as when he was working on opening the hatch. What started out as his hatch, with him delegating the tasks and setting up shifts for who would press the button, quickly became Jack's domain, with Jack lording it over Locke, demanding to know the combination to the armory, and setting up clandestine meetings with people behind Locke's back. Meanwhile, Locke believed that maybe he was meant to help other people, but then he discovered Charlie was lying to him. He tried to make Jack look like an idiot when he paired up with Sawyer, and he ended up looking like the idiot instead.

Then came Henry Gale. Henry very quickly realized the main tension in the camp was between these two men, and he used it to his advantage. Locke's faith in Jack, the hatch, and the button waned as Henry worked his verbal manipulation on him. He believed Henry's story and Henry's actions afterward convinced him he was right. When Sayid discovered the truth, Locke was momentarily floored. Henry changed tactics and soon Locke believed in Henry again and doubted that the button did anything. And now, in this episode, he returns to the hatch to discover Henry has shot his way out of captivity, proving Sayid right all along. That discovery *nearly* destroys him, but his discovery of the Pearl station finishes the job. What's inside is too much for him. As far as he's concerned, Locke has finally gotten an answer to the question he's been asking all season, and he's gutted to find out that what he's been doing the entire time he's been on the island has been as useless as bonding with Anthony Cooper or training for a walkabout tour.

Eko, on the other hand, is still the way Locke was in season 1. He interprets the Pearl station in a completely different way, and his wide-eyed enthusiasm and

The church that Eko (and Charlie) built. (RYAN OZAWA)

excitement reminds us of the determination Locke had in season 1. Just like Locke, Eko had lost his faith in his past life. He lived his life as someone else — Mr. Eko — the murderer and drug runner from Nigeria. The gold cross he wore around his neck as a child was ripped from his throat the moment he crossed the line, and he saw it as a symbolic gesture that meant God had abandoned him. But just as he is given a sign from his brother Yemi to bring Locke along on his quest to help restore Locke's faith, the monsignor at the church where Eko preaches in Australia sends Eko on a mission of his own to help Eko believe again. Eko investigates a claim that a girl who died came back to life a day later. What he discovers is both eerie and revelatory.

The big surprise of the episode happens when zombie girl's dad comes out to confront Eko, and it's none other than Richard Malkin, the psychic who put Claire on the plane. He admits to Eko he's nothing but a sham, which either completely ruins Claire's backstory in "Raised by Another," or, more likely, he's lying, and not only did he manage to get Claire on the flight, but he was able to indirectly get Eko on the same flight. Is the living dead girl an actress Malkin hired? Eko's passport is issued in April, and he doesn't board the flight until September, so the investigation clearly caused him the delay. Did Malkin use his psychic abilities to find out what Eko wanted to hear about Yemi, and did he pass it on to the girl? Who *is* this guy? As Claire figured out in season 1, Malkin clearly knew the plane was going to crash, and now he's managed to force two people onto it. Was he doing it to save them, or was he doing it to save the rest of the world *from* them?

In "What Kate Did," Eko tells Locke, "Do not mistake coincidence for fate." At that time, Locke believed it was fate that made them land on different parts of the island, discover separate parts of the orientation film, and then find each other to put it together. The cynical Eko saw it as coincidence. But in this episode, the tables are turned, showing how much each man has changed in the course of a few weeks. Is it a coincidence that both of them had dreams that led them to the plane? That they are now having dreams for each other? That the plane landed in such a way as to make a dot in a question mark that was drawn on the ground? That underneath the plane was an important Dharma station? That the plane was originally commandeered by Eko? That both Locke and Eko found something on the island that gave them a renewed lease on life? Eko interprets all of these things as destiny, with the plane crash in the water providing his baptism. When he put the gold chain around his neck, it signaled a return to the innocence that he once had, and all of his sins were cleansed.

Locke, the man who has lost his faith, sees these events as bitter coincidences, mocking him from afar. He turns into Jack, and challenges Eko the same way Jack mocked, taunted, and raged at Locke early in the season. What he hates more than anything is that Jack was right — that's the bitterest pill to swallow.

Highlight: Hurley apologizing to Libby for forgetting the blankets. Usually he has the funniest line in the episode, but here he has the saddest.

Did You Notice?:

- When Ana Lucia speaks to Eko in his dream, she says, "You need to help John," but she says "John" strangely, so it almost sounds like "Jack."
- In Eko's dream, he sees a flash of images pass by him in less than five seconds that represent the significant moments of his life: the original crash on the island with the bits of plane; black smoke; a crash victim floating face down in the water; the gold cross in the dirt from his childhood after he shot the man; a child's feet as he walks by with a teddy bear; fire; Jin blindfolded; nine Mary statues sitting in front of his brother's church; Charlie

and Eko staring at the burning Beechcraft; Yemi; the Dharma Arrow station; Eko holding the bible he found in the station; a closeup of his Jesus stick; looking at the corpse of the thug with the gold tooth; Locke staring at him surprised; Eko staring at the images in the black smoke; seeing the gold cross on his brother's chest; the plane flying away from him on the tarmac; the military vehicle driving up to him; Yemi yelling to him; Marvin Candle talking on the orientation video.

- When Yemi speaks to him in his dream, he keeps saying "brother" the same way Desmond did.
- When Eko says, "To receive God's forgiveness you must be penitent for your sins," he echoes Yemi's comment to him in "The 23rd Psalm" when he tells Eko, "For confession to mean something you must have a penitent heart." Eko repeats it in his flashback like it's rote, but his heart isn't yet in it. But now he believes it, because in "Maternity Leave" he confessed to Henry, and was truly sorry.
- In "The Whole Truth," Locke said the bunker was *his* hatch, but in this episode, he's given up, and says it's not his hatch at all.
- Locke's map has the Staff station to the northeast, but on the blast door map it looked like it was more directly north.
- This time last season, Jack never would have trusted Kate to accompany Sawyer alone to get the guns. It's amazing how much their relationship has changed.
- In Locke's dream, Eko is limping as if *he* is Locke.
- In "The Whole Truth," Jin tells Bernard there are no pearls on the island. Clearly he was wrong.
- In the Swan station's orientation video, the speaker called himself "Candle," and here he changes it to "Wickman," which is a play on Candle. The actor is uncredited in both episodes, as if the producers want to keep us guessing whether or not he's the same guy.
- When the video ends, Eko asks Locke if he'd like to see it again, and Locke says no, he's seen enough. This echoes the conversation between Locke and Jack in "Orientation," when Jack asks Locke if he's going to watch it again, and Locke says, "Aren't you?" and Jack says, "No, John, I'm not."
- Locke says they're nothing but rats in a maze, which echoes the B.F. Skinner experiment (see page 187).
- The language that zombie girl used when she spoke to Eko was interesting:

she says she spoke to Yemi when she was "between places." On the island, the castaways are literally between places (between Sydney and L.A.) and many of them are emotionally, psychologically, and theologically between places. Only there, according to her, can you find what you've been looking for. (Cue the U2 music.)

- When Libby is gasping for breath, she looks at Hurley and appears to be terrified, like she thinks Michael will come for Hurley next.
- The Virgin Mary statues actually do bring comfort to Libby (their original purpose), but they also bring death.
- In "Lockdown," when we saw the blast door map, there was a comment on the right-hand side, "The Pearl?" but the comment is unconnected to the question mark in the center of the map.

Interesting Facts: The story of the dead girl who lived echoes the story of Lazarus from John 11. In this parable, Jesus arrives after Lazarus' death (he travels 15 furlongs to get there), and Lazarus has been in the tomb for 4 days. Lazarus' sister Martha approaches Jesus, and he tells her Lazarus will rise again. This section contains the oft-quoted passage, "I am the resurrection, and the life: he that believeth in me, though he were dead, yet shall he live: And whosoever liveth and believeth in me shall never die." He tells the mourners to roll away the stone in front of the tomb, and calls out for Lazarus to come to him, and Lazarus walks out of the tomb.

Pearls symbolize purity, innocence, and honesty. In Eastern cultures, they are believed to bring about spiritual transformation. The Japanese believe they bring good luck. St. Augustine believed the pearl symbolized Jesus Christ, which may be why Eko finds such serenity in the station. Heaven is often referred to as having pearly gates, another reference Eko might find soothing. "Pearls of wisdom" is a popular phrase that fits here — the station's denizens watch the other station and impart the knowledge they've gained.

In the orientation video, Wickman says they have to put the journals into pneumatic tubes to send them to their headquarters. Pneumatics is the science of the mechanical properties of gas. Pneumatology is the branch of theology concerned with the Holy Ghost and other spiritual concepts.

Nitpick: Jack's bedside manner hits an all-time low: as Libby gasps for breath, he tells Kate to keep pressure on the wound, and then he nonchalantly wanders out wiping his hands on a towel to ask Michael questions about Henry Gale. I'm glad the dying woman in the next room comes second to finding his escaped convict.

And, while the technique of filming a character learning about another character's death without any audible dialogue was successful with Shannon finding out about Boone, it somehow doesn't work in this episode with Hurley. Jorge Garcia just drops his head, and looks like Kate just told him his favorite television show was canceled. Finally, zombie gal has the worst Australian accent we've heard yet.

Oops: Hurley's sideburns were very thin in "Dave," and the action here takes place a couple of days later and they're very thick and full. Also, at the Pearl station, Eko opens one of the journals and blows on it, and we see dust fly up off the pages. No dust would have accumulated *inside* the books, if they'd been closed. And if you look closely at the printouts, the final numbers are all exactly 108 minutes different from each other, showing that every time the numbers were input correctly (i.e., every 108 minutes) they were accepted by the computer in the Pearl station. However, this calculation isn't accurate, because the numbers could be input at any time after 104 minutes. So the times should have ranged from 104–108 minutes, rather than making it look like everyone punched in the numbers at the last second.

4 8 15 16 23 42: Eko's passport number is 223652. It contains 32 pages (a reverse **23**), and says he was born **08/23/1968**. The passport was issued on **04/16/04**, and expires **04/15/14**. When Eko goes to see the coroner, on the autopsy tape he says the girl is **161** centimeters tall. In the orientation video, Mark Wickman says the participants will work in **8**-hour shifts.

It's Just a Flesh Wound: Eko headbutts Locke when Locke refuses to listen to him.

Any Questions?:
- Why is Eko in Australia?
- The coroner looks a little shifty. What isn't he telling us about all of this? Is he lying? Is the tape something that's been made up?
- The psychic tells Eko there are no miracles to be had, "Not in this world, anyway." What does he mean by that? Is the island the next world? Is death the next world?
- Does Hurley suspect Michael of any wrongdoing, or is he genuine when he says he's glad Michael's okay?
- There appears to be a cigarette on the table beside one of the chairs. Was it smoked recently?
- A tour of duty in the Pearl station is three weeks: why such a short period? Do they worry someone will learn too much about what is going on?

"?" Whisper Transcripts

Surprisingly, the two fans who transcribed the whispers found some in the autopsy tape Eko listened to in Australia. How is that possible? What's more interesting than the whispers, though, is what Charlotte Malkin says when she comes back from the dead:

Doctor: This is a Caucasian female. She's 161 cm, 51.3 kilos, body prepped and washed by the very lovely Valerie McTavish.
Assistant [*chuckling*]: Ian, stop it.
Doctor: Commencing with the post.
Whisper: That's her (*or*) That's enough
Doctor: This is a clear case of drowning. I'll begin with a thoracic . . .
Charlotte Malkin: John! [*screaming*]
Whisper: She's alive
Whisper: How will we know
Assistant: Oh my God!
Doctor: Valerie!
Assistant: She's alive!
Doctor: I think she's trying . . .
Charlotte Malkin: Let John Locke go (*on*)!
Whisper: She's not dead
Whisper: I found it
Doctor: Try and calm down.
(*Assistant screaming "Stop, stop"*)
Doctor: Valerie get . . . she's crying, don't just stand there, do something!
Whisper: We're sending them in (*or*) Let's hear what she says

- When the orientation film begins, the speaker is Marvin Candle from the other orientation film, but he says his name is Mark Wickman. Is he an actor making up both names? Is this part of the psychological experiment? Or are the two men twins?
- Rickman says that they will proceed to the Pala ferry. What's that?
- Like the Swan station's orientation film, this video appears to have something missing after he says, "to prepare your next . . ." What was cut, and why?
- Is the Pearl station computer the one Walt or someone else used to talk to Michael?

Ashes to Ashes: Libby (no known last name) was a clinical psychologist who spent some time at the Santa Rosa Mental Health Center, and had just found love when her life was unexpectedly cut short.

1984 by George Orwell (1948)

1984 is probably the most well-known example of dystopian literature, which are stories describing a hellish existence. Orwell wrote the book shortly after WWII as a warning to people of what could happen under a totalitarian regime. In the novel, set in an England now called Oceania, the Party rules by instilling fear and paranoia in its citizens. People are watched everywhere, including in their own homes, through telescreens mounted on the walls. Posters and billboards with the face of Big Brother (the figurehead of the Party) peering out remind everyone that they can never escape the eyes of the Party. Thought Police roam the streets, searching for anyone who is transgressing the will of the Party, whether in word, deed, or thought.

The novel follows Winston Smith, a cynical member of the Outer Party who works in the Ministry of Truth, which is in charge of fabricating history to make it seem like the Party was always in power. (Similarly, the Ministry of Plenty is in charge of organizing economic shortages, the Ministry of Peace conducts the wars, and the Ministry of Love is where dissidents are tortured.) He notices that the citizens of Oceania seem to accept whatever rhetoric the Party throws at them, but he's not so convinced. He's been having snatches of memories coming back to him that tell him the world wasn't always the way it is now. When he buys a diary and begins writing in it nasty things about the Party and its slogans (War Is Peace; Freedom Is Slavery; Ignorance Is Strength), he becomes convinced he's going to get caught. His transgressions build, because he assumes that if he's already essentially dead, there's nothing worse they can do to him. He suspects another worker in the Party, Julia, to be a spy when he discovers her following him everywhere, but she eventually tells him she loves him, and they begin an affair (according to the Party, sex should be considered an unpleasurable act that is an unfortunate necessity to produce future generations of Party members).

The Brotherhood is the rebel party (that may or may not exist) led by Emmanuel Goldstein (who may or may not exist) that is trying to usurp the Party's power. Every day, citizens are subjected to the "Two Minutes' Hate," where pictures of Goldstein are projected onto telescreens and everyone has to shout expletives and curses at him. O'Brien, another member of the Party, often looks disconcerted during these two minutes, and Winston wonders if O'Brien might actually be part of the Brotherhood. When he gets an invitation to see O'Brien at his house, Winston's prayers are answered, and O'Brien welcomes him into the Brotherhood and begins explaining their mission. He gives Winston a book to read written by Goldstein, and Winston takes it back to the small telescreen-less room where he and Julia have been carrying out their affair. He reads the book with some excitement, and, still convinced that there's no hope for him, he hopes the next generation of "proles" (the lower classes or proletarians who aren't under the thumb of the Party the way he is) might be the army that eventually unseats Big Brother and his Party. As he and Julia look at each other and say, "We are the dead," they suddenly hear a voice say, "You are the dead" from behind a picture in the room, and realize there was a telescreen behind it the whole time. The army descends on them, beats them, and drags them off to the Ministry of Love.

As Winston awaits his fate, O'Brien comes into the room, and Winston's shocked that they've caught him, too. He quickly realizes, however, that O'Brien was a spy who tricked him into revealing his mistrust of the Party. O'Brien begins the torture and brainwashing of Winston, trying to get him to accept anything the Party hands him. When Winston finally agrees that 2 + 2 = 5, O'Brien is convinced until Winston has a breakdown and admits that he hates Big Brother. O'Brien takes him into the dreaded Room 101, where he tells him his worst fears will happen, and they strap him into a chair and set a cage of rats on the table (Winston's deepest fear is of rats). He says he will open the cage and let the starving rats loose, and they will eat Winston's face. Winston shouts, "Do it to Julia!" and O'Brien is satisfied that the Party has prevailed. Winston is set free.

At the end of the novel, Winston and Julia meet up again, and she admits that she, too, wanted them to torture Winston to stop her torture. Winston has no feelings for her anymore, and they go their separate ways. He sits in a café and sips his coffee, awash in the feelings of love for Big Brother.

Winston's major flaw in the novel is his fatalism, his insistence that no matter what he does, he cannot escape the Party. He has no faith in himself or his beliefs, even though he knows that what the Party is doing is wrong. Julia, on the other hand, lives in the moment, and she never worries about being caught. She admits that she's slept with many Party members, and has evaded the eye of the Party until she begins a relationship with Winston. Every once in a while Winston has a small glimmer of hope that he might be okay, but deep down, he still believes he won't be, making that false hope his worst enemy. When O'Brien forces Winston to give in under torture, Winston realizes the Party can control his body, and therefore his mind. And he gives up, and gives in. The Party's slogans suddenly make sense to him: by keeping the people convinced they're in a perpetual war, they maintain peace on the home front; by giving the people the freedom to be protected by Big Brother, they become slaves to the Party; and by keeping the people completely ignorant of the truth, the Party gains its strength.

1984 has definitely influenced *Lost*. From the "84" Chinese symbol on Boone's shirt throughout season 1 to the fact there were 48 survivors (a reverse 84) of the crash, the writers have been giving subtle shout-outs to Orwell's masterpiece. In "?" the writers draw the most obvious parallels to the book. Eko and Locke discover a Big Brother-like hatch where everyone in the Swan station is being constantly monitored and watched. It's unclear whether the people in the Swan station are the subjects of the experiment, or if it's the people in the Pearl; but where the Thought Police in *1984* can read the thoughts of citizens, Locke's discovery of this hatch will affect his thoughts and force his actions in upcoming episodes. The television screens in the Pearl station mirror the description of the telescreens in *1984*.

Just as Winston believes in a false hope, it was Locke's false hope in the redemptive qualities of the hatch that led to his downfall. Similarly, in "S.O.S." Rose admonishes Bernard for instilling false hope in the people on the beach, and at the same time she gave Bernard false hope that her cancer was actually gone after she'd met Isaac.

In many ways the very idea of Big Brother was more destructive than the Party's actual activities, reinforcing the mantra that fear itself is the biggest thing we have to fear. As the characters come to a realization that they are actually being watched in the jungle, in the hatch, and on the beach, their paranoia will become increasingly destructive, until the discovery of the Pearl station sparks what could be the most devastating thing to happen on the island.

2.22   Three Minutes

Original air date: May 17, 2006
Written by: Edward Kitsis, Adam Horowitz
Directed by: Stephen Williams
Guest cast: Michael Bowen (Pequot), April Grace (Miss Klugh), Tania Raymonde (Alex)

Flashback: Michael

Michael insists that Hurley, Jack, Kate, and Sawyer — and no one else — should accompany him north to find the camp of the Others.

When Michael committed the unthinkable at the end of "Two for the Road," his actions left fans buzzing about the possibilities of what could have happened to him. In "Three Minutes," we flash back almost two weeks to the events of "The Hunting Party," and we see the events that forced Michael's hand. He is behaving irrationally and often seems panic-stricken, and for someone who claims to want to take down the Others, he's not putting together the army he should. His actions seem to go unnoticed by Jack, who chalks his behavior up to those of a distraught dad, but Sayid finally sees through the smokescreen, and guesses what has been going on. Eko, too, seems to have figured out what Michael has done, and delivers a parable that taps in to Michael's current distress.

Michael *did* find the Others, and his description of the camp was accurate. The village of the Others is an exciting thing to finally see, and looks very much like a

Michael will do anything it takes to get Walt back. Anything. (SUE SCHNEIDER/MOONGLOW PHOTOS)

Viking village, with small huts right by the water, salted fish being the staple food (served in palm leaves), and two weird guys standing guard in front of a pair of Dharma doors. The Others seem to conduct experiments and have the ability to test blood. There is a hierarchy of sorts, where some of the Others answer to higher members, yet they each seem to have a different purpose in the camp. We are introduced to Miss Klugh (pronounced "Clue," which is about as subtle as putting a blue paw print on her forehead), a condescending, straightforward, psychological torturer, who asks Michael a myriad of questions (creating many new questions for the viewer) and delays giving him the one thing he really wants — his son. When Walt finally does walk into the hut, it's a shock for any viewer who thought he was dead, and the look on Michael's face proves he'd thought his son was gone, too. Just as he had finally given up, here is his chance for redemption standing right in front of him.

Similarly, Charlie finds a sort of redemption in this episode, which has been a long time coming. His low point on the island was in "Fire + Water," where he put Aaron's life in jeopardy, alienated Claire, and was publicly humiliated by Locke. Since that moment he's become an outcast among the Lostaways, and bides his time building a church with the guy everyone else is too scared to talk to. He has gone from being one of the most-liked characters to a bit of a

Tania Raymonde plays the kind and helpful Alex. (CHRISTINA RADISH)

weasel, and the "is he or isn't he using" question has become tired. At this point, it's difficult to care anymore: if he is using, then he's not worth anyone's time, and if he isn't, then he has a serious attitude problem. He's gone from being that guy who will do anything to be liked, wanting to take care of everyone around him, to a self-serving little man who keeps people at arm's length, and the moment they don't do things the way he wants them to — like Eko in this episode — he turns his back on them. When Vincent drops an unexpected "gift" at his feet (prompting the admittedly hilarious line, "Are you kidding me?") he follows him to the stash, and once and for all answers our question. Charlie undergoes a baptism of sorts, where he literally tosses his old life to the ocean, letting the water wash away his sins, and it is important that Locke witnesses Charlie's renewal. But is it enough? Does this mean Charlie's a new man? Or is he going to be even more smug and insufferable than he's been for the latter half of this season? Not only does he throw away the heroin, but the Virgin Mary statues that contain it, as if to suggest he's also giving up his spirituality.

This episode was more of a teaser for what was to come in the big season

Michael finally sees the camp where the Others have been living on the opposite side of the island. (RYAN OZAWA)

finale the following week, but it did show us how Michael was given his mission by the Others. The scene where Walt rushes to him, begging his father to save him, is heartbreaking. Michael is unable to hug Walt or talk to him privately, and the things his son tells him are terrifying and infuriating. What parent wouldn't almost be driven mad by the suggestion that their child is being abused mentally and possibly physically by strangers? In saving Walt, Michael gets the chance for the redemption he was seeking when he got on the plane — he can finally be the father his son always wanted. But he will sacrifice the lives of others — and his own soul — to do so.

Highlight: Sawyer opening up to Jack and telling him he's his only friend, and confessing that he and Ana Lucia "got caught in a net."

Did You Notice?:

- When Mr. Friendly and the Others attack Michael, we hear the same shots go off that Jack, Locke, and Sawyer had heard in "The Hunting Party."

- When Eko talks to Michael about the boy in his English parish, he again sounds like Locke in season 1. Throughout that first season, Locke would suddenly appear and tell a parable that made the listener look within himself to find an answer. Similarly, Eko's story rings true with Michael.
- Jack's becoming a more democratic leader in the group. When Michael makes a case to Jack that he must trust him on this one because of his emotional connection to the situation, Jack agrees and steps back. (Unfortunately, it was the wrong time to do so.)
- "Maternity Leave" only contained the suggestion that the dark-haired girl was Alex, but this episode offers the proof, when we hear her called Alex (and it's interesting that hers *wasn't* the arm we saw in "The Hunting Party").
- Many of Miss Klugh's questions to Michael echoed the questions Susan's attorney asked him in "Adrift," when she asked what his first words and favorite foods were.
- Eko doesn't attend the funeral, just like Locke didn't attend Boone's. Both thought their purpose on the island was more important.
- Sun's sudden comment, "Boat," is the same first English word Jin says in ". . . In Translation," though it seems strange coming out of her.

Nitpick: The constant flash of "13 Days Ago" and "Today" became repetitive and annoying. They should have flashed it on the first flashback, and then assumed their viewers were intelligent enough to know that Michael with a sling and a burgundy shirt was present-day Michael (in Claire's flashback, they didn't feel the need to put "Today" at the bottom of the screen). Also, Michael sits and waits at the computer for Walt's response for about five seconds, and suddenly this rather large reply comes back. How could a 10-year-old type that quickly?

Oops: When Klugh holds up the list, from Michael's point of view it's folded in half, but from her perspective it's a flat piece of paper.

4 8 15 16 23 42: Sawyer says they have 11 guns, and that the others took five, so that means there were originally **16**. Miss Klugh writes **4** names on a sheet of paper.

It's Just a Flesh Wound: Mr. Friendly throws a rock and hits Michael, and he's hit in the head with the butt of Alex's gun.

Any Questions?:
- Michael asks Jack if he has a son, and Jack seems taken aback and waits a beat before saying no. Is he lying?

- Since everyone now knows about the magnetic anomaly on the island, why would Michael have used a compass to go north on the island? Was he really going north?
- Why was Eko in a parish in England?
- Who does Charlie think he is, grabbing a box of vaccines from the pallet that was dropped on the island and just handing it off to Claire? Shouldn't he have shown that to Jack? Why would he inject it into himself without running it by the doctor first? And what if it isn't the vaccine he thinks it is — did he just put Aaron's life in serious jeopardy? Why would Claire just accept Charlie's word, after everything he's done?
- Why doesn't Michael bring Vincent with him? Is he worried that the dog's intuition will pick up on his betrayal? If he really believes he's returning to the camp to retrieve Walt and leave the island, wouldn't Walt want his dog, too?
- Miss Klugh's questions are very pointed, and make us wonder if there's a reason she's asking them: *Is* Michael really Walt's father? As I mentioned earlier, Walt says to him rather vehemently the morning of the flight that he's not his father, and that's immediately after Michael had touched him. Klugh wonders how old Walt was when he started speaking: does she sense that he has a certain genius that she's never seen before? The illnesses and fainting spells question would suggest she thinks he's telepathic. Michael looks disconcerted when she asks if he'd ever seen Walt anywhere he wasn't supposed to be. Did he?
- What kind of tests did they make Walt take? What does Klugh mean when she threatens to put Walt into "the room" again? What room? What does Walt mean when he says the Others are just pretending, and they're not who they say they are? Is this proof they are actors in some way?
- If the Others wanted Jack, Hurley, Sawyer, and Kate, then why did they let Sawyer, Kate, and Jack go in "The Hunting Party"?
- Walt appeared to Shannon three times, and each time he did he was dripping wet and trying to warn her about things. Was he astrally projecting himself to her of his own will? Why was he always wet? Were the Others keeping him somewhere that was wet? Were the Others manipulating him to make him appear to her like that? Why did he appear to Shannon in particular? Did Vincent have anything to do with it, since he always disappeared right before Walt emerged?
- During the eulogy for Ana Lucia, Jack says she did the best she could, and

A Dog's Life

Vincent the dog is a major character but no one really thinks about him (he's actually played by a female dog named Madison). But the dog has a mysterious quality to him, and whenever he makes an appearance and then leaves, something bad usually happens. Even *Lost* writer Javier Grillo-Marxuach referred to him as "the dog of doom" during an online chat. If Vincent turns his back on you, you'd better watch out.

Pilot, Part 1: When Jack wakes up in the jungle and is about to see the plane crash, Vincent is sitting beside him. When Charlie, Kate, and Jack are out looking for the cockpit of the plane, Vincent sits in the jungle and watches them.

Walkabout: Vincent stands near the fuselage barking, which brings everyone over to look at it, and then a bunch of wild boar run out at them.

Special: Vincent growls and begins running in the jungle, breaking his leash and leaving Walt alone. Moments later, Walt is attacked by a polar bear.

Homecoming: Vincent trips the alarm they set up around the perimeter of the camp, and distracts everyone from the real concern — the fact that Steve is dead on the beach.

Exodus, Part 1: Walt gives Vincent to Shannon, and as the raft pulls away, Vincent tries to chase it, but then turns his back. Soon after, the raft is sabotaged and Walt kidnapped.

Man of Science, Man of Faith: Shannon runs out into the jungle after Vincent, and she sees him, but he turns and runs away. As Sayid runs after Vincent, Shannon sees Walt standing there, dripping wet, and warning her of something.

Abandoned: Shannon lets Vincent sniff one of Walt's shirts, and tells him to find Walt, but he gets away from her. As she chases him through the jungle, Ana Lucia emerges, mistakes Shannon for an Other, and kills her.

The Hunting Party: Ana Lucia shoos Vincent away from her tent, and gives him a piece of apple that will make him turn and run away from her. She's killed a few days later.

The Long Con: Sun is working in the garden when Vincent runs out to see her. He runs back into the jungle, and someone attacks Sun from behind and hurts her.

Three Minutes: Vincent runs up to Charlie and drops a Virgin Mary statue at his feet, and leads Charlie back to the stash as if he's trying to tempt him.

it wasn't easy for her being on the island. Was this a subtle reference to himself?

- Who is on the boat at the end of the episode?
- In "Lockdown," in the northeast corner of the blast door map next to a station marked "C3," the cartographer has written, "Why so many DharmaTel relays in such an untenable location?" Could the Others have rigged the DharmaTel communication system so that they can contact people in the Swan station from this location?

2.23, 2.24   Live Together, Die Alone

Original air date: May 24, 2006
Written by: Carlton Cuse, Damon Lindelof
Directed by: Jack Bender
Guest cast: Clancy Brown (Kelvin Inman), Tania Raymonde (Alex), Michael Bowen (Pequot), April Grace (Miss Klugh), Alan Dale (Charles Widmore), Sonya Walger (Penelope Widmore), Stephen Page (Master Sergeant), Len Cordova (Man #1), Alex Petrovitch (Man #2)

Flashback: Desmond

Desmond returns to the island, and we finally see what brought him there in the first place. Meanwhile, Jack, Hurley, Kate, and Sawyer follow Michael to the Others' camp, and Locke decides to risk it all and find out what happens if the button doesn't get pushed.

So, after everything the castaways have been through, it seems it all comes down to love. Through Desmond's flashback we see a true Romeo and Juliet scenario, with a guy in love with a girl whose father hates him. Just like all the other characters on the island, Desmond needed to redeem something when he landed on the island — his honor — and after three years of being trapped in the place, he believes that no amount of honor can ever get him back to the woman he loves. What did Desmond do that was so terrible? They don't reveal that tidbit in this episode (making a regular appearance next season inevitable) but it sounds like something that seemed far worse to him than to Penelope Widmore, the woman he loves. His flashback reveals a surprising link to not one character in the past (besides Jack), but two. The first is Libby — meeting her inspires him to try to get Penelope back, which involves taking something away from Widmore.

The second is Kelvin Inman, whom we first saw in "One of Them," encouraging Sayid to torture one of Sayid's own people. Inman drags Desmond into the bunker and asks him the same riddle that Desmond had asked Locke, and has the same dismal realization that the new guy isn't his savior. Watching the subsequent scenes between Desmond and Kelvin are frustrating in a sense, because we realize the society on the island never progresses because no one shares the information they acquire to anyone else. Desmond didn't tell Locke and Co. what he knew about the button, the blast door map, or the quarantine; and sim-

No, it's not Desmond. Clancy Brown (seen here in the mid-1990s), who plays Inman, is a prolific actor whose distinctive look and voice have earned him roles in *Highlander*, *Shawshank Redemption*, and *Carnivale*. Cartoon fans will recognize his voice as that of Lex Luthor. (SUE SCHNEIDER/MOONGLOW PHOTOS)

ilarly Desmond is with Kelvin for three years before Kelvin tells him what happened to his former partner.

The revelations of the past show us how much quicker the large group of people were able to obtain the information than one person could, but the revelations in the present show us how much quicker that knowledge has driven them to drastic action. Where Locke frantically pushed that button for the first half of the season, now Eko finds serenity in his new task, and believes saving the world every 108 minutes is a *gift*, not a burden. Where Jack, the holier-than-thou, condescending non-believer, had taunted Locke's belief, Locke refuses to respect Eko's conviction entirely, and physically removes him from what Eko thinks is his destiny. By attempting to use Eko's "Jesus stick" to destroy the computer, Locke takes the symbol of one of Eko's beliefs to destroy another. Locke's determination to prove his theory comes from his humiliation at Jack's hands and what he believes to be his own stupidity for ever having faith in the first place. But what Locke fails to recognize is that wavering faith can be far more destructive than a misguided one.

Locke's declaration to Eko that they're nothing more than puppets on a screen brings to mind the cave allegory in Plato's *Republic*. In this famous allegory, Plato

Sawyer and Jack: Best Friends Forever. (STHANLEE MIRADOR/SHOOTING STAR)

describes a group of people who have been chained in a cave their entire lives, watching shadows on the wall. They come to believe the shadows *are* the actual thing. Plato then says to imagine if one of these people were suddenly "freed." He would be pushed out into the world, where the sun would at first blind him, but he would eventually understand how important the sun was, and how the world worked. He would also realize, to his horror, that he'd spent a lifetime staring at shadows. If he tried to return to tell others, however, they wouldn't listen to him, because venturing into the unknown is a frightening prospect. They would become hostile to any suggestion that what they believe is wrong, and they wouldn't listen to him. The allegory comments on our impulse to accept status quo and not ask enough questions of the world around us. Locke has gone out into the world, he's come back with an idea, and he's trying to tell Eko, but Eko won't listen because he wants to believe the computer has a purpose. The difference between their situation and that of the cave dwellers in Plato's allegory is that Eko, too, has gone into the world, and he is likewise

Henry Ian Cusick makes a rare public appearance at the 2006 Creative Emmy Awards. (SUSAN SCHNEIDER/MOONGLOW PHOTOS)

Sayid makes a surprising discovery at the Others' camp. (RYAN OZAWA)

trying to convince Locke of its veracity, but can't get through to him either.

But why does Desmond help Locke? We've seen in his flashback that he's already seen what happens when the clock counts down to zero, and it's not pretty. At the beginning of the episode, he's suicidal, but Locke forces him to sober up before helping him, if only to prove that Desmond is acting consciously. Has Desmond spent the last two months going over that day in his mind, until he's convinced himself it might have been nothing but a hoax? If a bunch of metal objects suddenly stopped flying across the room, did it have anything to do with him entering the numbers, or was it just another experiment put on by the Dharma Initiative? Perhaps Desmond follows Locke because Locke has saved him once already. Each man saw the presence of the other as his salvation, but it was only when they came face to face they realized they were harboring a false hope. Now perhaps they both think they can save the other again. And again, they're wrong. Once Desmond takes a look at the printouts and realizes the electromagnetic anomaly was real, he knows they're all in big, big trouble.

Jack, the ever-reluctant leader, takes his unwitting team to what could very well be their deaths and when the truth finally comes out, it's a tense and terrifying moment. All of the actors are superb in this scene: we feel Evangeline Lilly's shock, Josh Holloway's vengeful anger, Matthew Fox's fury, Jorge Garcia's injured resignation, and Harold Perrineau's panic. Viewers were spellbound, wondering if Sawyer was going to pull a Sayid on Michael, or if Hurley was finally going to snap and do it himself. But instead, Jack steps up and says he has a plan, but it's a flawed plan at best. Sayid wants to use a smoke signal to give the Others a message that the Losties were coming. Knowing how wily the Others are, that's got to be the worst plan anyone's ever come up with on this show.

Speaking of which, The Artist Formerly Known as Henry Gale appears to *be* Keyser Soze, after all (see page 267), as he steps out of the motorboat and the rest of the Others let him do all the talking. Knowing that he's probably the most important of them suddenly makes a lot of sense. In "One of Them," when Rousseau first captured Henry, she told Sayid that he would lie for a long time, and she was right. He's misled them throughout his captivity; even when they discovered he was one of the Others, he continued to make them think he was an insignificant member of the group. We learn that in "Lockdown" he didn't run away, because he had purposely planted himself there in the first place. If he is the leader of the group (the "him" Tom referred to in "Maternity Leave") then he's clearly become fed up with the screwups of other people in his group, like Ethan, and he's decided to just do the job himself. How he was able to withstand the torture that Sayid put him through is still unclear, but we saw that Ethan had superhuman strength, so perhaps he's taking the same vitamins. (Considering the vaccines and experiments the Others have been doing, it wouldn't be surprising to discover they're all on something that makes them different, or that their long time on the island has given them the extra strength.)

Henry makes an interesting comment to Michael at the end of the episode, when he says, "We're the good guys." In "Dave," after the real Henry has been found, Not-Henry pleads with Sayid, "You can't do this. I'm not a bad person!" In "Two for the Road," Henry tells Locke that he's one of the good ones, and that he had been on a mission to come and get Locke. They regularly take innocent children, who are also "good ones." When Henry tries to kill Ana Lucia, it's because she killed two "good people," which seems to infuriate Henry. Henry tells Ana Lucia that Goodwin believed that she was inherently good, and obviously "he was wrong." Henry wasn't the only Other to talk like that: In "The Other 48 Days," Goodwin referred to people as good and bad. He told Ana that they only took good people, and that he had to kill Nathan because Nathan was a bad person. Ethan strung Charlie up and left him for dead, suggesting the Others thought Charlie was a bad person (and after his behavior this season, who could blame them?), and in "Maternity Leave" Ethan reassures Claire that they're "a good family."

The Others seem to see the world in black and white, good and bad. What are their criteria for good and bad? From their point of view, they discovered a plane crashed on the island, and they knew the victims needed a vaccine but they didn't have enough for all of them. They watched the castaways fighting and torturing one another, and eventually decided the one who deserved the vaccine was the one who hadn't yet been born — the only one who wasn't corrupt. So they took Claire and brought her to a facility to help her and her unborn baby. When she got away, one of them went after her, and had to face the hostile, horrible people who had crashed on the island — and they ended up killing him. They took Walt for his own "protection," and fed him and tried understand his powers. When Henry was in the castaways' prison, on the other hand, they tortured him and beat the snot out of him. *Now* who are the bad guys? (Of course, it's difficult to take the high ground when you're snatching children away from their parents, blowing up rafts, and killing people like Steve in cold blood.)

As the Locke clock finally counts down to zero, fans all leaned forward in anticipation of the moment we'd been waiting for all season — is the button real, or is it all a psychological hoax? Unfortunately for everyone in the hatch . . . the button really does something. The frenzied scene of the metal objects flying and the room shaking and the countdown clock crumpling is absolutely terrifying, and Terry O'Quinn's performance (as always) is note perfect. All his life, John Locke has been a loser in everything. His parents gave him up, he was tossed him from one foster home to the next, he had few friends at school, he worked a series of odd jobs, and either remained a bachelor or had failed relationships (it's not clear yet), when his parents came back into his life it was only to serve their own selfish purposes, he met a woman but lost her due to his bad decision-making, he lost the use of his legs, he ended up in a dead-end job with a condescending boss, his only way of connecting with a woman of the opposite sex was through a dial-a-date line, he trained for a walkabout tour of Melbourne but was turned away when they realized he was paralyzed. But on the *island*, everything has been flipped. He's respected by the other castaways, if perhaps a little feared. He's regained the use of his legs. He discovered a hatch that he thought would be his salvation. He found faith. When the hatch was opened, it's like his old life came sailing back to him, and again he was questioned and disrespected by other people on the island, he was kept out of important decision-making, he became a slave to a computer, he lost the use of his leg, he was conned by Sawyer, and he discovered that everything he had been doing for months was a sham. Now he's certain for the first time in his life that he is making the absolutly correct decision, and no one is going to stop him, not even dynamite.

And he's wrong. What will this do to Locke in season 3? Considering the importance of the character to this series, it's safe to assume he's survived Desmond's obliteration of the station, so what will become of him?

Or Eko? Eko has had his faith fortified by everything he's encountered on the island, and he has yet to doubt anything. Locke's huge mistake simply proves Eko's convictions are correct, and if he survives the explosion as well, it'll be interesting to find out what will happen between him and Locke.

Charlie was the other person who was in the hatch when it exploded, yet he wanders out, a little deaf but mostly unhurt, and appears to have no recollection of anything. Where we've watched Locke's faith disintegrate all season, we've watched Charlie's very character deteriorate over the latter half. Yet there's always been something slightly off about Charlie. He uses people to try to prove something to himself. He believes that he's doing the best for others, but never asks if they want what he's trying to give them. He walks through life feeling sorry for himself and the way he was treated in Drive Shaft, without ever stopping to think of his own culpability in what happened. After kicking his heroin habit, Charlie is given a second chance, but in the second season, he decides to keep the heroin nearby, and as a result, his friends move further away. The sad thing is, Charlie never touched the stuff, and the lack of trust he feels from everyone around him is hurtful to him. Locke publicly disgraces him, and since that time Charlie's been looking to bring Locke down. His humor is no longer cheerful, but biting. On the one hand, he's upset everyone doubts him. But on the other, he can't move past his anger. In "White Rabbit," Charlie publicly punched Boone yet Boone didn't cop the mercenary attitude Charlie has shown to Locke. The way he revels in finding Locke broken and crying in the jungle in this episode is sinister. When he wanders out at the end of the episode, he generates a lot of questions: does he have some sort of amnesia? Does he know that Eko and Locke didn't make it and doesn't want to panic anyone? Does he know they might be alive, but considering neither of them showed Charlie any respect, this is his horrifying revenge, to leave them in the rubble? Is he in shock and genuinely doesn't know what happened? Is Charlie really dead and we saw his ghost walk out? The act of giving Claire the vaccine in "Three Minutes" has changed her mind about him, which is baffling (but then again, this is a woman injecting some unknown substance into her newborn child, so she's not exactly an ace decision-maker these days). Will their relationship become far more important in season 3?

Hurley's been sent away from the Others, and has gone from being one of *the* important people on a list to being a messenger boy for the tribe. How will the events of season 2 affect Hurley in season 3? He's no longer Mr. Happy Fun Guy. He's lost Libby, he's been betrayed by someone he thought was his friend, he's seen the darkest side of human nature, and he's left his friends behind on a dock while he's returned to the group. He's had to face his demons all season, whether it's his past psychosis or his present nightmare.

Jack, Kate, and Sawyer have been captured by the Others. Henry's made it clear they're only interested in the good guys, so does he think these three are inherently good? What sets them apart from everyone else in the group? The three of them have formed a love triangle, and perhaps the Others are intrigued by their actions within that dynamic. Or is it because all three of them have had even more serious parent issues than the rest of the survivors? Does it have to do with their capacity to love? That they've each lost a father? Sawyer tells Charlie in "The Long Con," "I'm not a good person, Charlie. Never did a good thing in my life," so it would be strange if the Others actually thought he was one of the good ones. The possibilities are endless. One thing is for certain: that look of understanding that passed between Jack and Kate will no doubt fuel an even more bitter Sawyer next season.

Michael and Walt are finally reunited, and many fans noticed that Malcolm David Kelley appeared to be a foot taller. Having the actor continue to play his role will be increasingly difficult for the production team, since an adolescent actor will grow quickly and his voice will change soon, so that might be the last time we're going to see Walt (unless we're to believe the Others injected him with a super-fast growth hormone). But what of Michael? There's still so much to be resolved with his character. The question of his biological paternity to Walt still hangs in the air, as do several questions about his past and what really happened to him in the years he didn't see Walt. Will he ever return, just like Desmond was brought right back to the island?

Sayid, Sun, and Jin are out on a boat sailing around the island, and Sayid has discovered that the camp where the Others held Walt and Michael is just a false front of a shantytown. There's no other hatch, there's no laboratory. What they *do* find, however, is a mysterious statue that suggests several possibilities: a former civilization once lived there and they erected a monstrous statue to their leader (who was apparently Homer Simpson, if the four toes are anything to go by); or that the Dharma Initiative is attempting some new psychological experiments and perhaps erected the statue as a foot only; or that the foot originally had five toes and one of them has crumbled away (though there's no sign of damage on the foot); or that it was indicative of a weird mutant anomaly on the island, perhaps as a result of the electromagnetic radiation; or that someone is a huge Monty Python fan. *Lost* fans immediately pointed out a similar-sounding phrase from Thomas Love Peacock's first novel, *Headlong Hall*, where someone states, "Here you see the pedestal of a statue, with only half a leg and four toes remaining: there were many here once. When I was a boy, I used to sit every day on the shoulders of Hercules: what became of him I have never been able to ascertain." Carlton Cuse and Damon Lindelof have both stated the statue will have great significance in season 3.

In the end, the one character we cannot forget is Desmond. No matter what criteria the Others use to determine if someone is good, Desmond is one of the good ones. People have killed, fought, and maimed in the name of love on this island, but no one has given up their life for it. After almost giving up, thinking that he'll never reclaim his honor, Desmond suddenly realizes there *is* a way to get his honor back, and that is to sacrifice himself to save everyone else. (It's not coincidence that Desmond looks like Christ in this episode.) As he stares at the termination switch — the thing that will end everyone's slavery to the godforsaken button, but will also probably end his life — he thinks back to the one person who means anything to him.

Desmond's love for Penelope has kept him going for many years, through many kinds of prisons, both physical and emotional. But in the shocking and jarring closing moments of the show, we realize Desmond hasn't been the only one searching and pining for his lover. The moment where Penelope receives a frantic phone call in the middle of the night is the first and only time we've ever seen life continuing off the island, and it immediately destroys the purgatory/time warp/aliens/alternate universe/nuclear holocaust theories, and many others. Just as Desmond's been searching in his heart for the way to make Penelope love him, she's been faithfully searching the globe, and now, with one blast, he's given her

The very long pier where we leave three characters and the Others at the end of season 2 is Waikane Pier near Kualoa. The pier has been a favorite shooting location for several movies and television shows. (RYAN OZAWA)

a brief look at the island, which seems to have been invisible to her before. Will it be too late when/if she finds him? Or will love prevail?

Season 2 has explored issues of faith and what happens when one loses it, the search for truth, vengeance borne of humiliation, and most of all, the triumph of love. "Live Together, Die Alone," was a brilliant season finale, and while it answered a lot of questions for us, it left many open, and created new ones for the next season that lay ahead. Which is exactly what a season finale should do.

Highlight: Locke's understatement of the century: "I was wrong."
Did You Notice?:
- When Jack throws open the door in the boat and looks down, Desmond simply says, "You." It's the same thing Jack said when he first saw Desmond in the hatch in "Man of Science, Man of Faith."

- Desmond says they're stuck "in a bloody snow globe," which was actually a fan conspiracy theory.
- Penelope lived in Knightsbridge, which is where Lucy Heatherton also lived.
- Eko says to Locke, "Do not tell me what I can't do," which echoes Locke's season 1 mantra.
- There have been several twists on the name Elizabeth on this show (Libby is a short form of Elizabeth). Kate mentions her friend Beth, who is a huge fan of Drive Shaft. Christian's patient who dies in "All the Best Cowboys" was also named Beth. When Michael loses Walt in the adoption process, Susan's lawyer's name is Lizzy.
- Libby's husband's name is David, which echoes Hurley's Dave.
- Libby's wearing a gold cross.
- This is the third time we've heard the phrase "live together, die alone," on the show (see notes for "Man of Science, Man of Faith").
- When the power goes out in the station, Eko is etching "922 Revelations" on his stick. He's probably indicating Revelations, chapters 9 to 22, which is the majority of the book of the Bible that explains what will happen on Judgment Day.
- The flashback of Desmond meeting Kelvin for the first time is almost exactly Desmond's explanation of it in "Orientation," only in that episode, he said Kelvin met him on the beach and told him to come to the hatch, instead of finding him on the beach and dragging him there.
- In "One of Them," Inman showed Sayid a videotape marked "Eyes Only Top Secret, Property of DIA." It's interesting that Inman went from the **D**efense **I**ntelligence **A**gency to the **D**harma **I**nitiative, which has the same initials.
- Kelvin talks about the sickness the same way Rousseau does, but it's interesting to note the *opposite* can be said of the island. No one has gotten sick since the plane crash — no colds, flu, nothing — except for Aaron, who was actually vaccinated against the healing properties of the island.
- Sawyer talks about how he believes the Others are aliens, which is a writer's joke about one of the fan conspiracies circulating on the Internet.
- This is the first time we've seen Sayid doing his afternoon prayers since the crash.
- Just as Locke gave Charlie three chances in "The Moth," Eko knocks on

the blast doors and asks Locke to open them before he blows them open, and says if Locke complies he will forgive him. Charlie gave in and did the right thing, but Locke doesn't, showing his hypocrisy and arrogance in the situation.

- When Desmond finds Pen's letter, and you can hear her voice reading it, there's a line in the letter after "the only person who can ever take it off is you" that the voice doesn't actually say, which is "Sorry to be so dramatic, but these are dramatic times, are they not?"

- The Others seem to be the opposite of a civilized society — where most people bum around the house in old clothes but dress up to go out, they are clean-shaven and well dressed when no one is looking (like in "Maternity Leave") and put on their tattered clothes, wipe dirt on themselves, and go barefoot for a night out on the town. Notice how Henry Gale looks *worse* now than when he was a prisoner in the armory.

- After everything he's done to Jack, Kate, Hurley, and Sawyer, Michael refers to them as his friends when talking to Henry Gale, yet in ". . . And Found," when Libby asked Michael about his friends, he told her he never thought of them that way. On the contrary, when Desmond asks Locke about his friends, Locke bluntly retorts, "They're not my friends."

- Henry Gale sending Hurley back to give a message to the Losties is reminiscent of Eko sparing the little boy's life in "The 23rd Psalm" and telling him to send a message back that Mister Eko let him live.

- One of the two Portuguese men at the end in the blizzard looks so much like Jack, many fans thought it was actually Matthew Fox playing the character until the producers confirmed that it was not.

- One of the men asks if it's happened again, and wonders whether it's another false alarm. He's probably talking about the two other false alarms from Desmond's late response on September 22nd, and Locke's in "One of Them."

- In season 2 we never saw a single flashback of a Tailie while they were on the plane.

- There is a whisper scene in this episode, but the transcript was not ready when this book went to press.

Interesting Facts: Penelope was the name of Odysseus' wife, and there is one major similarity between her and Penelope Widmore: they are both faithful to the men they love. Odysseus goes away to fight in the Trojan War, and doesn't return for 20 years. During that time Penelope is visited by 108 suitors (there's that number again) and refuses all of them. Odysseus eventually returns, dressed as a beggar, and she doesn't recognize him. He watches as she comes up with various impossible tasks for her suitors, and he knows that she's been faithful to him. She finally declares that whoever can string a very difficult bow will be the man she will marry, and all of them fail except for Odysseus, who then uses the bow and arrow to slaughter Penelope's suitors.

Possibly the most important recurring name that doesn't belong to a major character is "Tom." There have been five of them so far, all for significant characters: Thomas is the name of Aaron's biological father; Tom was Kate's childhood sweetheart before he died, with her by his side; Tommy was Charlie's drug dealer; when Ana Lucia and Christian Shephard choose names for each other, she names him Tom; Tom is the real name of Mr. Friendly. Why do the writers keep coming back to this name? Considering we have a Rousseau and a Locke, it's surprising that so far there's no Thomas Hobbes (see page 147). Perhaps the recurrence of this name suggests that there are many Hobbesian tendencies on the island and off, and those philosophies have shaped these characters their entire lives.

Henry Gale was the name of Dorothy Gale's uncle in *The Wizard of Oz*. When Dorothy traveled to Oz to meet with the wizard, she discovered that there was no wizard, just a simple man who had traveled there . . . in a hot air balloon. In an interesting twist, *Lost*'s "Henry Gale" didn't actually travel in a hot air balloon — he's the real wizard.

Nitpick: Desmond meeting Inman for the first time happens a decade after Sayid encountered Inman in "One of Them," yet Inman definitely doesn't look 10 years older. Also, throughout season 2 several episodes had big, resonant endings that didn't really go anywhere. Jack asks Ana Lucia what she knows about putting together an army in the final moments of "The Hunting Party," and then nothing ever comes of it. Sawyer comes out of the jungle in "The Long Con" and announces there's a new sheriff in town, but then other than being the guy with the guns, he doesn't act any differently than he ever did. Sayid asks Charlie at the end of "One of Them" if he remembers what the Others did to him, as if he's trying to recruit Charlie for an army of his own, but nothing comes of that, either. Hurley seemed to go off the deep end in "Dave," and by the next episode was acting like nothing had happened. This season had a lot of anticlimactic moments.

Oops: Just before Desmond inserts the key, we hear Pen's voice reading the letter, but it's a different reading than we heard earlier.

4 8 15 16 23 42: On the envelopes that Widmore shows to Desmond, you can see that Penny's street number is **23**, and Desmond's is **42**. Libby gives Desmond **4** dollars, and he asks her if she has **42**,000 more. He tells Libby the race is in **8** months. Sayid spots a statue with **4** toes. Just before Desmond finds Kelvin under the computer room with the key, he found the countdown clock at 48 seconds (**4** & **8**). When Locke tells Desmond about his low point when he was at the hatch door and Desmond saw him, the clock is at 32 minutes (a reverse **23**). When Kate reads the journal, the entries are for 0400, and 0**415**. Desmond looks at the printout and realizes the system failure happened on September 22, 2004, at 4:16. Henry tells Michael to keep bearing 325 (another reverse **23**). The most interesting number, however, happens at the end, when we see 7418880 on the computer screen detecting the electromagnetic anomaly. This number is the product of multiplying **4** x **8** x **15** x **16** x **23** x **42**.

It's Just a Flesh Wound: Eko punches Locke and leaves a mark; Sawyer kills one of the Others; Sawyer, Kate, Jack, and possibly Hurley are hit with poisonous darts; Charlie and Eko are knocked out by a fireball, leaving Eko hurt and Charlie with ringing ears and a bloody arm.

Any Questions?:

- Why doesn't Jack's hair ever grow?
- Knowing the strength of the electromagnetic anomaly on the island, why doesn't Desmond assume that his boat came right back because his compass was faulty and just kept pointing to the island?
- What did Desmond do to become dishonorably discharged from the army?
- Widmore calls Desmond a coward, and later Desmond says Widmore believed him "unsuitable" for Penelope. Why?
- What is Widmore's connection to the island? We've seen several Widmore products showing up on the island, and if Widmore was a "philanthropist," was he connected to the Hanso Foundation in some way? *Is* he Alvar Hanso?
- Why does Desmond go to the U.S. if Widmore is in England?
- How did Libby's husband die? Is it possible she's an actress, who tries on different parts and plays them in public to see if people will buy the routine? Perhaps the writers have read the 2003 novel, *May Not Appear Exactly as Shown*, by Gordon j.h. Leenders, which is about a group of people who

appear to be one thing, but turn out to be quite another. One character in the novel plays different roles to people every day to test her acting chops. Perhaps Libby's just acting when she's in the mental institution, and again on the island, and here she's playing the part of the aggrieved widow. (Or maybe she's telling the truth, and the death of her husband caused her to go off the deep end and end up in a mental institution.)

- What the heck was that Hurley bird? Did it really say his name?
- When Pen asks Desmond about her letters, why doesn't he tell her the truth? Is he worried she won't believe him?
- Why did Kelvin join the Dharma Initiative? Is he a knowledgeable participant in the goings-on on the island (i.e., is he behind the experiments) or is he as big a schmuck as Desmond and the castaways? In "One of Them," Kelvin seemed pretty sure of himself, and assured Sayid that he would need the tools he'd given him one day, as if he knew he would end up on that island. Inman tells Desmond to take the vaccine because he's worried he might have caught the virus, yet he goes outside and takes his protection gear off, showing he knows it's safe outside.
- If Desmond sees that Inman was safe after all this time, why did he continue to shoot himself with vaccine and refuse to leave the hatch?
- Did Inman and Radzinski come to the bunker together? Or did Inman show up the same way Desmond and the castaways did?
- How did Charlie and Eko get the dynamite down the ladder and into the hatch without pulling an Arzt?
- Did Kelvin ever encounter Rousseau in his travels?
- What part of the map did Kelvin paint? What part did Radzinski paint? Did they take turns going out and exploring the island and then painting it, or was Radzinski as hard-assed with Kelvin as Kelvin is with Desmond? Were there other cartographers before them? Why does Kelvin use materials that can only be seen under black light? Did he know how to turn on the black light to read his map?
- How did Eko and Charlie survive the fireball?
- In "Everybody Hates Hugo," Sayid showed Jack the tunnels underneath the bunker. Why didn't Sayid ever find the system termination lock? Also in that episode, Sayid says the last time he saw concrete poured over an entire area like the bunker was in Chernobyl, which is an apt comment to make in light of this episode.

- Kelvin *finally* explains that the computer discharges the electromagnetic energy every 108 minutes. Why isn't there just a program to reset the clock every 108 minutes, rather than making it a manual thing?
- The discovery of the open grave full of pneumatic tubes and journals seems to prove Eko's suggestion that it was actually the Pearl station that was the psychological experiment. How many different people worked at the station? Why hasn't anyone else (like Rousseau) found this collection of tubes before?
- Kate reads from one of the books, "S.R. moved the Ping-Pong table again." Who is S.R.? Radzinski?
- Kelvin admits he saw Desmond as a "sucker" who would save the world after he left. Did Desmond feel the same about Locke?
- In all that time on the island before the events of "Orientation," why didn't any of the Lostaways find Desmond's boat?
- Desmond believes he crashed the plane. Did he?
- In Eko's dream in "?" we saw the computers all shaking like they were about to explode, and you could hear the beginning of the electromagnetic surge, which foreshadows what happens in this episode.
- When Desmond turns the key and we see the effect of the noise on everyone, Sayid, Sun, and Jin are on the boat. Did Sayid actually light the fire, and if so, why did he hop back on the boat rather than wait for Jack and Co. to arrive? Did the Others light it instead to draw Jack away from Sayid?
- Why doesn't Charlie remember anything?
- Did Eko, Desmond, or Locke survive? If so, how did the electromagnetic surge affect them? What forced the quarantine door to fly off and land on the beach?
- Henry comments that they got "more than they bargained for" with Walt. What does he mean by that? Was Walt a pleasant or unpleasant surprise? Did they find a way to isolate and remove his powers? Or did his gifts overwhelm them and they're happy to be rid of him?
- In various episodes Henry referred to an important, brilliant, unforgiving man whom he had to answer to; was he immodestly referring to himself or is there a much bigger person above him?
- Why did the Others choose Hurley as their messenger boy? Because it's always him who relays information to people?

- Where is that hut at the end? In Siberia? The men are speaking Portuguese, so is it Brazil? Was there some weird nuclear explosion and now Brazil has blizzards? The fact that Penelope appears to be in a comfortable bed probably rules out the idea of a holocaust of some kind.
- What happened at the end? Was the island being hidden by the electromagnetic rays, and now that it's gone the island is suddenly visible? What did Penelope have the men looking for?

Ashes to Ashes: ???

Music/Bands: When Sayid, Jack, and Sawyer find Desmond on his sailboat, he's playing Mozart's aria "Voi Che Sapete," from *The Magic Flute*. The aria is about the pain of love, and how it burns the singer's soul, yet it's a comfort. When Desmond and Kelvin bring down the blast doors in the hatch, they're playing B.B. King's "Chains and Things" (*Indianola Mississippi Seeds*).

Henry Ian Cusick (Desmond David Hume)

Actor Henry Ian Cusick was best known for a recurring role on the hit series *24* before emerging from the hatch as the character of Desmond on *Lost*.

Born in 1969 to a Peruvian mother and an Irish-Scottish father, he actually grew up in Trinidad and Scotland and was raised as a staunch Roman Catholic. Trained in the Royal Scottish Academy of Music and Drama, he began his career as a stage actor, appearing in numerous roles in Scotland, including star turns in *The Portrait of Dorian Gray* and *The Country Wife*. His performances in the theater won him numerous accolades, including the Ian Charleston Award in 1995 for outstanding performance by a young actor in a theater role.

As his career progressed, Cusick began appearing more regularly in television and film productions. This included the role of Jesus Christ in the film production of *The Gospel of John* (2003), an important role given his spiritual nature. "Apparently, the Vatican is being asked to approve the film," he said during the film's release. "My mother would be so thrilled if I could tell her the Pope had seen me play Jesus. The whole experience has rubbed off on me, too. It's made me think more carefully about who Jesus was. I go to Mass more often, and when the priest reads from the Gospel of John, I find myself saying: I know every word of this."

He also played the role of German agent Theo Stoller throughout the fifth season of the terrorist drama *24*. After toiling in relative obscurity on the English theater circuit, Cusick got the role of Desmond at the beginning of the second season of *Lost*, a part that would recur. His character's first appearance was a shocker, and finally laid to rest the summer-long question of what was in the hatch. Cusick, who had only infrequently worked in the U.S., was thrilled that the part would allow him to use his real Scottish accent.

He found shooting *Lost* to be refreshing. "It was quite good not knowing anything when I arrived in Hawaii," he said. "I find, with the whole L.A. thing, that ignorance is pretty cool. It means that you're not fazed by people."

However, it didn't take long for Cusick to gain some recognition. During the 2006 Emmy nomination upset, in which *Lost* was shut out of any major awards, Cusick got a much-deserved nod for his guest appearance as Desmond. "I don't think anyone could have predicted just how big the program would be," he said. "I was in the States when my episodes were on there and people would stare in the supermarket. It was kind of weird. The occasional person would come up and say, 'Are you Desmond from *Lost*?' But there are so many famous people in L.A. that nobody bothers that much."

Our Mutual Friend by Charles Dickens (1865)

In an interview in 2005, author John Irving talked about his love of Charles Dickens, and deemed him the most important influence on his own writing. He said, "I have read his books many times, and have even purposely not read one of them. I am saving it for a severe illness or a near-death experience. Something I will read when I have to despair of doing anything else. I have not read *Our Mutual Friend*. That's the one I have saved." Just like a certain character on *Lost*. Someone should probably warn both of these guys about the book: The second half of this 800-page behemoth is a fascinating social commentary on the harsh conditions of London's Industrial Age. But if someone decided to read this book during a severe illness, the first 200 pages will probably kill them from sheer boredom before they can get to the good stuff.

Our Mutual Friend offers several similarities to *Lost*, but Dickens' characters work toward a different purpose than those on the show. In the book, we meet a series of characters who seem to have no connection to one another but who end up being linked in various ways the reader doesn't immediately anticipate. Three characters perpetuate a "long con," as *Lost's* Sawyer would put it, that isn't revealed until the closing pages of the book. Most of the characters are impelled to do things through greed. And love — as with Desmond and Penny — is the force that drives most of their actions.

In the main plotline, John Harmon Sr., who has worked in the "dust" business his whole life (a dustman collects up the city garbage and then sifts through it for items that can be resold) has somehow amassed a fortune of $100,000 before he dies. His son, who had run away from home years earlier, is in line to become the heir to most of his father's fortune — with the exception of one of the "Mounds" (of garbage) and a small house at the foot of it, which is left to Mr. Boffin, a dustman and a loyal foreman to Harmon. But the old man's will stipulates that the only way John Harmon Jr., can come into the money is to marry one Bella Wilfer, and if he doesn't, all of the money will instead go to Boffin. The younger Harmon hears about his father's death and mentions it to a colleague, and the colleague pretends to befriend Harmon, and then tries to kill him to pass himself off as Harmon and take the money. Harmon gets the better of him, and the other man dies instead. However, because Harmon doesn't know Bella Wilfer and isn't sure he wants to be married to someone he's never met, he decides to let people think the dead man is him, and the money all goes to Boffin.

The book opens with Lizzie Hexam and her father, Gaffer, who is a waterman (while a dustman dredges through the earth for treasure, a waterman searches the waters). They are poor and live a difficult life, and they are the ones who find the body of "John Harmon." The news travels to a posh dinner party at the Veneerings, a nouveau riche couple who are hosting a dinner party for their "bran-new friends," among whom are Mortimer Lightwood and Eugene Wrayburn, two lawyers who receive word of Gaffer's find. Thus Dickens establishes the worlds of the stupidly rich and the abjectly poor, as he does in most of his novels, and shows how these worlds remain separate but can collide through unfortunate events such as the death of a man. Lizzie is established immediately as a good woman who has raised her brother Charley to move up in the world, giving him his earliest lessons and saving her pennies for his education, while Charley is an ungrateful brat who takes the money she offers to him and goes off to become a "better" person, thinking himself far above his sister. Gaffer is a good man who is suspected of the murder of Harmon, and ultimately he dies in an accident on his boat while trolling the river. Another waterman, Rogue

Riderhood, is set up as the obvious "bad guy," the one who tries to pin the murder on Gaffer and is likely a murderer himself.

Meanwhile, the Boffins have come into a considerable amount of money, and they are a pair of seemingly naïve and sweet people who are deserving of the riches but are obviously lost as to what to do with it. Mr. Boffin hires Silas Wegg, a rascal who runs a street stall where he sells ballads for pennies, to come to his house in the evenings and read to him (Mr. Boffin, like most of the poor at the time, is illiterate). Wegg sees the vulnerability in Boffin and charges him far more money than he's worth.

Mr. Boffin quickly realizes he is unable to keep track of the money he has, and Mr. John Rokesmith appears to offer his services as Boffin's secretary. He had been staying at the Wilfers' house, a respectable family with a shrew of a mother, a "cherub" of a father, an argumentative younger daughter, and a beautiful but haughty older girl (Bella, the one who had been betrothed to John Harmon). Boffin hires Rokesmith, and the Boffins also take in Bella Wilfer as their charge, becoming her guardians and lavishing her with gifts and clothes and a rich lifestyle. Bella becomes a little too comfortable in her lifestyle, however, and starts to look for a husband who is rich, confessing to her father that she has become accustomed to a certain lifestyle, and no longer wants to marry for love, but solely for money. We discover that Rokesmith is, in fact, John Harmon, and he's living in disguise to find out if his betrothed is really as mercenary as she suggests she is and to see how happy his beloved Boffins are. He doesn't want to reveal himself because to do so would strip the Boffins of their wealth, and he believes they deserve all of it. When he asks for Bella's hand in marriage, she rebuffs him, angry that someone of so little money would dare to ask her, though it's clear she has feelings for him.

The wealth of the Boffins soon becomes a curse, and Boffin becomes increasingly erratic and cruel, and demands that Wegg read him books only about misers who squirrel away their savings and become penny-pinchers. He becomes openly hostile and pushy with Rokesmith, much to Bella's despair, and Mrs. Boffin seems to be suffering daily at the sudden change in her husband, wringing her hands and pleading with Rokesmith and Bella to realize that he really is a good man. Bella turns to her father, complaining that there has been a distinct change in Mr. Boffin, and she's very upset to see how money has corrupted him, and is beginning to change her mind about how she wants to live. If money can destroy a man as kind as Boffin, what might it do to her?

Mr. Boffin finds out through a couple of con artists (the Lammles) that Rokesmith has asked Bella to marry him, prompting Boffin to call Rokesmith into his office and fire him in a heartless way. Bella, devastated to see such a change in Boffin, swallows her pride, gives up her riches, and tells the Boffins she can no longer stay in a place where they treat people in such a way. She leaves the house to return to her own, runs into Rokesmith along the way, and he, finally knowing that she's a good person, again asks her to marry him, and she accepts.

In a secondary plot, Lizzie Hexam, daughter of the waterman, gains the unwanted attentions of Eugene Wrayburn when her father dies. He often comes to comfort her. At the same time, her brother Charley has come under the tutelage of schoolmaster Bradley Headstone, who falls in love with Lizzie the instant he sees her. She's not interested in either one of these men. Eugene is a sarcastic wit — he knows just which of Headstone's buttons to push — and he mocks Headstone for his affections. Lizzie goes to live with Jenny Wren, arguably the most fascinating character in the book, a small, physically handicapped girl who is a doll's dressmaker. She lives with her alcoholic father, whom she refers to as her "naughty child," and treats him as if she were his parent, and not vice versa. When Headstone makes his affections clear to Lizzie and she rejects him, Charley confronts her and tells her what an ungrateful sister she is for not marrying someone her brother has chosen for her. Headstone, in a violent rage, utters a threat, saying he hopes he won't have to kill "him," and Lizzie fears that someone's life is in danger if she sticks around. She flees London to a paper mill in the countryside where she can work in peace, away from the men who pursue her. Headstone, in a jealous rage, begins following Wrayburn everywhere, but Wrayburn is onto him instantly and has some fun with it, leading him into strange places, looping around, and bumping right into him just to drive him mad.

Jenny Wren keeps in touch with Lizzie, and when Wrayburn offers Jenny's father 60 "threepenny'orths" of rum in exchange for Lizzie's whereabouts, he gets the information. Wrayburn follows the directions . . . and Headstone follows *him*. Wrayburn arrives at the mill, confronts Lizzie, who tells him she's not interested in him at all. She tells him to go away, and he leaves her, wondering what he should do. On his way back to his boat, he's attacked by Headstone, who beats him bloody with a board and throws the body into the river. Lizzie hears the cries, leaps into a boat as she'd seen her father do many times, and rows out onto the river, retrieving the body and getting Wrayburn to a doctor. On his deathbed, he asks for Lizzie's hand in marriage. She accepts and sends word to Bella and

Rokesmith through Mortimer Lightwood, but only Bella comes (Lightwood knows Rokesmith through his other identity, and Rokesmith doesn't want Lightwood to see him). They marry, but Wrayburn doesn't die the way everyone thought he would. When Headstone hears what has happened, he goes half mad with fury. After he had beaten Wrayburn, he had changed his clothes at the waters' edge, but Rogue Riderhood watched him from the bushes and went fishing in the water when Headstone left, found the clothes, and kept them to use as blackmail against him. He presents his findings to Headstone a few months later and attempts to use it to get money out of Headstone, but Headstone instead walks him to a bridge, and, deciding Riderhood doesn't deserve to live and he has nothing to live for himself, begins wrestling with him and pulls him off the bridge along with him, to their deaths.

Speaking of blackmail, Wegg has discovered a box that Boffin has buried in one of the mounds in the middle of the night, containing a *second* will that John Harmon Sr. had drawn up after the first one, changing it to read that if Harmon the Younger doesn't marry Wilfer, then one Mound will go to Boffin and the rest of the money will go to the Crown. Wegg shows his discovery to his scoundrel-in-arms, Mr. Venus, and the two of them try to figure out how to best go after Boffin. Venus keeps the document on his premises, and behind Wegg's back he reveals the finding to Boffin, and it appears the two men will try to out-blackmail each other. Wegg's main obsession becomes a bottle that he sees Boffin dig up one night and take home, and he demands to know what was in it, and he finally confronts Wegg and demands his money in exchange for Wegg's silence.

But soon, all is revealed. Rokesmith and Bella run into Lightwood in the street, and Lightwood takes Rokesmith to be Julius Handford (yet another identity that Rokesmith has assumed, which is that of the suspected murderer of John Harmon). Bella discovers, to her horror, that Lightwood believes her husband to be a murderer, but she stands by Rokesmith, and says she will continue to do so no matter what. Finally satisfied that Bella will always be true to him, Rokesmith arrives home one afternoon to say they are moving. They pack up their belongings to go to . . . the Boffins. Bella is baffled as they walk into the house, and mutters that she doesn't want to see these people ever again, but as Rokesmith escorts her up the stairs to the dream nursery he has put together for their baby, she finds a jolly Mr. and Mrs. Boffin sitting in the room, with Mrs. Boffin practically bursting at the seams to tell Bella the real story. It turns out, Mrs. Boffin recognized John Harmon early on, and revealed his true identity to her husband.

Harmon asked them to keep his identity a secret, and told them he was in love with Bella, but worried that she was a woman only interested in money. Boffin had agreed to play the part of the miserly old coot to show her the dangers of what too much money could do to a person. Harmon watched Bella's reaction and waited to see if she would be faithful to him no matter what, and she was, so now he is finally giving her the riches she deserves. Wegg and Venus are called to the house where it is revealed that Venus was actually honest with Boffin and told him of Wegg's intentions. We discover the bottle that Boffin had dug up was in fact the most recent will of Harmon Sr., in which he renounced his children completely and didn't leave a penny to them. Boffin had been hiding it because, despite Harmon's children being dead, he didn't want their names to be disgraced. Harmon threatens Wegg and Sloppy, the Boffins' adopted son, physically throws him into a cab. Wegg is presumably never heard from again. The reader knows that the Boffins will always be comfortable (and that they're both quite pleased to be rid of the bothersome money). The Harmons live happily ever after, as do the Wrayburns, the Veneerings, and even Jenny Wren seems to take a shine to Sloppy (who returns the affection) by the end of the book. The good are rewarded, the bad are punished. Ah, the neatness of Victorian literature.

While happy endings are not in the cards for most of the characters on *Lost*, the book's underlying message of what happens to people who are greedy, vengeful, and cruel is also explored on the television show. Sawyer's vengeance has destroyed him morally, and he now cons people for money. The "long con" that the Boffins and Rokesmith play on Bella (which seems over-the-top; Boffin is a bit of a buffoon at the beginning of the book, and I doubt he could have ever pulled off something as elaborate as this scheme) is done for love, which is why it ends well. Just as the Others have divided the island's inhabitants into the good people and the bad people, so too does Dickens make his characters either very bad or very good, with the exception of Eugene Wrayburn, who is an unlikable character who gets his happily-ever-after by the end of the novel. Jenny Wren's difficult relationship with her father echoes Jack's relationship with Christian, in that the son had to become the parent when the parent was acting like a child.

In Desmond's case, the book's power comes from the examination of how the rich become ugly through their riches. Widmore has become a miserly old man who controls what his daughter does, and Penny goes out of her way to thwart the future that Widmore has planned for her. Desmond's situation is the opposite of Harmon's — Harmon is betrothed to a woman whom he doesn't immediately want to marry, and his father tries to force him to marry her. Desmond, on the other hand, is in love with a woman whom he has been forced to avoid, though she uses her father's money to track him down, showing that wealth can be used for good. Widmore is known as a philanthropist while actually being a misanthropist, just as the wealthy socialites in Dickens' novel present themselves one way to the public, but in fact are a bunch of mindless gossips at their dinner gatherings. At the end of the book — and the end of "Live Together, Die Alone" — love prevails. The question is, will the *Lost* writers be as generous with their happy endings as Dickens was?

"The Greatest Finale I Have Ever Heard": The End of Season 2

It would appear 2006 could be a pivotal year for *Lost*. It started out strongly, with the cast winning the Golden Globe in January for Best Television Series, and Naveen Andrews and Matthew Fox were nominated for their work on the program. "It's been a crazy evening, and I wish the whole cast were with us, but a lot of them are here," said executive producer Bryan Burke, who attended the Golden Globes with Fox, Andrews, and Evangeline Lilly. "All of us are amazingly surprised that we won. We're such huge fans of the nominated shows — and if I were a betting man, I thought *Grey's Anatomy* was going to win."

With new episodes of *Lost* showing infrequently as the winter turned to spring, fans began to grumble about how a show that's as complex as this one was suffering from too many breaks, unlike the successful *24*, which recognized the importance of no repeats in a serialized drama, and ran it without any. Before the end of season 2, the producers of *Lost* announced that season 3 would run in two blocks of unrepeated episodes, with the first seven episodes airing in October and November, and the remaining 16 airing from late January until early May.

As the show's mysteries began to deepen (which, coupled with the repeats, caused a drop-off in viewership), many began speaking about how the season would conclude. Though cocreator J.J. Abrams had only been peripherally involved with the second season of *Lost*, he told many that he was thrilled with how the season ended. "The ending of this year in *Lost* blows the ending of last season out of the water. It's an incredible finale," he told the press.

The cast of *Lost* picks up a SAG award for best dramatic ensemble on January 29, 2006.
(SUE SCHNEIDER/MOONGLOW PHOTOS)

He acknowledged that cocreator Damon Lindelof and the program's writers had upped the ante, but that they were also starting to tie up some of the many loose ends left by the show's expansive plot. "You'll see what happens, but I can tell you that a lot of it has been there and been building from the beginning of this season," Abrams added. "It's not out of the blue, but what happens at the very end of this year, for me, it's the greatest finale I have ever heard." Abrams announced in April that he would be helming the next *Star Trek* movie, with Lindelof helping out.

As the season continued toward a conclusion, ABC's marketing department began to push beyond the ordinary commercials to promote the show. One concept they developed was *The Lost Experience*, a marketing promotion that utilized some of the elements of the show and conceptualized them as if they were real. Included among the promotional gimmicks was a Hanso Foundation Web site (www.thehansofoundation.org) and a toll-free number that could be called (877-HANSORG) for the fictitious organization "devoted to the advancement of the human race," that said it had a 105-year-old orangutan as part of its life-extension program.

Though no one was saying for certain, the notion of external Web sites that referred back to elements of the show was something J.J. Abrams had toyed with since creating a site for a character on *Felicity*. *Lost*'s marketing team said the response to the site and toll-free number had been remarkable, adding that they planned to continue with the ruse into season 3. "What the Hanso Foundation did was just the beginning of this thing," noted Mike Benson, ABC marketing chief, who said the massive response shut down call centers in the UK and USA.

One of the other creative elements dreamed up to promote *Lost* and add interest to the convoluted plot was the creation of a book, *Bad Twin*, supposedly written by Gary Troup (see page 302). To join the two endeavors, the Hanso Foundation took out newspaper ads denouncing *Bad Twin*, and Hugh McIntyre, a character in *The Lost Experience*, appeared on Jimmy Kimmel to say the marketing department on *Lost* was giving his very real and honorable foundation a bad name. It was a brilliant marketing campaign. What was so groundbreaking about it was that many of the clues were in television spots that aired during *Lost*. All TiVO and PVR users were suddenly forced to sit through the commercials to find the clues, rather than skipping them outright. Advertisers were thrilled, and it was a great ploy to bring in more advertising dollars.

With a third season still months away, the creators of *Lost* had managed, without new shows, to do something few in television have managed: they kept up the buzz for a program that wasn't showing new episodes (the *Lost Experience* advertisements aired during summer repeats) and expanded the show's audience during television's dead months, no doubt setting up a new legion of fans to tune in come season 3.

It's a Small World After All

In "Exodus, Part 1," Sawyer says to Jack, "Small world, huh?" and he doesn't know how right he is. The following is a list of the links between the castaways before they boarded the flight, and as you can see, the chance meetings form a chain linking everyone:

- Kate's friend Beth is a fan of Drive Shaft (Pilot, Part 1)
- Hurley knew Drive Shaft's music, but didn't like them (Everybody Hates Hugo) whereas Locke was a fan of the music (House of the Rising Sun)
- Charlie yells at Hurley from the elevator in the hotel (Exodus, Part 2)
- The woman that Sawyer is with in the hotel room (Outlaw) is the lotto girl who calls the numbers when Hurley is watching (Numbers)
- After winning the lottery, Hurley becomes the owner of Locke's box company in Tustin (Numbers), and Hurley's former boss Randy at Mr. Cluck's (Everybody Hates Hugo) eventually becomes Locke's boss (Walkabout)
- Locke and Rose crossed paths at the airport (S.O.S.)
- Locke's mother stayed at the Santa Rosa mental hospital (Deus Ex Machina), which is also where Hurley and Libby were staying (Dave)
- Libby gave Desmond the boat that brought him to the island (Live Together, Die Alone)
- Desmond ran into Jack in a stadium (Man of Science, Man of Faith; Live Together, Die Alone) before seeing him again on the island
- When Jack is in the airport yelling at the ticket agent he is standing in front of Jin, Sun, and Ana Lucia, whom he later talks to in the hotel bar (Exodus, Part 1)

- Ana Lucia accompanies Christian Shephard to Australia (Two for the Road), where he enters a bar and meets up with Sawyer (Outlaw)
- Sawyer is dragged through into a police station where Boone is reporting that someone is abusing Shannon (Hearts and Minds)
- Shannon's father is killed in the car accident that paralyzed Jack's wife Sarah (Man of Science, Man of Faith; Abandoned)
- Shannon gets Sayid into trouble at the airport (Exodus, Part 1)
- Sayid is detained by Kate's father in Iraq in 1991 (One of Them), and we see Sayid on a television behind Kate when she goes to see her father years later (What Kate Did)
- Kate slams into the same car (Born to Run) that previously hit Locke (Deus Ex Machina) and Michael (Special)
- Locke did a home inspection for Sayid's former girlfriend Nadia (Orientation)
- Sayid was turned into a torturer of his own people by Inman (One of Them), who later shares the hatch with Desmond (Live Together, Die Alone), and who worked alongside Kate's father
- Kate's mom is the waitress at the diner where Sawyer meets up with Gordie (The Long Con)
- Michael (Adrift) and Claire (Raised by Another) were in the same law office, giving up their children
- Eko investigated a miracle claim of a girl (?) whose father is the psychic who put Claire on the plane (Raised by Another)
- Libby walked up to Eko in the airport and asked if everything was okay with him

Lost . . . on the Web

Over the past 10 years, water cooler talk the morning after the broadcast of a favorite show has become online discussion moments after the broadcast has ended. Arguably, the Internet has never been more important to a single television show than it is to *Lost*. In the summer of 2006, to sate fans' need for new episodes, the writers on *Lost* created an online game called *The Lost Experience*, directing fans through a maze of sites inspired by the show's mention of The Hanso Foundation. But *Lost* had an important online presence long before the game began. Forums allow fans to decipher clues in that game and on the show itself, online searchable resources enable fans to look up obscure references and discuss them with other fans, and fan-run sites help connect the dots and draw links between the seemingly disparate events on the show. You'll find transcripts, databases, lists, podcasts, and blogs. There are literally thousands of sites on the Net, and I'm only going to list a small handful, but if you begin with the basics and make your way through these ones, you'll inevitably find an entirely new dimension to *Lost* in cyberspace.

Official sites:

abc.go.com/primetime/lost/
www.oceanic-air.com/

The Basics:

www.tv.com
www.imdb.com
www.wikipedia.org

The Rest:

www.docarzt.com
Run by Jon "DocArzt" Lachonis, this excellent site brings together various bloggers in the online *Lost* community who collectively post updates, news, reviews, and analyses of that week's episode. A fantastic one-stop site for all *Lost* fans.

www.thefuselage.com
This is a forum that is supported by the cast and crew, and you can register to chat with the stars and crew members of the show. Expect quick responses from people like Jorge Garcia, and the sound of crickets if you try to contact Josh Holloway.

www.4815162342.com
A great forum that explores the numbers and a million other conspiracy theories on *Lost*.

www.lost.cubit.net
One of the best *Lost* resources around, this site usually puts up clues spotted in the new episodes first thing the following morning. Screen captures point out Easter eggs and other revelations, and there are several opportunities to comment and discuss the episode.

www.lost-tv.com
A great site that posts transcripts of the episodes usually within a week of its broadcast, as well as new articles and information about merchandise and the show itself.

www.lost-media.com
If you're looking for screen captures of the episodes or the latest tidbit of news on the show or the stars, look no further. This site has it all.

www.lostpedia.com

Because Wikipedia was becoming an essential resource for all *Lost* fans, a group of fans decided to create this offshoot that looks exactly the same as its much-larger encyclopedic counterpart, but is devoted solely to all things *Lost*. Fans can post information in the same way they can on Wikipedia, and it's built up a massive collection of speculative theories and information.

www.losthatch.com

A searchable database of transcripts, quotations, and recurring motifs and themes. The best site I found for listing the music in the episodes.

www.televisionwithoutpity.com

Always a fun site no matter what the show. You can choose to read recaps of the *Lost* episodes, or enter the forum area to discuss it with other fans. Some of the funniest forum discussions involve the people who hate the show.

www.hawaiiup.com/lost

The Transmission is a great *Lost* fan site featuring podcasts of the first two seasons, audio and video clips, links, an interactive map of the *Lost* locations, and much more.

www.islostarepeat.com

In the midst of the frustration fans felt about the chaotic broadcast schedule of season 2, one brilliant fan put up this site. Don't bother checking *TV Guide* or looking through your onscreen TiVO guide, simply type in this URL and a one-word answer will let you know.

jopinionated.blogspot.com

Jo Garfein, a.k.a. JOpinionated, is one of my favorite *Lost* bloggers. Every week she posts brilliant and funny insights into the episodes, while providing the latest news about the show.

darkufo.blogspot.com

Another fantastic *Lost* blog, DarkUFO's site is updated constantly with some of the best stuff out there. Spoilers are safely hidden away in one corner of the site, where spoiler-hounds can find them, but spoilerphobes won't see them.

www.lostblog.net

One of many *Lost* blogs online, this is one of the best.

lost.about.com

Hosted by About.com, this site has up-to-date *Lost* news, quizzes, reviews, games, and much more, written in a blog format.

Get Lost:

● ●

A Guide to Oahu and the *Lost* Filming Locations

Through the characters' flashbacks on *Lost*, we've visited South Korea, Sydney, Melbourne, New York City, Los Angeles, Tennessee, New Mexico, Baghdad, Manchester, Nigeria, Michigan, and Edinburgh. But in reality, the actors have never actually left Hawaii; all of these foreign locales have been played by various locations on Oahu. Ryan Ozawa, a resident of Oahu, runs a Web site called The Transmission (www.hawaiiup.com/lost/). An avid fan of the show, Ozawa has traveled around his home island taking photographs of the *Lost* filming locations, and has generously offered them for use in this book. John Fischer is the Hawaii travel guide for About.com (gohawaii.about.com) and he, too, offered up some of his photos and helped me map out an island that I have, sadly, never actually been to. If you have a chance to go to Hawaii and want to see where Sawyer conned the guys at the gas station with the jewelry, or Jin and Sun got engaged, or Kate held up the bank, just follow the map and the instructions below. Most of the locations are in Honolulu, unless otherwise indicated. Some of these places are private property, so please respect the privacy of the people who own (or live in) the buildings, and take your photos from afar. All photos are by Ryan Ozawa unless otherwise indicated.

1 The crash site of Oceanic Flight 815, and the setting for most of season 1, is the Mokuleia Beach on Oahu's north shore. Driving west on the Farrington Highway, the beach is on your right. (Photo by John Fischer)

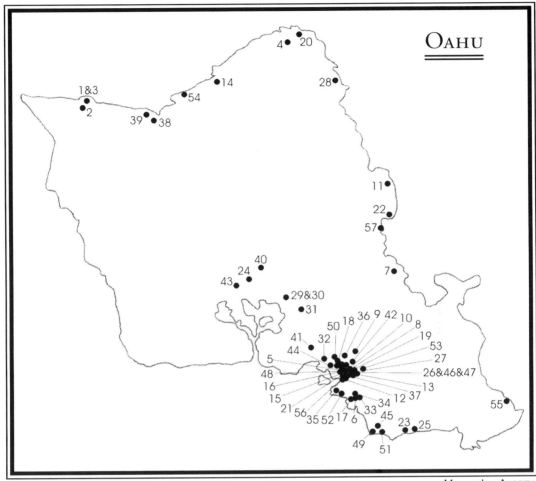

OAHU

MAP BY IAN ANDREW

2 Most of what's left of the fuselage of the Oceanic Flight 815 widebody jet is being stored on a back lot of Dillingham Airfield, a commuter airstrip in Mokuleia near the northeastern point of Oahu (68-760 Farrington Highway). The airfield also played a Nigerian airport for a Mr. Eko flashback in "The 23rd Psalm." (See also page 10.)

3 The first night on the island, the survivors encounter the monster, and the camera is facing the Valley Inland of Mokuleia Beach as we see the trees begin to disappear. (Photo by John Fischer)

4 As Charlie, Kate, and Jack flee the monster that has just eaten the pilot in "Pilot, Part 1," they run through the West/Green Trail, Turtle Bay Resort. Along this trail you'll find the banyan tree where Jack and Kate find Charlie strung up by Ethan ("All the Best Cowboys Have Daddy Issues") and where Walt tries to find refuge from a polar bear ("Special"). (Photo by John Fischer)

5 The "Walkabout" travel agency where Locke is forbidden to go on the tour ("Walkabout") is in downtown Honolulu (1 N. King Street), now home to McClain's Auctions. (See also page 29.)

6 The Sydney international airport has been seen several times throughout the series, and is actually the Hawaii Convention Center, which does bear a striking resemblance to an airport (1801 Kalakaua Ave). (See also page 34.)

7 The temple where Jin and Sun are engaged is the Byodo-In Temple (47-200 Kahekili Hwy), located in the Valley of the Temples off the Kahekili Highway (Highway 83) in Kaneohe. (Photo by John Fischer)

8 The church where Charlie goes for confession and talks with his brother in "The Moth," is Parke Chapel, next door to St. Andrew's Cathedral on the edge of downtown Honolulu (229 Queen Emma Square). (See also page 47.)

9 The Victorian-style home in Sydney where Charlie's brother Liam lives is part of the historic Ripley Homestead, located on Gretchen Lane in Nuuanu.

10 The restaurant where Sawyer pulled Jessica's husband into his con game in "Confidence Man" is the excellent Indigo restaurant (1121 Nuuanu Ave.), known for its creative Eurasian dishes as well as its after-dark, after-theater crowd.

11 Hurley's golf course ("Solitary") is located in the Kaaawa Valley. (Photo by John Fischer)

12 The house used as the dwelling of the psychic that Claire visits in "Raised by Another" and that Mr. Eko meets in "?" is the historic Manoa Valley Inn near the University of Hawaii (1001 Vancouver Dr.).

13 The law office where Claire meets Aaron's would-be adoptive parents in "Raised By Another" and where Michael fights for custody of Walt in "Adrift" is a conference room at the Hawaii State Supreme Court (Aliiolani Hale, 417 S. King St.).

14 The waterfall where Sawyer and Kate take a dip and find the Halliburton in "Whatever the Case May Be" is part of the Waimea Valley Audubon Center (formerly known as Waimea Falls Park) in Haleiwa (59-864 Kamehameha Highway).

15 The bank that Kate robs in "Whatever the Case May Be" is the Chinatown Branch of First Hawaiian Bank, that boasts old-fashioned teller stations (2 N. King St.). (See also page 76.)

16 The police station where we saw Boone and Sawyer in "Hearts and Minds" was a vacant retail space downtown at the time of filming (50 N. King Street), and is now Do's Formals.

17 The yacht harbor where Boone pays off Shannon's boyfriend to leave her alone in "Hearts and Minds" is the Ala Wai Small Boat Harbor.

18 The SoulLenz Gallery, located upstairs near the corner of King and River streets (186 N. King St.) was used as Michael's apartment in "Special."

19 The busy intersection of Bishop Street and Hotel Street in downtown Honolulu was dressed as New York City and used in "Special" when Michael steps off the curb after an angry phone call and is hit by a car.

20 The shrimp truck where Sawyer meets Frank Duckett in "Outlaws" is the famous Kahuku Shrimp truck located on the north shore of Oahu, east of the Turtle Bay Resort.

21 The unwelcoming office of Sun's father in "...In Translation" was the mezzanine gallery space inside First Hawaiian Center, the tallest building in the state (999 Bishop St.).

22 The picturesque shore in "...In Translation" that was meant to be Namhae, Jin's father's fishing village, is the historic Molii Fishpond, situated within Kualoa Regional Park.

23 The large house that Hurley bought for his mother ("Numbers") is located on Hunakai Street between Onaha and Koloa streets in Kahala (808 Hunakai St.) (See page 115 for photo.)

24 The store where Locke works and where he confronts his mother in the parking lot in "Deus Ex Machina" is the Costco Wholesale warehouse in Waipio (94-1231 Ka Uka Blvd.).

25 The hotel and beachfront gazebo where Jack and Sarah are married in "Do No Harm" is the Kahala Hotel and Resort (5000 Kahala Ave.)

26 The Laniakea restaurant at the YWCA in downtown Honolulu (1040 Richards Street) served as the interior of Sayid's mosque in "The Greater Good." The YWCA is also the setting for Hurley's mental institution in "Numbers" and "Dave." The restaurant is not open on weekends.

27 The park where Sayid and Essam play a game of soccer in "The Greater Good" was filmed on the northwest lawn of the Hawaii State Capitol Building (415 S. Beretania St.).

28 The motel where Kate dyes her hair at the beginning of "Born to Run" is the Laie Inn, situated next door to the Polynesian Cultural Center in Laie (55109 Laniloa St.) A vast cornfield was digitally inserted in the background of the episode.

29 The hospital parking lot that Kate flees in "Born To Run" is the parking structure at Pearlridge Center. The gate she crashes was set up at the entrance nearest Inspiration Interiors (98-1005 Moanalua Road).

30 The canal in "Born to Run" where Kate escapes the scene of Tom's death on foot runs past the shopping center, behind Sears and California Pizza Kitchen.

31 The stadium where Jack meets Desmond ("Man of Science, Man of Faith") and Pen meets Desmond ("Live Together, Die Alone") is Aloha Stadium in Honolulu (99-500 Salt Lake Blvd.).

32 Mr. Cluck's Chicken Shack, where Hurley, Johnny, and Randy work in "Everybody Hates Hugo," is the Popeye's Chicken in Iwilei (1515 Dillingham Blvd.). (See page 190 for photo.)

33 The spot where Jin and Sun first meet in "...And Found" and the spot where Sun is confronted by their doctor in "The Whole Truth" are directly opposite each other along the Ala Wai Canal near the Kalakaua Ave. bridge, on the west end of Waikiki.

34 The "Seoul Gateway Hotel" where Jin briefly worked in "...And Found" is the Royal Garden at Waikiki Hotel (440 Olohana St.).

35 The police headquarters building where Ana Lucia and her partner arrive after responding to a domestic dispute in "Collision" is the old Gold Bond Building (677 Ala Moana Blvd.).

36 The diner where Kate stops to see her mom after "taking care" of her in "What Kate Did" is the famous Liliha Bakery (515 N. Kuakini St.).

37 The bus station where Kate is captured by the marshal in "What Kate Did" is actually the historic downtown Honolulu post office (335 Merchant St.).

38 Waialua town has been used to portray Mr. Eko's Nigerian village ("The 23rd Psalm"), the home of Rose and Bernard's psychic Isaac ("S.O.S."), and the spot where Sawyer and Cassidy plan the jewellery con ("The Long Con"). The surrounding roads have also been used in several episodes, including Kate's truck crash ("Tabula Rasa").

39 The gas station where Sawyer and Cassidy pull off their jewelry con in "The Long Con" was Eric's Expert Service in Waialua (67-016 Farrington Hwy.). The station's actual name and sign were used in the episode.

40 The suburban home where Sawyer and Cassidy shack up ("The Long Con," Ep. 2x13) is a model home in Mililani Mauka., specifically, developer Castle & Cooke's "American Classics" showcase Residence Two (Lehiwa Dr.).

41 The diner where Sawyer met with Gordy in "The Long Con," is Bob's Big Boy in Mapunapuna (2828 Paa St.).

42 The cemetery where Anthony Cooper is "buried" in "Lockdown" is Oahu Cemetery (2162 Nuuanu Ave.)

43 The suburban home that Locke inspects for Nadia in "Lockdown" is in Waikele (94-1003 Alelo St.).

44 The bar where Locke meets Anthony Cooper to discuss the safe deposit box in "Lockdown" is Murphy's Bar & Grill (2 Merchant St.).

45 The Flightline motel where Locke meets Anthony Cooper and where Helen confronts them in "Lockdown" is the Hale Hana apartment complex off Kapahulu Avenue near Waikiki (3410 Leahi Ave.).

46 The mental institution where Hurley meets Lenny and imagines Dave is the downtown YWCA (1040 Richards Street).

47 The exterior of the YWCA is seen briefly at the end of "Dave" when Dave escapes.

48 The snowy street where Bernard first meets Rose in "S.O.S" is Marin Lane in downtown Honolulu. The crew trucked in the snow. (See page 290 for photo.)

49 The restaurant overlooking "Niagara Falls" where Bernard proposed to Rose in "S.O.S." is Michele's at the Colony Surf Hotel (2885 Kalakaua Ave.).

50 The rooftop LAPD parking lot in "Two for the Road" is at the Dole Cannery complex (753B Iwilei Rd.).

51 The modest Sydney home where Christian Shephard demands to see his daughter in "Two for the Road," is located at 3022 Makini St., near Waikiki. The film was flipped to make it look like Ana Lucia was driving an Australian car with the steering wheel on the right side, so the door appears to be on the opposite side of the house.

52 The waterfront bar where Ana Lucia and Dr. Shepherd part company in Sydney in "Two for the Road" is Fisherman's Wharf, situated at the end of Ward. Ave. (1009 Ala Moana Blvd.).

53 The Sydney church where Mr. Eko conducts confession in "?" is the Cathedral Church of St. Andrew (229 Queen Emma Square), on the edge of downtown Honolulu.

54 The graves for Libby and Ana Lucia are next to "Tent City," which was the season 2 beach location on the show. The beach is Papailoa, also known as Police Beach, past Haleiwa on the North Shore of Oahu. The beach is beautiful but remote (no direct access) and the shoreline is rocky. While you can see the tents from the beach, they are technically located on private property, so tread carefully.

55 The Others camp that Michael is taken to in "Three Minutes" is located on Makapuu Point, a very popular hiking spot. In summer 2006, a new parking lot and improved rail access were put in by the state. The crew of *Lost* originally intended to rebuild the Others camp for season 3 (it was taken apart at the end of season 2) but if there is increased foot traffic in the area, that might have to change.

56 Dina's coffee shop, where Desmond runs into Libby, is actually the Honolulu Cafe (741 Bishop St.).

57 The long pier where The Others hold Jack, Kate, and Sawyer but release Michael and Walt is Waikane Pier near Kualoa. The pier has been a favorite shooting location for several movies and television shows. (See page 331 for photo.)

Sources

"5 questions for: Harold Perrineau." *Ebony*. April 2006.

"10 Things You Now Know About Terry O'Quinn." *X-pose*. 2004.

"About Dharma." Aboutdharma.org. Online. Accessed June 19, 2006.

Adams, Richard. *Watership Down*. London: Penguin, 1972.

"A *Lost* Hunk's Ordeal." ETonline.com. Online. November 9, 2005.

Amatangelo, Amy. "Holloway finds recognition as bad guy on ABC hit *Lost*." *Boston Herald*. December 8, 2004.

"Apollo." *Encyclopedia Mythica*. www.pantheon.org. Online. Accessed May 2, 2006.

"Apollo (Son of Zeus)." The Zodiac Master. www.thezodiac.com Online. Accessed May 1, 2006.

Avary, Roger. "Ian Somerhalder." *Contents Magazine*. November 2002.

Baracaia, Alexa. "Found . . . *Lost* star's past." *Evening Standard*. August 12, 2005.

Barker, Lynn. "Maggie Grace: *Lost* in The Fog." TeenHollywood.com. Online. October 12, 2005.

Barker, Lynn. "Malcolm David Kelley — *Lost*'s Lost Boy." TeenHollywood.com. Online. September 14, 2005.

"Beach Boys: Naveen Andrews." TVGuide.com. Online. April 15, 2005.

Berni, Christine. "DDK interview." LOST-TV.com and DanielDaeKim.org. Online.

Bierce, Ambrose. "An Occurrence at Owl Creek Bridge." Online. eServer.org.

Bishop, Julie. E-mail interview with author. March 15, 2006.

Blackwelder, Rob. "From Prison Blues to High-Heeled Shoes." Contactmusic.com. Online. September 7, 2000.

Boeree, C. George, Dr. "B.F. Skinner." *Personality Theories*. Online. Accessed May 2, 2006.

Brown, Bob. "In an Ivy League of their own: Stadium provides ultimate workout." *Boston Globe*. November 14, 2004.

Cafferty, Leslie. "Maggie Grace: from a hot cult show to this season's clammy cult film." *Interview*. October 2005.

Chia, Elisa. "No pants, no problem for Matthew Fox." *Today*. August 18, 2005.

Choi, Moon Yun. "*Lost* Star Daniel Dae Kim." *Ain't It Cool News*. Online. March 25, 2006.

Chung, Philip W. "Daniel Dae Kim is Busy in Acting Career." *Korea Times*. January 31, 2000.

———. "A Korean American TV Invasion?" Asianweek.com. Online. October 28, 2005.

Conrad, Joseph. *Heart of Darkness*. New York: Penguin Modern Classics, 2000.

Craig, Olga. "The man who discovered *Lost* — and found himself out of a job." *London Telegraph*. August 14, 2005.

Crook, John. "Rodriguez Puts Films on Hold for *Lost*." Zap2it.com. Online. October 9, 2005.

"Cynthia Watros." Touchstone Television Press. Online.

Daniel Dae Kim. www.danieldaekim.org

DavidFury.net

"David Hume." *Stanford Encyclopedia of Philosophy*. Online. Accessed June 28, 2006.

Dawson, Angela. "Actress back in action with *S.W.A.T.*" Entertainment News Wire. August 7, 2003.

De Moraes, Lisa. "ABC's 'Six Degrees' Of Calculation." *Washington Post*. May 17, 2006.

———. "In the Church of J.J., a Congregation of *Lost* Souls." *Washington Post*. July 14, 2004.

"Deus Ex Machina." *Starlog*. January 2000.

"Dharmic Religions." Answers.com. Accessed June 19, 2006.

Dickens, Charles. *Our Mutual Friend*. London: Oxford World's Classics. 1998.

DiLullo, Tara. "Terry O'Quinn." *SFX*. February 2005.

"Dominic and Evangeline's Hush-Hush Love Life." People.com. Online. January 21, 2006.

"Dominic Monaghan Wants To Settle In Hawaii." *Toronto Fashion Monitor*. November 4, 2005.

"Dominic's Teenage Money-Making Schemes." Contactmusic.com. Online. November 1, 2004.

DuBois, Stephanie. "*Lost* and Found." Compuserve.com. Online. May 2005.

Duffy, Mike. "No Mystery about this hit." *Detroit Free Press*. July 2004.

"Early Lilly Ad Makes Airwaves." Contactmusic.com. Online. August 9, 2006.

Edwards, Gavin. "Little Girl *Lost*: Evangeline Lilly is the ultimate desert-island fantasy." *Rolling Stone*. September 22, 2005.

Emilie Online. www.emilie-online.net.

Eng, Dinah. "*Lost* world created by diverse writing staff." Gannett News Service. November 26, 2005.

Eun-jung, Han. "Kim Yun-jin to Play Major Role in ABC's New Series." *Korea Times*. June 22, 2004.

"Exclusive: Secrets Of *Lost* Star Matthew Fox." Mirror.co.uk. Online. August 15, 2005.

"Fascinating Fact 1368." Contactmusic.com. Online. April 12, 2006.

Fienberg, Daniel. "Akinnuoye-Agbaje Is *Lost* Mystery Man." Zap2it.com. Online. November 7, 2005.

———. "Burly Hurley of *Lost* Gets Cryptic." Zap2it.com. Online. January 4, 2005.

———. "'Get Rich' Baddie Finds Character in a 'Pure Place.'" Zap2it.com. Online. November 9, 2005.

Finn, Natalie. "*Lost* Star Finds Herself in Jail." E! Online. April 25, 2006.

Florence, Bill. "The Fourth Alien." *Starlog*. June 2001.

Fossell, Eric. "Actor Matthew Fox wraps filming in Huntington." *The Herald-Dispatch*. April 7, 2006.

Gard, Laura. "Sexy Naveen Andrews Swears Off His Bad Boy Image." *Nirvana Woman*. Spring/Summer, 2005.

Golding, William. *Lord of the Flies*. London: Penguin, 1954.

Good News Bible: Today's English Version. Toronto: Canadian Bible Society, 1976.

"Google Earth Hi-Jinks." *Quadlasers*. Online. Accessed May 28, 2006.

Gregory, Deborah. "Chit Chat & All That — Actor Harold Perrineau." *Essence*. November 2000.

"Hey, Mr. Deejay." *People*. June 8, 2005.

"Holloway Considered Playboy Lifestyle." Contactmusic.com. Online. April 13, 2006.

"Holloway Created *Lost* Heartthrob." Contactmusic.com. Online. September 26, 2005.

"Holloway feared he would be fired." Contactmusic.com. Online. February 8, 2006.

"Holloway Recalls Abrupt Introduction to Wife." Contactmusic.com. Online. December 1, 2005.

"Holloway Stole to Survive." Contactmusic.com. Online. February 8, 2006.

Hong, Caroline. "Daniel Dae Kim." *Yolk*. 2002.

Hughes, Mike. "Sweeps time winds up with TV's 2 hit shows facing off tonight." *Detroit News*. May 2005.

———. "Versatile actor gets used to *Lost*." IndyStar.com. Online. November 13, 2005.

"Ian Somerhalder." *Arena UK*. September 2003.

"Ian Somerhalder Interview." *Adorable Magazine*. October 2002.

"Ian Somerhalder Interview." *Cosmopolitan Magazine*. May 2005.

Internet Movie Database. Imdb.com. Online.

"Interview with Daniel Dae Kim." CNN.com. Online. Accessed April 14, 2006.

"Is *Lost* Too Scary?" *Variety*. July 14, 2004.

James, Henry. *The Turn of the Screw*. Electronic Text Center. Online.

"Jean-Jacques Rousseau." *The Internet Encyclopedia of Philosophy*. Online. Accessed May 26, 2006.

Jenkins, Elizabeth. "Runaway Bride." *InStyle Weddings*. Summer 2005.

Jensen, Jeff. "War of the Worlds." *Entertainment Weekly*. May 19, 2006.

"John Locke." *Internet Encyclopedia of Philosophy*. Online. Accessed April 3, 2006.

"John Locke." *Stanford Encyclopedia of Philosophy*. Online. Accessed March 29, 2006.

"Jorge Garcia: TV's most lovable castaway." Associated Press. November 15, 2005.

Josh Holloway Fan. www.josh-holloway.com

Juba, Scott. "Daniel Dae Kim." *The Trades*. Online. March 8, 2005.

—. "Harold Perrineau." *The Trades*. Online. March 14, 2005.

—. "Harold Perrineau: *Lost* Star." *The Trades*. Online. October 24, 2005.

—. "Jorge Garcia: By the Numbers." *The Trades*. Online. February 24, 2006.

Keck, William. "Actress Kim gets *Lost* in generous gifts, jewels." *USA Today*. January 15, 2006.

—. "De Ravin: *Lost* in Transformation." *USA Today*. April 2005.

—. "Fame's a breeze for Holloway." *USA Today*. November 29, 2005.

—. "She's Not *Lost* in a Fog." *USA Today*. October 19, 2005.

—. "She Shot Shannon, What's Her Next Target?" AOL News. November 19, 2005.

Keveney, Bill. "The many aliases of J.J. Abrams." *USA Today*. January 4, 2005.

Kim, Ju Yon. "Daniel Dae Kim." *KoreAm Journal*. May 2003.

—. "Man of Action." *Audrey Magazine*. Online. May/June 2003.

Knoll, Corina. "Daniel Dae Kim." *KoreAm Journal*. October 2004.

Knutzen, Eirik. "Somewhere in paradise." Copley News Service. November 6, 2005.

Kuhn, Sarah. "*Lost* has found actor Jorge Garcia." *Back Stage West*. May 1, 2005.

L'Engle, Madeleine. *A Wrinkle in Time*. New York: Random House, 1962.

Levin, Gary. "Serials Keep the Clock Ticking." *USA Today*. May 21, 2006.

"Lilly Failed to Spot Merry Monaghan." Contactmusic.com. Online. April 10, 2006.

"Lilly Hates Hawaiian Winters." Contactmusic.com. Online. April 5, 2006.

"Lilly Loathed Good Looks." Contactmusic.com. Online. April 13, 2006.

"Lilly loved being an extra." Contactmusic.com. Online. March 20, 2006.

"Lilly's Character Crisis." Contactmusic.com. Online. March 23, 2006.

"Lilly to quit acting in ten years." Contactmusic.com. Online. March 21, 2006.

Lorenzi, Rossella. "Michelangelo's David Marble Said Flawed." Discovery News. Online. September 12, 2005.

"*Lost* Actor Proud Of Show For Putting Asian Characters Front And Centre." *National Post*. September 20, 2005.

"*Lost* Actresses Arraigned in DUI Cases." December 30, 2005.

"*Lost*'s Andrews finds himself at home in L.A." Associated Press. April 7, 2006.

"*Lost* and Found." *Backstage*. Online. October 4, 2004.

"*Lost* Bad Boy Josh Holloway Finds Feature Film." *Extra TV*. February 11, 2006.

"*Lost* Cast Interviews." *IGN*. Online. September 6, 2005.

"*LOST* — Inside Scoop on Lethal New Beauty Ana Lucia." TVGuide.com. Online. November 27, 2005.

Lost Links. www.lostlinks.net

"*Lost* Role Changed For Fox." Sci-Fi Wire. Online. July 16, 2004.

"*Lost* Star Almost Ditched Acting." Contactmusic.com. Online. September 27, 2005.

"*Lost* star finds himself in Mexico." *Tonight*. Online. September 22, 2005.

"*Lost* star finds love, home in L.A." CNN.com. Online. April 10, 2006.

"*Lost* Star Named As TV's Top 'Hunk.'" Associated Press. January 26, 2006.

"*Lost* Star Wants Johansson's Career." Contactmusic.com. Online. April 12, 2006.

"*Lost*'s Naked Doc." Sky News. August 15, 2005.

"*Lost* star's real life airplane courage." Contactmusic.com. Online. April 5, 2006.

"*Lost*'s True Survivor." *Tonight*. September 14, 2005.

Louie, Rebecca. "Michelle fights bias on the domestic front." *NY Daily News*. September 1, 2003.

Louie, Rebecca. "*S.W.A.T.* star pulls no punches." *The Province*. August 8, 2003.

"Maggie Grace Victim of *Lost* Set Prank." *Monsters & Critics*. September 7, 2005.

Mahopec, Doug. "The Meaning of Pearls." Exchangenet.com. Accessed June 16, 2006.

Malcolm, Shawna. "Holloway Champions Sawyer's *Lost* Cause." TVGuide.com.

Online. February 8, 2006.

"Matthew Fox's *Lost* Audition." Extra TV. August 18, 2005.

McFarland, Melanie. "Shedding light on a *Lost* villain." *Seattle Post-Intelligencer*. November 29, 2005.

M.D.K. www.mdkofficial.com

Michelangelo Buonarotti. www.michelangelo.com. Accessed April 9, 2006.

"Michelle Rodriguez." *Interview Magazine*. September 2000.

"Michelle Rodriguez: Nothing Added." *Risen Magazine*. January 2006.

Miguel, Christine. "Class Act." *Jasmine*. Spring/Summer 2004.

Miller, Bruce R. "From 'Hobbit' to TV habit." *Sioux City Journal*. August 27, 2004.

"Million Dollar Mami." *Fuego Magazine*. Summer 2005.

Mitovich, Matt Webb. "Dominic Monaghan Has the Dope on *Lost*." TVGuide.com. Online. January 25, 2006.

———. "Will Hurley Get *Lost* in Love?" TVGuide.com. February 1, 2006.

"Monaghan's Character Lures Committed Fans." Contactmusic.com. Online. September 10, 2005.

"Monaghan's Girlfriend a 'Terrible' Driver." Contactmusic.com. Online. May 26, 2005.

"Monaghan's LOTR Depression." Contactmusic.com. Online. September 22, 2005.

"Monaghan's Sweet Side Effect." Contactmusic.com. Online. September 11, 2005.

Moore, F. "*Lost* helps O'Quinn find elusive star turn." Associated Press. February 2005.

Morris, Clint. "Josh Holloway." Moviehole.net. Online. November 28, 2005.

Morrow, Terry. "Monaghan finds himself *Lost*." Scripps Howard News Service. September 30, 2004.

Murray, Rebecca. "Michelle Rodriguez Talks About *Blue Crush*." About.com. August 9, 2002.

Naveen-andrews.net.

"Naveen Predicts Short Run for Hit Show." *National Ledger*. March 23, 2006.

"No debate: *Lost* a hit." *Variety*. October 14, 2004.

O'Brien, Flann. *The Third Policeman*. Illinois: Dalkey Archive, 1967.

Ogunbayo, Modupe. "Adewale Akinnuoye-Agbaje." OnlineNigeria.com. September 1, 2005.

O'Hare, Kate. "A Day in Monaghan's *Lost* Life." Zap2it.com. Online. February 12, 2006.

——— . "Kim, star of Korean cinema, finds a new home on *Lost*." Zap2it.com. Online. October 11, 2005.

——— . "Kim Talks About the *Lost* Art of Being Jin." Zap2it.com. Online. February 17, 2005.

——— . "*Lost*'s Boone and Locke Become Buddies." Zap2it.com. Online. January 2, 2005.

Oldenburg, Ann. "Kim surfaces as sex symbol on *Lost*." *USA Today*. March 21, 2005.

Olim, Charles de. "A Sheppard's *Lost* Flock." *Tonight*. Online. February 17, 2006.

"One Man and a Baby Box." Urban Legends Reference Page. www.snopes.com. Online. Accessed May 2, 2006.

Online Symbolism Dictionary. Online. Accessed May 12, 2006.

"O'Quinn Knows *Lost* Secret." Sci-Fi Wire. Online. July 2004.

Orwell, George. *1984*. New York: Signet, 1950.

Pearlman, Cindy. "Andrews gets *Lost* in latest roles." *Sun Times*. February 20, 2005.

Percy, Walker. *Lancelot*. New York: Picador, 1977.

Phillips, Brian. *SparkNote on The Brothers Karamazov*. June 25, 2006 www.sparknotes.com/lit/brothersk

Polly, John. "If His Looks Could Kill, We'd All Be Dead!" *Ocean Drive Magazine*. March 2001.

Post, Chad. E-mail interview with the author. June 13 and 14, 2006.

Rankin, Bill. "Canadian actress with no real acting experience lands leading role in hit U.S. network series." *The Province*. October 13, 2004.

Reardon, Patrick T. "Lost book mention may be good for small press." *Chicago Tribune*. September 29, 2005.

Riley, Jenelle. "Out of the Blue." Backstage.com. Online. May 2005.

Ripley, Ian. "Josh Holloway Biography." PopStarsPlus.com. Online.

Rizzo, Monica. "*Lost*'s Yunjin Kim." People.com. Online. October 19, 2005.

Ryan, Tim. "Actors explore Korean heritage in *Lost*." *Honolulu Star Bulletin*. September 22, 2004.

——— . "Michelle Rodriguez welcomes the change of scenery as she joins the TV hit *Lost*." *Honolulu Star Bulletin*. September 15, 2005.

Sacks, Ethan. "*Lost* star finds calling." *New York Daily News*. February 12, 2006.

"Saint Sebastian." *Patron Saints Index*. Online. Accessed June 17, 2006.

Schwartz, Missy. "*Lost* and Found." *Entertainment Weekly*. March 4, 2005.

"Shakespeare's Sonnets." www.shakespeares-sonnets.com. Online. Accessed May 30, 2006.

Shimabukuro, Betty. "Castaway: Monaghan of *Lost* is no longer an innocent, furry-footed hobbit." *Honolulu Star-Bulletin*. August 24, 2004.

Skinner, B.F. "A Brief Survey of Operant Behavior." B.F. Skinner Foundation. www.bfskinner.org. Online. Accessed May 2, 2006.

Slaughter, Adele. "Cynthia Watros nurtures breastfeeding awareness." *USA Today*. March 8, 2001.

Sloane, Judy. "Two Against Nature." *Starburst*. February 2005.

Snierson, Dan. "Almost Paradise." *Entertainment Weekly*. December 3, 2004.

Song, Jaymes. "Daniel Dae Kim Loving *Lost* Blessings." *The Seattle Times*. January 21, 2006.

Sorkin, Amy. "Ian Somerhalder." *BRNTWD Magazine*.

SparkNotes Staff. *SparkNote on The Turn of the Screw*. June 20, 2006. www.sparknotes.com/lit/screw.

Spelling, Ian. "Going Ravin Mad!" *Expose*. January 2001.

—. "Naveen Andrews on acting, epics and stardom." *Sun News Services*. March 29, 2006.

"St. Sebastian." *Catholic Online*. Online. Accessed June 17, 2006.

StarDom. www.dommonaghan.com

Steinberg, Scott. "So it was written." *Alternative Press Magazine*. January 2003.

Stein, Joel. "Fox." Men.Style.com. Online. 2006.

Stipp, Christopher. Trailer Park. Online. October 14, 2005.

Strachan, Alex. "*Lost* now biggest cult hit since *X-Files*: It's a show with real substance." *Vancouver Sun*. December 8, 2004.

—. "Strength of character a rocket to stardom: Actress looking for walk-on gets lead." *Vancouver Sun*. December 8, 2004.

"Strange Days." *X-pose*. 1996.

"Terry O'Quinn Web Chat." Channel 4. Online. December 12, 2005.

"The Beach Boys." *Entertainment Weekly*. April 15, 2005.

"The Friday Five." IanSomerhalder.net. Online. December 31, 2004.

"The Philosophy of David Hume." *Classic Philosophers*. Online. Accessed June 28, 2006.

"The Secrets of the *Lost* Phenomenon." E! Online. May 6, 2005.

"Transcript of Jorge Garcia's Live Webchat." Channel 4. Online. December 4, 2005.

Troup, Gary. *Bad Twin*. New York: Hyperion, 2006.

Tsai, Michael. "Actor in the zeitgeist." *Island Life*. December 28, 2005.

Tseng, Ada and Eyvette Min. "Interview with Daniel Dae Kim." Online. December 16, 2004.

TV.com. Online.

"Two *Lost* stars charged with drunken driving." Associated Press. December 2, 2005.

"We Want Answers! Jorge Garcia." *Maxim*. March 2006.

Wikipedia. Wikipedia.org. Online.

Wilkes, Neil. "*Lost* actor Perrineau 'stalked.'" Digital Spy.com. Online. October 19, 2005.

Williams, James. "Hollywood men the next generation." *Glamour UK*. October 2003.

Winfrey, Yayoi Lena. "Indian-British actor smolders onscreen." *Northwest Asian Weekly*. November 27, 2004.

"Yin and Yang." AZN-TV.

Zeitchik, Steven. "Inside Move: It's a Shames: *Lost* Finds Forgotten 'Twin.'" *Variety*. June 18, 2006.

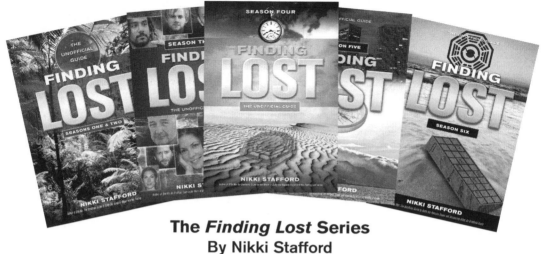

The *Finding Lost* Series
By Nikki Stafford

"Nikki Stafford [is] . . . one of the show's leading scholars."
– *Newsday*

"Nikki Stafford is a godsend to *Lost* enthusiasts in particular and TV lovers in general. I've written about TV for several years, and have always valued her opinion and insights on all things television."
– Amanda Cuda, *Connecticut Post*

"The *Finding Lost* series is quite simply the best resource for fans."
– Jon "DocArzt" Lachonis

"[A] top-notch *Lost* blogger."
– EW.com

"It is impossible to imagine a better guide than Nikki Stafford for the viewer exploring the incomparable complexities of the now completed series. Stafford never fails to be funny, candid, informative, and brilliant."
– David Lavery, co-author of *Lost's Buried Treasures* and editor of *The Essential Cult TV Reader*

The only books that offer an in-depth guide to every episode of each season of *Lost*, Nikki Stafford's *Finding Lost* series goes beyond the show itself to explore all of the references and allusions the writers work into the scripts. Each book explores the season's literary references (including *Watership Down*, *A Wrinkle in Time*, *The Third Policeman*, *Of Mice and Men*, *Slaughterhouse-Five*, *Ulysses*, and many more); historical and philosophical facts within the framework of the episodes; behind-the-scenes information; fan and critical reactions to each season; sidebars with fun trivia; exclusive behind-the-scenes photos of filming in Hawaii; bios of the actors on the show; and much, much more.

Find more from Nikki Stafford at her blog, Nik at Nite:
nikkistafford.blogspot.com